'This pioneering volume gives us a widescreen account of the profound, complex, and fast-moving world of disability and social media. Essential reading for anyone interested in understanding the cutting-edge of Internet, communication, and society, not to mention the rich area of disability, which opens up new perspectives on key questions in technology, design, participation, democracy, and social justice.'

– Gerard Goggin, University of Sydney, Australia

'This vibrant collection highlights the inherent variety and variability of social media, drawing attention to disability in multiple forms and contexts. Touching on technological design, educational contexts, communication, community, and activism, it will be of interest to scholars in media, communication, and disability studies. Furthermore, it marks an important global extension of social media research. Fascinating, diverse, and engaging.'

– Elizabeth Ellcessor, Indiana University, U.S.A.

Disability and Social Media

Social media is popularly seen as an important media for people with disability in terms of communication, exchange and activism. These sites potentially increase both employment and leisure opportunities for one of the most traditionally isolated groups in society. However, the offline inaccessible environment has, to a certain degree, been replicated online and particularly in social networking sites. Social media is becoming an increasingly important part of our lives yet the impact on people with disabilities has gone largely unscrutinised.

Similarly, while social media and disability are often both observed through a focus on the Western, developed and English-speaking world, different global perspectives are often overlooked. This collection explores the opportunities and challenges social media represents for the social inclusion of people with disabilities from a variety of different global perspectives that include Africa, Arabia and Asia along with European, American and Australasian perspectives and experiences.

Katie Ellis is Senior Research Fellow in the Department of Internet Studies and convener of the Critical Disability Studies Research Network at Curtin University. Her research focuses on disability and the media extending across both representation and active possibilities for social inclusion. Her books include *Disability and New Media* (2011 with Mike Kent), *Disabling Diversity* (2008), *Disability, Ageing and Obesity: Popular Media Identifications* (2014; with Debbie Rodan & Pia Lebeck), *Disability and the Media* (2015; with Gerard Goggin) and *Disability and Popular Culture* (2015).

Mike Kent is the head of department and a senior lecturer in the Department of Internet Studies at Curtin University. His main research interests focus on the two overlapping areas of people with disabilities and their access to communications technology as well as tertiary and online education. He is co-author, with Katie Ellis, of *Disability and New Media* (Routledge, 2011), and co-editor (with Tama Leaver) of *An Education in Facebook? Higher Education and the World's Largest Social Network* (Routledge, 2014). His current research includes the forthcoming books *Massive Open Online Courses and Higher Education: Where to Next?* (Routledge) with Rebecca Bennett and *Chinese Social Media Today: Critical Perspectives* (Routledge) with Katie Ellis and Jian Xu.

Interdisciplinary Disability Studies
Series editor: Mark Sherry
The University of Toledo, USA

Disability studies has made great strides in exploring power and the body. This series extends the interdisciplinary dialogue between disability studies and other fields by asking how disability studies can influence a particular field. It will show how a deep engagement with disability studies changes our understanding of the following fields: sociology, literary studies, gender studies, bioethics, social work, law, education or history. This ground-breaking series identifies both the practical and theoretical implications of such an interdisciplinary dialogue and challenges people in disability studies as well as other disciplinary fields to critically reflect on their professional praxis in terms of theory, practice, and methods.

For a full list of titles in this series, please visit www.routledge.com/series/ASHSER1401

Disability and Social Media

Global perspectives

Edited by Katie Ellis and Mike Kent

Routledge
Taylor & Francis Group

LONDON AND NEW YORK

First published 2017
by Routledge
2 Park Square, Milton Park, Abingdon, Oxon OX14 4RN

and by Routledge
711 Third Avenue, New York, NY 10017

First issued in paperback 2017

Routledge is an imprint of the Taylor & Francis Group, an informa business

British Library Cataloguing in Publication Data
A catalogue record for this book is available from the British Library

Library of Congress Cataloging in Publication Data
Names: Ellis, Katie, 1978– editor. | Kent, Mike, 1969– editor.
Title: Disability and social media : global perspectives / edited by
    Katie Ellis and Mike Kent.
Description: Abingdon, Oxon ; New York, NY : Routledge, 2017.
Identifiers: LCCN 2016026589 | ISBN 9781472458452 (hardback) |
    ISBN 9781315577357 (ebook)
Subjects: LCSH: Accessible Web sites for people with disabilities. | People
    with disabilities—Means of communication. | People with disabilities—
    Social networks. | Online social networks. | Sociology of disability.
Classification: LCC HV1568.4 .D57 2017 | DDC 302.23/1087—dc23
LC record available at https://lccn.loc.gov/2016026589

ISBN 13: 978-1-138-49440-4 (pbk)
ISBN 13: 978-1-4724-5845-2 (hbk)

Typeset in Times New Roman
by Apex CoVantage, LLC

For Stella Young, disability activist social media superstar. We dedicate this book to you and all that you did to teach us how to use social media.

Contents

Figures

Tables

Contributors

Meryl Alper is an Assistant Professor of Communication Studies at Northeastern University, a Faculty Associate at the Berkman Klein Center for Internet and Society at Harvard University, and the author of *Digital Youth with Disabilities* (MIT Press, 2014). She studies the social and cultural implications of communication technologies, with a focus on children and families' technology use, disability and digital media and mobile communication. Prior to joining the faculty at Northeastern, Alper earned her doctoral and master's degrees from the Annenberg School for Communication and Journalism at the University of Southern California. She also holds a bachelor's degree in Communication Studies and History from Northwestern University.

Najma Al Zidjaly is Associate Professor of Sociolinguistics (Intercultural Communication) in the Department of English Language and Literature at Sultan Qaboos University, Oman. She is the author of *Disability, Discourse and Technology: Agency and Inclusion in (Inter)action* (Palgrave Macmillan, 2015), and the editor of *Building Bridges: Integrating Language. Linguistics, Literature and Translation in English Studies* (CSP, 2012). Her other publications include articles in *Language in Society*, *Multilingua*, *Visual Communication*, *Communication & Medicine*, *Multimodal Communication*, *Disability Studies Quarterly* and *Intercultural Management Quarterly*. Al Zidjaly is on the Editorial Board of *Multimodal Communication*. Her research interests focus on multimodality's role in illuminating the connections between human agency and social media, as they manifest in the relationship between people with disabilities and new forms of technology, on one hand, and the relationship between creative media and the ever-complex identity of (Omani) Arabs, on the other.

John E. Armenta is a Ph.D. Candidate in the Department of Communication at UC San Diego where he teaches writing in the Culture, Art and Technology programme. His research is focused on understanding the transition narratives of Post 9/11 veterans. Prior to his academic career he served nine years in the US Army Reserve with deployments in Bosnia and Herzegovina, Iraq and Afghanistan. He served as a co-organizer of the exhibition *Senses of Care: Mediated Ability and Interdependence* at the CALIT2 gallery at UCSD (Spring 2014).

Paul M. A. Baker is the senior director of research and strategic innovation and a principal research scientist at Georgia Tech's Center for Advanced Communications Policy; he is also an adjunct professor in the Centre for Disability Law & Policy at the National University of Ireland, Galway. His research interests include higher education and disability policy, accessible information technology, post-secondary workforce development and virtual/online communities. Baker has a Ph.D. in public policy from George Mason University and a Masters in Theological Studies from Emory University.

Owen Barden is a lecturer in disability and education. His research interests include the relationship between dyslexia and digital literacies and emerging methods for studying digitally mediated networks and learning.

DeeDee Bennett, Ph.D. is an Assistant Professor at the University of Nebraska at Omaha in the Emergency Services Program within the School of Public Administration. Her primary research areas include emergency management, socially vulnerable populations during disasters, emergency communications, disaster policy and mobile wireless communications. Dr. Bennett was previously employed as a Research Scientist in the Center for Advanced Communications Policy (CACP) at the Georgia Institute of Technology. She received her Ph.D. from Oklahoma State University's Political Science Department in Fire and Emergency Management and both her M.S. in Public Policy and B.S. in Electrical Engineering from the Georgia Institute of Technology.

Tom Bieling is a visiting professor in Applied Sciences and Art at the German University in Cairo. Research Fellow and Ph.D. candidate at Berlin University of the Arts (Design Research Lab). Author of the book 'Gender Puppets' (Lit, 2008). Chief-Editor at *Designabilities.org* and Co-Founder of the Design Research Network. www.tombieling.com

Andrea Bundon (Ph.D.) is an Assistant Professor in the School of Kinesiology at the University of British Columbia (Canada). Her work, which spans the fields of sport sociology and critical disability studies, uses digital qualitative methods to explore the intersections of sport, physical activity, disability and social inclusion. She has published in peer-reviewed journals including *Qualitative Research in Sport, Exercise and Health, The Journal of Sport and Social Issues, Disability and Society* and *Ageing and Society.* She has also contributed chapters to forthcoming handbooks, including *The International Handbook of Qualitative Methods in Sport and Exercise* and *The Palgrave Handbook of Paralympic Studies.*

Lucy Burke is Principal Lecturer in English at Manchester Metropolitan University. Focusing specifically upon dementia and learning disability, her research explores contemporary cultural responses to cognitive disability and the role of the arts and creativity in challenging particular conceptions of value, meaningful life and personhood. She is co-investigator on the AHRC funded D4D project (2016–2020) exploring disability and community and on the editorial board of the *Journal of Literary and Cultural Disability Studies.*

Craig Collinson is a Ph.D. candidate at Edge Hill University. Craig's thesis is on 'lexism' in recent English Educational policy documents. He has published in the British Journal of Special Education, Disability and Society and Studies in Higher Education.

Liz Crow is a British artist-activist working in performance, film, audio and text, and drawn to the potential of creative work as a medium for social and political change. She is founder of Roaring Girl Productions (www.roaring-girl.com) and a former NESTA (National Endowment for Science, Technology and the Arts) fellow. Her work has shown at Tate Modern and Washington, DC's Kennedy Center for the Performing Arts, as well as on the Trafalgar Square Fourth Plinth, the Thames foreshore, and through social media. She is currently a doctoral candidate at the University of the West of England, undertaking practice-led research into methodologies of activism.

Katie Ellis is Senior Research Fellow in the Department of Internet Studies at Curtin University. Her research focuses on disability and the media extending across both representation and active possibilities for social inclusion. Her books include *Disability and New Media* (2011 with Mike Kent), *Disabling Diversity* (2008), *Disability, Ageing and Obesity: Popular Media Identifications* (2014; with Debbie Rodan & Pia Lebeck), *Disability and the Media* (2015; with Gerard Goggin) and *Disability and Popular Culture* (2015).

Juliet Goldbart is Director of the Research Institute for Health and Social Change and Professor of Developmental Disabilities at Manchester Metropolitan University. Her research interests focus on communication and people with profound intellectual impairment, models of service delivery in the UK and in underserved countries and issues in research methodology.

Brian Goldfarb is Associate Professor of Communication at UCSD. His research and creative production focus on visual/digital culture, disability and education. His book, *Visual Pedagogy*, considers media technologies used in the 20th century to advance models of pedagogy in the US and globally. Goldfarb's current projects include *Global Tourette*, a documentary and media exchange project engaging cultural and professional responses to Tourette Syndrome internationally; and, *Carescape*, a digital book exploring patient communities in the digital age. As a curator at the New Museum of Contemporary Art (1993–1997) he organised exhibitions such as alt.youth.media and initiated their online programming. He recently organised the exhibition *Senses of Care: Mediated Ability and Interdependence* at the CALIT2 gallery at UCSD (Spring 2014).

Beth Haller, Ph.D., is Professor of Journalism/New Media at Towson University in Maryland, USA. She is the author of *Representing Disability in an Ableist World: Essays on Mass Media* (Advocado Press, 2010) and *Byline of Hope: Collected Newspaper and Magazine Writings of Helen Keller* (Advocado Press, 2015), as well as numerous academic articles and book chapters. She is the former co-editor of the Society for Disability Studies' scholarly journal,

Disability Studies Quarterly, (2003–2006). She currently maintains a blog on disability issues in the news, Media dis&dat, http://media-dis-n-dat.blogspot.com/, as well as a website on media and disability research at http://www.media-disability.net

Scott Hollier, Media Access Australia's Director of Digital Accessibility, is a leading authority in the area of access to computers and the internet for people with disability. Dr. Hollier authored a doctoral thesis titled "The disability divide: A study into the impact of computing and internet-related technologies on people who are blind or vision impaired". He can also provide a personal perspective as he is legally blind and relies on assistive technology to use computers. Dr. Hollier represents Media Access Australia on the advisory committee of the World Wide Web Consortium (W3C).

He is the author of Media Access Australia's *SociABILITY: social media for people with a disability* resource which is now used by the US government to help agencies improve the accessibility of social media. He is also author of the *Service providers accessibility guide*, funded by Department of Families, Housing, Community Services and Indigenous Affairs to assist DisabilityCare providers in making their communications accessible for clients and employees using mainstream technology.

Dr. Hollier is also co-lecturer of the Professional Certificate in Web Accessibility, an industry course for Web professionals, run jointly by the University of South Australia and Media Access Australia. He is also an Adjunct Senior Lecturer within the School of Computer and Security Science at Edith Cowan University.

Amanda Hynan is a senior lecturer in the Speech and Language Therapy Department of Leeds Beckett University and completed her doctoral research with Manchester Metropolitan University. Her research interests focus on the discipline of augmentative and alternative communication (AAC) with a particular focus on how social media is used within the field.

Gesche Joost is Professor for Design Research at Berlin University of the Arts; Head of the Design Research Lab. Chairwoman of DGTF e.V. [German Society for Design Theory and Research] and board member of Technologiestiftung Berlin. In 2014 she was appointed as a Digital Champion for the EU commission, where her priorities are to improve and enhance diversity in the digital society and an open internet. www.drlab.org

George Julian is an independent knowledge transfer consultant who works with universities, researchers and charities to help their research make an impact. She is also a Visiting Fellow at Personal Social Services Research Unit (PSSRU) at London School of Economics and Political Science (LSE).

Muneo Kaigo is an associate professor in the Faculty of Humanities and Social Sciences at the University of Tsukuba. He teaches in the Graduate School of Humanities and Social Sciences, the Graduate School of Business Sciences and the College of Comparative Culture at the University of Tsukuba, Japan. He is currently leading a joint research project on social media uses among local municipalities in Japan with cooperation from the municipal government of Tsukuba and Intel Corporation Japan. His recent research interests are also centred on the positive and negative information aggregation and flows in cyberspace.

Mike Kent is the head of department and a senior lecturer in the Department of Internet Studies at Curtin University. His main research interests focus on the two overlapping areas of people with disabilities and their access to communications technology as well as tertiary and online education. He is co-author, with Katie Ellis, of *Disability and New Media* (Routledge, 2011), and co-editor (with Tama Leaver) of *An Education in Facebook? Higher Education and the World's Largest Social Network* (Routledge, 2014). His current research includes the forthcoming books *Massive Open Online Courses and Higher Education: Where to Next?* (Routledge) with Rebecca Bennett and *Chinese Social Media Today: Critical Perspectives* (Routledge) with Katie Ellis and Jian Xu.

Tiago Martins is a researcher and creative technologist at Berlin University of the Arts (Design Research Lab). Lecturer in Programming, Physical Computing and Game Design at the University of Arts and Industrial Design in Linz (Austria).

Anneleen Masschelein is professor of Literary and Cultural studies at the University of Leuven, Belgium. In *The Unconcept* (SUNY Press, 2011), she studied the history of the concept of "the uncanny" in the late 20th century. Her current research focuses on two contemporary cultural practices: on the one hand, handbooks for creative writing, on the other, different forms of shaping illness and dying in contemporary media society.

Leanne McRae is a lecturer in Internet Communications at Curtin University. She has written extensively on education, work, city imaging and popular cultural studies. Her current research interests include disability, social media, gaming and e-learning.

Helena Mitchell is a *Regents' Researcher,* the highest status within the University System of Georgia, in tandem Executive Director of the Center for Advanced Communications Policy (CACP) at the Georgia Institute of Technology and the Principal Investigator for the Rehabilitation Engineering Research Center for Wireless Technologies – part of CACP – funded to support equal access to innovative wireless technologies and products. She held senior positions in Washington, DC at the Federal Communications Commission (FCC) and at the National Telecommunications and Information Administration, where she received the prestigious US Department of Commerce Silver Medal, twice. Dr. Mitchell received her doctorate from Syracuse University.

Janice Murray is Professor of Communication Disability at Manchester Metropolitan University and Chair of the International Society of Augmentative and Alternative Communication (ISAAC). Her research focus is language development through aided communication, language development in aided speakers, outcome measurement, AAC and memory.

Laurence Parent is a Ph.D. student in Humanities at Concordia University in Montréal. She holds a MA in Critical Disability Studies from York University and a BA in Political Science from Université du Québec à Montréal. She is currently working as a research assistant at the Mobile Media Lab at Concordia University.

Jeffrey Preston, Ph.D., is a professor of Digital Marketing at Fanshawe College in London, Ontario and a disability and culture correspondent on AMI Accessible Media Inc. A long-time advocate and motivational speaker, Jeff's work focuses on the intersection of disability, subjectivity and culture.

D. Andy Rice is a Visual Communication Ph.D., nonfiction filmmaker and post-doctoral fellow at UCLA in Undergraduate Education Initiatives. He develops courses in documentary production for social change as interdisciplinary capstones and practicums for liberal arts majors, including "Documentary Production for Social Change: Mobility in Los Angeles" cross-listed in Disability Studies and Urban Planning, the focus of his chapter in this volume. His research centres on aesthetics and digital media technologies in documentary film and reenactment performance. He is also the Co-Producer, Cinematographer and Editor on *Spirits of Rebellion: Black Cinema from UCLA*, a feature documentary directed by Zeinabu irene Davis about a collective of radical black independent filmmakers known as the L.A. Rebellion, and the Co-Director of *Unhooked* with choreographer Victoria Marks, a movement-documentary created with members of fraternities and sororities at UCLA about hookup culture and sexual violence in college.

Sara Ryan is a sociologist, and focuses largely on experiences of disability, autism and mothering. She is the Research Director in the Health Experiences Research Group, Nuffield Department of Primary Care Health Sciences, University of Oxford.

Kudzai Shava is a blind disability activist and Lecturer in the Faculty of Education and Social Sciences at Reformed Church University in Zimbabwe, teaching Disability and Inclusive Education.

Leni Van Goidsenhoven is a doctoral researcher of the FWO-Flanders at the Literary and Cultural Studies department at the University of Leuven, Belgium. She is preparing a Ph.D. on autism and self-representation. She has already published several articles on this topic as well as on outsider art. Her research interests cover illness and disability representations, the institutionalisation of the self-help culture, autism and outsider art.

Marie-Eve Veilleux is a disability activist and Bioethics student at Université de Montréal. She holds a BSc in Microbiology and Immunology, a Certificate in Translation and a Graduate Diploma in Translation from McGill University in Montréal. She works as translation coordinator for the Canadian Longitudinal Study on Aging.

Jian Xu is a joint visiting scholar at the Centre for Global Communication Studies and the Center for the Study of Contemporary China at the University of Pennsylvania. He is an associate in the Sydney Democracy Network at the University of Sydney and recently completed Endeavour Postdoctoral Research Fellowship in the China Research Centre at the University of Technology Sydney. Dr. Xu researches Chinese media and communications with a particular interest in the mediated social-cultural-political changes caused by digital media. His research areas focus on China's internet activism, internet governance, authoritarianism 2.0, and micro-charity. He is the author of *Media Events in Web 2.0 China: Interventions of Online Activism* (2016, Sussex Academic Press).

Magdalena Zdrodowska, Ph.D. is an assistant professor in Institute of the Audiovisual Arts, Jagiellonian University, Cracow, Poland. Her main research fields are media studies and anthropology. An author of *Television on the Borderlines* (*Telewizja na pograniczach*) (2013, Wydawnictwo Universytetu Jagiellońskiego) devoted to the representations of the otherness in global, regional and local television programmes. She currently researches the complicated relations between the d/Deaf and technology.

He Zhang is a doctoral candidate at the School of Media, Culture and Creative Arts in the Faculty of Humanities, Curtin University. She holds a MA in translation studies from Shanghai International Studies University. Her research interests include digital literacy, co-creative media practices, cultural citizenship and migration activities of Chinese young people.

Acknowledgements

We would like to thank the authors both for their contributions to this collection and also for acting as anonymous readers of this book. Everyone offered both insightful and encouraging feedback at every stage – it has been a pleasure working with you all.

A number of people have read or heard pieces of this book and generously gave of their time to discuss ideas with us: Kai-Ti Kao, James Boyd, Gerard Goggin, Leanne McRae, Lucy Montgomery and Susan Leong. Fiona Kumari Campbell also offered valuable mentoring for some of our authors. It was rewarding also to have been invited to present this work at the Curtin University Faculty of Humanities Research Day in the three minute research challenge. We would also like to thank our colleagues from the Department of Internet Studies for their valuable feedback, tolerance and the vibrant research culture they enable that facilitates our disability media collaborations.

Katie would like to thank her family – Chris and Stella now veterans of a few books and Connor who was born just as the chapters for this book first started arriving. I am grateful for your love, support and understanding. Special thanks to Gail Pearce for stepping in as a last-minute babysitter in the final hours of work on this collection. And of course Mike, for a great partnership. This book is a testament to your work and enthusiasm for the subject.

Mike would like to thank the friendly staff at Epic Expresso where much of his editing work was done. He is also grateful for the support from his family and friends, and for his cat Cameron, who generously chose to share her valuable desk space with him throughout this project. Mike also needs to acknowledge Katie's vision for this book, and her incredible commitment to the project.

Vital research assistance was provided by Melissa Merchant, Paul McLaughlin, Kathryn Locke, Francis Shaw and Erin Stark. Ceri Clocherty has been invaluable helping to prepare the final manuscript for publication.

Research for this collection was funded by a number of sources. While individual contributors acknowledge a number of funding bodies in their individual chapters, as editors we thank the following bodies for seeing the importance of disability media research and for awarding us invaluable research funds:

- Curtin University and the School of Media Communication and Creative Arts for providing a Publications grant to complete the manuscript.

- The Australian Research Council Discovery Early Career Research Award (DE130101712) on Disability and Digital Television.
- The Australian Communications Consumer Action Network grant Accessing Video on Demand: A study of disability and streaming television (2015048)
- The National Centre for Student Equity in Higher Education and the Australian Government grant Access and barriers to online education for people with disabilities.

Finally, we offer our deepest thanks to our commissioning editor Claire Jarvis for the initial approach, series editor Mark Sherry for his leadership in disability studies and for inviting us to be part of this important series, Interdisciplinary Disability Studies, and Lianne Sherlock for shepherding the book through its final stages. Working with Routledge has been a pleasure, as always.

1 Introduction

Social disability

Katie Ellis and Mike Kent

Background

Social media has become a vital element of how we communicate with each other. It has, in a short space of time, risen from the obscurity of dialup bulletin board discussion pages to platforms like Facebook where 936 million people log on every day (Internet World Statistics, 2015). These networks are increasingly integrated into our everyday lives through the proliferation of smartphones and the integration of social media apps that now form the backbone of many of these platforms. However, while social media is becoming an increasingly important part of our lives, its impact on people with disabilities has gone largely unscrutinised. Are people with disabilities using social media in the same way as the majority of the population? Are they able to, or are they excluded from social media spaces in the same ways they are excluded from much of public life and participation? Importantly, how are people with disabilities in different parts of the world engaging with social media? Furthermore, how can an investigation of disability and social media advance interdisciplinary disability studies?

When we began planning this book we surmised that social media was popularly seen as an important media for people with disability in terms of communication, exchange and activism (Ellis & Goggin, 2015). Social media sites, we suggested, potentially increase both employment and leisure opportunities for people with disabilities who are one of the most traditionally isolated groups in society. However, we were also aware that, despite this potential for social inclusion, there is the potential that these platforms replicate the inaccessibility and discriminatory attitudes people with disabilities regularly experience offline (Ellis & Kent, 2011), particularly on social networking sites. Social media has the potential to both enable and further disable people with disability. For example, despite recognised benefits of social inclusion for people with disabilities, Scott Hollier notes the continuation of inaccessibility in social media in his seminal report *Sociability: Social media for people with a disability:*

> all of the popular social media tools remain inaccessible to some degree. Facebook, LinkedIn, Twitter, YouTube, blogging websites and the emerging Google+ all feature limited accessibly, denying many consumers with disabilities the opportunity to participate in social media.
>
> (Hollier, 2012, p. 11)

Although Hollier paints a dreary picture regarding accessibility in social media, his report holds much scope for optimism, as did we as we embarked this project:

> Fortunately, users have often found ways around the accessibility barriers such as alternative website portals, mobile apps, additional keyboard navigation shortcuts and online support groups. This is a rich source of expertise, and social media users with disability continue to find creative ways to access the most popular platforms.
>
> (Hollier, 2012, p. 11)

With Hollier's observations firmly in mind, we have compiled a collection which explores the opportunities and challenges social media represents for the social inclusion of people with disabilities all over the world. It is a long book, longer than we thought it would be as we began planning. It is a long book because disability and social media is a large topic and does, as we thought, encompass communication, exchange, activism and leisure, and the way it is used by different groups in different locations contains much diversity.

Core values

In January 2011 the American president Barack Obama stated that 'there are certain core values that . . . we believe are universal: freedom of speech, freedom of expression, people being able to use social networking' (Ackerman, 2011, para. 7). While this statement was made in response to protests in Egypt against the rule of Honsi Mubarak, it highlights the increasing importance of web-based platforms that allow people to construct a public profile, connect with others and thereby participate in society.

Previously in 2009 at the *More Than Gadgets Conference* in Fremantle, Western Australia, Graeme Innes, the Australian Disability and Race Discrimination Commissioner, spoke of the link between disability and social media. He suggested that social networking had the potential to open up vast opportunities to people with disability to participate in society. He also cautioned that, in the future, people who were not using these networks, including those without a disability, would find themselves effectively disabled by a lack of access to information and communication.

Similarly Beth Haller argues social media is particularly important for people with disabilities:

> and this explosion of [social media] has included many people with disabilities. It is a way to organize disability rights actions, let others know about disability related news, promote events, or just find like-minded disability rights advocates. It also has the advantage of mitigating some disabilities, like providing an easy communication system for people who are deaf or have speech disabilities. On the other hand, text-heavy social networking

sites that require being computer savvy might create barriers for people with intellectual disabilities, serious learning disabilities, or those who have visual impairments.

(2010, p. 5)

In a recent survey of 341 Australians with a disability (see Ellis, Chapter 11 this volume) it emerged that 20 per cent of respondents had been profiled by the mainstream media, 6 per cent maintained a disability blog, 12 per cent contributed articles to disability blogs, 3 per cent made YouTube videos about their lives and 47 per cent commented on social networking sites or blogs related to disability issues. While this is a high amount of political engagement online related to disability, 36.5 per cent of the cohort also claimed to blog, tweet, YouTube and Facebook but not about disability issues. These figures show people with disabilities are using social media in both political and non-political ways.

Disability stories

This finding is also evident in a recent Storify compilation of the power of #SocialMedia and #DisabilityStories where people participating in the conversation identified both new types of disability narratives becoming available, and the potential to connect with others online. The conversations emphasised both the opportunities and challenges of the most popular social media platforms, for example communicating via 140 characters on Twitter or feeling limited by Facebook's constantly changing platforms (see Wong, 2015).

However, while Haller and these people participating in social media conversations emphasise recreation and advocacy, it important to first consider whether people with disabilities are able to access social media.

This introductory chapter first explores how an understanding of disability is transformed when it is applied to the use of the internet, and particularly social networks – termed digital disability. We outline four different stages of digital design in relation to accessibility of internet platforms. These four stages describe how an online platform can be accessible but not widely distributed, widely distributed but not accessible, widely distributed and retrofitted to be accessible, or 'born' accessible and widely distributed. These different approaches can be illustrated through the recent history of social media by the approach taken to accessibility by MySpace, Facebook, Twitter and Google+.

Digital disability

The social model of disability distinguishes between disability and impairment. It maintains that disability is the result of decisions made by society and their impact on an individual with a specific impairment (see Finkelstein, 1980; Oliver, 1996). For example, a person may have a specific impairment that means that they use a wheelchair to aid mobility; however, they are disabled when they come to a set of stairs with no alternate access.

Disability is activated differently online compared to the analogue world and has uneven effects on different impairments. Whereas a person who uses a wheelchair for mobility may not necessarily experience disability when accessing the internet, people with various perceptual and cognitive impairments, as well as those that relate to manual dexterity, may require accessible websites and assistive technologies. Just as the absence of a ramp disabled the wheelchair user in the analogue world, these users are disabled by inaccessible web design. The way that different aspects of the internet and world wide web are constructed – choices made by society – will then determine the disabling impact of these different impairments (see Goggin & Newell, 2003; Ellis & Kent, 2011).

At its most fundamental level, information stored digitally online should be able to be accessed in a wide variety of ways that will best suit any potential users. For example, it can be presented visually on a screen, or audibly as spoken word, music or any other noises that might aid in the operation or navigation of a particular platform, it can also be delivered through touch such as with a Braille tablet or a Lorm glove. As well as retrieving information in this way, it can also be inputted and digitised through any of these mediums. As Foley and Ferri (2012, p. 192) observe:

> Technology is often characterised as liberating – making up for social, educational and physical barriers to full participation in society. Often viewed in very utopian ways, technology promises to liberate us from the confines of embodiment and provide us with a futuristic antidote for impairment. Through technological advancements, disability would simply fade away or become largely inconsequential difference.

Social media and four stages of digital accessibility

However, the way information is stored and formatted can constrain a person's ability to access it, and will have a disabling impact on people with different impairments. In the past we have observed that there are four broad stages to digital design/accessibility on the internet (see Ellis & Kent, 2011).

At the first stage, an online platform will be accessible, but not highly distributed or used. In these cases, design decisions that will exclude people have yet to be made. As Jaeger (2012, p. viii) observes, 'Ironically, the pre-Web Internet – an environment in which content was mostly limited to electronically readable text – was more accessible to many users with disabilities than is the contemporary Web-enabled Internet.' For social media this stage is evident in the earliest forms of online social networks in dialup bulletin board enabled chatrooms, and the discussion forums of Usenet where the simple text-based interface could be easily interpreted by assistive technologies.

The second stage of digital design is where a particular platform or service is highly popular, but not accessible. In this case a platform has achieved a large distribution before any thought has been given to accessibility for people with disabilities. As Annable, Goggin, and Stienstra (2007, p. 146) have questioned:

> If there is much more acceptance of disability as a social, rather than purely medical, phenomenon, and greater public support for the removal of barriers and for an end to discrimination and exclusion of people with disabilities, why are information technologies – often the newest, most heralded ones – still disabling?

From the perspective of social media this can be seen in MySpace. The social networking site that overtook Google as the most visited site on the internet in 2006, was also notoriously inaccessible and resistant to any pressure to change the network to make it more accommodating (Ellis and Goggin 2014).

The third stage occurs when one of these platforms that was previously inaccessible is then changed – retrofitted – to become accessible and inclusive. As Wentz, Jaeger, and Lazar (2011) observe, this process of retrofitting technology is inevitably more expensive than planning a project with universal access in mind from the beginning. In 2010 Facebook became the most visited site on the web. The year before, in consultation with the American Foundation for the Blind, it had overhauled the platform to make it more accessible for people with disabilities who rely on assistive technologies. Twitter initially had a different approach with Dennis Lembree in 2009 famously designing his own site *Accessible Twitter* as a workaround to what was, at the time, Twitter's own inaccessible web interface (Ellis & Kent 2010). As Scott Hollier demonstrates in Chapter 6 of this book, Twitter has subsequently undergone its own retrofit for accessibility.

A final, fourth stage avoids this retrofit by having platforms that are born accessible, with accessible design for people with disabilities applied from the foundation and then maintained as the platform becomes widely distributed. When in 2011 Google launched its latest social networking platform Google+ it seemed initially that there had been effort put in to make the site accessible (Google Accessibility, 2011; Romack, 2011; Toor, 2013), and as Hollier shows when the final product was audited by Boudreau in 2011, it was as accessible as its competitors such as Facebook without any need for a retrofit.

People with disabilities have engaged with social media at all these stages of accessibility. Facebook was used as the venue for a protest on the inaccessibility of Facebook through the *Official petition for a more accessible Facebook* page (see Ellis & Kent, 2011, pp. 101–105). People with disabilities have become accomplished at using work-arounds like *Accessible Twitter* or utilising the mobile-optimised social media sites to bypass inaccessible features. This book brings together chapters that look at how people and groups with disabilities access social media, and the uses they put it to. As Hollier notes, many of the 'mainstream' social media sites such as Facebook, Twitter and Google+ have taken great strides in their approach to accessibility and the disability community (others, such as MySpace, have ceased to operate). However social media increasingly delivers a feast of different options, with a troubling array of commitment to accessibility. In the face of this rapidly evolving area, this book provides a snapshot of how social media today is being accessed and utilised by people with disabilities. It considers the specific and, at this stage, largely unexplored impacts of our increasing reliance on social media for people with disability through the perspective of a number of international case studies.

Outline of this book

Figure 1.1 is a word cloud of the contributions to this book. It reveals a large number of social media platforms – from Facebook to WhatsApp to the China-focused WeChat. It also communicates a large number of impairments – from quadriplegia, to stroke, to autism, to vision and hearing impairment, to children with communications impairments. We have sought to give voice to a large number of groups in this book, including people with various impairments, their allies – such as parents of children with disabilities and teachers of students with disabilities – as well as to include perspectives from as many countries as possible.

A number of common themes and topics emerged throughout the book, including the Paralympics, the inadequacies of the mainstream media, the importance of education and new ways to communicate both new stories and old stories.

Figure 1.1 Word cloud of disability and social media: Global perspectives

While we sought to give voice to as many people interested in the nexus between disability and social media as possible, and particularly introduce new insights, there were some areas that were more challenging than others, the introduction to Chapter 13 demonstrates some of the difficulties faced by authors with disabilities in second and third world countries, and while we were grateful to be able to publish that chapter, it is one of the few voices in the book from the global south. Our authors from South America had to withdraw from the project, and getting voices from Asia also proved challenging. However we are pleased by the level of diversity we were able to find across different disability groups, nationalities, and social media platforms.

The book is divided into six sections each consisting of three or four chapters. The first section concerns the potential for advocacy using social media. It addresses the use of Facebook by the deaf community in Poland (Chapter 2), the potential for subversive action via social networks following tragedy and governmental neglect (Chapter 3), the problem with images of people with disability being shared via social media as an example of what Stella Young described as 'inspiration porn' (Chapter 4), and the intersections between disability performance art and social media to offer an unseen narrative of disability (Chapter 5).

A chapter authored by Scott Hollier, whom we have cited extensively throughout this introduction, heads up the second part of the book which addresses the theme of access. Throughout this section, accessibility is addressed both in terms of the importance of assistive technology (Chapters 6, 8 and 9) and the use of social media to advocate for access to public space and essential infrastructure (Chapter 7).

The third section of the book – communications – seeks to use the topic of disability and social media to advance a number of theories in communications studies such as the basic model of communication itself (Chapter 10), collaborative media (Chapter 11) and feminist ethics of care (Chapter 12). Chapter 13 addresses the importance of new avenues of communications and media in the global south when inaccessibility, unavailability and unaffordability of social media, or even survival itself, dominate the lives of people with disabilities.

Throughout part IV – education – chapters both celebrate (Chapter 14) and criticise (Chapter 16) the potential for social media to offer inclusion for students with disabilities. Chapters 15 and 17 introduce new styles of pedagogy and methods of communication for students with disabilities using social media in the classroom.

While community has been a key theme of the book so far, part V – community – considers explicit case studies around the ways people with disabilities have created communities online for sport (Chapter 18), self-representation (Chapter 19) and increasing awareness of local government initiatives (Chapter 20).

We finish the book with a section on new directions. This part includes chapters on topics we see as under-represented in the disability studies and social media studies literature. They include analysis of people using augmentative and alternative communication (Chapter 21) and case studies located in the Middle East (Chapter 22) and China (Chapter 23).

The book celebrates and complicates the increasing visibility of disability through social media, by acknowledging and analysing the opportunities and challenges social media represents for the social inclusion of people with disabilities.

Conclusion

In 1976 the Union of the Physically Impaired Against Segregation (UPIAS) stated in their manifesto:

> What we are interested in, are ways of changing our conditions of life, and thus overcoming the disabilities which are imposed on top of our physical impairments by the way society is organised to exclude us. In our view, it is only the actual impairment which we must accept; the additional and totally unnecessary problems caused by the way we are treated are essentially to be overcome and not accepted.
>
> (para. 16)

This statement was made long before the internet and world wide web were a part of people's everyday lives; however, this call to social justice still resonates in the digital arena where the struggle for access for people with disabilities is ongoing. In this struggle, access to online social networks is important, particularly as they become an ever increasingly significant part of the online environment. Wentz, Jaeger, and Lazar (2011, para. 1) caution:

> Current disability rights laws which are supposed to exist for the protection and well-being of individuals with disabilities are often too close to the heart of the problem, as they can actually promote a separate but unequal online environment. If current U.S. laws were revised to encourage born-accessible technology and there was consistent enforcement of such laws, the online experience of millions of individuals with disabilities could be drastically improved.

As Obama observed, access to these networks can now be seen as a part of a universal set of core values. Innis similarly predicted in 2009 that for people to be excluded from these networks is increasingly becoming a disability in its own right. This, through lack of accessible design, is then being imposed on people with disabilities who are excluded and disadvantaged. As people with disabilities are increasingly recognised as a potential market, social networking sites are taking different approaches to accessibility from retrofits, to work-arounds, to what we hope is the future of the web – born accessibility.

As the chapters in this book show, while limitations caused by impairments are accepted, social media is used to reveal the 'additional and totally unnecessary problems caused by the way we are treated.' They also demonstrate that it is totally unnecessary to create additional problems for people with disabilities seeking to participate in social media through inaccessible platforms.

References

Ackerman, S. (2011, January 28). Egypt's internet shutdown can't stop mass protests. *Wired*. Retrieved from http://www.wired.com/dangerroom/2011/01/egypts-internet-shutdown-cant-stop-mass-protests/#more-39575

Annable, G., Goggin, G., & Stienstra, D. (2007). Accessibility, disability, and inclusion in information technologies: Introduction. *The Information Society: An International Journal, 23*(3), 145–147. Retrieved from http://dx.doi.org/10.1080/01972240701323523

Boudreau, D. (2011). Social media accessibility: Where are we today? AccessibleWeb, Paper presented at a11ybos 2011, Boston (17 September). Retrieved from http://accessibiliteweb.com/presentations/2011/a11yBOS/#7

Ellis, K., and Goggin, G. (2014). Disability and social media. In J. Hunsinger, and T. Senft, (eds) *Handbook of Social Media*, New York: Routledge, 126–179.

Ellis, K., & Goggin, G. (2015). *Disability and the media*. New York, NY: Palgrave Macmillan.

Ellis, K., & Kent, M. (2010). Community accessibility: Tweeters take responsibility for an accessible Web 2.0. *Fast Capitalism, 6*(2). Retrieved from http://www.uta.edu/huma/agger/fastcapitalism/7_1/elliskent7_1.html

Ellis, K., & Kent, M. (2011). *Disability and new media*. New York, NY: Routledge.

Finkelstein, F. (1980). *Attitudes and disabled people: Issues for discussion*. New York, NY: International Exchange of Information in Rehabilitation.

Foley, A., & Ferri, B.A. (2012). Technology for people, not disabilities: Ensuring access and inclusion. *Journal of Research in Special Education Needs, 12*(4), 192–200.

Goggin, G., & Newell, C. (2003). *Digital disability: The social construction of disability in new media*. Lanham, MD: Rowman and Littlefield Publishers Inc.

Google Accessibility. (2011, June 30). We considered accessibility of Google+ from day 1. Find something we missed? Press Send Feedback link & let us know [Tweet]. Retrieved from https://twitter.com/googleaccess/status/86442474523992065

Haller, B. (2010). *Representing disability in an ableist world: Essays on mass media*. Louisville, KY: Advocado Press.

Hollier, S. (2012). Sociability: Social media for people with a disability. Retrieved from http://mediaaccess.org.au/online-media/social-media

Innes, G. (2009). Creating welcoming school communities. Paper presented at the More Than Gadgets Conference, Fremantle, Western Australia, August 2009.

Internet World Statistics. (2015). *Facebook stats for the years 2013–2015*. Retrieved from http://www.internetworldstats.com/facebook.htm

Jaeger, P. T. (2012). *Disability and the internet*. Boulder, CO and London, UK: Lynne Rienner Publishers.

Oliver, M. (1996). *Understanding disability: From theory to practice*. Hampshire, UK: Palgrave.

Romack, J. (2011, June 30). Accessibility of Google+: Will blind users be +1ing? *No Eyes Needed*. Retrieved from http://noeyesneeded.com/2011/06/accessibility-of-google-will-blind-users-be-1ing/

Toor, A. (2013, March 1). Google+ Hangouts adds sign language app and new shortcuts for disabled users. *The Verge*. Retrieved from http://www.theverge.com/2013/3/1/4042964/google-hangout-adds-sign-language-app-keyboard-shortcuts

UPIAS. (1976). *Fundamental principles of disability*. London: Union of the Physically Impaired Against Segregation. Retrieved from http://disability-studies.leeds.ac.uk/files/library/UPIAS-UPIAS.pdf

Wentz, B., Jaeger, P. T., & Lazar, J. (2011). Retrofitting accessibility: The legal inequality of after-the-fact online access for persons with disabilities in the United States. *First Monday, 16*(11). Retrieved from http://www.firstmonday.org/htbin/cgiwrap/bin/ojs/index.php/fm/article/view/3666/3077

Wong, A. (2015, July). Power of #SocialMedia & #DisabilityStories. Retrieved from https://storify.com/SFdirewolf/power-of-socialmedia-disabilitystories

Part I
Advocacy

2 Social media and deaf empowerment

The Polish deaf communities' online fight for representation

Magdalena Zdrodowska

Social media brought change in the communicational, cultural and social practices of many internet users including marginalised and minority groups – for some acting as a great emancipatory force, for others as another frontier filled with disabling features. In this chapter, I explore the profound impact of social media on the Polish deaf community, with a special focus on two aspects. The first one concerns the welcoming milieu for the alternative public space for the deaf – one that gives space for debate outside the majority/hearing domain as well as outside the official deaf agenda. The second is the possibility of mainstreaming the deaf cause with the skillful usage of the social media viral mode of communication. I will start, however, with a brief introduction to the history of the Polish deaf organisation model that will shed some light on how electronic media (not only social ones but so-called Web 1.0 as well) dramatically reshaped the deaf community, making grass-roots initiatives not only successful but possible in the first place.

One state, one party, one deaf organisation

Before World War 2 (WW2), deaf communities in Poland developed in parallel to those in other parts of Europe and the United States. There were a great number of diverse deaf associations including Christian, Jewish and others based around sport and charity. Most were run by deaf people.

The situation changed after WW2 when the communist party came to power. Centralisation became the determining factor of the new economic and social order. Grass-roots initiatives seemed suspicious and potentially threatening to the ruling party, which governed every aspect of public life. All local, minority, cultural and social (not to mention political) institutions became victims of the 'one nation, one state, one viewpoint' perspective. The variety of local deaf organisations was reduced to one official, centralised Polish Association of the Deaf (Polski Związek Głuchych – PZG) which had a typical hierarchy consisting of a directorate in the capital city and a multitude of local branches. The same idea of one organisation for each social group was also applied to blind people and ethnic and national minorities, but whereas the latter were managed by representatives of these groups, associations for deaf and blind people were governed by the hearing and seeing authorities. Both deaf and blind people were regarded as not only physically but also socially impaired, and were deemed not able to govern their own associations. The PZG served as a charity and an educational institution which set up cooperatives that were granted tax reductions in exchange for hiring deaf people as unqualified workers. The PZG also promoted and taught signed Polish (a signing system invented and developed by hearing linguists) instead of Polish Sign Language, which is the native language of Polish deaf people. This created a situation in which the deaf, banned from setting up their own, independent organisations, were turned into passive beneficiaries of state support.

Due to the iron curtain, the Polish deaf did not experience or benefit from the social movements and changes that took place in the twentieth century in the West, especially in the United States. The gaining of respect and representation, the recognition of sign language (Stokoe 1960; Caterline & Cronenberg 1965), social protests (for example the Deaf President Now! campaign at Gallaudet University in 1988) and the expressions of cultural individuality by deaf communities were all components of the gradual process of 'Western' deaf emancipation; an emancipation that did not take place in Poland until the late 1990s. After the fall of communism in 1989, Poland's borders opened to people and ideas, including new perspectives on deafness and on deaf people's role in society. The vision of Deaf World (the concept of a unique, social Deaf realm) and of deaf cultural separateness and self-determination that had slowly evolved for more than half of the century in the West appeared in Poland as a ready-made set of ideas and attitudes. These concepts and social processes were also closely related to the development of analogue technologies – movies, videos (Bauman, Nelson & Rose, 2006; Peters, 2000), the TTY (Lang, 2000) and captions. Changes in the Polish deaf community started in the late 1990s and converged with the appearance of new media that was quickly followed by a shift from the analogue to digital.

Web 1.0 – the emergence of an alternative public sphere

Jürgen Habermas (1999, 2008) perceived the public sphere as an ideal discursive milieu of consensus achieved by representation of all actors and their willingness to negotiate. The free exchange and criticism of ideas, concepts and values are the core elements of the Habermasian public sphere. However, they need several prerequisites – common access to the discursive sphere, representation of the Other and the goodwill of all participants.

Outside the idealistic Habermasian concept, the accessibility of the physical public sphere is limited by physical obstructions, whereas the public sphere distributed through press, radio and television is ruled by audience ratings and advertising. Therefore, minorities (which in Poland constitute a very small percentage of society) are not considered to be a significant audience group, especially in terms of commercial media. In public media, governed by its mission to provide information, entertainment and representation to the whole spectrum of society, it is slightly easier to find content designed for the ethnic and national minority audiences, but still the coverage of minority needs are far from sufficient. Disabled people are hardly ever considered a distinct audience group and media is even less accessible for many deaf Poles as their native language is not the same as the national one. Many deaf Poles do not comprehend the Polish language well enough to freely participate in the media sphere, follow captions on television (if there are any) or read the press. This excludes them from active as well as passive participation in the public sphere. The deaf who lack both access and a common communication mode are sorely unrepresented and become the marginalised Other. The internet has the capability to serve as an alternative public sphere to those who suffer lack of access to the mainstream public sphere, namely minority groups, including the disabled and the deaf.

The internet, which is not free of barriers and disables many users (Ellis & Kent, 2011), provided new opportunities for the deaf in terms of participation and access to information, albeit for users whose language skills allow them to read in Polish. It enabled the first stage of an alternative deaf public sphere – representing the deaf community online in the same mainstream domain as the hearing majority. The official deaf organisations which were based offline were the first to transfer to the internet and form 'communities online' (Kozinets, 2010, pp. 13–15) which mirror the landscape of the offline deaf community. However, communities originating online (Kozinets's 'online communities') soon started to emerge and had a new, bottom-up quality. These formed the second stage of the online alternative public sphere – grass-roots, unofficial collectives that proposed views alternate, not only to the hearing majority, but also to the dominant discourse of deaf organisations which are run by the hearing and hard of hearing authorities, and consequently represent a medical attitude toward deaf and deafness. I will briefly describe two online platforms designed for deaf users that have played an important role in the evolution of the online deaf community.

The first one is the Association of Deaf and Hard of Hearing Internet Users (Organizacja Niesłyszących i Słabosłyszących Internautów – ONSI). They run onsi.pl, a typical variety portal which offers a wide range of information, from politics and economy, through to culture and trivia. Its main role is to filter internet content to find, translate and publish information that may be of interest to the Polish deaf. In 2008 the platform expanded its offerings by launching onsi.tv, the first news service in Polish Sign Language. While this is far from a professional news service, it plays an important, if auxiliary, role by providing narratives in sign language that serve as the basis of its recognition and unification. Sign language's usage in a context wider than interpersonal communication builds its importance and makes it a tool for self-recognition. Also, its use in movies causes it to develop in the same way that writing influences oral cultures. The role of analogue technologies of moving pictures and video for Western sign languages (most profoundly for American Sign Language [Krentz, as cited in Bauman, Nelson & Rose, 2006, p. 51–70]) in Poland was taken over by internet video files posted on YouTube and distributed via Facebook.

There is no formal organisation behind the second platform, glusi.pl; instead it is run by a group of enthusiasts. Glusi.pl was one of the first deaf platforms in Poland to make extensive use of YouTube. Volunteers translate videos concerning deaf issues, but what is more interesting is that glusi.pl has two versions – one in written Polish, another in Polish Sign Language, which includes a signed forum. The idea seemed brilliant at first as it allowed users to express themselves in their native language, thereby creating a totally separate discursive sphere for the deaf. This initiative, however, was surprisingly unsuccessful – only a few films were uploaded by users and most of them are singular statements, tales or jokes that do not engage one another or constitute real discussion.

There are two reasons for the signed forum failure. First, when it was launched, the signed forum was an island of Polish Sign Language in an ocean of written Polish. For those deaf people who have significant problems with comprehension of the Polish language, the forum might have been hard to find. The second reason for its failure was the appearance of YouTube and Facebook, establishing a perfect communication milieu for deaf people, with the first serving as a publication platform and the latter as a powerful distribution tool.

Web 2.0 – between networking and the filter bubble

The social media boom in Poland started in the mid-2000s, with grono.net (launched in 2004) or nasza-klasa.pl (launched in 2006) as local answers to the global phenomenon of social media sites. But in 2009–2010 the landscape of Polish social media was shaped by just two sites – Facebook and YouTube. Facebook became extremely popular in 2009 after the Polish language version of the platform appeared in 2008 (Rusza polska wersja Facebooka, 2008). YouTube's popularity among Polish internet users consequently rose from 23% in 2006, to 61% in 2010 and to 67% in 2013 (www.gemius.pl).

At that time the main internet platforms for deaf people were still web 1.0 sites, with the powerful deaf.pl forum serving as an online agora and counterweight to the offline domination of the pathologised vision of deafness. deaf.pl (a forum associated with the aforementioned onsi.pl) was created in 2004 and attracted deaf users who were the 'proud deaf', meaning they identified themselves with a cultural attitude towards deafness which contrasted with the aforementioned PZG. As one of the few Deaf Culture asylums, the forum soon became a rather extremist and unfriendly environment for the hard of hearing and deaf people that do not use Polish Sign Language, leading to a drop off in users. Painful as this was, it created a coherent and highly motivated group of Deaf people who were eager and ready to take up offline action. For them the idea of Deaf Culture was not an extravagant Western fad but a shared value that was worth putting into social and political practice.

Before the hyper popularity of social media in Poland, Facebook was used rather instrumentally by Web 1.0 platforms, serving as a tool for visualising the community gathered around sites such as glusi.pl and onsi.pl. As these sites did not have many other instruments with which to create a sense of belonging for their participants, they employed the graphic capabilities of their Facebook fan pages to showcase photos of users and the quantity of 'likes' their organisations received. At onsi.pl there was information showing the number of views of each article, and the deaf.pl forum provided statistics. In both cases, information was anonymous and strictly quantitative, but it gave users a sense of participating in a bigger group of (presumably) deaf users. The software simply counted and displayed the number of times each page had been viewed. The display of the number of likes on Facebook together with fans' photos presents something more – it counts people who have deliberately clicked the 'like' button and identify with the set of ideas and values regarding deafness, as well as the model of the deaf person represented by the site and consequently by its Facebook profile. Otherwise, the popularity of onsi.pl's Facebook fan page is difficult to explain as it does not offer much – no stimuli in the form of additional information, questions or moderating discussions. The content is self-referential and consists of links to articles and videos published on onsi.pl and onsi.tv. The much smaller and less organised group behind glusi.pl had to try much harder to gain an equal number of fans of their Facebook fan page.

The deaf media landscape changed after deaf users combined YouTube as an expression tool for sign communication, and Facebook as a distribution and discursive instrument. After this fusion, the fate of Web 1.0 sites was sealed. They demand a high level of Polish language comprehension as everything is written, which results in a paradoxical stratification – the most active members who praise and fight for Polish Sign Language are those who are the most fluent in Polish. The vast majority of deaf.pl users are in fact passive readers. On one hand, this is typical of online participation. Prosumerism, so praised by the first researchers of social media (e.g. Tapscott & Williams, 2010), turned out to be more optimistic than realistic. Counter to expectations and enthusiastic predictions, most internet users participate passively more than by actually creating content.[1] On the other hand, when reading deaf.pl threads intended for everybody to express themselves (e.g. who is who or the dating section) it can be clearly seen that the users who do not post regularly have great difficulties with the Polish language and in fact are on the verge of illiteracy. For them, the YouTube–Facebook combination was a liberating communication environment. The two work in tandem – YouTube allows signing, and Facebook offers a variety of non-verbal communication possibilities such as liking, sharing and commenting with easily posted gifs, memes, images and links to YouTube videos. The dynamics of Facebook encourage uncomplicated, short statements followed by icons displaying mood, physical location or the activity the user is undertaking. All this makes Facebook far more welcoming to deaf people who do not know verbal language than any Web 1.0 platform.

In 2013 the deaf.pl forum started to die off, while deaf groups on Facebook were mushrooming. The deaf.pl community was aware of this fact and accurately pointed out that Facebook was the source of the forum's rapid popularity decrease. On 27 February 2014, a special thread was created which was devoted to the forum's decline due to Facebook. As a remedy, pasting Facebook's deaf-related content into deaf.pl was proposed. The idea of cataloguing Facebook's content was suggested not only as a tactic for the revival of deaf.pl, but also as a means of addressing what some users experienced as Facebook's overwhelming and chaotic interface. Facebook communication is rapid, intensified by the practice of frequent status updating, which is much easier than writing long and complex forum posts. At the same time, the multitude of posts, status changes and replies to posts often make it impossible to follow. This is especially true in the case of very large groups and fan pages where the number of comments is so large that debate is practically impossible. The perceivable elements of the communication are the flows and changes in direction of discussions, rather than single comments that are easily overlooked and eventually hidden, as Facebook's structure shows only the most recent comments.

Apart from the confusing overabundance of constantly updated content, Facebook has another paradoxical feature – although the platform creates an ideal environment for representing diversity (creating multiple groups and fan pages which gather people around ideas and concepts that are hard to promote and distribute otherwise) it also makes it extremely difficult to engage in substantive discussion of different viewpoints. On the deaf.pl forum, the deaf used to discuss, negotiate and often argue within one space, all organised in a neat and ordered thematic structure – here the practice of meeting and exchanging viewpoints was the basis of the public sphere concept. The deaf community is highly heterogeneous with regards to age, gender, education, social background and, most importantly, in terms of deafness and deaf identity. This diversity caused friction in the forum, which led to conflicts and schisms. Although deaf.pl needed strict regulations by moderators, it was still one common discursive space.

On Facebook, different deaf factions have formed their own groups – the Deaf Unity Front (Polityka Jedności Głuchych) and the Social Movement of the Deaf and Their Friends (Społeczny Ruch Głuchych i Ich Przyjaciół) or anti-PZG (PPZG) seem the most influential and antagonist ones. Most of them require acceptance of new members by administrators, are isolated from each other, and act as cliques. Cooperation and the exchange of ideas is rather difficult because this separatism reinforces the 'filter bubble effect' (Pariser, 2012) which is a consequence of new media variability (Manovich, 2001). Variability may be understood in two ways – as the ability of new media objects to adjust to different types of equipment (e.g. web browsers or mobile devices), and as content being adjusted to the user's interests, preferences and browsing history. Content is personalised to protect the user from unwanted information, but at the same time it creates a 'you loop' (Pariser, 2012) in which the user's point of view is constantly reassured. One's worldview is not challenged due to the established practices designed to provide users with content tailored to their perceived interests, tastes and points of view. The division of the Polish Facebook deaf community into numerous, separate groups does not promote social networking – on the contrary it deepens the lack of contact, making it harder to encounter the Other who might challenge what we regard as obvious.

Although the deaf community seems more dispersed and divided on Facebook than it used to be on deaf.pl, it is easier to organise offline events in social media than it was several years earlier on deaf.pl. The deaf community has changed, gaining self-consciousness and social skills since 2010. On 14 May of that year members of the deaf.pl forum took their first offline action by manifesting their discontent of the lack of captions in front of the Polish public television building. The protest originated in February on the forum and ended in June, when the last of many highly critical posts regarding the manifestation appeared. This was the first grass-roots event of this scale organised by the deaf community, during which the deaf made a clear statement of their cause. Unfortunately, the protest was judged as unsuccessful mainly due to the poor attendance. However, the organisation of the event provided real experience in both the managing of a social action (e.g. contact with media) and active participation in public life.

One of the most memorable events of the Facebook era was the founding of an alternative to the official PZG. In 2013, the Social Movement of the Deaf and Their Friends was inaugurated. The Movement's online home was launched in in April 2013 at g.klyo.net, and served as a publication forum for YouTube videos uploaded by the group's leaders. At first the site made it possible to collect videos uploaded by different people into one place. This reflected the lack of trust in social media platforms as mechanisms for focusing the concerns and conversations of deaf people. As an 'official' site, g.klyo.net was still perceived as something more accurate than a YouTube profile. The first videos are no longer available, but their titles (*Heading toward reform: the Deaf fighting for their rights,* or *Spring is coming: time to build deaf power*) clearly portray the movement's objectives of both recognition, and social and organisational change. The number of posts per month declined after the Movement was officially registered in December 2013 and the Facebook profile appeared in January 2014.

It is interesting that when the move occurred from g.klyo.net to Facebook, the logo of the Movement was changed from two hands signing to two clenched fists – from communication to fight. The new logo accurately reflects the Movement's attitudes and targets – social and political change regarding services and welfare for the deaf and profound opposition to the PZG, the organisation blamed for almost all the negligence, bad organisation, mismanagement and discrimination that the deaf community suffers. The dissatisfaction with PZG was (and still is) a powerful impetus to the Movement whose unofficial name, anti-PZG, underscores PZG's role as a unity-building enemy.

In February 2014, the biggest (and second in the short history of the organisation) protest against the PZG was held – the deaf organised a march through the streets of capital city with its climax in front of the PZG building. Marching, protesting and occupation are a form of gaining attention in order to voice expectations or demands towards the other side of the conflict; however, collective presence in the same physical space works for the protesters themselves as well, it is a tool which displays the size of the groups. As I have mentioned before, Facebook was used to achieve the same effect by Web 1.0 sites but, as Eric Kluitenberg argues, social media lets people know how many similarly thinking people are out there, as well as revealing their identities (Kluitenberg, 2011, pp. 7–8). Taking into consideration all the critics of the digital dualism (Jurgenson, 2009, 2011a, 2011b, 2012) there is a difference between so-called cyberactivism and offline actions, such as marching and temporarily occupying physical space – just like the Arab Spring or the Twitter-originated #occupywallstreet. Social media does not release users from their social roles and images, on the contrary it highlights them with the timeline, the list of liked pages and groups and eventually with their social locus by revealing their friends, workplace or location, accordingly to what

Manuael Castells calls 'mass self-communication' (Castells, 2009). Co-presence in a physical (urban) space allows a group of individuals, whose biographies and preferences are not revealed, to transform into a crowd, and eventually into a public or political entity. Meeting outside social media results not in individual, social roles but in public ones driven by one cause, and allows people to act as a citizen or a social movement's member.

The demonstration by the Movement was based around Facebook, which served as a powerful information board and navigation centre. Organisers maintained the high level of emotions every day by uploading a daily countdown to the demonstration on the Facebook page, as well as documents such as the official permission for the demonstration, its route and the set of postulates. Information was published numerous times both in Polish and Polish Sign Language. While its online origin makes this deaf demonstration similar to #occupy and the Arab Spring (in its own scale), the usage of social media in preparing the offline action makes the deaf demonstration strikingly different. Even though the Arab Spring and #occupy were pronounced as cyber revolutions, they were far from that – in those instances social media was not used extensively due to the fact that it is an extremely easy object of surveillance. The Polish deaf could use both Facebook and YouTube as their gathering was legal.

This legality of the protest allowed both actors of the conflict – protesters and PZG – to use social media as a communication tool before the demonstration took place. PZG made use of the unofficial communication strategies used in the social media by the deaf community. The vibrant Polish deaf community expresses quite a lot of aggression and hostility online – communication is often highly emotional and quarrels are quick to escalate. On the deaf.pl forum the discussions were strictly moderated and all manifestations of aggression and vulgarity were noticed and deleted, with persistent offenders eventually being banned. Even though allegations of censorship were voiced, the forum was a sphere of calm, factual discussions, even if the peace was constrained.

Some Facebook groups and fan pages are moderated, but on individual walls or unmoderated pages, personal, highly offensive quarrels often take place not only in written Polish (as on deaf.pl), but also in Polish Sign Language through YouTube videos, which seems to make the communication even stronger, as on YouTube the author's face is clearly visible and recognisable, as opposed to written messages on deaf.pl. As users involved in the rows do not belong to the same groups and fan pages, and are not Facebook friends, their quarrels have to rely on the social media viral mode of spreading the content. The harsh discussions are conducted by properly addressing the YouTube videos (that are later shared in Facebook groups) to the intended recipients, e.g. 'To [name and surname]', 'Answer to [name and surname]'. The 'share' function combined with networking does the rest in delivering the video to the right person even if he/she is not in the circle of friends of the sender of the message.

This method of individual communication between conflicting parties was used by the Movement and PZG just before the demonstration; information exchange took place online through YouTube. The PZG authorities addressed the organisers in a series of YouTube videos (with comments disabled) that were later distributed among Facebook users. Previously, the PZG YouTube channel, which was founded in March 2013, was filled with videos covering official statements, legal issues and trivia. One month before the demonstration, the PZG channel became more intense, starting with an 'open letter' to all deaf organisations supporting the event. In 2014 YouTube became an official medium of communication between PZG and the demonstration organisers. As PZG were the common enemy, they had to adapt to the unofficial mode of communication of the Movement in order to at least try to stop it from organising the demonstration.

Three weeks before the demonstration, morale-building posters appeared on the Facebook page. Similarly to the famous #occupy call to action poster with a ballerina dancing on the Wall Street bull, the deaf posters remodelled the mental environment of the deaf, as Kalle Lasn put it in the case of the #occupy poster (White & Lasn, 2011). The posters and memes used by the organisers made extensive national references, including the national flag, the shape of Poland and the national colours (white and red). A local symbol was used as well, the Warsaw mermaid, the symbol of the capital city, a woman with a raised sword with 'PJM' (the abbreviation for Polish Sign Language) on her shield.

The Movement's Facebook page was stimulated by the demonstration for a long time. Administrators gave detailed information about all media coverage and uploaded video material whenever possible. However, the demonstration and the Movement did not gain much media attention in contrast to the famous Deaf President Now! protest at Gallaudet University in 1988, which attracted the nationwide media to deaf issues. In Poland the protest did not resonate to this extent; however, it caught the attention of the left wing politicians of the progressive Your Movement (Twój Ruch). The party appeared on the Polish political scene in 2011 with great and unexpected (for a conservative Poland) success. Strongly anti-clerical while supporting woman rights, LGTB groups and transgender people, the party presented itself as a supporter of the excluded. Deaf people struggling for emancipation and standing up against powerful institutions caught Your Movement's attention, especially in 2014, when it had already lost its freshness and the image of uncompromising young politicians. Your Movement's interest in the deaf cause was short and fruitless, but it remains as one of the most visible public consequences of the demonstration.

Mainstreaming the deaf cause

The second feature of social media in respect to minority/excluded groups that I want to mention is the 'boomerang effect'. This is the process of strengthening a minority's voice and increasing its influence on the majority of society. This is done by the institutions mobilised to support the expectations, interests or aspirations of the minority, which is a weaker party on the social scene. The result is the multiplexing of the minority and the balancing of the initial unequal state (Porębski, 2010, pp. 44–48). All this may be achieved with the support of NGOs, the government, political institutions and the media. The same effect can be stimulated by the skillful usage of the mainstream online communication channels in order to gain the interest of the majority/mainstream media. The viral interest of users often attracts media researchers to minority issues. Even though social media platforms are divided into groups and circles of interest, they are in the public sphere, where the content of deaf users can be exposed to the hearing majority's eyes. Social media comes to the rescue of the traditional media as press and television follow the infotainment pattern and struggle with the difficulties of constant news production. Both television and press in Poland extensively leverage user-generated content as a source of information, media drama and lighter topics. All this creates quite a favourable milieu for the deaf message getting through to public opinion.

Surprisingly, the boomerang effect of deaf issues in traditional Polish mainstream media was not achieved by the deaf demonstrating against the PZG (which seems an ideal topic for long-term media interest), but by a group of pupils at a school for the deaf. They formed a performing group called Young Sign Music (Młodzi Migają Muzykę – MMM) after a workshop in 2012 at which they translated popular Polish songs into Polish Sign Language and made videos. The results of the workshop (signed songs and backstage materials) were uploaded on YouTube with the first video appearing in March 2013. The group appeared on the platform as a fully formed phenomenon with a name, logo and Facebook profile (created in February 2013). The sequence of events suggests that the idea of forming a recognisable 'brand' was intended from the beginning and social media was used to gain popularity and attention. The first video uploaded on YouTube (and shared on Facebook) was a short presentation from an existing group in which its members sign and a Polish transcription is presented on the screen, which was a real rarity for videos uploaded online by the Polish deaf. Even onsi.tv does not have captions, which excludes both the hearing and the deaf who do not know Polish Sign Language.

The first videos with signed translations of songs were a rather modest success, but a brilliant PR move had been undertaken. In October 2013, Polish Humanitarian Action (PAH), the most recognised Polish charity organisation, celebrated its twentieth anniversary and several Polish artists recorded a song together to promote and celebrate the anniversary. MMM decided to translate the song into Polish Sign Language and present it at a meeting with Janina Ochojska, the founder and leader of PAH. They recorded and uploaded the song translation to YouTube, where it spread virally with the extensive help of the PAH Facebook page as well as the fan pages of the artists who performed the original song. This attracted media attention to MMM, and, on 25 December, a news item about MMM was broadcast on one of the largest public television news services. The group's decision to join the celebration of PAH brought it to the attention of the public media and made a perfect, heart-warming Christmas story of young creative people who overcame their disability. It was also a curiosity story, a 'wonder of humanity' tale, in which deafness combined with music made a miracle paradox that worked extremely well for audiences gathered at home and watching the news during the Christmas break (for a critique of these stories see Haller and Preston, Chapter 4 this volume).

Two months later, the Polish pop band Video invited MMM to join them and take part in a video promoting their single (consequently the band gained not only media interest but also a nomination for the Stars of Charity Award). The publication of the video was the element that got MMM on television via the news services and breakfast television programmes. Now it was official – MMM was part of mainstream, popular culture. They were no longer a group of school kids having fun during some extra classes, but a nationwide, recognised phenomenon who worked as ambassadors of the deaf cause and Polish Sign Language in mainstream media. In 2015 MMM performed with Video during a large and popular music festival. Whenever they make a public appearance, the issues of deafness and Polish Sign Language come into the limelight with them. In addition, the YouTube comments that accompany the videos show that the aforementioned elements can reach more and more representatives of the mainstream society.

Social media has profoundly changed the media landscape; in particular, it has had a great impact on minority groups, especially the ones whose members are dispersed nationwide or globally. Social media created the chance for mainstreaming minority issues – in contrast to earlier Web 1.0 platforms that, although serving as minorities' discoursive agoras, were also likely to constitute online ghettos.

Conclusion

In this chapter I have showcased studies of Polish deaf social media initiatives that succeeded in introducing the deaf cause to the wider public and were a tool of the deaf emancipation. The powerful Facebook–YouTube cooperative is a bitter–sweet phenomenon. It comes to the communicational rescue for those internet users who prefer to interact in visual and performative sign language. However, due to algorithms intending to craft the social media content to the personal interests of their users, it creates the filter bubble which makes social networking seems more difficult than through Web 1.0 platforms.

There is still a long way to go before the Polish deaf community gains respect and is able to independently shape its own representation and social and political fate. Undoubtedly, the first steps have been taken in making extensive use of electronic media. These steps may seem irrelevant or even trivial in comparison to other deaf actions, such as the Deaf President Now! protests, but one must remember that the Polish deaf community is waking up from a very long and passive sleep. Taking over governance is a slow and painful process in which social media plays an important role as a matchless tool for communication in sign language as well as a battlefield for practising both social and citizenly behaviours.

Note

1 TubeMogul research shows that only 17% of YouTube content is created by the users themselves. The rest is the commercial content – advertising, YouTube partners and piracy. www.tubemogul.com/research/report/31 citing after: *Obiegi kultury. Społeczna cyrkulacja treści. Raport z badań*, Centrum Cyfrowe, Warszawa 2012, s. 31–32.

References

Bauman, H-D. L., Nelson, J. L., & Rose, H. M. (Eds.). (2006). *Signing the body poetics: Essays on American sign language literature*. Berkeley, Los Angeles, London: University of California Press.

Castells, M. (2009). *Communication power*. Oxford, NY: Oxford University Press.

Ellis, K., & Kent, M. (2011). *Disability and new media*. New York, London: Routledge.

Habermas, J. (1999). *Teoria działania komunikacyjnego*, t. 1, Wydawnictwo Naukowe PWN, Warszawa (*Theorie des kommunikativen Handelns)*. Frankfurt am Main 1981.

Habermas, J. (2008). *Strukturalne przeobrażenie sfery publicznej*, Wydawnictwo Naukowe PWN, Warszawa (*Strukturwandel der Öffentlichkeit)*. Hermann: Luchterhand Verlag, Darmstadt-Neuwie, 1962.

Jurgenson, N. (2009). Toward theorizing an augmented reality. Retrieved September 23 2014 from http://thesocietypages.org/sociologylens/2009/10/05/towards-theorizing-an-augmented-reality.

Jurgenson, N. (2011a). Digital dualism and the fallacy of web objectivity. Retrieved September 23 2014 from http://thesocietypages.org/cyborgology/2011/09/13/digital-dualism-and-the-fallacy-of-web-objectivity.

Jurgenson, N. (2011b). Digital dualism versus augmented reality. Retrieved September 23 2014 from http://thesocietypages.org/cyborgology/2011/02/24/digital-dualism-versus-augmented-reality.

Jurgenson, N. (2012). When atoms meet bits: Social media, the mobile web and augmented revolution. *Future Internet, 4*(1), 83–91.

Kluitenberg, E. (2011). *Legalicies of tactical media: The tactics of occupation: From Tompkins Square to Tahir*. Amsterdam: Institute of Network Cultures.

Kozinets, R. V. (2010). *Netnography: Doing ethnographic research online*. London, Washington: Sage.

Lang, H. G. (2000). *A phone of our own: The deaf insurrection against MA Bell*. Washington: Gallaudet University Press.

Manovich, L. (2001). *The language of new media*. Cambridge, MA: MIT Press.

Pariser, E. (2012). *The filter bubble: How the new personalized web is changing what we read and how we think*. London: Penguin Books.

Peters, C. L. (2000). *Deaf American literature: From Carnival to the Canon*. Washington: Gallaudet University Press.

Porębski, L. (2010). Internet jako narzędzie mobilizacji politycznej mniejszości. In Ł. Kapralska & B. Pactwa (Eds.). *Agora czy Hyde Park. Internet jako przestrzeń społeczna grup mniejszościowych* (pp. 107–120). Kraków: Nomos.

Rusza polska wersja Facebooka. (2008). Retrived December 20 2014 from www.wirtualne media.pl/artykul/rusza-polska-wersja-facebooka.

Stokoe, W. C. (1960). Sign language structure: An outline of the visual communication systems of the American deaf. Studies in linguistics. Occasional Papers 8.

Stokoe, W., Casterline, C., & Croneberg, C. (1965). *A dictionary of American sign language on linguistic principles.* Silver Spring, MD: Linstok Press.

Tapscott, D., & Williams, A. D. (2010). *Wikinomics: How mass collaboration changes everything*. New York: Portfolio Trade.

White, M., & Lasn, K. (2011, September 19). The call to occupy Wall Street resonates around the world. *The Guardian*. Retrieved May 4 2014 from http://www.theguardian.com/commentisfree/cifamerica/2011/sep/19/occupy-wall-street-financial-system.

3 Personal reflections on the #107days campaign

Transformative, subversive or accidental?

Sara Ryan and George Julian

Introduction

In this chapter, we describe the emergence of a social movement for justice in an area little engaged with in social media; learning disability. This movement, in which we both played key roles, began in response to the preventable death in 2013 of a young man, Connor Sparrowhawk (also known as LB or Laughing Boy), in a National Health Service (NHS) assessment and treatment unit. Typically his death would not be widely known as learning disabled people are marginalised within the UK and fail to generate much coverage in mainstream media. However, LB's mother (SR) had been writing a blog, *My Daft Life*, about family life since 2011 and this created an unusual space in which a diverse range of people knew of LB before he died. Mobilising a social movement around 'learning disability' has offered both challenges and fascinating insights into the logistics of online campaigning, the ways in which people choose to become involved (or not) and the processes of engagement, disengagement and social networking. Here we highlight and reflect on how social media ensured that learning disabled people were central to and active participants in a campaign that increased recognition of the humanity of a quirky young man who loved buses. It also demonstrated a mobilisation potential we did not foresee and which contradicts pervasive views about learning disability within the UK. The broad engagement and ongoing support given suggests that learning disabled people do matter to (many) people.

In the UK, there are an estimated 1.14 million people with learning disabilities and this group have consistently limited opportunities in all aspects of life. For example, the median age of death for learning disabled people is 24 years younger than those without a learning disability and only 7.1% of learning disabled people are in paid employment (Emerson et al. 2013). Learning disabled people are also likely to experience prejudice, discrimination and abuse (Emerson et al. 2013). Periodically, scandals within institutional settings have penetrated UK media coverage (for example, the Ely Hospital Enquiry, 1968–1969; the Longcare Inquiry, 1998 and the Cornwall Partnership NHS scandal, 2006) but the interest generated is generally short lived.

The uncovering in 2011 of abuse at the Winterbourne View assessment and treatment unit by an undercover journalist generated public outcry and condemnation when televised on British television. It also seemed to provoke serious attention and action by the UK government. Ultimately, however, this action led to little or no change (Parish 2014) with the Minister responsible for Social Care simply condemning the programme as 'an abject failure' (Brindle 2014).

Background to #JusticeforLB

LB was a hilarious and quirky 18–year-old boy who was diagnosed with epilepsy, autism and learning disabilities. He lived at home with his family and attended the local special education school. Towards the end of 2012, LB became increasingly anxious, distressed and uncharacteristically aggressive. There was little support available and he spent the next three months in and out of school. On March 15, 2013 he punched his teaching assistant and four days later was admitted to a specialist, local, short-term assessment and treatment unit close to his family home. This unit had a specialist team of staff including psychiatrists, occupational therapists, psychologists and learning disability nurses. There were five patients with four staff always on duty.

SR had been blogging about her experiences of family life with LB since 2011, documenting funny everyday happenings as they occurred; at meal times, on day trips out, waiting to catch the school bus, shopping and on holiday. Once LB was admitted to the unit, the blog became less about family life and more of a record of life at the unit with entries numbered from Day One of LB's incarceration.

These entries documented how LB's identity as a much loved member of a large, extended family, was stripped away by the unit staff who made much of his status as an adult. There was little assessment or treatment and much of LB's time was spent watching DVDs in his room. In May, SR told staff that LB was having seizures (the staff changed his medication without concern about sensitivity to medication change) but her concerns were largely dismissed, despite his diagnosis of epilepsy. On the morning of July 4, 2013, Day 107, LB drowned in the bath.

At some point that afternoon, SR posted a one liner on the *My Daft Life* blog stating that LB had died. This caused considerable shock among readers who felt that they had got to know LB through this virtual space. Within days, a human rights barrister got in touch, via Twitter, and strongly advised the family to contact INQUEST, a small independent charity providing advice for bereaved families. It transpired that the NHS is not above covering up catastrophic events like this and strong legal representation was needed for the inquest at an estimated cost of £25,000. The family set up a fund (LB Fighting Fund) to raise money and began to sell postcards and prints of LB's artwork via a new blog.

Social media usage

In understanding the emergence of online activism around learning disability in response to this event, it is important to consider social media usage and how campaigns derive from and depart from earlier forms of activism which encompass both movements and moments of collective action (Harlow 2012). Activism can involve a prolonged contesting of authority with interactions between challengers and power holders (Tarrow 1998) and the aim of achieving social change. Writing before the development of the internet, Tilly (1978) argued that successful activism depends on the degree of the group's common interests and shared identity, available resources, political power, opportunities and threats and level of governmental repression. Social media has enabled the emergence of new forms of activism and collectivism and, for the disabled people's movement, within the context of austerity and welfare cuts, a new politics of disability is emerging (Morgan 2013). A new community of activists has reinvigorated the disabled people's movement and broadened its membership to include many previously excluded or marginalised from disability activism (Ellis & Goggin 2013; Morgan 2013). Social media has provided disabled people with a voice, and a larger audience that those in power may find harder to ignore:

> It's been a magic bullet. It's given us political influence, media respect and international impact. . . . In the disabled and long term-sick, social media has found a section of society simultaneously targeted and excluded from mainstream politics. In social media, disabled people have found themselves a voice.
>
> (Ryan 2014a)

While social media allows for the creation of new forms of activism and resistance (Ellis & Goggin 2013; Morgan 2013; Van Laer & Van Aelst 2009) as well as supporting more traditional forms (through offering fast and cheap channels of communication, for example), there is some caution around the use of the internet in activism. This includes the suggestion it encourages a type of 'Slacktivism' or less than dedicated campaigners (Morozov 2009), involves challenges in developing trust, and there is an enduring belief that face-to-face relationships are more durable and easier to sustain (Diani 2000). Overall, these concerns can be summarised as social media offering a less valid or authentic space of engagement.

We began #JusticeforLB as a campaign to gain justice for the preventable death of LB but, from the start, had broader stated aims around the social change needed to improve the lives and experiences of learning disabled people. One way of considering #JusticeforLB, and the use of social media in learning disability, is through the framework of three phases of activist campaign management identified by Gerhards and Rucht (1992); diagnostic, prognostic and motivational. These involve defining the problem, suggesting possible solutions and inciting mobilisation. There has to be both mobilisation potential and activation which Gerhards and Rucht suggest occurs at both a meso and micro level. The aims of #JusticeforLB are captured in a document known as the 'Connor Manifesto' and fall into three sections. First, for those directly related to LB, to seek justice for his death including staff disciplinary action, a corporate manslaughter charge against the NHS trust Southern Health and meaningful involvement at the inquest into his death. Second, questioning commissioning practices and previous deaths within the Trust's care. Third, broader aims including prevention of the misuse of the Mental Capacity Act, an assimilation of learning disabled people into mainstream NHS provision and an informed debate around the status of learning disabled people as full citizens in the UK.

So the problem was clearly defined at the outset of the campaign and the manifesto presented some potential solutions. The approach to mobilisation, however, was undefined, especially given that, historically, learning disabled people have been effectively socially, economically and politically marginalised from meaningful engagement with the various issues and policy that concerned their own wellbeing. We had no idea of the potential that existed for meso and micro mobilisation.

Early campaign activity: Setting the scene for #107days

For the seven months following LB's death, the family and their solicitor fought a battle with the NHS Foundation Trust responsible for LB's care, demanding an independent investigation into his death. After much delay and prevarication, the investigation was conducted by Verita, an independent consultancy, and was scheduled to be published on February 24, 2014.

GJ was one of the people who read SR's blog and purchased postcards from the LB Fighting Fund, setting up a Google map to document how far the postcards travelled. In early February, GJ contacted SR to discuss whether there were plans to increase awareness of what was happening in the family's quest for answers. We decided, via an email exchange to formalise the campaign in advance of the publication date. In mid-February a #JusticeforLB twitter account (@JusticeforLB) was created and we started to use #JusticeforLB in our tweets.

At this stage we used our personal blogs to let people know what was happening. As anticipated, the publication of the report was later in the day than could have been reasonably expected. There was a lot of activity at #JusticeforLB from 9am as people gathered online to wait for the report which wasn't released by the hospital trust until after 6pm. The report clearly stated that LB's death was preventable. In this interval an online network of supporters had formed that shared the anxiety of anticipation born by SR and LB's family. This network witnessed the delay, tweeted their anger and annoyance and started to publicly challenge and question the inappropriate behaviour, the power relationships at play and the treatment of a grieving family seeking answers.

As much as one would hope the preventable death of a young man with a learning disability would provoke a societal outrage, this outrage was confined to LB's family and friends and local community up until this point. However, analysis of the social media activity that week in February 2014 (see Figure 3.1) suggests that the prevarication by a professional state-owned provider of care led to an international outrage as people heard about what had happened.

> There has been a lot of anger and incredulity expressed on social media over the past two weeks. A twitter account http://www.twitter.com/JusticeforLB was established the day before the report into Connor's death was published, in less than two weeks it has gained 885 followers. It has shared 3,929 tweets, averaging about 300 tweets a day. . . . In addition to the twitter account, the hashtag *#JusticeforLB* has been in use. Analysis using topsy suggests that the delay by Southern Health in publishing the report enabled a huge spike in usage of the hashtag, which may well have kick started the momentum for JusticeforLB.

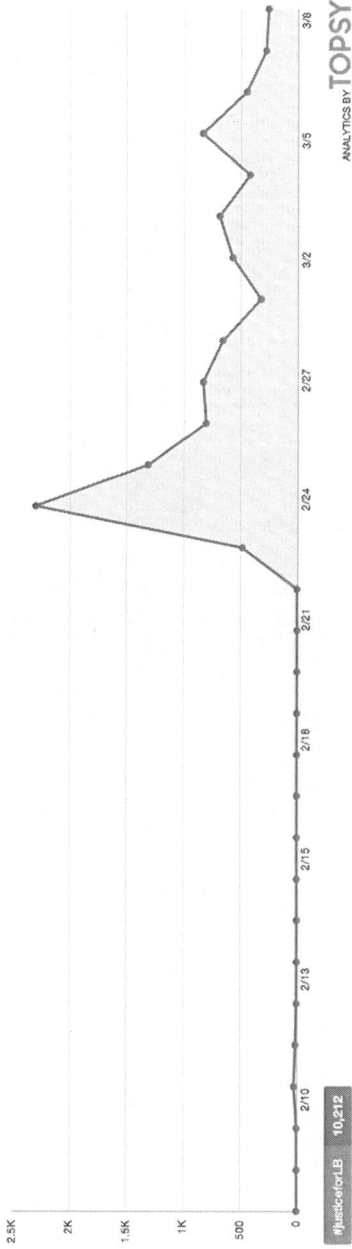

Tweets per day: #justiceforLB
February 7th — March 9th

2.5K
2K
1.5K
1K
500
0

#justiceforLB   10,212

2/10 2/13 2/15 2/18 2/21 2/24 2/27 3/2 3/5 3/8

ANALYTICS BY TOPSY

Figure 3.1 Tweets per day: #justiceforLB

The hashtag has been used 10,212 times and there has been a lot of discussion. . . . In an attempt to engage more people, and widen the conversation from just happening on twitter, a JusticeforLB facebook page was established six days ago. Facebook insights data shows that so far it has been viewed 13,422 times and received 770 likes and 468 people are talking about it.

(Julian 2014)

Background to #107days

In the weeks that followed the publication of the independent report into LB's death the network of supporters continued to grow. Numerous blog posts by supporters were published in the aftermath of the report's publication. These posts offered multiple perspectives and reflections on what had been found, while situating it within a wider societal issue of poor healthcare and premature death of learning disabled people. The initial responses also demonstrated the range and breadth of support for #JusticeforLB, in terms of the roles held by supporters, the influence they had, the networks they were connected to, and the wide geographical spread they were situated within.

The focus for us at this stage was two-fold, to raise awareness of the need for #JusticeforLB and raise funds to cover LB's family's legal costs. Conversations on Twitter between supporters focused on how they might help with these two causes and a suggestion was made that people raise money a year on from when LB entered the unit. This then became the idea to mark the time LB spent in the unit with 107 days of action, as described on the #107days blog:

> #107Days seeks to inspire, collate and share positive actions being taken to support #JusticeforLB and all young dudes. We want to harness the energy, support and outrage that has emerged in response to LB's death and ensure that lasting changes and improvements are made.
>
> #107Days of action will start on Day 0: Wednesday 19 March, and will continue until Day 107, the first anniversary of LB's death, Friday 4 July 2014. This blog will be used to share information, ideas and evidence of the changes made, big and small.
>
> (#JusticeforLB 2014)

The blog was set up on 13 March 2014, less than a week before the start of the #107Days campaign. It was shared on Twitter, Facebook and on the email distribution list established to keep people informed of campaign developments.

Structure of the #107days activity

We produced an open invitation to '*get involved with #107days, and take actions, large and small, individual or collective. We need your help to share responsibility for the actions that take place*'. People could 'adopt' one of the 107 days available and use it to raise funds or awareness or they could set a target to be completed within the 107 day period.

We did not wish to be prescriptive about the actions people should take and were therefore intentionally open. This allowed people to be creative and use their own talents, while collectively contributing to #107days. This was particularly important because we wanted to be as inclusive as possible. Given only 61% of disabled people live in households with access to the internet, compared to 86% of non-disabled people and 3.5 million disabled adults in the UK have never used the internet, representing 30% of the adult population who are disabled (ONS 2014), we did not anticipate that many learning disabled people would necessarily engage with the online activity. That said, we wanted to ensure that they could participate as fully as possible in the campaign activity.

We also did not want the campaign to be perceived as something that was purely for one group e.g. learning disabled people, or for activists, for academics, for professionals, for parents or carers. We believe we need a wholesale change in how society views, engages and involves learning disabled people, and that this change, which will inevitably involve social media, requires a new, truly collaborative approach.

The only thing that we were prescriptive about was the need to be positive:

> We would like the focus to be on positive actions at this stage. You could choose to raise funds to support legal costs, to have conversations, to write letters or blog, we need fundraisers, conversationalists and writers. We also welcome social media evangelists, artists and reflectors.
>
> (#JusticeforLB 2014)

It was important that actions were positive to ensure that the family's grief was not worsened or added to throughout this period; for authenticity's sake, so that LB was remembered in a positive fashion as the quirky, funny and acerbic person he was; and also because we believed #JusticeforLB itself would only grow and maintain support if a positive approach was taken to a challenging situation.

Adopted days and campaign activity during the #107Days

Within a relatively short period of time, with little promotion, all 107 days were adopted for activity. Towards the middle of the period it became clear we would run out of days and decided to share days. By the end we were doubling and trebling up days so as many people as possible could be included.

The actions taken were wonderfully varied and diverse. Some examples are included here and the full range of activities can be found at *https://107daysofaction.wordpress.com/*. Fundraising activities included donations in lieu of christening presents, party nights and social evenings, sales of cakes, art, plants, notebooks and pencil cases, and a crowd-funded head shave. There were a number of attempts to share the perspective of living as, or with, a learning disabled person, mostly through blog posts, but also through a sibling manifesto and film. Creative activities included a hair competition entry inspired by LB's artwork, a comedy night, an animation, a wall hanging and the Justice Quilt (see Figures 3.2 and 3.3).

First Note Luton, an all-ability community music group performed in memory of LB, lamentations were sung in Oxford and an EP for LB was recorded and released for sale online. There were events and actions focused on improving and documenting current practice including a film with Peter Walsh from Action against Medical Accidents and the launch of the Oxfordshire Family Support Network Health Watch report.

Events with an academic focus took place at the Universities of Kent, Lancaster, Cardiff, Aston, London School of Economics, Manchester Metropolitan and East Anglia mostly aimed at undergraduate students in nursing, psychology, social work, education and disability studies. Sporting activity included cycling, running, triathlon and kayaking. Events with a specific political dimension included a meeting at the House of Commons, a letter with over 600 signatures published in the Guardian and a collective approach to encourage letters to MPs.

LB had a particular love of buses and transport and this was reflected in a number of the days. Three school buses and an Earthline truck were named after LB. There was a sponsored bus ride around London and one contributor travelled 107 buses in a day. Children of the Oxford Woodcraft Folk drew buses and a group of young learning disabled people visited one of LB's favourite places, the Oxford Bus Museum. Internationally, days were adopted in France, New Zealand, Canada, USA and Ireland.

Throughout the campaign duration a number of people took daily actions including a tweet a day to share learning from those supporting people to move from assessment and treatment units into the community; a daily blog post of learning from a parent whose son had been in a unit; a daily blog post reflecting on lessons from someone else's career; and a tweet with a photo a day of the LB Bus postcard.

The beginning and end of 107days

We started #107days by inviting people to send postcards highlighting 'what is awesome' about themselves or someone they know with a learning disability. Submissions were collated across the 107days and shared at a later date. It was important to start with positive action and it enabled us to merge online media and offline physical artefacts. Encouraging people to actively engage early on enabled us to grow the network further.

The requests for Postcards of Awesome coincided with a double page colour spread in a national newspaper (Salman 2014). This comprised an article about what had happened to LB and a personal perspective constructed from extracts from SR's blog (Ryan 2014b). This national coverage, in print and online, provided a welcome impetus at the start of the #107Days.

How the last day would be marked was left open given it coincided with the first anniversary of LB's death. One suggestion made was to march on parliament, however it felt important to choose an activity that enabled LB's family to be out of the spotlight if they wished.

About a week before the end of the campaign we shared the request that people change their social media profile pictures to a black and white picture of LB on the anniversary of his death. Hundreds of people did so, with some changing just before midnight and others in the morning. SR described it as:

> Friday was a day I dreaded with every bit of my being. When I woke, very early, I was surprised to see that overnight, people had begun to change their photos on twitter. Some couldn't wait till the day. . . . A couple of times during the day I had a quick peek at twitter/facebook and was astonished at the sea of black and white pics of LB. It was absolutely brilliant and so incredibly moving. The next morning, I lay in bed reading through all the tweets. Hundreds of people. Stepping up in solidarity with 'the quirky guy who should still be here'.
>
> (Ryan 2014c)

The campaign blog was visited over 7,000 times on the final day and while we do not have an exact count of the number of people who changed their profile picture, we know hundreds did. Simultaneously supporters were invited to leave a comment on the blog reflecting on what their take-away point from the campaign would be.

The reach of #107days

Throughout #107Days the blog received an average of 550 hits per day, totaling 63,000 visits. In terms of geographical reach, Figure 3.2 shows that our global reach was vast.

At the time of writing, October 2015, the blog has been visited 104,263, by 49,381 visitors. Of these, 23,267 were referred by Twitter and 21,805 by Facebook.

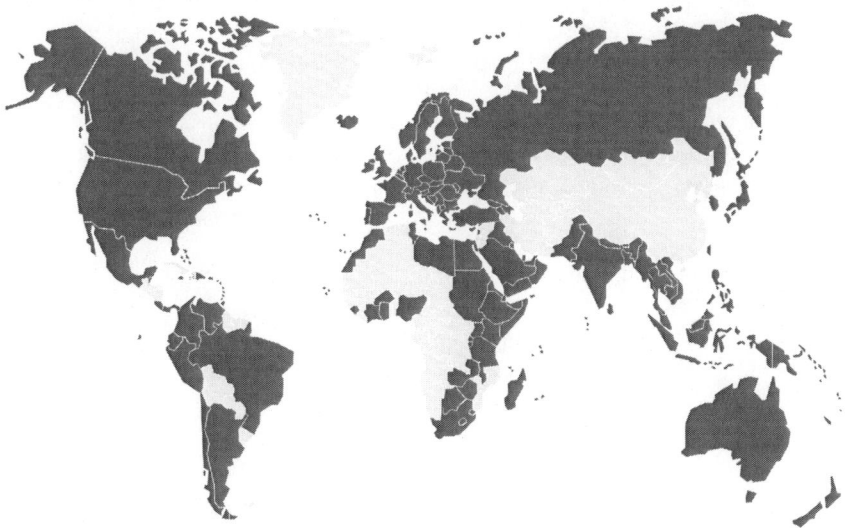

Figure 3.2 Geographical reach of #107days blog

These statistics suggest that having a number of channels for social media allows for a stronger campaign.

Supporter's views of #107days

Comments made about #107day on the final day also speak to the spread and impact of what was an intense, but relatively short, campaign. These took the form of acknowledging the power and inspiration and the potential impact that it has on disability rights movements:

> The *#107days campaign has been powerful, moving and has inspired many to stand up for disability rights.*

Others made specific mention of the role of social media as a vehicle to effective campaigning:

> *I've been a campaigner for 15 years but I've never seen anything like 107 days. Sara, George and everyone involved have finally fulfilled the promise of social media campaigning – by challenging everyone's righteous anger about a preventable tragedy into real actions for change at so many different levels.*

Mention was made of the positive developments from LB's death, and also of the positive role modelling that SR speaking out provided to other parents in similar situations:

> *It has blown me away that such a horrendous event as the preventable death of a young, vibrant man has brought so many people from different walks of life together in such a passionate and loving way. These people and this campaign has had more impact on changing crap use of ATUs than years of waiting for the system people to change it! But to me the most important thing about the campaign is seeing other families who have been in the same situation as Sara or are still in living hell with their child in an ATU get strength, come forward and grow in confidence about shouting from the rooftops that it is not acceptable and they are not putting up with crap anymore! Thank you for allowing me to be part of all this.*
>
> Sam x

Parents of learning disabled children also acknowledged the positivity to have come from LB's death, while sharing their fears for the future:

> *#JusticeforLB and the #107days campaign has been amazing and inspirational. To see so many people come together behind a cause shows something of what might be achieved in terms of a real and lasting legacy. It*

*has made me feel hopeful that it is possible to change the way people with
disabilities and learning difficulties are treated. As a mum to a little 'dude' I
am constantly thinking of how to keep him safe and cared for in the future. I
cannot imagine how difficult the last year must have been for Connor's family, without him. I have a red bus postcard framed on the wall in my home.
The sight of so many LB profile pictures on Twitter today was a very fitting
way to round off the #107days. A reminder of the person at the centre of it
all. A handsome, quirky, funny, unique and special 18 yr old young man. He
should not have died x.*

Much was also made of the collective nature of the campaign. It seemed many
felt that through bringing people together into a network, we had strength and
voice to challenge the status quo, generating optimism of a new way of doing
things and hope that it might actually lead to improvements.

We suggest some impact supporters recall could be attributed to social media
usage. Following Segerberg and Bennett (2011), Twitter, Facebook and blogs were
the key elements of our protest ecology, with Twitter particularly serving two
purposes, as networking agent and organising mechanism, while also serving as a
window onto our protest space. Social media enabled us to maintain a spotlight on
an issue that the mainstream media would only have visited fleetingly. This was
possible due to its low resource requirements, but also due to the connective nature
of communication it facilitated. As the campaign progressed, actors within our
networks increasingly took on the role of promoters and challengers, magnifying
our messages and helping to increase and maintain pressure on the UK government
to address this issue.

The people's artwork

Day 59 was adopted by three stitching enthusiasts who invited people to send
in small patches celebrating LB, or the campaign, to create a Justice Quilt. With
organisational skills that matched their creativity, the trio, led by Janet Read,
organised a mail box, issued instructions for patch size and spent months creating
a quilt. This quilt was produced very much in the tradition of resistance stitching
and, in particular, the Aids Memorial Quilt (Lewis & Fraser 1996) albeit on a
small scale. With details of the request for patches shared via social media and in
face-to-face interaction (a workshop was hosted at the University of Cardiff, for
example, which involved opportunities to create patches). It generated responses
from a diverse range of people including learning disabled people, children, professional stitchers and artists, and many others. The finished quilt, measuring 9 × 4
ft is a stunning, visual representation of LB and the campaign, dotted with images
of buses, sparrowhawks, human rights quotations, exclamation marks and questions. This piece of people's artwork will be exhibited in different locations across
the UK in the next year and is a remarkable symbol of resistance, hope and collective action.

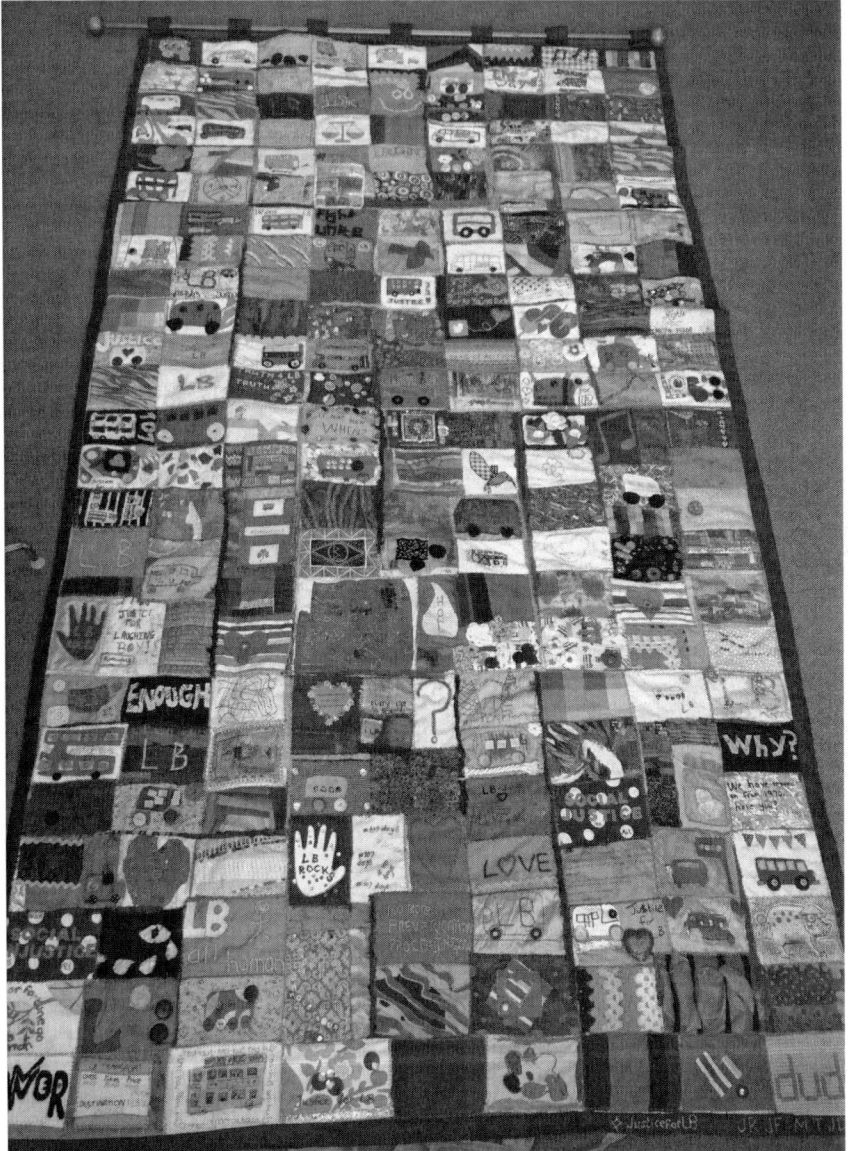

Figure 3.3 The Justice Quilt

Discussion

#JusticeforLB continues to be a ground-breaking and organic social movement that draws together two unlikely bedfellows in learning disability and social media. Kent (2008) suggests that blogs are useful as research tools and as message or issue framing and persuasion tools. *My Daft Life* was the initial driver behind the campaign enabling an understanding of LB as a person and drawing in people who had not, necessarily, engaged with learning disability previously. It widened the potential for mobilisation and worked against the siloing of learning disability as an unpopular and often ignored category even within disability activism and disability studies (Goodley & Moore 2000; Walmsley 2001). In writing LB as a very human young man, the blog gained a range of followers and readers. In time it became a space to document the unfolding events, structures and processes that accompany a preventable death, and the negative actions of the NHS Trust.

We suggest #JusticeforLB is an exemplar in the development of new forms of activism and resistance despite, or perhaps in some ways because of, the ad hoc way in which we acted. As mesomobilisation actors we (accidentally) introduced a level of organisational flexibility that Gerhards and Rucht (1992) identify as a mobilising facilitator. At the same time, we had considerable experience in research and knowledge exchange which we were able to draw upon as well as access to skills, experience and resources we did not possess via social media.

Earlier we discussed how successful activism depends on the degree of the group's common interests and shared identity, available resources, political power, opportunities and threats and level of governmental repression (Tilly 1978). #107Days cut across typical boundaries and silos, drawing together a diverse range of people and groups who do not, necessarily have common interests. This included academic networks, self-advocacy groups, disability activists, human rights activists, learning disabled people, carers and families, journalists, patient safety campaigners, information specialists and so on. We did not anticipate the cross-cutting themes that LB's death generated including law, criminal and social justice, human rights, patient safety, disability, citizenship and discrimination and these mediating factors increased mobilisation potential substantially.

We were able to crowdsource resources, engage with political power largely through the democratising characteristic of social media, and tap into spaces that offer potential to circumvent the layers of failed social action through more traditional routes.

> Disabled people's exclusion from society is such that, too often, they're even excluded from the traditional means to protest what is being done to them. Tweeting, Facebook, below-the-line comments, or blogging, has given many a new way.
>
> (Ryan 2014a)

Moreover, we argue #JusticeforLB and #107days provide no evidence of 'slacktivism'; the focus on an area characteristically ignored and the mobilisation of support demonstrates more rather than less dedication. Our experience is that people unfamiliar with, or disconnected from, learning disability are appalled and outraged on learning how people are typically treated. *My Daft Life* became an effective tool of issue framing and persuasion, a mediating factor, allowing an unusual engagement with the humanity of LB and others.

A key issue has been how to effectively engage with learning disabled people who may not use social media. This was overcome to some extent with the flexible design of #107Days which allowed anyone to adopt days. Several days were adopted by learning disabled people or their advocates and there was fluidity between on and offline activity throughout the campaign mirroring other studies (Harlow 2012). We agree with Jurgenson (2012) that 'digital dualism' is not an accurate way to describe differences between on and offline activity. In our experience, the digital and physical enmeshed with little apparent effort to generate collective spaces. There were also benefits to using physical artefacts, such as postcards of awesome, quilt patches and LB's artwork, to move from the virtual to the physical, engaging new audiences and supporters. The Justice Quilt, literally and figuratively, stitched together a wonderful range of individual and unique contributions using crafting as political protest. It enabled an acknowledgement of LB's life denied by mainstream media and society (Newmeyer 2008).

In the months after #107Days, there was a slight lessening in activity although we continued to document the actions of the Trust and broader discussions continued around learning disability provision. As part of these discussions and reflections, Mark Neary, the father of a young autistic man, questioned why the law could not be changed to make it harder for residential accommodation to be the default position for people who were deemed to have behaviour that 'challenges'. This idea grew into a draft Private Members Bill, known as the #LBBill. As the campaign develops and becomes more sophisticated, easily read materials and films have been produced and activists have organised meetings to discuss with learning disabled people the draft bill. This further demonstrates how new forms of online activism can generate serious potential for social change (contrasting with the largely ineffective substantial programme of work devised in the wake of the Winterbourne View scandal).

As the protagonists behind the campaign, we have been both recipients of and, to some extent, contributors to the shape and form of action taken, encouraging, capturing and presenting the #107Days. In shaping an inclusive campaign ecology that actively sought to engage and involve learning disabled people, their advocates and their allies, we believe we have made some progress to achieving #JusticeforLB, while simultaneously bringing together social media and learning disability.

References

Brindle, D. (2014). Post-winterbourne view transfer plan branded 'abject failure' by minister, *Guardian*, 25 May 2014, Retrieved from http://www.theguardian.com/society/2014/may/25/winterbourne-view-transfer-plan-branded-abject-failure-by-minister [12/01/15]

Diani, M. (2000). Social movement networks virtual and real. *Information, Communication & Society, 3*(3), 386–401.

Ellis, K., & Goggin, G. (2013). Disability and social media. *The Social Media Handbook,* 126–146.

Emerson, E., Hatton, C., Robertson, J., Baines, S., Christie, A., & Glover, G. (2013). *People with learning disabilities in England 2012.* Improving Health and Lives: Learning Disability Observatory.

Gerhards, J., & Rucht, D. (1992). Mesomobilization: Organizing and framing in two protest campaigns in West Germany. *American Journal of Sociology,* 98(3), 555–596.

Goodley, D., & Moore, M. (2000). Doing disability research: Activist lives and the academy. *Disability & Society,* 15(6), 861–882.

Harlow, S. (2012). Social media and social movements: Facebook and an online Guatemalan justice movement that moved offline. *New Media & Society,* 14(2), 225–243.

Julian, G. (2014). JusticeforLB: A movement for change, 9 March 2014. Retrieved from http://www.georgejulian.co.uk/2014/03/09/justiceforlb-a-movement-for-change/ [11/01/15]

Jurgenson, N. (2012). When atoms meet bits: Social media, the mobile web and augmented revolution. *Future Internet,* 4(1), 83–91.

#JusticeforLB (2014). About #107Days, 13 March 2014. Retrieved from http://107daysofaction.wordpress.com/about-107days/ [11/01/15]

Kent, M. L. (2008). Critical analysis of blogging in public relations. *Public Relations Review,* 34(1), 32–40.

Lewis, J., & Fraser, M. R. (1996). Patches of grief and rage: Visitor responses to the names project AIDS memorial quilt. *Qualitative Sociology,* 19(4), 433–451.

Morgan, H. (2013). #disabilitysnotworking: The evolution of the disabled people's movement in an era of colonisation, disabling corporatism and austerity, Nordic Network on Disability Research, 12th Research Conference, Naantali Spa, Finland. 30–31 May 2013.

Morozov, E. (2009). Texting toward utopia: Does the internet spread democracy? *Boston Review*, March/April. Retrieved from http://bostonreview.net/BR34.2/morozov.php.

Newmeyer, T. S. (2008). Knit one, stitch two, protest three! Examining the historical and contemporary politics of crafting. *Leisure/Loisir,* 32(2), 437–460.

ONS (2014). *Internet Access Quarterly Update, Q1 2014.* Retrieved from http://www.ons.gov.uk/ons/rel/rdit2/internet-access-quarterly-update/q1–2014/stb-ia-q1–2014.html#tab-Disability [13.01.15]

Parish, C. (2014). Minister refuses to cover up lack of progress in rehousing: Winterbourne view concordat has failed to ensure clients have accommodation close to their families. *Learning Disability Practice,* 17(4), 7–7.

Ryan, F. (2014a). Social media means the voices of the disabled can no longer be ignored by those in power, *New Statesman,* 7 August 2014. Retrieved from http://www.newstatesman.com/2014/07/social-media-means-voices-disabled-can-no-longer-be-ignored-those-power [12/01/15]

Ryan, S. (2014b). My son died in an NHS residential unit: Every day I wake to the pain, *Guardian,* 17 March 2014. Retrieved from http://www.theguardian.com/society/2014/mar/19/connor-sparrowhawk-death-nhs-residential-unit-fight-justice [14/01/15].

Ryan, S. (2014c). Progress towards #JusticeforLB in #107days, 7 July 2014. Retrieved from http://107daysofaction.wordpress.com/2014/07/07/progress-towards-justiceforlb-in-107days/ [15/01/15].

Salman, S. (2014). Why did Connor Sparrowhawk die in specialist NHS Unit? *Guardian,* 17 March 2014. Retrieved from http://www.theguardian.com/society/2014/mar/19/connor-sparrowhawk-death-nhs-care-unit-slade-house-learning-disabilities [14/01/15].

Segerberg, A., & Bennett, W. L. (2011). Social media and the organization of collective action: Using Twitter to explore the ecologies of two climate change protests. *The Communication Review, 14*(3), 197–215.

Tarrow, S. (1998). *Power in movement: Social movements and contentious politics.* Cambridge, MA: Cambridge University Press.

Tilly, C. (1978). *From mobilization to revolution.* New York: McGraw-Hill.

Van Laer, J., & Van Aelst, P. (2009). Cyber-protest and civil society: The internet and action repertoires in social movements. *Handbook on Internet Crime*, 230–254.

Walmsley, J. (2001). Normalisation, emancipatory research and inclusive research in learning disability. *Disability & Society, 16*(2), 187–205.

4   Confirming normalcy

'Inspiration porn' and the construction of the disabled subject?

Beth Haller and Jeffrey Preston

Introduction

While the disabled body has long been a source of curiosity for the non-disabled, whether it is casual stares on the street or organised exhibitionism at freak shows, a more recent cultural imagination of disability has been as a source of inspiration to the non-disabled. Both online and off, countless stories and images circulate depicting the struggles faced by those (often children) with disabilities and the courage of those strong enough to 'overcome' their inadequacies and strive to be 'normal'. These fantasies of survival have exploded with the advent of social media, with personal stories from disabled people touching the non-disabled user deeply, motivating them to share these tropes on Facebook and Twitter. These tropes are perceived as quiet celebrations of human strength and promises of human resilience, but they serve to objectify the disabled individuals caricatured within. This chapter seeks to reveal the ways disability manifests on social media as the memetic trend known as 'inspiration porn', which marks the disabled subject as a source of inspiration for the non-disabled, an imagination of disability commonly promoted in events such as the Paralympic Games. In addition, this chapter will look at how social media allows disabled people to fight back, engaging in what Kalle Lasn dubs 'memetic jujitsu' (Vaske, 2009), to resist inspiration porn memes through their own harnessing of social media spaces.

Defining inspiration porn

Inspiration porn has been popularly defined by Stella Young, an Australian disability activist/editor/writer and TEDx presenter (2014), as being 'an image of a person with a disability, often a kid, doing something completely ordinary – like playing, or talking, or running, or drawing a picture, or hitting a tennis ball – carrying a caption like "your excuse is invalid" or "before you quit, try"' (Young, 2012). Young, who was a wheelchair user, explains the problem with these inspiration porn memes:

> These modified images exceptionalise and objectify those of us they claim to represent. It's no coincidence that these genuinely adorable disabled kids in

these images are never named: It doesn't matter what their names are, they're just there as objects of inspiration.

(Young, 2012)

Inspiration porn can manifest in several formats, from a type of online poster with an image of a disabled person doing something ordinary with an inspirational tagline, or it can be a YouTube video of a disabled person doing something that non-disabled viewers perceive as being extraordinary (and as inspirational as seen through viewers re-posting, titling or commenting), or it can be an article from a website like Upworthy, which even has a story category called 'Inspirational' (Upworthy, 2014). These forms of inspiration porn have fit easily into the social media space because, with a click, they can be posted, shared, liked or tweeted.

Inspiration porn as media frame

Media framing is relevant to inspiration porn because media shape how disability images are understood by audiences (Goffman, 1974; Davis & Kent, 2006; O'Malley, 2009; Haller, 2010). O'Malley explains frame theory as referring to the expectations of the world, 'based on prior experience, against which new experiences are measured and interpreted' (2009, p. 21).

Media frame disability through images and words that are often stereotypical and filled with ableism – the white man in a wheelchair succeeding at his job, a person with schizophrenia as ill and detached from reality or inaccurate and condescending terms such as 'confined to a wheelchair' (Linton, 1998; Davis, 1999; Weeber, 1999; Ross, 2001; Schneider, 2003; Haller, Dorries, & Rahn, 2006). One of the more significant media frames that intersects with inspiration porn is that of the 'supercrip'. In Clogston's categories of framing (1989, 1990), he defines the 'supercrip' frame in the news as stories depicting disabled people 'overcoming' their disabilities to live regular (or 'normal') lives. Dajani (2001) calls the supercrip frame the 'handicap role', which is often employed when someone is presented as having overcome limitations from a disabling condition (p. 198).

Ross (2001, 1997) points out that one person's attempt to fight a particular impairment becomes the benchmark frame, implying that anyone else with that impairment should be battling it as well. As Haller (2010) explains, dominant societal beliefs shaped by an ableist culture influence media content which, in turn, impacts the global understanding of disability. Images of inspiration porn posted throughout social media can both reflect and shape social attitudes towards disability, as well as reveal ableist tropes populating that media space.

Inspiration porn memes and ableism

While many believe the cultural products found on the internet, like user-generated images and video, have little intrinsic value, new media expert

Dr Limor Shifman believes internet memes are an important site of inquiry. Shifman explains in her book *Memes in digital culture*: 'While memes are seemingly trivial and mundane artifacts, they actually reflect deep social and cultural structures. In many senses, internet memes can be treated as (post) modern folklore, in which shared norms and values are constructed through cultural artifacts such as Photoshopped images or urban legends' (Shifman, 2013, Chapter 2).

This chapter uses qualitative textual analysis (McKee, 2003) to understand the framing of disability within inspiration porn on social media, as well as to evaluate the reactions from disabled people on social media when they counter these narratives that are seen as patronising and demeaning. This chapter uses Shifman's definition of a digital meme, which is '(a) a group of digital items sharing common characteristics of content, form, and/or stance, which (b) were created with awareness of each other, and (c) were circulated, imitated, and/or transformed via the internet by many users' (Shifman, 2013, Chapter 1). More than just reflecting social and cultural structures, memes are also about delineating those 'in' and 'out' of a specific culture and encouraging those outside to decrypt the code and become part of the discourse. As this chapter seeks to reveal, memes, particularly those focused on the idea of a disabled person as an inspirational subject, are inherently political, as they are often reductionist, rely on stereotypical media frames, and reinforce dominant ableist ideology through repetition and participation.

'Like my status'

Disability representations such as the supercrip or inspiration porn are really just different framing of pity narratives, i.e. a non-disabled person feels better about pitying someone if they also see them as inspirational. 'People with disabilities are put on pedestals because of their inspirational quality in doing ordinary things, which is actually a patronising way to laud people, imbued with charity. Presenting someone as inspirational is just another way of pitying them for the "tragedy of their fate"' (Haller, 2000). These memes are clearly rooted in the long tradition of pity and paternalism that drives much of the charity work and poster child narratives in the West (Haller, 2010; Longmore, 2013). An early manifestation of social media disability frames was a series of digital memes asking users of social networking sites to share images and fan groups dedicated to sick children with the hope of raising funds. As Emil Protalinski explains:

> This type of hoax involves photographs of ill and/or disabled children in hospitals being shared virally across Facebook. Sometimes the hoax asks Facebook users to donate for the child's medical expenses and other times it promises that sharing the photo will result in donations from Facebook itself. Both claims are false: if you donate money, you're just giving it straight to the

scammer, and if you share the photo, you're only helping the hoax become viral, since Facebook will never donate money based on the number of shares.

(Protalinski, 2012b)

At the height of their popularity, these memes reached hundreds of thousands of users, often being shared countless times before it is discovered the entire post was a fake – there was no sick child, no fundraiser, it was just an elaborate hoax. The most common motivation behind creating and spreading these hoaxes is money – the creators rely upon the charity of others to spread the meme far and wide, accumulating large numbers of fans to dedicated Facebook groups before selling those groups to other companies, who rebrand the page and use it to promote their own products to these newfound followers (Findlay, 2013). Worse, the creators of these memes offer links to fake donation pages, gathering thousands of dollars in donations from sympathetic people who believe their money is actually going to help save an ill child.

For example, a 2012 hoax claimed Facebook would personally donate 3 cents for every share to help a child with cancer; the plea used a popular image of a child with a facial birthmark (Protalinski, 2012a). Sometimes only 'likes', not money, are involved. A photo that went viral of a young woman with Down syndrome, allegedly named Mallory, with the caption, 'This is my sister Mallory. She has Down syndrome and doesn't think she's beautiful. Please like this photo so I can show her later that she truly is beautiful', gathered more than 3.5 million likes (Findlay, 2013). The sick child needing donations meme is not new, as the memetic potential of photos of sick children and calls for money have long been deployed with varying levels of success by charity organisations around the world. For instance, the hoax sick child meme occurred in pre-internet days as a chain letter (Kelley, 1999).

Despite these memes' popularity, counter memes have emerged in recent years that seek to protect people from these hoaxes. Most notably is the way mainstream media reports on these hoaxes, particularly focusing on the 'crime' of stealing these pictures and the re-victimisation of a disabled or ill child. As Protalinski explains, 'Families often find it very unsettling to learn photos of their sick relatives have been used to perpetuate these scams and hoaxes' (Protalinski, 2012b). Findlay agrees: 'These Facebook photo memes tug at heart strings. But they hurt real people – the photographed children and their families' (Findlay, 2013). This counter narrative of the victimised disabled child plays into Susan Wendell's notion of disability as belonging to the private realm and that non-disabled people believe to draw disability into the public, to have it seen, is inappropriate or wrong (Wendell, 1996). This frame also implies a distinct shame attached to disability, that being seen publicly is upsetting and disabled people must be protected from this experience. A more progressive counter meme that has emerged in the last few years are sarcastic photo macros that joke about people dying because these photos did not receive enough likes on Facebook. One popular example depicts a concerned doctor with the text 'I'm sorry, we didn't get enough likes in time. Your little boy is going to die' (Jpegger Supreme [pseud], 2012). This meme openly criticises the manufactured seriousness of the sick child hoaxes, revealing the absurdity of connecting one's health with the number of likes or shares they receive on social networks.

The fecundity and longevity of these memes reveals something important about the traditional non-disabled encounter with disability. This meme is passed on because society pities these children, seemingly suffering without just cause, and those on social media are willing to do something as simple as clicking the share button or donating a few dollars if it will mean ending their 'suffering'. More significant for this chapter, though, these memes actively confirm several assumptions about disability and the disabled body, given memetic weight by the sheer volume of people who share the content. First, this meme confirms the link between disability, suffering and dependency. Second, this meme confirms the link between disability and death and inspires the non-disabled to action – click now or this child will die! This, in turn, confirms the charity model of disability, validating the role of the non-disabled as obligatory caretakers of disabled people, illustrating that only the non-disabled have the power to help 'needy' disabled individuals (Oliver, 1990). The non-disabled are given an opportunity to show their humanity, their compassion for *all* humans, by donating their time and money, which will make them feel good about themselves. So while this meme is not inspirational in the traditional sense, it does inspire the non-disabled to assume the role of saviour, which in turn positions the non-disabled in a place of authority (and superiority) over the disabled subject. Finally, all of these memes validate the medical model of disability and the belief that the ultimate objective must be to cure disability. All of these hoaxes rely upon the notion that cure is a desired outcome for all disability and that, by inference, disability is a problem needing to be fixed. In the same way that charities like the Jerry Lewis Telethon rely upon clichés of sickness and urgency to generate funds (Haller, 2010; Longmore, 2013), these memes rely upon the accepted belief that all disability must be cured, returning the child to a normative level of function.

Well-known inspiration porn memes

Several inspiration porn memes have become representative of this memetic trend. This inspiration porn message uses the achievement of a disabled person as inspirational motivator for the non-disabled. Although deployed through a variety of meme vehicles, this inspiration porn generally consists of a stock image of a disabled individual, particularly those engaging in some sort of sporting activity, with the caption or overlaid text 'The only disability in life is a bad attitude' (Willitts, 2012). Interestingly, this popular quote used in much inspiration porn is actually from the non-disabled US gold-medal-winning Olympic figure skater Scott Hamilton. In 1997, Hamilton found out he had testicular cancer and vowed to get back on the ice after his chemotherapy. That was the context of his quote, which has a second sentence: 'The only disability in life is a bad attitude. I feel 100% confident that I can overcome this disease and be back on the ice within a few months' (Scott Hamilton Cares Initiative, 2014). This is significant because it directly links disability with sickness, in this case cancer, and is coming from the perspective of an Olympic medal winner, someone in peak physical form who is heavily involved in charity and wrote a book about overcoming challenges called *The great eight* (2009). His background shapes the way society interprets the meaning of the quote and the way it is deployed. While the quote has spread to a variety of images, it is most commonly connected with an image of Paralympic runner Oscar Pistorius running beside a girl with his style of prosthetic blades – this image and the quote are bound together by ideas of bodily supremacy. This popular Pistorius meme can be traced back one step further, with an earlier photo of a boy running on blades made famous by Pistorius with the caption, 'Your excuse is invalid' (Coble, 2012). As Coble explains:

> Most people look at that and see the boy's smile, his human feet replaced with prosthetics and the fact that he's about to bust through the slogan like the winner's tape at the end of the run. The natural reaction is to think 'what a darling child!' and 'if he can run without feet, I can make it until 5:00pm and deal with this annoying coworker!' So they pass it on.
>
> (Coble, 2012)

Central to this meme is the belief that disabled people are encountering harsh barriers throughout their life and their ability to overcome them *and* partake in traditionally normative activities like track and field serves as an inspiration to the non-disabled. While the 'Your excuse is invalid' meme would later spread to a photo of Pistorius, it was not until the image of Pistorius running beside the disabled girl that this meme would truly become viral, as it began circulating at the same time as Pistorius's historic entry into the Summer Games of 2012 (Willitts, 2012). These memes were not created in a vacuum, but, in fact, reflect the very messaging of the Paralympic Games itself, as seen in both its offline and online marketing (see Bundon, Chapter 18 this volume).

Inspiration porn and the Paralympics

The athletic competition for elite disabled athletes has become a major source of inspiration porn in recent years. The International Paralympic Committee (IPC), which runs winter or summer Paralympic Games after the Olympics every two years, embraces the notion of 'inspiring' in its mission. The stated vision of the IPC is 'to enable Paralympic athletes to achieve sporting excellence and inspire and excite the world' (IPC, 2014). Interestingly, its version of inspiration tries to focus on bringing about equality as Paralympic athletes 'touch the heart of all people for a more equitable society' (IPC, 2014). The IPC says its mission is about aspiration:

> Athletes and the Paralympic Games are at the heart of our Movement. Their performances and incredible stories teach the values of acceptance and appreciation for people with an impairment. The Paralympic Movement builds a bridge which links sport with social awareness thus contributing to the

development of a more equitable society with respect and equal opportunities for all individuals.

(IPC, 2014)

The IPC defines the 'courage' of disabled athletes as the 'unique spirit of the para-athlete who seeks to accomplish what the general public deems "unexpected" but what the athlete knows as "truth". The Paralympic brand and its values are tangible manifestations of what it means to push oneself beyond expectations' (IPC, 2014).

On the surface, this IPC mission fits clearly with many other athletic endeavours globally that try to uplift people and better society through athletic competition. For example, the International Olympic Committee (IOC) has a video from Namibia on its website about how 'sport can generate hope and joy among refugees' (IOC, 2011). The IPC goals, however, often lose their nuance when reshaped into marketing campaigns, become videos posted on social media, or are rejiggered as internet memes. Media research about the Paralympics has identified this contradiction. In her study of human interest profiles of Paralympians, Ellis (2009) says those profiles represent the supercrip frame of disability in which disabled people are presented as 'overcoming' their disabilities by living regular lives, participating in sports, or just creating a cool Halloween costume out of being a leg amputee (Clogston, 1990, 1991; Barnes, 1992; Goggin & Newell, 2005; Haller, 2010; Thrastardottir, 2014). Ellis says: 'Such media representations purport to offer new identities for people with disabilities, but may actually perpetuate the biomedical model of disability as it discursively situates disability as deficit. By locating disability in the body and emphasizing the personal attitude of these individuals with disability, these profiles individualize disability' (2009, p. 32).

British disability sport researchers Purdue and Howe (2012) describe what they call the Paralympics paradox as 'see the sport, not the disability' (p. 189). They interviewed people involved with the Paralympic community about their social perceptions of the disabled athletes. Some of the people they interviewed discussed emotion as an important reason for being involved with Paralympic sport. Interestingly, the IPC cites fostering an emotional response as one of its key values: 'The stories and accomplishments of para-athletes induce intense and personal emotions' (Paralympic Committee of Punja, 2016). Barry, a non-disabled former coach of sports for blind people, explained to Purdue and Howe (2012): 'There is another appeal to Paralympic sport which is really quite moving and uplifting and that is the spectacle of people struggling with impairment to perform as performers, as athletes. That can be quite moving. It's a bigger emotional charge I think than you get in the Olympic Games' (p. 200).

Several of their interview subjects mentioned they felt the media patronised Paralympic athletes. Disability researcher Nathan, who has a spinal cord injury, described the Paralympic images bluntly: 'I often feel the Paralympics is shown as "after the lord mayor's show". This will sound crude, but occasionally when I read some of the media and listen to people talking about it they're almost discussing it in a way that they would discuss a poodle walking on its hind legs' (Purdue and Howe 2012, p. 201). This patronising structure also informs inspiration porn, but those who find these images inspiring believe they are lauding the disabled athlete in the photo.

Purdue and Howe's research teased out the contradictions in elite disability sport. Their interview with Abigail, a former wheelchair basketball player at the 2000 Sydney Paralympic Games, illustrated their point. Abigail said she felt the media's focus on her physical body, rather than her sports achievements, was insulting: 'I can remember the first sort of press releases and stuff I had done. They were so patronizing. It was brave [name of athlete] does this and that, and you're like "no"! It was all about that kind of sob story and I'm like "no, I don't want that, I'm playing a sport and I'm training hard, that's the message"' (2012, p. 202). But even though she wanted her sports ability emphasised, not her impairment, she also said: 'I think people need to see it's not straight forward. It's not as easy as being an able-bodied athlete, because you've got all sorts of things to take into account . . . you want people to have an understanding of the disability but you want people to see the sport first' (p. 202). DePauw (1997) explains that, in reality, no contradiction exists between having an impairment and participating in sports at the highest level, but the non-disabled spectators don't see this. She says disability sports will only be transformed when spectators understand it is just difference of style, not substance, and when they don't assume a disability means an 'impaired athletic performance' (p. 428).

Silva and Howe's research explored the iconography of supercrip frame in the Paralympics by looking at promotional campaigns disseminated through the media in Britain and Portugal (2012). They believe the supercrip frames have a negative impact on disabled people, as well as giving incorrect information about disability to media audiences. Their findings concluded:

> The complexity of disability experiences is ignored when one assumes disability can be overcome by individual effort alone. In the world of sports, stereotyped images of disability constitute a lost opportunity to acknowledge the pervasiveness of difference. The exceptional character of some athletes has to be assessed against criteria that respect the specific ethos of the Paralympic Games and must not be based on the premise that impairments make people special. In order to treat athletes with impairments as true athletes, media coverage must play a crucial educative role in increasing public knowledge on the specificities of the Paralympics, namely, classification, new sports, records, and performances in order to develop an informed and educated audience.
>
> (2012, p. 191)

So Paralympics promotional efforts may be feeding supercrip narratives and inspiration porn images that then flow throughout the internet via social media.

Paralympics promotions

The promotion of the Paralympics in several countries clearly connects to inspiration porn and the promotion of a supercrip status among the athletes. In the London summer Paralympics 2012, Channel 4, the official TV network carrying the games, created a marketing campaign, called *Meet the superhumans* (Channel 4, 2012). It was broadcast on 78 TV channels across Great Britain. Set to the track, *Harder than you think* by hip hop artists Public Enemy, the promotional film depicts Paralympians training or competing in their sports, with many shots focused on prosthetics, wheelchairs and other markers of an impairment, and, in the middle of the film, there is a disturbing montage that shows a battlefield bomb blast, a sonogram, a pregnant woman, a horrible car crash and then a double leg amputee sitting next to a crashed car. The film's tag lines say, 'Forget everything you thought you knew about strength. Forget everything you thought you knew about humans. It's time to do battle. Meet the Superhumans' *(Meet the superhumans* video, 2012).

The press release about the promotional film says it 'shows the herculean efforts that have gone into their preparation for the Games' (Channel 4, 2012). Dan Brooke, Channel 4's chief marketing and communications officer, tied the film into the network's desire to get an emotional response from viewers: 'London 2012 is a coming of age moment for the Paralympics. This campaign will help bring a whole new audience to it and may even raise a goosebump or two along the way' (Channel 4, 2012).

The promotional film's framing as inspiration porn is further clarified by the comments on YouTube. Commenter Gaith Bader, who commented 6 November 2014, said: 'Amazing . . . this add never gets old. . . . Awesome then, even better now . . . totally inspirational (*sic*)' (2014). And a commenter in July 2014 wrote: 'Hats off to whoever associated that music with these clips and did the whole thing. You moved and inspired millions' (Stevenbadman, 2014).

Another British promotional campaign tied to Paralympics sponsor Sainsbury, a supermarket in the UK, was even called 'Paralympic heroes 2012 – What inspires you?' Interestingly, it doesn't really fit the definition of inspiration porn because the Paralympians themselves are describing what inspires and their answers are what any athlete might say, 'swimming', 'my family' or 'winning' (Sainsbury, 2012).

Many disabled people have spoken out against the inspiring supercrip frames they see in the Paralympics. British wheelchair user Robert Jones (2012) says he is concerned about young disabled people who were having their needed disability benefits slashed in the midst of a London Paralympic event that might have made them feel inadequate. 'I worry about the young – those who can no more choose work than choose not to be disabled, but will have their benefits slashed anyway. As a spectacle, the Paralympics might inspire them, but as a symbol of what society thinks disability means, it will hurt them', he explained. An American college student confronted her university's diversity initiative when it hosted a Paralympian and used a poster saying, 'Blake Leeper was raised to believe that the only disability in life is a bad attitude'. University of Chicago student Kiran Misra explained:

> This inspiration porn only exists so that nondisabled people can put their worries into perspective. It exploits the assumption that no matter how bad something is in a nondisabled person's life, it could not possibly be as bad as having a disability. These feel-good tools, as 'inspiration,' are based on the

assumption that people with disabilities have terrible lives, and that it takes extra courage to live them. In fact, it is rare to find any representation of disability in popular media that doesn't use the derogatory language: 'suffers from,' 'victim of,' 'defying the odds,' 'wheelchair bound/confined,' or the ever-misleading 'overcoming disability.'

(2014)

Australian disability advocate and writer/editor Stella Young discusses many examples of Paralympian inspiration porn in her articles and TEDx talk. She says:

Inspiration porn shames people with disabilities. It says that if we fail to be happy, to smile and to live lives that make those around us feel good, it's because we're not trying hard enough. Our attitude is just not positive enough. It's our fault . . . .So next time you're tempted to share that picture of an adorable kid with a disability to make your Facebook friends feel good, just take a second to consider why you're really clicking that button.

(Young, 2012)

As a result of this prominent meme of inspiration porn on social media, digital spaces such as Facebook, Tumblr and Reddit have become a location of oppositional struggle (Hall, 1973) between many disabled people and those on the internet who want to 'feel good' and be inspired by images of visibly disabled people doing everyday activities.

The promise of social media – the George Takei incident

While the disabled population rarely gets the opportunity to openly respond to inspiration porn memes that co-opt their lives, package them and distribute for the entertainment and inspiration of the non-disabled, a 2014 social media incident involving original *Star Trek* actor/social media humourist George Takei provided hope for some disability activists as a platform was finally provided to think and talk critically about a famous disability meme.

But to understand the firestorm that would erupt on Takei's wall, this chapter tracks the original development of the meme. The earliest copy of the photo in question was posted to the '/r/pics' subreddit of link aggregator Reddit in April 2011 by user 'shotty1058'. It was a candid picture of a woman standing up from her wheelchair to reach an alcohol bottle on a store's top shelf. Shotty1058 titled the image 'Praise the Lord! Miracle in the alcohol aisle!' That post received 117 votes in total, of which 69 were upvotes (shotty1058 [pseud], 2011). The top comments in the thread were all negative, criticising the original poster for being insensitive. Several months later, the same picture would be submitted to the '/r/pics' subreddit by user 'kopo27' with the title 'It's a miracle', which received 76 votes, 44 of which were upvotes (kopo27 [pseud], 2011). Again, the top comments were negative. After being reposted several more times throughout 2011 and 2012, the meme was posted to the '/r/funny' subreddit in 2013 by user 'miss_maryjane' with the title 'praise the lord, hallelujah!' and the overlaid text 'There has been a miracle in the alcohol isle (*sic*)'. This post would receive 1499 votes, 1139 of them being upvotes (miss_maryjane [pseud], 2014). Despite the popularity of the post, with far more users upvoting the image than downvoting it, the top comments were all dominated by critics asserting that some wheelchair users can stand and that this image was perpetuating a negative stereotype of disability.

On his Facebook fan page in August 2014, Takei would post presumably this very meme, given the style of the text and the misspelling of the word 'aisle' with the caption 'She was filled with the holy . . . spirits' (Thompson, 2014). While many would like this post and comment positively, there was a flurry of negative comments, similar to those made by people on Reddit previously, around the perpetuation of stereotypes and insensitivity towards people with disabilities. Takei would eventually respond to this criticism, posting on his Facebook page, 'Fans get "offended" from time to time by my posts. There hardly is a day where something I put up doesn't engender controversy. Concerned fans, worried the sky may fall, ask me to "take it down". . . . So I'm also going to ask them also to take it down – a notch, please' (Alexander, 2014). When Takei refused to remove the meme, the controversy grew, as more and more users began flooding his page with negative comments. Again, Takei would rebuff the criticism, this time commenting on his own post:

> If I had to 'take down' everything that some section of the Interverse found offensive, this would be lonely and barren page indeed. Think of this way, Matt. The picture allows people to have a conversation about stereotypes they wouldn't otherwise have. I'm not 'mocking' a disabled person. I am laughing at the fact that someone who appears to be disabled is rising from the chair to get alcohol. Doesn't that indicate that not every person in a chair is unable to stand?
>
> (Thompson, 2014)

Within his very defence, Takei appears to contradict himself, assuring his fans that he is not 'mocking' the disabled person, but simply laughing at them standing up to get alcohol.

Despite Takei's continued refusal to remove the image, his comment does point to a very real outcome from the posting of the meme – a public conversation about ableism and the ways we imagine and produce disability culturally. The more Takei refused to acknowledge what was wrong with the original meme, the more opportunity disabled activists had to open up conversations in the comments section of his fan page around stereotypical perceptions of disability, such as if someone is able to stand she is faking her disability. In addition, it provided an active example of ableism in action. Activist Andrew Pulrang pointed out Takei's apparent obliviousness to his own ableist attitude:

> They probably know what ableism is, but they don't recognize it when it bites them in the proverbial ass . . . or comes out of their literal mouths. And, when

they are called out for it, their first reaction is the kind of defensiveness they would normally criticize in others for different prejudices.

(Alexander, 2014)

What became apparent in this moment for those outside of the disability community is that ableism is operating in much the same way as other-isms (sexism, racism, etc.) and requires the same level of serious consideration. Several days after the original skirmish, Takei would post a formal apology, explaining that he had not intended to hurt anyone and is now more conscious of ableism and the types of discrimination faced by disabled people (Thompson, 2014). For all intents and purposes, this would serve to show that while social media memes *can* form the ways society imagines disability, social networks also provide the opportunity for memetic warfare, with the ideas of disability studies brought directly to bear on the systemic ableism interwoven into popular Western culture.

Nowhere is this resistance more apparent than in a 2012 disability community Facebook page, 'This is what disability looks like'. Inspired by Stella Young's article on inspiration porn and growing to more than 6,900 members, this page provided a social media space where disabled people posted photos of themselves or their disability heroes with the slogan 'This is what disability looks like' and a tagline that describes the individual, such as a wheelchair user with her young son that says, 'Parenting'. These images counter the typical frames of inspiration and sickness imbedded within inspiration porn memes (Hitt, 2013). The Facebook page says, 'This is a visual culture project featuring images of people with disabilities that do NOT pander to sentimentality, inspiration and/or paternalism like many images that have circulated around social media of late' (Stevens, 2013). In many ways, this Facebook page embodies McRuer's call to 'crip' everything (McRuer, 2006), as it injects radical disability discourse into social media, actively drawing into question the frames postulated by the memes discussed previously in this chapter. So while social media provides the opportunity for ableist inspiration porn to go viral, it also provides a platform for disability activists to resist these images through online content of their own.

Conclusions

Despite the promise of the internet to provide an opportunity to glimpse the world outside of the frames mainstream media wrap around disability, imaginations of disability online are deeply imbued with the same type of ableist content present offline within the mainstream media. Just as the entertainment media focus on heroes and villains, inspiration porn memes are similarly focused on sickness, survival and supercrips, with viral hoaxes promising cures for sick children and popular images of disabled people urging the non-disabled to let go of their bad attitudes.

While these imaginations may seem positive, albeit simplistic, they are still damaging to disabled people. Many of these social media memes are infantilising, marking disabled people as children in need of protection and strengthening the hold of the charity model that encourages paternalism from non-disabled people (Oliver, 1990). Others present disability as a binary – either you overcome your disability to become a hero or succumb to it to become a villain. Inspiration porn, like that stimulated by the Paralympics, shifts the disabled subject into an object of inspiration, whose struggle against systemic barriers is converted into a moment of reflection and encouragement for the non-disabled to better themselves. Worse still, these inspirational images devalue critical voices from within the disability community, marking those who speak out *against* these systemic barriers to be deficient compared to those inspirations who appear to 'make do just fine'. Despite the fact that social media enable this inspiration porn to circulate and strengthen, Facebook especially has also provided a platform for resistance, with disability activists confronting inspiration porn memes head on through their own pages, like 'This is what disability looks like', their own posts on their individual pages and comments on other people's posts. By countering inspiration porn through producing empowering memes, disabled people imagine disability on their own terms and live up to the rally call of disability rights activists everywhere – nothing about us without us.

References

Alexander, E. (2014, August 11). George Takei branded 'offensive' and 'ignorant' for sharing controversial disabled meme – Not that he cares. *The Independent.* August 11. Retrievedfromhttp://www.independent.co.uk/news/people/george-takei-branded-offensive-and-ignorant-after-sharing-controversial-disabled-meme—not-that-he-cares-mind-you-9661754.html.

Bader, G. (2014, November 6). Comment on meet the superhumans YouTube video. Retrieved from https://www.youtube.com/watch?v=kKTamH__xuQ&list=PLeiohMuC FIoFf8TzWfzGpnx3wVBNgvoqo&index=2.

Barnes, C. (1992). *Disabling imagery and the media: An exploration of the principles for media representations of disabled people.* Krumlin, Halifax: Ryburn Publishing Ltd.

Channel 4. (2012, July 18). Meet the superhumans. [Press release]. Retrieved from http://www.channel4.com/info/press/news/channel-4-takes-over-tv-with-meet-the-super humans-campaign.

Clogston, J. S. (1989). *A theoretical framework for studying media portrayal of persons with disabilities.* Paper presented at the Annual Meeting of the Association for the Education in Journalism and Mass Communication, Washington, DC.

Clogston, J. S. (1990). *Disability coverage in 16 newspapers.* Louisville, KY: Advocado Press.

Clogston, J. S. (1991). *Reporters' attitudes toward and newspaper coverage of persons with disabilities.* Unpublished doctoral dissertation, Michigan State University.

Coble, K. (2012, January 27). Your excuse is invalid: Just another pretty farce. Retrieved from https://mycropht.wordpress.com/2012/01/27/your-excuse-is-invalid/.

Dajani, K. F. (2001, Summer). What's in a name? Terms used to refer to people with disabilities. *Disability Studies Quarterly, 21*(3), 196–209.

Davis, L. (1999). J'accuse: Cultural imperialism – Ableist style. *Social Alternatives, 18,* 36–41.

Davis, D., & Kent, K. (2006). *Framing theory and research: Exploring the implications for the practice of journalism.* Paper presented at the International Communication Association Conference, Dresden, Germany.

DePauw, K. (1997). The (in)visibility of disability: Cultural contexts and 'sporting bodies'. *Quest, 49*, 416–430.

Ellis, K. (2009). Beyond the aww factor: Human interest profiles of Paralympians and the media navigation of physical difference and social stigma. *Asia Pacific Media Educator, 19*, 23–36.

Findlay, C. (2013, July 1). Facebook's 'sick child hoaxes'. *Daily Life*. Retrieved from http://www.dailylife.com.au/life-and-love/real-life/facebooks-sick-child-hoaxes-20130701–2p77g.html.

Goffman, E. (1974). *Frame analysis: An essay on the organization of experience.* London, UK: Harper and Row.

Goggin, G., & Newell, C. (2005). *Disability in Australia: Exposing a social apartheid.* Sydney, Australia: UNSW Press.

Hall, S. (1973). *Encoding and decoding in the television discourse.* Birmingham, UK: Centre for Cultural Studies, University of Birmingham, pp. 507–517.

Haller, Beth A. 2010. *Representing disability in an ableist world: Essays on mass media.* Louisville, KY: The Advocado Press.

Haller, B., Dorries, B., & Rahn, J. (2006, January). Media labeling versus the US disability community identity: A study of shifting cultural language. *Disability and Society, 21*(1), 61–75.

Hamilton, S. (2009). *The great eight* (2nd ed.). Nashville, TN: W Publishing Group.

Hitt, A. (2013, June 7). #cwcon 2013. *Accessing rhetoric.* Retrieved from https://allisonhitt.wordpress.com/2013/06/07/cwcon-2013/.

International Olympic Committee (IOC). (2011). See how sport can generate hope. [Video]. Retrieved from http://www.olympic.org/videos/see-how-sport-can-generate-hope.

International Paralympic Committee (IPC). (2014). The IPC – Who we are. Retrieved from http://www.paralympic.org/the-ipc/about-us.

Jones, R. (2012, August 30). Sorry, the Paralympic spirit insults disabled people like me. *The Guardian.* https://www.theguardian.com/commentisfree/2012/aug/30/paralympic-spirit-insults-disabled-like-me

Jpegger Supreme (pseud). (2012). I'm sorry we didn't get enough Facebook 'likes.': Your boy is going to die. *JPEGY.* Retrieved from http://jpegy.com/lol/im-sorry-we-didnt-get-enough-facebook-likes-your-boy-is-going-to-die-3383.

Kelley, T. (1999, July 1). Internet's chain of foolery. *The New York Times*, sec. Technology. Retrieved from http://www.nytimes.com/1999/07/01/technology/internet-s-chain-of-foolery.html.

kopo27 (pseud). (2011, July 27). It's a miracle! • /r/pics. *Reddit.* Accessed July 27. Retrieved from https://www.reddit.com/r/pics/comments/j19f6/its_a_miracle/.

Linton, S. (1998). *Claiming disability: Knowledge and identity.* New York, NY: NYU Press.

Longmore, P. K. (2013). 'Heaven's special child': The making of poster children. In J. Davis Lennard (ed.) *The Disability Studies Reader* (4th ed., 34–41). New York, NY: Routledge.

McKee, A. (2003). *Textual analysis: A beginner's guide.* London, UK: Sage.

McRuer, R. (2006). *Crip theory: Cultural signs of queerness and disability* (Kindle ed.). New York, NY: New York University Press.

Meet the Superhumans. (2012). Channel 4 Paralympics – Meet the superhumans (annotated version). [YouTube video]. Retrieved from https://www.youtube.com/watch?v=kKTamH__xuQ&list=PLeiohMuCFIoFf8TzWfzGpnx3wVBNgvoqo&index=2.

Misra, K. (2014, October 17). Getting a rise out of RISE – Campus diversity initiative unknowingly reveals pervasiveness of ableism in our culture. *The Chicago Maroon.* Retrieved from http://chicagomaroon.com/2014/10/17/getting-a-rise-out-of-rise/.

miss_maryjane (pseud). 2014. Praise the Lord, Hallelujah! • /r/funny. *Reddit.* Accessed November 12. Retrieved from https://www.reddit.com/r/funny/comments/17vuz9/ praise_the_lord_hallelujah/.

Oliver, M. (1990). *The politics of disablement.* Basingstoke, UK: Macmillans.

O'Malley, M. (2009). Falling between frames: Institutional discourse and disability in radio. *Journal of Pragmatics, 41,* 346–356.

Paralympic Committee of Punjab. (2016). Vision, Values, & Objectives. [Website] http:// pcpunjab.org/our-objectives/

Protalinski, E. (2012a). Facebook hoax: This child's got a cancer. *ZDNet.* Accessed January 10 2012. Retrieved from http://www.zdnet.com/blog/facebook/facebook-hoax-this-childs-got-a-cancer/7137.

Protalinski, E. (2012b). Anti-Scam websites beg Facebook to remove sick baby hoaxes. *ZDNet.* Accessed February 5 2012. Retrieved from http://www.zdnet.com/blog/face-book/anti-scam-websites-beg-facebook-to-remove-sick-baby-hoaxes/8613.

Purdue, D. E. J., & Howe, P. D. (2012). See the sport, not the disability: Exploring the Paralympic paradox. *Qualitative Research in Sport, Exercise and Health, 2*(4), 189–205.

Ross, K. (1997). But where's me in it? Disability, broadcasting and the audience. *Media, Culture & Society, 19*(4), 669–677.

Ross, K. (2001). All ears: Radio, reception, and discourses of disability. *Media, Culture & Society, 23*(4), 419–437.

Sainsbury's YouTube channel. (2012, August 15). Paralympic heroes 2012 – What inspires you? – Sainsbury's. [Video]. Retrieved from https://www.youtube.com/watch?v=haoJx 3tWpZs&index=23&list=PLeiohMuCFIoFf8TzWfzGpnx3wVBNgvoqo.

Schneider, B. (2003). Narratives of schizophrenia: Constructing a positive identity. *Canadian Journal of Communication, 28*(2), 185–201.

Scott Hamilton CARES Initiative. (2014, November 11). About Scott Hamilton. [Cleveland Clinic website]. Retrieved from http://www.clevelandclinic.org/cancer/scottcares/scott/ about.asp.

Shifman, L. (2013). Memes in digital culture [Kindle version]. Retrieved from http://www. Amazon.com.

shotty1058 (pseud). (2011, April 5). Praise the Lord! Miracle in the alcohol aisle! • /r/pics. *Reddit.* Retrieved from https://www.reddit.com/r/pics/comments/gjcdo/praise_the_ lord_miracle_in_the_alcohol_aisle/.

Silva, C. F., & Howe, P. D. (2012). The (in)validity of *supercrip* representation of Paralympian athletes. *Journal of Sport and Social Issues, 36*(2), 174–194.

Stevenbadman. (2014, July). Commenter on meet the superhumans YouTube video. Retrieved from https://www.youtube.com/watch?v=kKTamH__xuQ&list=PLeiohMuC FIoFf8TzWfzGpnx3wVBNgvoqo&index=2.

Stevens, B. (2013). This is what disability looks like. [Facebook page]. Retrieved from https://www.facebook.com/ThisIsWhatDisabilityLooksLike.

Thompson, V. (2014). The George Takei disabled meme controversy: The offense, response and public apology. *Ramp Your Voice!* Accessed November 10 2014. Retrieved from http://rampyourvoice.com/2014/08/19/the-george-takei-disabled-meme-controversy-the-offense-response-public-apology/.

Thrastardottir, A. (2014). Paralympian Josh Sundquist already has the best Halloween costume this year. *Business Insider.* Retrieved from http://www.businessinsider.com/ josh-sundquist-halloween-costume-2014-2014-10#ixzz3IVp5TaTN

Upworthy. (2014). Topic. *Inspirational.* Retrieved from http://www.upworthy.com/ inspirational.

Vaske, H. (2009, March). Adbusters. *Kalle Lasn: Clearing the mindscape*. Retrieved from https://www.adbusters.org/blogs/adbusters_blog/kalle_lasn_clearing_mindscape.html.

Weeber, J. (1999). What could I know of racism? *Journal of Counseling & Development, 77*, 20–24.

Wendell, S. (1996). *The rejected body: Feminist philosophical reflections on disability.* New York, NY: Routledge.

Willitts, P. (2012, August 1). Bad attitudes do not cause disability any more than good attitudes guarantee health: Independent Editor's choice blogs. *The Independent*. Retrieved from http://blogs.independent.co.uk/2012/08/01/bad-attitudes-do-not-cause-disability-any-more-than-good-attitudes-guarantee-health/.

Young, S. (2012, July 2). We're not here for your inspiration. *ABC Ramp Up website*. Retrieved from http://www.abc.net.au/news/2012–07–03/young-inspiration-porn/4107006.

Young, S. (2014, April). Stella Young: I'm not your inspiration, thank you very much. *TEDx-Sydney online video*. Retrieved from http://www.ted.com/talks/stella_young_i_m_not_your_inspiration_thank_you_very_much?language=en#t-539335.

5 *Bedding Out*

Art, activism and Twitter

Lucy Burke and Liz Crow

@RGPLizCrow Against disability lies and myths, I will be defiant and disobedient
from my bed. Come and join me – it's no fun alone.

The main part of this chapter features extracts taken from a two-hour interview
between Liz Crow and myself conducted on the 1 February 2014, in the wake of
her touring performance of *Bedding Out*. Created and performed by Liz, *Bedding
Out* (Ipswich Arts School, November 2012, Salisbury Arts Centre, April 2013
and Edinburgh Fringe, August 2013) was a live durational performance piece that
took place over 48 hours. Taking to a bed (see Figure 5.1) in the centre of the performance space, Liz sought to draw attention to the usually hidden aspects of her
life in order to bring to light the complexity of her lived experience as a disabled
person.

   The performance took place in the context of the then UK Conservative and
Liberal Democrat coalition government's austerity agenda and the massive over-
haul of the benefits system and changes to support and eligibility criteria for disabled claimants. Formed in 2010, following the general election in which neither
the Labour Party or the Conservative Party managed to secure an overall parliamentary majority, what came to be known as the ConDem coalition promoted an
austerity agenda. Presenting the previous Labour administration's commitment to
public spending as profligate and responsible for a culture of welfare dependency,
the ConDem coalition promised to cut the budgetary deficit, the significance of
which was amplified by the global economic recession, and to cut public spending
which was presented as 'out of hand'. In a speech in 2010, Iain Duncan Smith,
the government minister responsible for the administration of the benefits system
at the Department of Work and Pensions, described his remit as one of fiscal
responsibility, ('We literally cannot afford to go on like this') and in terms of a
moral obligation to get people 'parked on inactive benefits' back into work.[2] What
followed was a series of massive cuts to the welfare budget, alongside broader cuts
to public spending and changes to the benefits system including the introduction
of sanctions so punitive that, for example, a man who had a heart attack during
a Job Centre assessment was sanctioned on the grounds that he had 'withdrawn'
from the interview.[3] The cumulative effect of these changes for disabled people

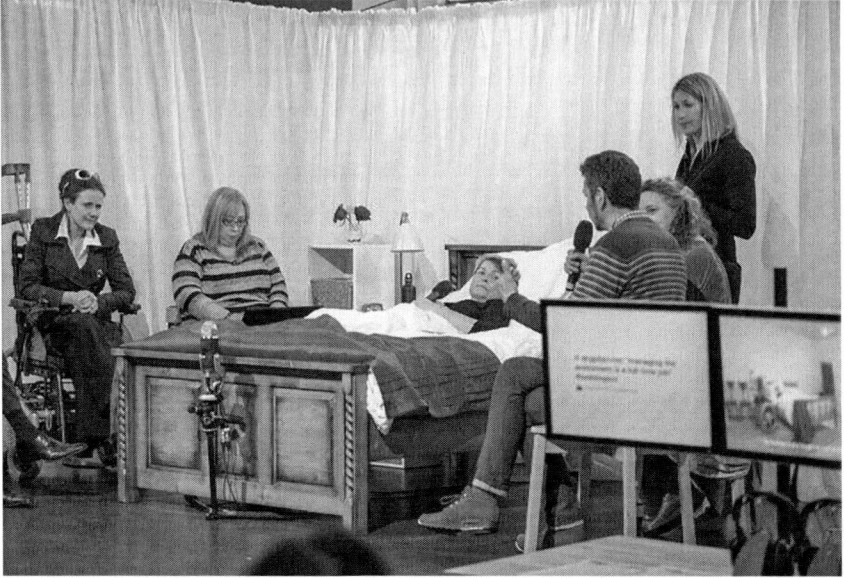

Figure 5.1 Image of Liz Crow lying in a wooden bed, centre stage, surrounded by six
        people, one of whom is speaking into a microphone

Still image from Liz Crow's *Bedding Out*, Salisbury Arts Centre, April 2013, reproduced by kind
permission of Roaring Girl Productions/Matthew Fessey.[1]

is at the centre of a number of campaigns including the work of DPAC (Disabled People
Against the Cuts) and the WOW (War on Welfare) campaign for a cumulative impact
assessment of welfare reform for disabled people.[4] Despite a series of scandals around
the numbers of deaths amongst disabled and ill benefits claimants deemed 'fit to work',
evidence of the fabrication of documentation at the Department for Work and Pensions
(DWP), and indications that the UN is planning to send a special rapporteur to the UK
to investigate whether welfare reforms have caused 'grave or systematic violations' of
disabled peoples' human rights, Iain Duncan Smith remained committed to making
further changes up until his resignation and apparent volte-face in March 2016.[5]

The overarching aim of *Bedding Out* was to challenge the ideological legitimation of austerity and benefit cuts in the rhetoric of cheats, scroungers and skivers
encapsulated in Chancellor of the Exchequer George Osborne's speech to the 2012
Conservative Party Conference in Birmingham. Here Osborne called on 'all those
who want to work hard and get on' and asked:

> Where is the fairness, we ask, for the shift-worker, leaving home in the dark
> hours of the early morning, who looks up at the closed blinds of their next
> door neighbour sleeping off a life on benefits?[6]

The rhetorical assertion of a stark distinction between strivers and skivers, hardworking families and those on benefits, continues to structure not only debates

about welfare in the UK but also mass cultural representations of benefit claimants in so-called poverty porn reality shows such as *Benefits Street* (UK, Channel 4, January – February 2014) and *On Benefits and Proud* (UK, Channel 5, October 2013). This contemporary iteration of what is essentially a much older nineteenth-century cultural discourse of the deserving and undeserving poor (O'Hara, 2015), has had powerful effects, not least in placing the question of whether a disabled person truly deserves state support at the centre of political and cultural debate. The consequence of the kind of language of scroungers and cheats has produced a kind of constitutive suspicion of disabled people that finds its apparent evidential veracity inscribed in outraged *Daily Mail* headlines. 'Benefit cheat who pocketed £100,000 by claiming to be wheelchair-bound for TEN YEARS is caught hula dancing on holiday' (*Daily Mail*, 19/08/12) or 'Benefits cheat who said disability made him a "hermit" suffering panic attacks when he went outside took 19 luxury cruises after falsely claiming £68,000' (*Daily Mail,* 01/09/15). However, actual levels of benefit fraud (across the entirety of the benefit system) in the UK are very low at 0.7%.[7]

It is in this context that *Bedding Out* set out to offer a counter narrative to the logic of 'austerity speak' and its consequences, one of which is arguably a significant increase in disability hate crime in the UK – the Crown Prosecution Service reported a 213% increase in reported cases of disability hate crime between 2007/8 and 2014.[8] In so doing, Liz invited members of the public to join in with a range of bedside conversations. Crucially, in the context of this collection, the conception of *Bedding Out* placed the potential of new social media – specifically, in this instance, Twitter – in conjunction with a continuous live stream at the centre of its exploration of the human consequences of austerity and changes to the benefits system for disabled claimants. Each performance set out to open up a dialogue between Liz, her audience and Twitter users. These conversations were not ancillary elements or supplementary extras but part of the performance itself. *Bedding Out* thus gained its energy from the temporal immediacy of Twitter and its capacity to generate and record multiple responses in real time. As such, the piece raises some important questions both around the ways in which the integration of new social media potentially transforms the ways in which we conceive of the arts-based political activism, the politics and ethics of artistic practice and the capacity of both to effect change in the world.

Twitter, art and activism – some preliminary reflections

Making sense of the political dimensions of Twitter in relation to social activism and, more particularly in this instance, to an arts-based disability activism is not straightforward. Despite Manuel Castells's (2015) compelling celebration of 'networked social movements' throwing off the shackles of 'economic distress, political cynicism, cultural emptiness and personal hopelessness' (p. 1), this kind of utopian investment in a virtual sociality fails to acknowledge the more complex and troubling convergence of democracy and capitalism in networked communication technologies (Dean, 2010). Van Dijck (2013) cautions against the fallacy of conceiving of 'platforms as merely facilitating networking activities' and of conflating 'human connectedness' with 'automated connectivity' (p. 13) particularly in relation to the commercial interests that underpin the development of platforms such as Twitter and Facebook. As he notes: 'social media services can be both intensely empowering and disturbingly exploitative; sociality is enjoyed and exercised through precisely the commercial platforms that also exploit online activities for monetary gain' (p. 18).

The imbrication of social media platforms with the monetising logic of late capitalism must therefore circumscribe the political optimism expressed by scholars such as Castells (2015), Jarvis (2011) and Papacharissi (2010). At the very least, it raises some important questions about the ways in which we might understand the role of these communication technologies in relation to the public expression of new forms of sociality. Van Dijck (2013) points to the process by which the boundary between the public and private has been increasingly elided; 'utterances previously expressed offhandedly are now released into a public domain where they can have far reaching and long lasting effects' (p. 12). If, this, on the one hand, subjects tweets and status updates to the regulatory and potentially punitive gaze of governmental surveillance mechanisms, then equally as insidious is the extent to which these platforms facilitate the incursion of the market into every aspect of life, even monetising affect and affective labour itself (Hardt & Negri, 2000).

The erosion of the very idea of private space in tandem with the sense that there is no longer any 'hinterland' or space outside the logic of capital (Jameson, 2005), has particular implications for disabled people in the specific context of the decimation of the welfare state and benefits system that we are witnessing in the UK. George Osborne's image of the closed curtains that must be torn asunder to reveal the previously hidden body of the slumbering, benefit claimant suggests that one of the conditions of state support is an acceptance that one must also relinquish any right to privacy, autonomy or choice. In other words, the ideological conflation of the concept of value with economic participation through 'hard work' and employment produces those whose quality of life and wellbeing is contingent upon additional support as essentially parasitical and thus profoundly vulnerable. This is the kind of thinking manifest in the preference utilitarian Peter Singer's support for the killing of disabled infants on the grounds that they will only ever 'take' from the available social and economic resources (Singer, 1996). Thus, we see disabled benefit claimants being subjected to increasingly intrusive and humiliating strictures and interventions, including the use of forms of surveillance encoded in the Regulation of Investigatory Powers Act (2000) as a means to reveal 'benefit fraud'. Alongside this, the DWP's 'Help to Work' programme demands a daily visit to the Job Centre or an enforced period of unpaid labour – disabled, chronically and terminally ill people must prove that they are unable to work, and anyone who misses an appointment or turns up late is sanctioned and thus impoverished for a designated time period.

In this kind of environment, the transformation of 'casual speech acts' into 'formalised inscriptions' (Van Dijck 2013, p. 7) and the merging of private and public communication on platforms such as Twitter is not without its risks. As

@Kewryta noted, 'Ooh, sneaky spying time! Hey Liz just smiled. Disabled people can't smile. Faker!!!'. Although clearly ironic, the tweet encapsulates the degree to which disabled people are currently subjected to constant scrutiny within a narrowly defined conception of what disability means and how it should look. In the interview that follows, we discuss some of the risks inherent in the project in the context of notions of public and private space and public and private selves in relation to the current austerity agenda.

It is also important to note here that the assumption that social media platforms are inherently democratised and democratising spaces of 'autonomy' (Castells 2015) also occludes and arguably reinforces an unacknowledged but constitutive ableism. In other words, if technology is inaccessible, then the possibility of the active participation and representation of disabled people is precluded from the outset, thus re-inscribing social marginalisation. Goggin and Newell (2003) have described the systematic exclusion of disabled people from the apparently 'friction free' 'utopia of cyberspace' (p. 11) and emphasise the regulatory aspects of contemporary digital communications and media technologies in determining the ways in which disabled people are able to 'access various parts of the social world' (p. 10). More recently, Ellis and Kent (2011) have drawn attention to the inaccessible features of Twitter in the context of its use as a tool of political mobilisation. They point, in particular, to the exclusion of people with visual impairments as an example of Goggin and Newell's concept of 'doing production', what they describe as the ways in which an 'underpinning moral order' intersects 'with technology and culture and digitally disables people with certain bodies' (p. 52).

Any engagement with *Bedding Out* must therefore acknowledge the limitations of Twitter in relation to its capacity to engage everyone whose lives and wellbeing are negatively impacted upon by austerity and changes to the benefit system. There is certainly more work to be done to address questions of accessibility and participatory democracy in relation to the use of communicative digital networks, not only by visually impaired people but also by non-verbal or non-literate people with cognitive impairments. However, although Twitter is not inclusive in this global sense, there is strong evidence to suggest that the performance of *Bedding Out* and the dialogue it generated had a significant impact upon Twitter participants to the degree that it enabled people to share their experiences, to connect with one another, and to forge a sense of communitarian solidarity:

> @janeysian Thank you for #beddingout. I have my own 'bed life' and feel less isolated today knowing you are out there
> @KathyOLearyAlways good to know we're not alone #oftensufferingin-silence x

Crucially, Twitter was used in this project in the context of other means of access (physical and virtual spaces, written and verbal – distance participation included via email, text and phone) and it offered a way of engaging those with their own bed-lives for whom attending the live event was difficult if not impossible. It remains challenging to garner sustained public attention to the high levels of social and economic suffering experienced by disabled benefit claimants. The release of DWP statistics (August 2015) that indicate that more than 2500 benefit claimants died after being found fit for work between December 2011 and February 2014 is indicative of the structural violence that underpins the changes to the benefits system that *Bedding Out* addresses. However, the marginalisation and isolation of disabled people that this system inscribes and reinforces also make it more difficult to gain widespread, popular, attention to the devastating and often deadly effects of austerity for this group. The circulation of tragic stories – such as that of the former soldier David Clapson who died, alone and hungry, from diabetic ketoacidosis, having had his benefits stopped entirely for missing two Job Centre appointments – is evidence of the impact of sanctions upon people who are already in a structurally vulnerable position (*Guardian*, 03/08/14). However, these stories necessarily foreground individual tragedy, victimhood and despair to make this point rather than fundamentally challenge the neoliberal ideological framework that produces people with additional needs as a drain on limited resources, deserving (i.e. tragic) or undeserving and so on. The achievement of *Bedding Out* was to refuse these prevailing conceptions of disability from the outset and to encourage participants to express the complexity of their experiences without reproducing the divisive ableist categories that dominate current political and cultural discourse:

> @RGPLizCrow #beddingout "This is not a work of tragedy, but of in/visibility and complication" in disability and welfare reform.

The Twitter conversations combine humour and mockery of the governmental agenda and of ministers such as Esther McVey (Parliamentary Under Secretary of State for Disabled People 2012–2013 and Minister of State for Employment 2013–2015) with important personal, emotional and political insights about the implementation and effects of the new benefits regime:

> @RGPLizCrow Have you anything you'd like #beddingout to say to 'la la la la, can't hear, won't hear, and won't speak to the disabled' @Esther McVeyMP?
>
> @ian_beckett @RGPLizCrow you speak for the many unlike Madam McVain.
>
> @RGPLizCrow If @EstherMcVey was here in the room, right now, what would you say to her? #beddingout would like to hear! Shout.
>
> @MisterNSandwich @RGPLizCrow @EstherMcVey I'd ask why she blocked me on Twitter. Because I challenged her ludicrous claims, or because I called her a tosser?
>
> @miltonorourke @EstherMcVey When 'diagnosiing', what emphasis will be placed on 'factual' medical evidence, as opposed to Capita [company assessing PIP claimants] opinion?
>
> @leonc1963 I would ask her to be my carer for a week!

@MyalgicEncephal I would ask why she implied cognitive and fluctuating are not physical.

@bloomer71 I'd want to know why she insists on telling lies – 50% DLA claims granted without medical info? Total bull.

The humour and passion in these exchanges – the capacity to laugh and to mock – is a rejection of the abject, tragic constructions of disability that give rise to the dominant attribution of disabled people as somehow intrinsically vulnerable rather than structurally vulnerable as a consequence of austerity. The circulation of counter narratives (i.e. the exposure of the much-maligned Esther McVey's 'total bull' and the questioning of the assessment criteria) also facilitate the development of a set of conceptual and political resources with which to resist the ideological powers of the scrounger/striver dichotomy established in George Osborne's speech discussed earlier. Whilst Twitter has its limitations, its use in this context remains an important tool in the forging of a sense of community and a shared sense of resistance amongst a constituency for whom networked communication platforms facilitate connectivity between people for whom face to face encounters are difficult. This is not to reject Goggin and Newell's emphasis on the regulatory and often exclusionary effects of apparently facilitative technologies but to identify spaces of resistance and positive political appropriation within them. The use of Twitter in *Bedding Out* is discussed in detail in the final section of the interview.

The following transcript is edited and extracted from what was a long interview between Liz Crow (LC) and myself (LB). In the interests of clarity and spatial constraints, I have excised unfinished sentences, ums and repetitions (mainly mine). I have also organised the transcript into sections that explore context, the issues of public/private selves and risk discussed earlier, and the participatory nature of the project. I use [. . .] to indicate where sections have been edited or removed for reasons of relevance to the topic.

Interview with Liz Crow, Bristol, 2 February 2014

Context

LB: What did you hope that *Bedding Out* would achieve in the initial planning stages when you were thinking about what you were going to do?

LC: Well the thing that triggered it was the newspaper reporting and the political briefings on benefit changes and this notion of claimants as being skivers and scroungers and that, you know that disabled people, if they set their minds to it could get out there and work. All the things I was hearing didn't tally with my own experience of it and my knowledge of other people's experience and I wanted to confront that. I wanted particularly to look at the idea that when people were making those judgements they were making judgements on what was visibly presented in public spaces. So if I'm aware that I've lived my life with this incredibly stark public/private divide, then clearly nobody can make a judgement about my life based on what they see of me down in the supermarket because that, that's where I'm performing. When I'm at home in my bed, that's where I'm not performing, that's where I'm closest to being me – whatever that is.

Whilst that had been my experience for 30 years, the stakes were suddenly much higher because of the kind of judgements that were being made about people, the ineligibility for benefits and the very precarious positions that people were being placed in and the rise in hate crime that was being associated with it. So suddenly we were talking about something that had been going on for forever and a day but had become much more dangerous. So I was working with that idea with the bed and I think, as with all my work, I saw it as potentially being a platform for those kind of conversations to be had. What I didn't realise, I think, was how far ranging the conversations would become, that it wasn't simply about those versions of ourselves that we present to kind of manage our lives; it became deeper and wider. So it became about the broadest politics, it became about the sort of society that we want to live in, it even became about what it means to be human.

My work is very much seen I think as having a disability focus and I'm not convinced that it does. In my films there's always a character who is a disabled person but the questions that arise in the films are simply about being human, about trying to find a place in the world amongst people who have to wriggle much more to find that place because the world doesn't admit them quite so readily. And I think that some of the conversations we had around the bed and through Twitter arrived at that point, of what kind of world do we want to live in? The biggest, most fundamental questions came out of that initial assertion that you need to understand more about me even to have the possibility of judging who I am. You can't make these sweeping judgements about a person on the basis of what they present publicly. One of the things I was trying to get across was that idea that my public self would be seen as striving [. . .] but if I reveal that private side of me, the real risk is that it is seen as tragic. Whereas what I wanted to say is that real life is a kind of complicated mishmash of elements, of both those things but also something completely different. I want to convey the idea that life is complicated for me because life is complicated. Actually at that level, the really simple message is that life isn't straightforward, it isn't this or that – extremes or absolutes or binaries – it's messy, and anybody who really looks at their own life will see that they are a mass of contradictions. One day I can do this or one day I choose to do this and I'm prepared to make a trade off and you, in public, will see me doing this physical exertion but what you won't see is the preparation or the recovery time. Reality for me is a constant juggling and calculation of that. It keeps coming back to the thing that if I make that public the risk is that people go 'oh yes I knew her life was awful, I knew her life was tragic' – but what I'm saying is that it is just an awful lot more complicated than the images that we are given.

LB: But this is in the face of a set of policies that attempt to simplify and reduce complexity, that are all about tick box exercises or reducing people's lives to passing or failing a test so it is probably very important that that's countered and that what you do counters that. But I'm also aware that there's risk, isn't there, for you – I suppose because, currently, if you are seen to be able to do anything then it's 'well, how can you possibly deserve support?'

LC: Absolutely, that's a huge part of it and those judgements are made every day, so the risk is that you spend a lot of time justifying the decisions you make instead of getting on with the decisions you make. What you just said about the kind of criteria that are applied, they've brought a particular urgency – the benefits changes have bought a particular urgency – to this whole public/ private thing and how we present ourselves. Because to a greater extent than previous benefits eligibility processes, they've relied on quantifiable factors. The form of measurement they use is akin to the form of measurement that's used on Paralympians to check their eligibility to compete, so there are measures of what you can do, how long you can exert in a particular action, whether you have a particular range of movement. [Things that] are all very measurable but are also based on bodies that predominantly function today as they will function tomorrow and as they functioned yesterday. They are predominantly physical impairment-based or sensory impairment-based, but again things that you can put a number on. The reality is that if most Paralympians – not all but most – roughly fit that mould, you are talking about a different group of people who are more likely to be on disability out of work benefits. They're the ones with the kind of nebulous, changeable, unpredictable, maybe invisible impairments that you can't quantify and very often rely on subjective reporting because there aren't tests to measure it. So what you find is that you've got a test that is completely unfit for purpose for the group of people it is supposed to measure because it doesn't deal in the complexities of real lives, and therefore the people who need it most are the ones who are most likely to fall through the net. So it's a system that is entwined in that public/private divide, judging a group of people on their public presentation and therefore failing to meet their needs.

LB: And it's complicated because it is a process that the government at least would present as being a fair one because it applies a standard set of criteria to measure and evaluate a group of people. So it looks from the outside as if it is doing all those things that seem to be fair.

LC: Yes and what I've described [. . .] doesn't even begin to look at the structural discrimination that's in society. You know if somebody goes through that claims process and is deemed fit to work then they are in a bunfight for jobs with someone who might have a postgraduate education, fantastic health, solid financial resources and a supportive family and no factors for which they are likely to be discriminated against. So, one person is actually much more likely to get off job seeker's allowance than the other, so to place the same expectations and requirements on those two people just doesn't represent life and isn't fair.

LB: Yes. It is fundamentally unfair [. . .] and it [comes back to] the reduction, to this simplification that we've talked about. The image that comes to me all the time when I think about *Bedding Out* is Osborne's image of the person behind the closed curtains staying in bed whilst the 'hardworking families' of the UK get up and go out to work. I think of all the things that *Bedding Out* challenges and questions it is precisely the power of that image to encapsulate this rhetoric around strivers and scroungers because it works by simplifying things in relation to particular ideas of what productivity is or what work is or what living is.

LC: I think that there's also a lot of symbolic stuff like the curtains that is used against us and I think with the *Bedding Out* piece [. . .] what I'm trying to do is to create a counter symbol so that there's a strong image that stays in the mind beyond the actual specifics of the performance or the actual conversations that are held; that [hopefully] that image can be held in people's minds next time they confront the kind of closed curtains thing.

Public/private selves

LB: So in *Bedding Out*, there is an endeavour to explore and to account for this [private self] that's often excluded or placed in parenthesis in some forms of activism, you bring that to the fore but it's still a performance. So when you were thinking about *Bedding Out*, how did you decide what you were going to perform? Was it simply enough to reference the fact that there is this private space? Or did you make conscious choices about how you would inhabit that space or what being in that space was about? I am thinking in terms of what is revealed and what continues – I guess – not to be revealed because it was also an extraordinarily tough task I think. I get the impression that the 48 hours that you describe were really, really hard work.

LC: It's known as durational performance work and I think it's just as valid to call it endurance – and there's really an element of that and yes, it was very hard and a lot of people said to me that they were amazed by how vulnerable I was willing to make myself. I think I only realised afterwards that it was a lot more exposing than I perhaps realised. On the other hand, it was a performance and therefore I was editing, so there were aspects of that private self that I didn't show and that I am not prepared to show in front of other people. Equally what I wanted to do was to present something that wasn't too specific, so for example had you seen me taking specific medication or talking about specific impairment stuff or making visible body stuff then I would have started to represent a much narrower constituency and I didn't want that private self to be labelled in that way. What I wanted to do was to provide an image, evidence of a life lived outside the public gaze. The majority of people are astounded at the idea that there are people who spend large parts of their lives in bed. Just that, just that simple thing, is so far beyond most people's knowledge, that there are lives like that. I wanted to present that as a symbolic thing and what happened, sort of immediately really, was that a lot of other disabled people whose experience was different from that still saw it as theirs. They recognised that process of editing themselves – so it wasn't that they spent their time in bed, but there were aspects of their impairment that they too felt the need to conceal. And with hindsight, I realise that a major vulnerability was not in the performance itself but in the 'holding' of other people's hurt.

LB: And it did enable people to talk about those things and to bring those things to light didn't it? I think in some of the Twitter responses you get a sense of people being able to suddenly say things publicly that they hadn't been able to say before.

LC: I think that with all of these things, if it is just some woman lying in bed in a public space, that doesn't go very far, but what it does is to provide a platform for other people to get involved in the conversations it triggers. In theory you could sit down and have any of those conversations that were had on the back of *Bedding Out*. However, there was something about the context in which they were held and the sense of integrity in the piece – that I was prepared to commit to doing this and to revealing this side of myself – that I think enabled those conversations to go deeper. When the conversations were held around the bed, there were some incredibly profound things said there and deeply personal things – very politically thoughtful things were said – and I'm not convinced they would be able to go to the depths they did if we'd been sitting round a table or in a training session.

[. . .]

What I would find in some conversations is that there would be other people [around the bed] who got hold of the conversation and could respond in ways that were incredibly helpful – the sense of support amongst every single person [in some conversations] was absolutely extraordinary and compelling. There was something about that whole setup of the person in the bed raising these issues that are not generally spoken about but evidencing them, and people gathered around the bed, and that taking down of barriers that [meant] that as a group we could move things forward.

Art, creation and participation

LB: I'm interested in how this relates to the ways we think about art and the production of art and art objects. Unlike say a film which might have a particular kind of narrative trajectory, a duration, an arc of some sort, or an exhibition that people move through in particular ways, [. . .] this is a very different way of thinking about art itself and of artistic practice. This is about being in a bed in a public space for a certain length of time. So in a sense you transform the idea of what art might be in that space, in doing this. Can you say something about the process by which you decided that this is what you were going to do, that *Bedding Out* was going to take this shape and form and how far your primary interest was in creating a piece of art or in the kind of dialogue, debate and discussion that it would generate?

LC: [. . .] For me, one of the key differences between the performance stuff that I do and the film stuff that I have done, and may return to, is risk and a kind of leap of faith. With the films [everything] is plotted. You know it can go awry but fundamentally you know what kind of story you are trying to tell, what kind of message you want to get over, what kind of conversation you are trying to trigger and to a very large degree you're in control of how that thing turns out. How the audience reacts is still not entirely in your control but you're giving a very strong lead in how it should be interpreted and potentially acted upon. With the performance, most of that goes. What you have rather than plot is intent. So if there are elements that can be controlled, in this case the setting of the bed, the location of it, how it was set up on the stage, the kind of cues that are given – you know, is it a domestic space that I'm setting up or is it a clear performance space, what's the lighting doing? – all those give some lead as to how people might respond. However, it is also a very unscripted piece of work and it involves live interaction with people that can make it into a very different piece. The risk for me in that is that it won't achieve what I'm hoping it will do, that even where the work is politically positioned very clearly, it will lead to what for me would be a misinterpretation that would undermine the values that are at its core. So it carries a risk that I don't think the films do nearly so much, but I also think when it works that risk means the impact can be far, far deeper, and I've seen that with Plinth[9] and I've seen that with *Bedding Out*. Where it works it does something that I wouldn't have dared hope for when I first came up with the idea.

[. . .]

LB: And do you think it [*Bedding Out*] fostered a kind of communal awareness? In other words, was there a sense that people were participating with you together to create something collectively? Because what strikes me is that it is an attempt to break down that distinction between performer and audience in that its whole conception is inclusive, about fostering a dialogue? So you cease to have that idea of the authority being in one place [with the artist].

LC: Yes but there is the potential for a conflict of interest there. Particularly in Salisbury where it was live streamed – anyone coming to the bedside knew it would be live streamed, that were would be visuals, and the sound would be relayed and it would be sign language interpreted and so on and they would be seen. But as you see on reality TV the implications of that don't automatically translate. People would come to the bedside and they would tell their own experiences of going through ESA assessments and pretty much in every conversation somebody would break down and cry. For me there was a kind of role in making that safe for them and in responding in a way that supported them whilst, particularly in the last conversation at Salisbury, I also had quite a clear agenda that I wanted to get across in that conversation for the wider audience. The conflict [of interest then] was that I moved through five bedside conversations and there had been a gathering momentum of ideas and it became really important that that fifth conversation looked outwards and forwards, that it didn't just reiterate how awful it is but gave us a launch pad to start improving things. I knew I needed to do this but that was also the conversation where a couple came along and told the most difficult story, a really hard story. [. . .] I was very aware of trying to manage these two agendas that could have conflicted. It was a very fine balance and I was concerned for them. Afterwards we got in touch and they said it was really hard but they were glad that they had done it so that was a real relief to know. That that was one of the dangers in those conversations, particularly with the live stream.

LB: So again, it is about that real balancing act between conceptions of tragedy, of public and private selves and performed and non-performed selves. It strikes me as a really difficult set of things to hold together and to portray and share with integrity.

LC: Yes, and it comes back to the risk thing. The reality is that with those kinds of conversations it could have gone very badly wrong, but it didn't. And it's a leap of faith; trying to trust that the process will be alright, but not having a clue whether it will be. What made it was the personal stories that people brought. We could have had a debate around the bed about grand theory about this stuff and everyone would have gone away with information and potentially deep thinking but they wouldn't have felt that connection to the issues that came through people bringing pieces of themselves to it.

LB: [. . .] In other words, it was about finding a way for people to bear witness and to do so publicly because that is central to the politics of what's happening right now. You need to have these stories and the stories need to be told. [. . .] *Bedding Out* provided people with a space to do that but in a space in which those stories are understood in relationship to bigger structures – things that aren't personal.

LC: The contextualising for me was absolutely at the core of it. There's a reason that newspapers turn to human issue stories because they connect with us, but it is really easy to do a human interest story that is superficial about one person's tragedy; it is much harder to put it into that political context, but for what I am trying to do it's critical.

The use of Twitter

LB: This leads me to the use of Twitter and its relationship to the performances because there's no bed on Twitter, no place around which people are sitting. Can you say more about your decision to use Twitter?

LC: Because a significant proportion of people on Twitter were in their own beds. In the first performance, in Ipswich, I was using Twitter only to report on the performance and not yet as an integral component of the work. But I was emailed by someone who said 'I love what you're doing, I'd love to come and see it but I'm in my own bed so that's not an option, but I'm still really happy that you're doing this and I feel represented'. So between conversations in Ipswich, I lay in bed, angst-ing on how I solve this. I'd done a tiny bit of Twitter and had had an account for a while, but wasn't using it on a grand scale, but I suddenly thought that I would look to Twitter and see if there was a possibility of developing something there, because I couldn't think of how else to get people participating virtually, of how to bring them into the performance space without their being physically present. I thought Twitter plus live stream could be a way forward and so I looked for recommendations of people who were really good on Twitter and found Dawn Willis who became my tweetmeister. It absolutely needed somebody in a dedicated role, but working very closely with me on it. I couldn't have done both. But her experience in social media really clinched that as a way forward.

LB: Was that an experience in connecting with people or with knowing how to tweet in the most effective ways?

LC: Both, and probably lots of other things too. Dawn already had a sizable following on her own account so she had a reputation, particularly in mental health circles, which meant that there was quite a nice [coming together] of mental health and physical impairment communities. We came from those different perspectives with a common political endeavour and so, where the two communities have traditionally been split, it was brilliant to bring them together. Our two communities brought quite a range of people into the same conversation. So she had a reputation and was well liked, so her putting information out on Twitter brought in people who didn't know about my work, but it also brought in people who did know my work already.

LB: Do you think that there are any disadvantages to Twitter in relation to the kinds of conversations that you might want to conduct?

LC: There is one thing I've observed in relation to the conversations that took place in *Bedding Out* and the work that takes place through In Actual Fact.[10] I think Twitter in *Bedding Out* was Twitter at its best, because what it did was facilitate conversation. I think Twitter at its weakest is something I've seen sometimes in In Actual Fact, where there would be a mass tweet against a programme such as *Benefits Street* and what you have is two opposing views shouting into the dark and no one listens to anyone and there's no conversation going on. So I think using Twitter to foster conversation was fantastic and it worked but I also think Twitter can be appalling. But even with those reservations, what I have realised with In Actual Fact is that it's not just those two opposing shouts, it's what happens to the whole stream of tweets afterwards and the way they get retweeted and retweeted, and commented upon, and therefore the net is cast wider. With each person who picks it up, their followers expand from the followers I have, so there is an increasing chance of reaching people who don't know about these issues and will be introduced to them.

LB: Perhaps, the aim of mass tweeting in relation to a TV programme isn't about having a conversation. Perhaps the aim is to say no, there are groups of people out here who are acting together to challenge what you are doing?

LC: Yes, it's about presence more than content. And it's also about solidarity with other who think as you do, a bolstering of your own resilience and ability to keep your activism going. But I'd thought its reach would stop at that point. But I was talking to someone the other day because I was feeling very despondent about In Actual Fact and he said people really like this, they are coming to it and they using it and he's still seeing tweets he sent two months ago being retweeted. So their reach is far bigger than we are ever going to know. So I do think it has value beyond that immediate moment when you tweet in response to a programme. But the *Bedding Out* Twitter conversations were so powerful in all sorts of ways. It required us to start things off, to introduce topics, to get people used to the idea of this forthcoming performance, but there was a point where people started to bring in their own ideas and to make suggestions about things, for instance, that people could submit their own *Bedding Out* photos and videos in solidarity. So these semi-independent projects happened, but there were also conversations instigated by other people in response, and there were conversations that went off at an angle and presumably carried on that we never heard about, so it became active in all kinds of directions.

The other thing is that we did is have two types of round the bed conversations. There was one where Dawn had earmarked all kinds of interesting Twitter comments and questions for me and she translated my responses back into Twitter. So you'd get the tweets coming in and the tweets going out, along with the live stream. The other thing we did was have Twitter conversations with particular groups. On the eve of the Salisbury performance we had a conversation with OT chat (a professional development group of Occupational Therapists). They were asking questions in relation to the performance and their own practice and it was a really interesting conversation that subsequently became a transcript that, along with all the other conversations, is now available as a reference tool.

LB: What kind of new things have emerged then on the basis of the conversations that happened on Twitter?

LC: It's hard to know, as in I think that many of the most significant things are not particularly tangible. A lot of people talked about the confidence they'd got from it, the friendships they'd built – and we are talking about people who in many instances are incredibly isolated, so to make social contacts through this is huge. There are people who have been introduced to a political perspective on their own lives or on policy changes, that's definitely come out of it. In Actual Fact has come out of it directly. There was a moment in the conversations when we had been talking and tweeting about media representation of disabled people within the whole benefits austerity thing and I'd mentioned the Daily Mail reporting that said 75% of people were faking it, when in fact it was 0.7%. As the conversation went on it became incredibly clear that one of things we needed to do was to start getting the facts out there, so on the second night we started (off the cuff) an additional hashtag #truefacts and started getting those facts out. Subsequently, I made that into a whole new project and called it #InActualFact. That has taken off as a completely independent entity and is perhaps the biggest tangible thing that has come out of it. It now has interns working on it and the intention is to make it a campaign of real influence. So a surprising number of things have come from it really, in ways I could never have predicted.

Notes

1 It is possible to access audio, images and the Twitter feed of *Bedding Out* here: http://www.roaring-girl.com/work/bedding-out/

2 Iain Duncan Smith 'Welfare for the 21st Century' speech (2010) See: https://www.gov.uk/government/speeches/welfare-for-the-21st-century [accessed 02/10/2015]

3 This is a widely reported incident. See, for example, http://www.mirror.co.uk/news/uk-news/sick-benefits-claimant-heart-attack-3098219 [accessed 02/10/2015]

4 See http://dpac.uk.net/ [accessed 02/10/2015] and http://wowpetition.com/write-to-your-mp-now/ [accessed 02/10/2015]
5 On mortality statistics see https://www.gov.uk/government/uploads/system/uploads/attachment_data/file/459106/mortality-statistics-esa-ib-sda.pdf [accessed 02/10/2015]. On the fabrication of the experiences of benefit claimants on a DWP leaflet see http://www.theguardian.com/society/2015/aug/18/dwp-admits-making-up-positive-quotes-from-benefits-claimants-for-leaflet [accessed 02/10/2015]; on UN investigation see http://www.independent.co.uk/news/uk/politics/un-to-investigate-uk-over-human-rights-abuses-against-disabled-people-caused-by-welfare-reform-10478536.html [accessed 02/10/2015]; on Iain Duncan Smith's resignation see http://www.bbc.co.uk/news/uk-politics-35848891 [accessed 09/09/2016]
6 George Osborne, speech to the annual Conservative Party Conference, Birmingham, 8.10.12, http://www.newstatesman.com/blogs/politics/2012/10/george-osbornes-speech-conservative-conference-full-text [accessed 20/08/15]
7 See https://www.gov.uk/government/collections/fraud-and-error-in-the-benefit-system [accessed 22/08/15]
8 See http://www.cps.gov.uk/publications/prosecution/disability.html [accessed 22/08/15]
9 *Resistance on the Plinth* was a 2008 performance by Liz Crow that took place as part of Antony Gormley's *One & Other* on the Trafalgar Square plinth.
10 In Actual Fact @InActualFact101 was a web- and Twitter-based social media campaign created by Liz Crow that set out to counter inaccuracies in austerity claims.

References

Castells, M. (2015). *Networks of outrage and hope: Social movements in the internet age* (2nd ed.). Cambridge, UK: Polity Press.

Dean, J. (2010). *Blog theory: Feedback and capture in the circuits of drive.* Cambridge, UK: Polity Press.

Ellis, K., & Kent, M. (2011). *Disability and new media.* London, UK: Routledge.

Goggin, G., & Newell, C. (2003). *Digital disability: The social construction of disability in new media.* Oxford, UK: Rowman and Littlefield.

Hardt, M., & Negri, A. (2000). *Empire.* Cambridge, MA: Harvard University Press.

Jameson, F. (2005). *Archaeologies of the future: The desire called utopia and other science fictions.* London, UK: Verso.

Jarvis, J. (2011). *Public parts: How sharing in the digital age improves the way we work and live.* New York, NY: Simon and Schuster.

O' Hara, M. (2015). *Austerity bites: A journey to the sharp end of cuts in the UK.* Bristol, UK: Policy Press.

Papacharissi, Z. (2010). *A private sphere: Democracy in a digital age.* Cambridge, UK: Polity Press.

Singer, P. (1996). *Rethinking life and death: The collapse of our traditional ethics.* New York, NY: St Martin's Press.

Smith, I.D. (2010) 'Welfare for the 21st Century' speech See: https://www.gov.uk/government/speeches/welfare-for-the-21st-century [accessed 02/10/2015]

Van Dijck, J. (2013). *The culture of connectivity: A critical history of social media.* Oxford, UK: Oxford University Press.

Television programmes

Benefits Street (first shown January – February 2014) Channel 4 and Love Productions, UK.
On Benefits and Proud (first shown October 2013), Channel 5, UK.

Websites

http://www.newstatesman.com/blogs/politics/2012/10/george-osbornes-speech-conservative-conference-full-text

https://www.gov.uk/government/speeches/welfare-for-the-21st-century

https://www.gov.uk/government/collections/fraud-and-error-in-the-benefit-system

https://www.gov.uk/government/uploads/system/uploads/attachment_data/file/459106/mortality-statistics-esa-ib-sda.pdf

http://www.cps.gov.uk/publications/prosecution/disability.html

http://www.roaring-girl.com/

http://dpac.uk.net/

Part II

Access

6 The growing importance of accessible social media

Scott Hollier

Introduction

The rapid evolution of social media in recent years has demonstrated that the web is no longer merely a passive information resource, but a gateway for conversational online interaction. As highlighted by Kaplan and Haenlein (2010), social media can be defined in technical terms as 'a group of internet-based applications that build on the ideological and technological foundations of Web 2.0, and that allow the creation and exchange of User Generated Content' or in the social context of 'engaging others in open and active conversation'.

While for most online users the technical implementation of social media through websites, apps and devices is rarely considered beyond being a mechanism for getting to the relevant social media tool, for people with disabilities the technical and the conversational are required in equal measure to truly achieve online participation, due to the assistive technology (AT) required to ensure that independent interaction with others online can be achieved.

This chapter focuses on the remarkable parallel developments of mainstream AT, the changing nature of social media requirements for people with disabilities, research undertaken to address accessibility issues, and the potential new benefits and barriers delivered by the cloud as more online elements entwine to provide new challenges in social engagement.

Mainstream AT evolution

The technical underpinnings of social media are vital in ensuring that people with disabilities are able to enjoy the benefits that the web, broadly, and social media, specifically, can provide. Software designed to run in popular computer operating systems that support people with disabilities was generally referred to as assistive technology or AT. Examples of popular AT include screen readers to provide audio navigation in a computing environment for people who are blind, screen magnifiers which enlarge on-screen content for people with low vision, and on-screen keyboards to assist people with a mobility impairment who may need to use a pointing device to type (Royal National Institute of Blind People, 2014; Microsoft, 2014a). While the benefits and availability of software-based AT gained prominence in the 1990s through products such as the JAWS screen reader for Windows, there were two fundamental issues with the initial AT offerings: first, they were notoriously unreliable due to the instability of the operating system on which they ran and, second, the software applications were extremely expensive, costing several thousand dollars on top of the cost of a desktop computer (Hollier, 2006).

However, both issues were addressed as a result of legislation in the United States of America. The *Rehabilitation Act of 1973*, Section 508, was a landmark public procumbent framework which required ICT sold to the Federal government to adhere to accessibility criteria, both in terms of products purchased and hosted web content (United States General Services Administration, 2014). As a result, companies responsible for creating popular operating systems began to incorporate accessibility features and AT into their mainstream products. Examples include the inclusion of Narrator, a screen reader with limited functionality in Windows 2000, and the VoiceOver screen reader in Mac OS X 10.4 Tiger (Hollier, 2013). With mainstream operating systems now including AT, the issue of stability was addressed due to the application programming interfaces (APIs) on the platform being optimised for AT. Furthermore, the availability of features for free on these platforms addressed much of the affordability issues.

In relation to social media specifically, it was the inclusion of accessibility features in the Apple iPhone 3GS in 2009 that had a particularly significant impact (Hollier, 2013). With the touchscreen interface on a popular mobile device now becoming accessible to people who are blind or vision impaired, due to the VoiceOver screen reader being integrated with the ability to explore on-screen elements by touch, social media apps were now available to people with disabilities, and people with disabilities were able to use key social media platforms in an on-the-go environment. Google Android also followed suit, introducing accessibility features into its ecosystem, which led to an ever-greater competition of affordability and accessibility.

The accessible web

With the parallel development of AT in mainstream mobile devices and the rise of social media, the potential had been created for people with disabilities to participate and enjoy the benefits of engaging directly using the relevant tools. Yet, while having the required AT represented an important part of the accessibility requirement, in order for AT to work effectively, it is also necessary for web content and apps to be built to relevant accessibility standards.

The current web and ISO standard is the World Wide Web Consortium (W3C) *Web content accessibility guidelines (WCAG) 2.0*, first published in 2008 (World Wide Web Consortium, 2008a; International Standards Organization, 2012). WCAG 2.0 consists of 12 guidelines, of which the simplified 'at a glance' version (World Wide Web Consortium, 2008b) is as follows:

Perceivable

* Provide text alternatives for non-text content.
* Provide captions and other alternatives for multimedia.

- Create content that can be presented in different ways, including by AT, without losing meaning.
- Make it easier for users to see and hear content.

Operable

- Make all functionality available from a keyboard.
- Give users enough time to read and use content.
- Do not use content that causes seizures.
- Help users navigate and find content.

Understandable

- Make text readable and understandable.
- Make content appear and operate in predictable ways.
- Help users avoid and correct mistakes.

Robust

- Maximise compatibility with current and future user tools.

In regard to social media, in order for people with disabilities to effectively use the web portal to popular social media tools, it is essential that the websites comply with the WCAG 2.0 standard.

Furthermore, in relation to non-web content, such as social media apps on popular mobile devices like iOS for iPad and iPhone or Android smartphones and tablets, there is also the advisory document WCAG2ICT which identifies the key elements of WCAG 2.0 relevant for software development (World Wide Web Consortium, 2013). For example, the first guideline that discusses text alternatives is also applicable to making sure that buttons in apps are labelled so that the correct information is provided by the screen reader when a user selects the button.

Personal engagement with social media

While the combination of AT and the implementation of web accessibility standards and techniques is critical to ensuring people with disabilities can gain access to social media from a technical standpoint, at its core the purpose for using social media remains focused on the conversational nature of the web through the fundamental need to create, modify, share, and discuss internet content in a particular situation (Kietzmann, Hermkens, McCarthy, & Silvestre, 2011).

To understand the direct experiences of people with disabilities in this area, I undertook a research project as part of my employment with Media Access Australia, Australia's only independent not-for-profit organisation devoted to increasing access to media for people with a disability (Media Access Australia, 2014). The research report was entitled *Sociability: Social media for people with a disability* (Hollier, 2012) and focused on interviewing people with disabilities who had an interest in social media across a variety of ages, experiences, and disabilities to determine why they used social media, the primary questions that needed answering to use social media more effectively, and any tips and tricks that experienced users has found which could assist novice social media users.

The research, which was largely qualitative in nature and took place between June 2011 and February 2012, focused on the responses of 49 participants with their input received by email, Twitter, and in-person interviews. The resource was funded by a grant provided by the Australian Communications Consumer Action Network (ACCAN) and all interviews adhered to the ACCAN ethics and written consent requirements (Australian Communications Consumer Action Network, 2011). It received international acclaim, including adoption by the USA Federal government as an important guide for its own social media communications (United States DigitalGov, 2014).

For online users broadly, people use social media for a variety of purposes such as personal use for engagement with family and friends using tools like Facebook, work-related purposes using tools such as LinkedIn, and personal reflections such as blogging tools or Twitter and entertainment through the sharing of videos on YouTube (International Telecommunication Union, 2010). For people with disabilities, the reasons are similar, but there are often additional disability-specific benefits that can also apply.

In the process of my sociability research (Hollier, 2012), I discovered several stories that encapsulated the power of social media for people with disabilities. The first was regarding a hearing impaired woman who relied heavily on the use of Facebook. Part of the benefit was for general discussion with friends, but a key disability-related aspect was that Facebook was a useful tool for helping her overcome the challenges of having little hearing in a loud social environment. When there was a social occasion such as a party, the young woman indicated that Facebook was very helpful as she could friend people going to the party beforehand, get to know them and explain her disability to them, then when she got to the party she felt more comfortable as people around her understood the nature of her disability and could engage with her in alternative ways such as hand gestures or writing things down.

Another story shared was by a blind man approximately 50 years of age who was unemployed at the time but was optimistic thanks to his social media use. The man indicated that by using LinkedIn he had an opportunity to put his résumé online to promote his qualifications, and could also keep up with conversations happening in his chosen industry by participating in online discussion forums. Given the high rate of unemployment among people who are blind and vision impaired (Vision Australia, 2012), the use of LinkedIn essentially provided optimism and hope

Other stories shared in the research highlight that humour is also an important mechanism in which social media can help people with disabilities share and discuss important information. A young vision impaired man indicated that he enjoyed YouTube because it allowed him to join in social conversations in the office where he worked about things they'd seen online such as cat videos even if he couldn't see them well, and an older man with a mobility impairment indicated that he found Facebook particularly useful because he was unable to drive, was not a particularly good cook, and really enjoyed using the pizza coupons found on a large pizza company's Facebook page.

What these experiences indicate is that people with disabilities are not seeking a specialist or disability-specific social media service, but rather wish to use the same popular social media tools used by the broader online community. There are, however, often disability-specific uses as part of that engagement.

Current accessibility barriers of social media

While the benefits of social media can be profound for people with disabilities, the ability to successfully interact with social media tools is heavily reliant on a successful combination of personal AT and the tools adhering to accessibility criteria such as WCAG 2.0. With AT support increasing in popular mainstream tools, attention turned to the level of WCAG 2.0 compliance in social media web portals and the accessibility of apps on popular mobile platforms.

When people with disabilities were asked in the *Sociability* report (Hollier, 2012) what information they needed to effectively use social media, there were a series of key questions that were collated from the participants that identified the information that was necessary to use social media effectively:

- What can the social media tool do?
- What are the specific benefits to me?
- What tips and tricks can help me get around the accessibility issues?
- How can I get set up to use it for the first time?
- How do I perform the necessary everyday tasks?
- How do I make my own content accessible?
- Where do I go for help?

While information relating to the purpose, setup and features of popular social media tools are readily available online, information on what accessibility issues are likely to appear, how people with disabilities can manage to get around them, and where to go for help continue to be critical information for effective social media engagement.

To provide answers relating to the questions of accessibility barriers and how to address them, it is necessary to find out which elements of WCAG 2.0 have not been implemented in popular social media platforms. Denis Boudreau of Accessibilité Web performed a landmark assessment of popular social media accessibility tools presented at the CSUN Technology and Persons with Disability Conference 2012, comparing five social media tools against the WCAG 2.0 guidelines and creating a customised percentage score of accessibility (Boudreau, 2012). Of the five tools – Facebook, Twitter, LinkedIn, YouTube, and what was at that time the recently launched Google+ – LinkedIn received the highest score of 29 per cent accessible followed by YouTube on 18 per cent, Google+ on 9 per cent, Facebook on 9 per cent, and Twitter receiving no accessibility score due to every element on the website having accessibility issues. While many accessibility issues remain in these tools several years later, improvements have been made, with Facebook, Twitter, and Google all providing accessibility improvements through their specific accessibility initiatives.

As Facebook grew into one of the world's most popular social media tools, it undertook work with the American Foundation for the Blind to start the process of making its website more accessible (Crum, 2009). While significant improvements were made at the time, tests conducted by BITV Test (2011) confirmed that several years later there are a number of accessibility issues in the primary Facebook website. Additional user testing by Media Access Australia in 2011 (Hollier, 2012) confirmed that accessibility issues at that time included a CAPTCHA during the sign-up process, difficulties with keyboard navigation and missing text alternatives. Furthermore, for deaf and hearing impaired users, videos uploaded to Facebook directly do not support closed captions. However, in the past two years Facebook appears to have taken accessibility issues more seriously and has begun providing monthly accessibility updates as it improves its web portal and the accessibility of its apps (Facebook, 2014).

While accessibility challenges remain, the proactive approach to addressing the issues appears to be successful, with some notable examples of recent accessibility improvements including the addition of captioned video for people who are deaf and hearing impaired and the inclusion of VoiceOver gesture support for the Facebook app on Apple iOS-based devices such as the iPhone and iPad. Furthermore, Facebook provides an AT helpdesk for users of popular products to help navigate users around particular accessibility issues (Facebook, 2012). While Facebook acknowledge accessibility issues remain, it is encouraging to see progress towards WCAG 2.0 compliance and integrated app accessibility.

As noted by Boudreau (2012), Twitter was one of the most inaccessible social media tools, which is ironic due to the text-based nature of the tool. The unwieldy interface, inaccessible elements, and lack of keyboard shortcuts support resulted in a difficult experience. This led people with disabilities to find new and creative ways to engage with Twitter without using its primary website, leading to the creation of an alternative portal, Easy Chirp (2014), to provide an accessible interface for people with disabilities. A number of third-party apps were also created on Apple iOS-based devices such as Twitterrific, Twittelator for iPad, Tweetosaurus, Tweetero, and TweetList Pro, as rated by the accessible crowd-sourced app review website AppleVis (2014).

However, as with Facebook, improvements to accessibility came in a dramatic fashion with an announcement by Twitter's engineering team in 2013 (Twitter, 2013) that there were significant accessibility improvements to the primary Twitter website based on a new interface that included improved timeline access, significant improvement to keyboard navigation, screen reader compatibility, and, arguably most importantly, the revealing of a specific Twitter accessibility team (Twitter, 2014). Tweets from the team in recent times have been similar to Facebook's monthly announcements, stating that there have been notable ongoing accessibility improvements to the main Twitter website and also improvements to its Twitter app on IOS, particularly around integration with the built-in magnifier and screen reader accessibility features.

YouTube is another tool that has significant accessibility issues but has seen significant improvements in recent years. An important distinction, however, is that Google provided many accessibility features to YouTube in terms of its video functionality such as its captioning playback feature and cutting-edge auto-mated captioning service introduced in 2009 (Google, 2009), based on its Google Voice system. However, as indicated in Boudreau's (2012) report and user test-ing conducted by Media Access Australia (Hollier, 2012), there were a number of issues at the time such as the inability to navigate around the player function using keyboard; unlabelled buttons in the player; challenges with the playback of Flash video causing instability with AT tools; and the automated captions. The latter, while a useful feature in assisting people to quickly caption their videos, were notoriously inaccurate, which YouTube itself used to highlight unfortunate examples of incorrect closed captions. To overcome these issues, as with Twitter, the community developed alternative portals to YouTube clips such as Accessible YouTube and Easy YouTube to create an accessible interface that would allow for effective video playback.

As with the other social media tools, significant improvements have been made since 2012, in part due to intentional improvements by Google to address acces-sibility issues in the YouTube player interface, thereby improving screen reader compatibility (Google, 2014). The improvements in video playback support are a result of the development of HTML5 which means YouTube playback does not have to reply on third-party plugins such as Flash (Google, 2010). While the move to incorporate HTML5 began in 2010, the HTML5 standard has only recently become a W3C recommendation (World Wide Web Consortium, 2014), meaning that the improvements in accessible video playback are likely to become stan-dardised across the browsers in the near future. While quality and accuracy issues still remain prevalent in the automated caption feature of YouTube, Google has provided an integrated captioning tool making it easier for users to modify the caption file to improve accuracy.

While in the case of Facebook, Twitter and YouTube there have been significant accessibility improvements in recent years, there has been little change to the accessibility of LinkedIn, although, as indicated by Boudreau (2012), this was generally considered to be the most accessible interface at the time.

While these are just a few of the extensive number of social media tools and plat-forms available, it is encouraging that when accessibility issues have appeared due to a lack of compliance with the WCAG 2.0 standard, people with disabilities have generally identified or created ways to overcome the barriers, while social media providers have also continued to improve the accessibility of their own content.

Cloud integration of social media

While effective access to social media is currently dependent on the accessibility of AT combined with the relevant tool complying with accessibility criteria, there is a notable move towards social media becoming integrated as a cloud storage service. This therefore suggests that future consideration of social media for people with disabilities should also consider the benefits, barriers and disability-specific initiatives around cloud-related accessibility.

For consumers, the need for the cloud is rapidly becoming an essential service due to our smartphones and tablets having limited storage. Since the arrival of the first Apple iPhone, global smartphone penetration had reached an estimated 22 per cent worldwide, with most of that rise consisting of approximately 1.3 billion smartphones in the last four years. By comparison, tablets have reached comparable global ownership in two years that it took smartphones to reach in four years. This translates to the equivalent of one in every five people owning a smartphone and one in every 17 having a tablet (Heggestuen, 2013).

With the need to access more content on the move, tools such as Facebook are no longer just a social media tool, but also a cloud storage service. Combining the benefits of creating, modifying, sharing, and discussing a picture or video with the ability to store it in an always-on, always-available location via a social media service such as Facebook or YouTube blurs the lines between personal and public data, but ultimately leads to the opportunity to be more social. Based on this definition, cloud-based applications such as Google Docs and Dropbox may also blur the lines as social media, due to the ability to share information with a specific group, therefore allowing for online collaboration.

For people with disabilities, the integration of mobile devices, the cloud and social media is of particular significance due to the need for all three to be accessible. In addition to the W3C standard WCAG 2.0 in partnership with the advisory note WCAG2ICT for app accessibility, it is also necessary to consider one other supporting accessibility element as it relates to the *Authoring tool accessibility guidelines (ATAG) 2.0* (World Wide Web Consortium, 2015).

ATAG 2.0 has two key elements which require that any authoring tool that supports the creation of web content must be able to be used by people with disabilities and also produce content that can be accessed by people with disabilities. This is particularly relevant to software which is integrated with the cloud as people with disabilities will need to be able to create content to be shared, and, in turn, be made accessible to people with disabilities that receive the content. While social media and cloud tools should consider WCAG 2.0, ATAG 2.0, and WCAG2ICT to ensure accessible web content and apps, it is an initiative focused on the future of the cloud that may offer the more significant potential for people with disabilities in accessing social media services.

A consortium of academic, industry and non-governmental organisations and individuals known as *Raising the floor* has created the global public inclusive infrastructure (GPII). The aim of GPII is to create a software and service enhancement to our broadband infrastructure which would then allow users to invoke and use the access features they need anywhere, anytime, on any device (Raising the Floor, 2014).

An example of GPII in action could consist of a person with low vision purchasing a ticket at a train station. After an identification process, the ticket machine downloads the relevant accessibility features required by the user and sets them up according to the predefined cloud preference, providing AT features such as a screen reader, high contrast, and large print. If another person with a disability used the same machine such as a person in a wheelchair, the interface would change based on their preferences, such as lowering the touch buttons so that they were in reach.

The potential of GPII is particularly profound if the cloud preferences could be applied to any device used so that the ticket machine, smartphone, tablet, desktop computer, and in-flight entertainment system could all change their interface based on the needs of the user. Instead of relying on the accessibility of the device and the content as is currently the case, the accessible software would change the content as required.

For social media, there are two particular areas of relevance to a cloud-based scenario similar to GPII. The first is that GPII would in itself assist in providing access to key social media tools for people with disabilities, creating an always-available, always-accessible environment for which true social participation without barriers could be achieved. The other potential benefit is that social media could play a role in helping to determine what preferences a user is most likely to require based on crowd-sourced social media feedback from family and friends. Analysis of social media content could interface with GPII to consider a number of viewpoints which could ultimately lead to better support of people with disabilities, particularly if the person with a disability was incapacitated in some way from fully identifying their own needs.

However, there are some significant issues regarding GPII. While the implementation of GPII itself is likely to be a difficult process due to the massive infrastructure rollout that would be required and the need to ensure that all devices and content have a consistent and accessible interface, the concept of storing or crowdsourcing personal data relating to the needs of a person with a disability raises important security and privacy issues. It may be the case that people with disabilities do not wish to have their details stored on the cloud due to concerns over data ownership – who is likely to view such information and privacy implications, particularly if the particular type of disability is relatively rare? The crowd-sourcing element, while potentially helpful, could be of even greater concern – will information about the individual's disability be freely circulating in online conversations, potentially leading to profiling which may be useful for GPII, but which could also be used for a variety of other uses such as advertising or more sinister purposes? As social media and the cloud continue to entwine, it is important to consider these issues – there is a potential for an even greater digital divide and accessibility barriers in the future if a GPII-style solution is available but the risks to personal security and safety lead a significant number of people to opt out.

While the GPII concept may seem distant, Microsoft is already incorporating cloud-based accessibility features into its Windows 8.x operating systems in which a user can change their accessibility features in real-time across multiple computers if they share the same login credentials (Microsoft, 2014b). As such, it is particularly timely to consider both the benefits and the implications of the interaction of cloud-based services.

Conclusion

The impact of social media is vital to ensuring that people with disabilities are given the opportunity to create, modify, share, and discuss with the tool of their choice. However, while AT and accessibility features are now available on most mobile platforms, accessibility issues remain in key web content.

Studies such as *Sociability* conducted by this author have highlighted that while the barriers are many, the determination by people with disabilities to benefit from the tools remains strong, with benefits ranging from the profound – gaining independence and employment – through to the simple – enjoyment of food and entertainment. When web accessibility issues have been present, the community has often created alternative portals to the same social media content, and in recent years the popular social media tools of Facebook, Twitter, and YouTube have led by example to continually improve the issues and ultimately ensure that people with disabilities can use their services.

While social media accessibility appears to be improving, its notable integration into cloud storage services due to limited storage functionality on mobile devices raises additional accessibility challenges, again requiring developers of web content, authoring tools, and device-based apps to ensure that they continue to improve the accessibility of social media and cloud services that allow users to share content. While the accessibility of social media remains a critical issue today, the GPII may provide some solutions in the future by using cloud-based preferences to assist in making interfaces accessible across multiple devices.

However, while technology benefits continue to provide increased support to people with disabilities, it is important to be aware that such benefits will be weighed against the issues of privacy and security.

References

AppleVis. (2014). AppleVis: Empowering blind and low vision users of Apple products and related applications. Retrieved November 6, 2014, from http://www.applevis.com
Australian Communications Consumer Action Network. (2011). 2011 ACCAN Grants Scheme projects announced. Retrieved November 6, 2014, from https://accan.org.au/news-items/media-releases/332–2011-accan-grants-scheme-projects-announced
BITV Test. (2011). The accessibility of Facebook. Retrieved November 6, 2014, from http://www.bitvtest.de/infothek/artikel/lesen/facebook-1-en.html
Boudreau, D. (2012). Social Media Accessibility: Where Are We Today? CSUN Technology and Persons with Disability Conference 2012. San Diego. Retrieved November 6, 2014, from http://www.slideshare.net/AccessibiliteWeb/20120301-web041socialmedia
Crum, C. (2009). Facebook works with the blind on accessibility. *Web Pro News*. Retrieved August 3, 2011, from www.webpronews.com/Facebook-works-with-the-blind-on-accessibility-2009-04
Easy Chirp. (2014). Easy chirp – web accessibility for the Twitter website application. Retrieved November 6, 2014, from http://www.easychirp.com

Facebook. (2012). Accessibility for people with disabilities. Retrieved January 21, 2012, from https://www.facebook.com/help/contact/169372943117927

Facebook. (2014). Facebook accessibility. Retrieved November 6, 2014, from https://www.facebook.com/accessibility

Google. (2009). Automatic captions in YouTube. Retrieved November 6, 2014, from http://googleblog.blogspot.com.au/2009/11/automatic-captions-in-youtube.html

Google. (2010). YouTube official blog – introducing YouTube HTML5 supported videos. Retrieved November 6, 2014, from http://youtube-global.blogspot.com.au/2010/01/introducing-youtube-html5-supported.html

Google. (2014). Using YouTube with a screen reader. Retrieved November 6, 2014, from https://support.google.com/youtube/answer/189278?hl=en

Heggestuen, J. (2013). One in every 5 people in the world own a smartphone, one in every 17 own a tablet. *Business Insider*. Retrieved March 19, 2014, from http://www.businessinsider.com.au/smartphone-and-tablet-penetration-2013-10

Hollier, S. (2006). *The disability divide: A study into the impact of computing and internet-related technologies on people who are blind or vision impaired.* Curtin University of Technology. Perth. Retrieved November 6, 2014, from http://espace.library.curtin.edu.au/R/?func=dbin-jump-full&object_id=17109&local_base=GEN01-ERA02

Hollier, S. (2012). *Sociability: Social media for people with a disability.* Media Access Australia. Sydney. Retrieved November 6, 2014, from http://www.mediaaccess.org.au/web/social-media-for-people-with-a-disability

Hollier, S. (2013). 10 milestones in the mainstreaming of accessibility. *.net Magazine Online*. Creativebloq. Retrieved November 6, 2014, from http://www.creativebloq.com/netmag/10-milestones-mainstreaming-accessibility-7135541

International Standards Organization. (2012). ISO/IEC 40500: 2012 Information technology – W3C Web Content Accessibility Guidelines (WCAG) 2.0. Retrieved November 6, 2014, from http://www.iso.org/iso/iso_catalogue/catalogue_tc/catalogue_detail.htm?csnumber=58625

International Telecommunication Union. (2010). The rise of social networking. Retrieved November 6, 2014, from http://www.itu.int/net/itunews/issues/2010/06/35.aspx

Kaplan, A., & Haenlein, M. (2010). Users of the world unite! Retrieved November 10, 2011, from openmediart.com/log/pics/sdarticle.pdf

Kietzmann, J., Hermkens, K., McCarthy, I., & Silvestre, B. (2011). Social media? Get serious! Retrieved November 12, 2014, from www.sciencedirect.com/science/article/pii/S0007681311000061

Media Access Australia. (2014). About us: Media access Australia – Inclusion through technology. Retrieved November 6, 2014, from http://www.mediaaccess.org.au/about/about-us

Microsoft. (2014a). Types of assistive technology products. Retrieved November 6, 2014, from http://www.microsoft.com/enable/at/types.aspx

Microsoft. (2014b). Top 5 benefits of cloud computing. Retrieved April 2, 2014, from http://www.microsoft.com/en-gb/business/community/hints-and-tips/top-5-benefits-of-cloudcomputing?WT.mc_id=Twitter_Small+Business_Vue+Sit_Awareness_Nov+2013_Office+365SMBPCA

Raising the Floor. (2014). GPII – how it will work. Retrieved April 16, 2014, from http://www.gpii.net/content/how-gpii-will-work

Royal National Institute of Blind People. (2014). Assistive technology. Retrieved November 6, 2014, from http://www.rnib.org.uk/information-everyday-living-work-and-employment-staying-work/assistive-technology

Twitter. (2013). Improving accessibility of twitter.com. Retrieved November 6, 2014, from https://blog.twitter.com/2013/improving-accessibility-of-twittercom

Twitter. (2014). Twitteral1y team. Retrieved November 6, 2014, from https://twitter.com/al1yteam

United States DigitalGov. (2014). Federal social media accessibility toolkit hackpad: Federal social media accessibility toolkit. Retrieved November 6, 2014, from http://www.digitalgov.gov/resources/federal-social-media-accessibility-toolkit-hackpad/

United States General Services Administration. (2014). United States Rehabilitation Act of 1973, Section 508. Retrieved November 6, 2014, from http://www.section508.gov

Vision Australia. (2012). Launch of vision Australia's Employment Report 2012. Retrieved November 6, 2014, from http://www.visionaustralia.org/about-us/news-and-media/latest-news/news/2012/10/09/launch-of-vision-australia-s-employment-report-2012

World Wide Web Consortium. (2008a). Web Content Accessibility Guidelines 2.0. Retrieved November 6, 2014, from http://www.w3.org/TR/WCAG20/

World Wide Web Consortium. (2008b). Web Content Accessibility Guidelines 2.0 at a glance. Retrieved November 6, 2014, from http://www.w3.org/WAI/WCAG20/glance/

World Wide Web Consortium. (2013). Guidance on applying WCAG 2.0 to non-web information and communications technologies (WCAG2ICT). Retrieved November 6, 2014, from http://www.w3.org/TR/wcag2ict/

World Wide Web Consortium. (2014). HTML5. Retrieved November 5, 2014, from http://www.w3.org/TR/html5/

World Wide Web Consortium. (2015). Authoring tool accessibility guidelines – W3C candidate recommendation. Retrieved November 5, 2015, from http://www.w3.org/TR/ATAG20/

7 *Transport mésadapté*

Exploring online disability activism in Montréal

Laurence Parent and Marie-Eve Veilleux

In December 2013, the *Société de Transport de Montréal* (STM), Montréal's public transit corporation, published a newsletter for paratransit users in which they proudly announced that 94 per cent of users were satisfied with the service. The Montréal disability rights organisation addressing public transit issues specifically, *Regroupement des usagers du transport adapté et accessible de l'Île de Montréal* (*RUTA de Montréal*), did not question that statistic. As paratransit users involved in the disability community, we knew that this statistic did not reflect disabled people's experiences. As regular users of social media, we also noted that the STM was increasingly using Facebook and Twitter to promote their services and to interact with their customers,[1] yet disabled clients and the accessibility features of their services were not taken into consideration.[2] STM's digital shift had left disabled users behind. Furthermore, the Montréal disability rights movement itself did not use social media to advocate for better public transit. History was repeating itself. Convinced that the use of social media by disabled people had to be an integral part of disability activism, we created a Facebook group called *Transport mésadapté* (Disabling transit).[3] Following Stella Young's (2013) observations that disabled people rarely tell their own stories, we hoped to create an online space for disabled people and their allies to share their experiences and discuss strategies to eradicate the discrimination they face in public transportation in the province of Québec.

In this chapter, we argue that *Transport mésadapté* has become a new space of disability activism where members address important critiques to public transit organisations, the STM in particular, and to the mainstream Montréal disability rights movement. We point out tensions and differences between traditional and online disability activisms. Additionally, we suggest that the group has built a new sense of community among disabled people in Montréal and beyond.

Situating the authors

We both started using the Montréal public transit in 2002. Laurence came from a small town and was excited to think she would finally be able to enjoy the freedom of movement that so many Montrealers take for granted. However, even if she lived close to a métro station, Laurence uses a motorised wheelchair and none of the stations were equipped with elevators at the time. Trying to use the bus, she would frequently be denied service because of ramp malfunctions, lack of training or simply because the bus did not have a ramp. She quickly realised that this freedom every young woman yearns for would not be for her. She was forced into a segregated transit system. Back then, using paratransit meant spending hours on the phone to book a ride and often being denied transportation due to the lack of vehicles. Cellphones were also a necessity if you were a paratransit user in order to call when a ride was late, which would happen on a regular basis.

Growing up in the suburbs where she depended entirely on rides from family and friends, Marie-Eve moved to Montréal hoping to learn to be independent. However, because of its lack of access, using regular transit was physically draining. She struggled to walk, climb the steps or keep her balance on the bus. Taking the métro also had its challenges with its ton of stairs, mechanical or not, heavy doors, people pushing and shoving and long standing time. Discouraged, like Laurence, she also ended up using the paratransit service. Dealing with the everyday constraints, challenges and frustrations that the Montréal paratransit service imposed on her and thousands of other users, caused her anxiety and stress which in turn affected her school, her work and her relationships.

We both learned to rely on our motorised wheelchairs for freedom, sometimes wheeling in extreme conditions, getting stuck in the snow, running out of battery in the middle of the night, kilometres from our apartments, and exposing our bodies to various dangers. We have experienced many of the issues that we will raise in this chapter. We experienced them alone – alone outside a building or in our apartment waiting for the ride to show up; alone in the car, bus or subway because of disrespectful behaviours; alone on the phone with customer service because we kept complaining and nothing would change. We tried to get involved in disability rights organisations and felt a reluctance to address discrimination in public transit. We were also disappointed by the lack of interest for connecting with the disability community online. It is in that state of mind that we created *Transport mésadapté*.

Disability activism and social media

Many disability studies scholars have pointed out that the internet brings about positive changes but also creates new barriers due to inaccessible design of websites as economic barriers to access (Goggin & Newell, 2003; Jaeger, 2011). Huang and Guo (2005) write that 'functioning within the boundary of existent social conditions and inequities, the Internet does not necessarily produce equal opportunities for people with disabilities.' (para. 4) Keeping these important limitations in mind and at the heart of our fight for equality and justice, we must acknowledge that many disabled people are already using the internet to promote change. Beth Haller, a disability scholar in the field of media and communications, claims that 'social media has become a requirement in the world of political communication' (2010, p. 4). She explains that 'Facebook is a way to organize disability-rights actions, let others know about disability related news, promote events, or just find like-minded disability rights advocates' (p. 5). Indeed, within the past few years, English-speaking disability activists have succeeded in challenging ableist ideas about disability by using social media. For example, in the spring of 2015, a public service announcement about osteoporosis prevention was released in the United States. The ad featured an empty manual wheelchair chasing down walkers in a shopping mall. Creepy horror film movie music played in the background. The message was 'Stand up to osteoporosis. Before you can't' (Ladau, 2015).

The campaign sparked outrage in the US disability activist community and beyond. Disabled people and their allies used Facebook and Twitter to critique this ad. The ad was removed from the air due to this mobilisation of the disability online community. Catherine Duschatel de Montrouge, a Ph.D. student in science and technology, claims that we need to realise that the 'revolution *is* being mediatized by disabled people: via Facebook statuses, Twitter hashtags, and Pinterest networks' (2014).

Despite the growing importance of the internet in disabled people's everyday life in the province of Québec, no study looks at the impact of the internet on disability advocacy. The last available statistic from the *Institut de la statistique du Québec* about internet use by disabled adults dates from 2005, which is an eternity in terms of the internet's history. In 2005, 39 per cent of disabled adults used the internet in their everyday life. A research conducted by Adaptech in the winter of 2009 surveyed 723 students and recent graduates with various disabilities across Canada (Asuncion et al., 2012). Seventy-four per cent of participants described themselves as frequent users of social media; 85 per cent of them indicated that they used Facebook. In addition, research published in 2014 about the participation of young disabled people within the Montréal disability rights movement indicated that 32 per cent of the participants post on a blog or on social media comments of political or social nature. These few statistics show that many disabled Quebeckers use the internet. However, we do not know how using the internet affects the way disabled people engage with disability activism through social media. Our experience with *Transport mésadapté* is offering a few answers and, more particularly, a lot of food for thought.

Three years after the creation of *Transport mésadapté*, the group has over 500 members. Since we do not have access to the personal information of group members, we do not have statistics like their gender, age, disability, sexual orientation or ethnicity. However, we observe that most posts on the group are in French; English-speaking members also contribute to the discussion, only less frequently. Most group members live in Montréal, but some live in other cities in the province of Québec. To participate in the group discussion, Facebook users must join *Transport mésadapté*. However, since it is an open group, posts are public and any Facebook user can read the discussion, giving it an unprecedented tribute to disabled people's experiences.

Québec disability rights movement: A brief overview

A brief overview of the history of the Québec disability rights movement is necessary to understand the importance of disability organisations in today's Québec disability politics. Before the 1970s, many disabled people living in Québec were institutionalised and subjected to the most horrible treatments (OPHQ, 1983). Religious and some philanthropic groups ran the various institutions in the province. The emergence of the Québec welfare state in the 1960s created a favourable social and political context for disabled people to organise and fight for their rights – many disability rights organisations were founded in the 1970s (Boucher, Fougeyrollas, & Gaucher, 2003). Early disability rights activists claimed that they were experts on disability issues and thus should be part of the decision-making processes that concerned them. They organised numerous protests. Over the years, disability rights organisations have gained in importance and in numbers.

In 1978, the Québec government adopted a law aiming to ensure disabled people's rights. This law also marked the creation of the *Office des personnes handicapées du Québec* (OPHQ), a government agency for disabled people. Many activists were against this new agency, claiming that it would be used by the government to weaken their movement and dictate the agenda of disability issues. According to Murielle Larivière, a disability rights activist, their fears turned out to be true. She remembers that after the adoption of *À part égale*, the first OPHQ policy aiming to remove obstacles and facilitate the participation of disabled people in Québec, disability rights organisations tempered their demands. She says:

> I feel like this policy has had a soporific effect on disability rights advocates. Many of them became silent. Before 1984, we used to go out in the streets and be heard from the public by using the media. After 1984 we were passably erased. [. . .] State grants were easier to get. Things were starting to get better. Who wants to bite the hand that feeds you, right? [. . .] Disability rights organisations representatives started to work in collaboration with the government which constantly asked them to wait because services were about to improve.
> (Parent, 2010)

OPHQ involved disability rights organisations in the development of policies aimed at responding to the needs of disabled people. About the impact of OPHQ on disability activism, Boucher, Fougeyrollas and Gaucher (2003) explain that 'In a more general sense, the disability movement has been affected in such a way that its advocacy role became more oriented to achievement of global policy objectives' (p. 154). This contributed to giving the disability rights organisations the opportunity to develop expertise regarding the political process and development of policies (p. 152). These organisations steered their actions to respond to government orientations.

In the past seven years, we have volunteered in a total of six different disability rights organisations in Montréal. As board members, we witnessed how disability rights organisations frame and present their demands to the city and government organisations. They mostly express their opinions on current issues by writing memoirs and letters and they sit on many committees and working groups chaired by community and government organisations. We noted that a particular set of skills is required to participate in the disability rights movement. Disabled people's expertise is not so much based on their lived experience but more on their ability to dissect and understand government jargon. We also noticed that the methods of knowledge production and dissemination used by many disability rights organisations have not changed with the arrival of new technologies such as social media. Documents and materials produced by these organisations are rarely available online. For example, *RUTA de Montréal* has a Facebook page on which they mostly relay news from the STM. The function for posting messages on their wall has been disabled, preventing disabled people and their allies to interact publicly with the organisation.

Traditional and online disability activisms meet

During the first months of existence of *Transport mésadapté*, staff members of some disability rights organisations, such as *Ex aequo*, *Regroupement des activistes pour l'inclusion au Québec* and Independent Living Montréal, sporadically took part in the conversation to either promote their events and activities or participate to the discussion. However, *RUTA de Montréal*, the main organisation whose mission revolves around accessible public transit in Montréal, was still conspicuously absent from the discussions and debates, as if the group was of no interest to them. In March 2014, *RUTA de Montréal*'s silence was criticised by a few people. Only then did the organisation manifest itself by claiming their existence. A few days later, a member of the group directly called out to *RUTA de Montréal* on a specific issue. However, their response was that they could only help the person if she contacted them directly by phone or email. Their response provoked an outrage for many members of the group. Even if *Transport mésadapté* members told *RUTA de Montréal* that the information given would benefit more than the person asking the question, they still did not answer questions publicly on the Facebook group. *Transport mésadapté* members who participated in that heated discussion argued that one-on-one support can provide some comfort to users, but, conversely, solving the issue for one person can result in hiding the potentially systemic aspect of the problem.

In April 2014, one of us attended a private meeting with *RUTA de Montréal*'s executive director where she told us they would not comment on any more posts and that they would even stop reading them. She claimed that the posts were full of lies and that reading them was driving them 'crazy.' This led us to question ourselves about stories shared on *Transport mésadapté*. What lies was the executive director referring to? What could be considered a story full of lies? Did we, ourselves, share lies without knowing it? After much thought, we suggest that RUTA's refusal to take part in *Transport mésadapté* points out the tensions and differences between traditional and online disability activisms.

Who participates?

RUTA de Montréal and *Transport mésadapté* both have disabled people and allies as members. The process to become a member differs. In order to become a member of *RUTA de Montréal*, one must get in touch with the organisation, fill out appropriate forms, meet the eligibility criteria and pay a membership fee of $5 for disabled people and $10 for able-bodied people. Only paratransit users can be voting members of *RUTA de Montréal*. To become a *Transport mésadapté* member, one needs a Facebook account and to send a request to the administrators. One click is necessary. This does not require much commitment for an already active user of Facebook.

RUTA de Montréal is composed of a board of directors elected by members. They also have paid employees. *Transport mésadapté* does not have such a structure and it operates differently. It is not a registered organisation, thus it does not exist legally. However, it also has administrators and members. Each Facebook group must be administered by at least one Facebook user and there is no minimum number of members required. People must join the group if they wish to post on *Transport mésadapté*'s wall or comment on others' posts. The group's wall is a constant source of information where disabled people are the main informants. *Transport mésadapté* members regularly ask questions about the access to public transit. Their questions are as diverse as whether someone under 18 years old pays the regular fare in paratransit or whether bus drivers are obligated to lower the bus when a disabled person asks for it. Members will then answer based on their own experience. Some answers will be wrong, but other members will correct them. This collective space allows members to access each other's knowledge of the system quickly and publicly since posts can be seen by other members who might have had the same question. With very little moderation necessary, the group is basically run by its membership. In addition, the group does not control which stories are shared publicly, therefore public transit narratives are available to the world.

Transport mésadapté members can also comment when they disagree with someone's perspective. Sometimes people try to find explanations for a specific situation due to the absence of knowledge available. They suggest explanations to the best of their knowledge, mostly gained through their own experiences with the system. For example, the payment process for paratransit changed recently. Payment options had already previously been limited to exact change or weekly/ monthly passes – as opposed to regular transit users who can also buy tickets or benefit from discounts such as unlimited evenings or weekends, three-day passes for a reduced price, etc. Over the last two years, STM have introduced a paratransit ID card with which they can remotely monitor whether the user has the correct payment option for paratransit. This new process raised a lot of questions and was the subject of many posts on *Transport mésadapté*. Disabled people who used a different 'anonymous' card for payment started to be questioned by paratransit drivers because the route sheet said they had to pay with exact change. One *Transport mésadapté* member asked why her companion was also questioned by the driver. Since the STM could not remotely access the companion's card to check for payment, they were expected to pay with exact change even if the companion already paid for a monthly pass. Her post elicited many comments from members who were not aware of the new process and started asking about confidentiality issues and profiling. At a meeting, when asked by one of us if the new process was explained to paratransit users, *RUTA de Montréal* said 'no' because users were not supposed to see a difference in their paratransit experience. Obviously, it did not take long before users indeed saw a difference in their experience and started asking questions. Unfortunately, neither STM nor *RUTA de Montréal* were ready to answer them.

Activism on the move

Transport mésadapté and *RUTA de Montréal* were created in different historical and technological contexts. *RUTA de Montréal* was founded in 1981. At that time, disabled people were just starting to be included in mainstream society. The public paratransit system in Montréal was only a year old. *Transport mésadapté* was created 32 years later during a historical period where many disabled people used mobile technologies and the internet.

Anderberg and Jönsson (2005) claim that the internet allows disabled people using mobility aids to overcome physical and social barriers. In a city where accessible public transportation is unreliable and winters are cold, disabled people spend a lot of time confined to their homes. Being able to participate in debates or tell stories from mobile devices and computers removes the burden of having to get to specific locations (e.g. to participate in disability rights organisations meetings) and, in some cases, having to rely on the assistance of personal attendants. When *Transport mésadapté* was created, sharing stories about transit discrimination on social media was something new to the disability community in the province of Québec. Within a few weeks, *Transport mésadapté* had already gathered dozens of stories, highlighting the impact of transit discrimination on disabled people's lives. These stories highlighted the fact that disabled people experience transit discrimination in various places and at different times. Their stories can be about a brief encounter with a customer service employee during booking or a series of different transit events that span the entire day. Possibilities are endless. Sometimes, you can follow members live as they are experiencing difficult situations.

In *The wireless spectrum*, Crow, Longford and Sawchuk (2010) argue that 'wireless technology has modified both individual and public life, transforming our experiences of space, time, and place, while reshaping our day-to-day interactions' (p. 3). The lived experience of disabled transit users has changed now that technology is part of these situations. The physical world and the virtual world are not two separate entities – they merge into each other. Frith (2012) argues that technologies modify users' mobility experiences and create hybrid spaces. Before the proliferation of mobile technologies and social media, disabled people would mostly share their experiences by attending disability rights organisations meetings and writing complaints and letters. These forms of expressions were distant from their lived experiences. For example, writing a letter of complaint about a transit discrimination event as it happens is not physically possible for many people; they would have to wait to be at home to write about their experiences.

Then, the letter would need to be mailed and it would eventually be read by only a few people.

On the other hand, mobile technologies and social media break down barriers and gaps between lived experiences and the telling and sharing of these experiences. They are changing how people experience transit discrimination. Büscher, Urry and Witchger (2011) argue that 'bodies sense and make sense of the world as they move bodily in and through it, creating discursively mediated sensescapes that signify social taste and distinction, ideology and meaning' (p. 6). Since the creation of *Transport mésadapté*, we noted that most stories told were happening live or had just ended: *Transport mésadapté* members who have mobile phones are able to track and share their experiences as they are happening. As members tell their stories, they do not have to project themselves into an imaginary space – they are already in it. By telling their story on *Transport mésadapté*, they are occupying two spaces at the same time – the oppressive space and the space of disability activism.

In contrast, *RUTA de Montréal* only operates during specific opening hours and people have to physically be there to take part in their activities, consultations, board meetings and assemblies. *Transport mésadapté* is not a physical space with opening hours or any time and space constraints. *Transport mésadapté* members have more flexibility and control on how they can share their stories and get information from other members. They can choose the moment to share their stories and still be assured that they will reach out to people. They assume full control over their stories. Posts can be modified or deleted easily.

Easier access to stories, information and feedback from other members contributes to empowering *Transport mésadapté* members. Anderberg and Jönsson (2005) claim that 'the Internet provides an opportunity to broaden and intensify your thought processes by providing immediate access to a range of facts and opinions. Previously unavailable or difficult-to-access information is now close at hand for everyone, including people with mobility impairments. You can get immediate answers to questions and spontaneously follow the thought patterns of others' (p. 720). Furthermore, the administrators have no particular control over which stories are published or which ones elicit many likes or comments. This differs greatly from conventional disability rights organisations where some narratives are chosen to represent their members' needs. If an issue is not considered a priority by the organisation, the stories told by the members on this issue are likely to be put aside. Choices have to be made and prioritised. In *Transport mésadapté*, the most popular stories will stay at the top of the Facebook page because they have the most recent comments. Which stories get more attention is not controlled by elected members and paid staff: it is in the hands of all members.

Building an online community

As participants and board members of different disability rights organisations in Montréal, we witnessed the difficulty of these organisations to reach the younger generations of volunteers. In 2014, Gysler and Racette presented their research findings about the participation of young disabled people within the Montréal disability rights movement. They found that disabled youth was poorly represented in the disability rights organisations. They also claimed that a majority of young people would like to be more involved but they do not have time to do so and obstacles related to their disability prevent them from doing so. These findings reflect our experiences as young disabled women. In most of the organisations we have been involved in, young people were a minority and their voices were seldom taken into consideration. This prevented us from developing a sense of belonging to the disability rights community. Furthermore, many organisations hold their meetings on weekdays. As students and part-time workers, this schedule does not meet our needs.

The rapid growth of *Transport mésadapté* shows that there is a real interest for disabled people to connect online with other disabled people. During its first year of existence, this group has already succeeded in creating a sense of community among many of its most active members. For example, between 1–14 December 2014, 41 posts were published on *Transport mésadapté*. On average, posts received five likes and seven comments, but some posts got as many as 48 comments. During this period, about 60 people commented on one or more posts. These numbers show that the group receives a constant input of information.

Many people admitted that for years they were isolated and would not share their public transit stories with anyone. No space was available to them. No community existed. This echoes one understanding of disability that is still dominant in Western culture. Imrie (1996) writes:

> The dominant strands of theory individualize the nature and experiences of disability, suggesting that it is akin to a medical condition that requires treatment and/or a cure. In this way, any negative experiences, which disabled people encounter in, for instance, moving around their environments or failing to obtain employment, is conceptualized as linked to individual impairment rather than resulting from forms of social and political discrimination.
>
> (p. 397)

Stories shared on *Transport mésadapté* almost exclusively frame the system as the problem, not the individual. Many stories spark a conversation between members who comment on how they feel and somehow seek to validate each other's experiences. They claim that finding *Transport mésadapté* has been like finding a space where their stories are welcomed and where they can support each other.

For example, in early December 2014, Montréal had its first major snow storm of the winter – the paratransit service was limited and priority was given to 'medical,' 'work' and 'school' rides. A *Transport mésadapté* member had to attend her father's funeral during this period. She was able to book a ride, but STM customer service employees could not confirm whether she would get it because it did not fit in one of the three prioritised categories. It actually fit in the fourth (and last) category – leisure. She turned to *Transport mésadapté* for comfort and explanations. Members suggested contacting one of the paratransit operations managers or its director, even the STM president. Another member said that she had no other choice but to lie and say the ride was for work or school. Some also started discussing alternative categories or criticising the lack of empathy shown by customer service employees. Everyone offered her their condolences and support during this difficult and stressful time. The member finally asked a colleague from work to write a note on the post to say she was thankful for all the support and that she was eventually able to confirm her ride to the funeral.

This example shows a community working together in a space they feel like their own. In *The practices of everyday life*, De Certeau (1984) describes belonging as a 'sentiment, which is built-up and grows with time out of everyday life activities and use of spaces.' The more often a space is used, the more one person develops feelings towards it. *Transport mésadapté*, as a space of disability activism, is certainly the most frequently inhabited space for many of its members because it is embedded in their daily routines of social media use.

Transport mésadapté has also succeeded in organising events in the physical world. We held one informal face-to-face meeting in July 2014 where about 15 members of the group discussed the current state of disability activism in Montréal and what actions they would like to do. In September 2014, *Transport mésadapté* members took part in a training session organised in collaboration with the Québec Human Rights Commission on discrimination based on disability. The group is also used to promote other events related to transportation and accessibility. On a few occasions, members organised themselves through *Transport mésadapté* to participate to a STM's public assembly.

Conclusion

Even 20 months after its creation, *Transport mésadapté*'s membership is still growing. We have noticed an increasing number of members adding their voice to the collective 'we're so far behind here, more should be done' expressed by many. Some people are regulars, posting almost every day, while others weigh in on issues that interest them. *RUTA de Montréal* does not participate to the discussions unless a member calls them out to answer a specific question. As the administrators of the Facebook group and activists, we learned that there is no false story. When someone shares information about paratransit that differs from the official procedures of the STM, it says something about how the information is conveyed to disabled people. It points out to failures.

What people think and feel also matters. Opening the space for ideas, thoughts and feelings gives us the possibilities to have a more meaningful understanding of disabled people's experiences. We suggest that *Transport mésadapté* represents a break in the model of activism in Montréal. By being hosted on a social media platform and being accessible virtually at any moment, *Transport mésadapté* removes some of the obstacles to social participation that disabled people often face. This then allows for a constant flow of information between members who ask questions, share news and personal stories or debate ideas. The group has become a new space where disabled people can brainstorm about transit discrimination.

On the other hand, we are also aware of the current limitations of Facebook as it is not accessible to all disabled people. Moreover, we note that some features of mobile media and Facebook, such as the possibility to post photos and videos, are rarely used by *Transport mésadapté* members. It would be interesting to do more research about the material produced and mediated by *Transport mésadapté* members. Overall, the popularity of *Transport mésadapté* shows that online disability activism is a new reality that needs to be taken in consideration by disability rights organisations such as *RUTA de Montréal*.

Notes

1 The STM started using social media in March 2010. The organisation is active on Twitter and Facebook. On 26 September 2015 the STM Facebook page counts 49,136 members.
2 For example, when the elevators were inaugurated at Jean-Talon métro station, the STM did not use social media to inform its clientele. The STM later claimed that this news was not of interest for the people following them on Facebook. We also note that the STM never use social media to share information about its paratransit service.
3 The choice of the group name was not innocent. We wanted to highlight the fact that the Montréal transit system was disabling us instead of enabling us. This critical perspective is rooted in the critique of the medicalisation of disabled people by numerous disability studies scholars since the mid-1970s (Oliver, 1990; Shakespeare, 2006). As many disabled individuals, we had our 'aha' moment when we were introduced to the social model of disability and came to realise that the discrimination experienced by disabled people was not caused by their impairments but by a disabling society.

References

Anderberg, P. & Jönsson, B. (2005). Being there. *Disability & Society, 20*(7), 719–733.
Asuncion, J. V., Budd, J., Fichten, C. S., Nguyen, M. N., Barile, M., & Amsel, R. (2012). Social media use by students with disabilities. *Academic Exchange Quarterly, 16*(1), 30–35.
Boucher, N., Fougeyrollas, P., & Gaucher, C. (2003). Development and transformation of advocacy in the disability movement of Quebec. In A. Wight-Felske & D. Stienstra (Eds.), *Speaking of equality: History of advocacy and persons with disability in Canada* (pp. 137–162). Toronto, ON: Captus Press.
Büscher, M., Urry, J., & Witchger, K. (2011). *Mobile methods.* London, UK: Routledge.
Crow, B. A., Longford, M., & Sawchuk, K. (2010). *The wireless spectrum: The politics, practices, and poetics of mobile media.* Toronto: University of Toronto Press.
De Certeau, M. (1984). *The practice of everyday life.* Translated by S. Rendall. Berkeley, CA: University of California Press.
Duchastel de Montrouge, C. (2014). Review of the book *disability and new media* by K. Ellis & Kent, M. *Canadian Journal of Disability Studies, 3*(2), 144–150.
Frith, J. (2012). Splintered space: Hybrid spaces and differential mobility. *Mobilities, 7*(1), 131–149.
Goggin, G. & Newell, C. (2003). *Digital disability: The social construction of disability in new media.* Lanham, MD: Rowman and Littlefield.
Gysler, D. & Racette, B. (2014). Rapport de recherche II – 'Vers où' s'engagent les jeunes en situation de handicap. Conference: *S'engager pour une voie sans obstacle* from Ex aequo, Montréal.

Haller, B. (2010). *Representing disability in an ableist world: Essays on mass media.* Louisville, KY: The Advocado Press.

Huang, J. & Guo, B. (2005). Building social capital: A study of the online disability community. *Disability Studies Quarterly, 25*(2). Retrieved September 11, 2016, from http://dsq-sds.org/article/view/554/731

Imrie, R. (1996). *Disability and the city: International perspectives.* New York, NY: St. Martin's Press.

Jaeger, P. (2011). *Disability and the internet: Confronting a digital divide.* Boulder, CO: Lynne Rienner Publishers.

Ladau, E. (2015). Beware the scare tactics: Stop negative portrayals of disability in PSAs. *Huffington Post.* Retrieved June 29, 2015, from http://www.huffingtonpost.com/emily-ladau/beware-the-scare-tactics-_b_7157054.html

Office des personnes handicapées du Québec (Producer & Director). (1983). *La grande sortie* [Motion picture]. Québec: OPHQ.

Oliver, M. (1990). *The politics of disablement.* London, UK: Palgrave Macmillan.

Parent, L. (2010). *The hegemony of stairs in the Montréal métro* (Master major research paper). Toronto , Ontario: York University.

Shakespeare, T. (2006). *Disability rights and wrongs.* London, UK: Routledge.

Young, S. (2013). Disability – a fate worse than death? *ABC Ramp Up.* Retrieved December 15, 2014, from http://www.abc.net.au/rampup/articles/2013/10/18/3872088.htm

8 Interactive inclusive – designing tools for activism and empowerment

Tom Bieling, Tiago Martins and Gesche Joost

Introduction

In the conceptualisation and development of information-communication technologies as well as in policy making, the needs, experiences and knowledge of socially marginalised people – especially those with disabilities – are still often not considered and incorporated. Targeting non-disabled majorities even reinforces the processes of social exclusion.

Strongly marginalised communities such as deaf–blind people are excluded from several forms of communication. In order to address the difficulties for deaf–blind individuals in using dominant social media technologies, a wearable translation and communication device has been developed – the Lorm glove. The prototype uses sensitive areas located on the palm of the glove to detect the wearer's touch and thus identify Lorm[1] alphabet signs, composing a message to be wirelessly relayed to a mobile device such as a smartphone or tablet. Conversely, messages received through the mobile device are wirelessly relayed to the Lorm glove and played back as simulated Lorm alphabet signs through haptic actuators, located on the glove.

This chapter draws from critical theories of design and technology to describe and situate a participatory action research process in which a research team and deaf–blind individuals developed the Lorm glove, the Lorm hand and orchestrated a series of public protest and performance events. The chapter is not specifically about social media, but the affordances of social media as online-mediated tools for active information access and exchange in virtual networks allowed this project to operate in a particular way.

Background

In recent years, the social[2] and political dimensions of design have gained increasing importance (Bieling, Joost, & Sametinger, 2014a). Critical and cross-cultural, as well as inclusive and socially informed, design approaches have helped form an understanding of design as a practice with a high potential for societal transformation. A strong characteristic of these approaches becomes obvious in their intention to satisfy the needs of underserved or marginalised populations (Margolin &

Margolin, 2002), as well as to improve and contribute to human wellbeing, participation, self-organisation or alternative forms of political action.

In previous publications we have discussed the different effects that occur when these marginalised communities are regarded as 'target groups' in terms of potential consumers instead of as an active source of innovative, socially sustainable development which contains added value to a broad range of non-intended use and originally non-addressed users[3] (Bieling, Gollner, & Joost, 2012a, 2012b; Joost & Bieling, 2012).

The research cluster 'social innovation' at the Design Research Lab at the Berlin University of the Arts unravels the social and political dimensions of design, prioritising interrogating design as an enabler and negotiator within social, cultural, economic, political, ecological and ethical parameters. Following an inclusive and diversity-based[4] approach for transformational change and activism in underrepresented and disadvantaged communities, this research cluster addresses issues such as dis/ability, poverty, ageing, health, gender, social movements, protest or intercultural dialogue. Within the framework of the social innovation cluster, the research project *Interaktiv Inklusiv* was raised, which focuses on the difficulty of access for visually or hearing impaired people to information channels and communication systems, all the while based on the assumption that developments in this field also bring an added value to a variety of other users (Bieling, Sametinger, & Joost, 2014b).

CASE STUDY

Interaktiv Inklusiv

In the project *Interaktiv Inklusiv*, the research team[5] has been exploring possibilities and challenges in the design of assistive technologies within a context of communication with or between deaf–blind individuals. The initial approach in this participatory design research project was not to come up with a 'solution' (e.g. a technical device) for a predefined 'problem' (e.g. a specific disability), but rather to – at first – explore, observe and understand the artificial world[6] from a deaf–blind perspective. Together with a group of deaf–blind people and institutions, including people who work or live together with deaf–blind people, everyday life situations were explored,[7] while a special focus was set on the specific forms of deaf–blind communication.

Deaf–blindness is a dual sensory impairment with a combined loss of hearing and sight. The lack of a common language makes it difficult for deaf–blind people to connect with the outside world. However, people with deaf–blindness acquired late in life – and who therefore have some basis of language – have the opportunity to learn to use the Lorm alphabet[8] for communication, which constitutes the main method of communication used by

deaf–blind individuals in Germany (as well as Austria, Poland, the Netherlands and the Czech Republic). Lorm, developed in the nineteenth century
by deaf–blind inventor Hieronymus Lorm,[9] is a tactile hand–touch alphabet,
in which every character is assigned to a certain area of the hand and requires
both interlocutors to be familiar with Lorm. The 'speaker' touches the palm
of the 'reader's' hand and draws Lorm alphabet signs onto it by tracing
points, lines and shapes. The Lorm alphabet also includes other gestures
such as squeezing the tips of fingers or drumming on the palm of the hand,
so physical contact is indispensable. These limiting preconditions often lead
the deaf–blind into social isolation and dependence on information relayed
by people around them. Furthermore both on- and offline social networking, as well as accessing information independently, is difficult, and is often
hardly possible.

The Lorm alphabet (Figure 8.1) is not strictly constrained to a single,
well-defined standard. Regional variations exist for certain gestures, and

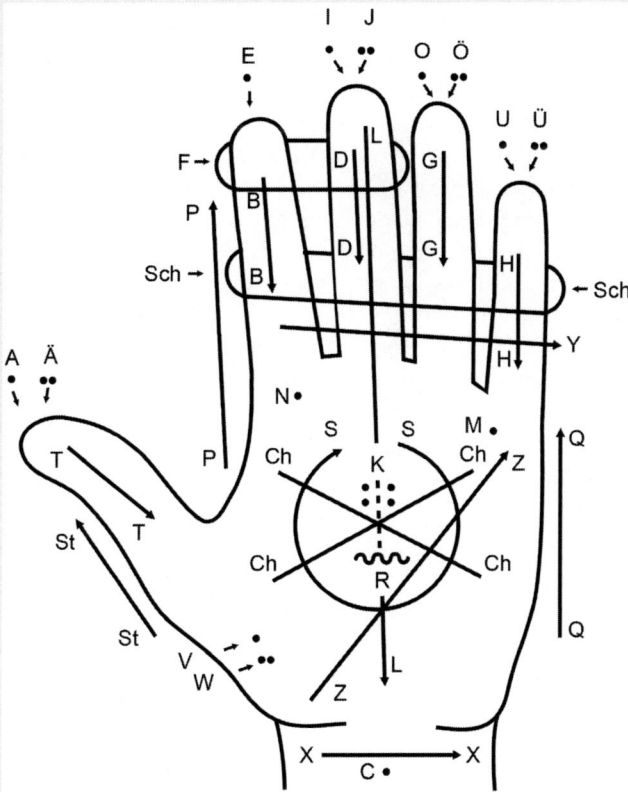

Figure 8.1 The Lorm alphabet

the exact form of each gesture can be highly variable between several individuals. The signing of numbers is conventionally done *in extenso* or by reproducing the number's shape, that is, drawing the numeral on the palm of the hand.[10] Some users opt on their personal abbreviations or even variations of gestures. Additionally, auxiliary and meta-communicative gestures are commonly used, such as signing the end of a word, holding the hand to signal 'please wait', or holding the hand and pointing with it to locate people, objects or events of interest in space.

As previously mentioned, using the Lorm alphabet implies physical contact between participants. It constrains conversations to individuals who are close at hand and on a one-to-one basis. Group conversations with and between several deaf–blind individuals are made very difficult. Conversations over a distance of even a few metres are impossible without the help of a translator. In order to have a conversation over a distance or to express themselves using digital media, deaf–blind individuals often depend on the help of an interpreter.

The research project *Interaktiv Inklusiv* addressed these issues with a sustainable impact in mind – with an ageing population the role of technology design changes. The raising of awareness towards accessible design and technology is also related to the global demographic development and the associated certainty that an increasingly ageing population will be confronted with a growing number of physical limitations such as age-related visual or hearing impairments.

As both a physical outcome and an object of reflective-practice in a collaborative research and design process (Schön, 1984), the Lorm hand has been developed. It is based on conclusions drawn from previous work on the Lorm glove,[11] a wearable interface for translating the tactile Lorm alphabet for the deaf–blind into text and vice versa (Bieling, Gollner, & Joost, 2012b). Given that it maps letters to haptic gestures, the Lorm alphabet is an adequate means to translate textual content and text-based media to a form understandable to sight and hearing impaired users.

In an iterative process through regular meetings, the participants participated in all project phases, starting from the first explorations (regarding everyday life challenges in a deaf–blind person's life or specifics of deaf–blind communication); to jointly formulating hypotheses and research questions; to ideating and conceiving (regarding potential design approaches/solutions); and finally to evaluating (process, methods and outcome).

The increasing importance of digital social media becomes especially obvious in the deaf–blind context, as mobile and web-based technologies can help to create interactive platforms through which communities and individuals can generate and share content (Agichtein et al., 2008).

Lorm glove

The overall aim of the Lorm glove concept is to create a portable communication device for Lorm alphabet users, including but not strictly limited to deaf–blind individuals. Such a device can provide deaf–blind individuals with better access to digital information and communication media, fostering autonomy and participation, both online and offline.

As a wearable device, it is able to detect and produce haptic stimuli. A microprocessor receives characters from a serial connection and reproduces them as Lorm gestures according to customised patterns[12] – triggering actuators according to sequences which match the Lorm alphabet. In the same way, recognition of gestures based on sensor data is done by the microcontroller and transmitted to the serial as readable characters.[13]

Thus the device (Figure 8.2) can work as a translator for those who are not proficient with the Lorm alphabet. The glove wearer can lend the device to another user to type in messages, which are sent to the glove, or to visualise messages recognised from the wearer's gestures. The user of the tablet or phone can choose to type in messages with the keyboard or to dictate them to the device. Furthermore, the facility of sending and receiving short messages over the text message service was added. Received messages are automatically queued and played back through the Lorm glove. To send a message, the user must first select a contact as destination. After the message is composed by 'lorming' on the glove's surface, a submit button will send the message as a text or voice message to the selected contact.

The Lorm glove has been frequently tested by the deaf–blind users and Lorm experts during development and provided observations of a qualitative nature during events. Some of the most important observations regarding the usability of the

Figure 8.2 Second prototype of the Lorm glove

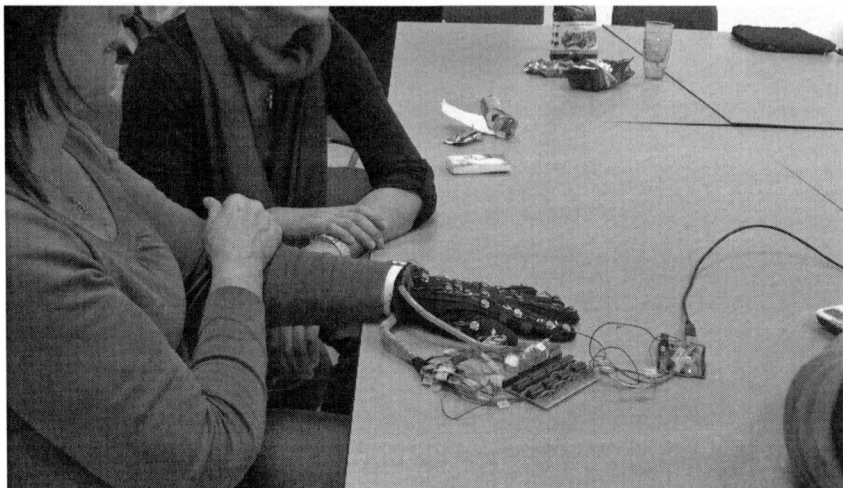

Figure 8.3 Deaf–blind user testing of the first Lorm glove prototype

revised versions of the Lorm glove have been gathered during public and semi-public events, focusing on quantitative issues. These observations have guided further efforts in improving the prototypes. The device was easily worn during events (see Figure 8.3), allowing us to observe and gather feedback from users in a variety of contexts, as well as to divulge the project and raise awareness – both towards the deaf–blind cause and to the possibilities afforded by design and technology in the service of accessibility in interactive, social and digital media.

Lorm hand

Concurrently, and furthering the work on the Lorm glove, an interactive installation for deaf–blind individuals was designed and built, taking the physical shape of a hand onto which users can sign Lorm alphabet characters, composing a message which can then be posted online. The installation, named Lorm hand, was initially developed to be integrated in the protest march Aktion Taubblind – Taubblinde in Isolationshaft[14] which took place on 4 October 2013 in Berlin, culminating at Potsdamer Platz (see Figure 8.4).

The installation was designed to allow deaf–blind individuals (and other Lorm alphabet users) to post messages on Twitter and Facebook. This created the opportunity for the deaf–blind and other attendants to share their thoughts, opinions and political demands with a wider audience, creating awareness towards the core topic of the protest, i.e. the experience of isolation that often accompanies the deaf–blind condition, while at the same time working against it. Additionally, the Lorm hand installation allows those unfamiliar with the Lorm alphabet to become acquainted

Figure 8.4 The Lorm hand at the Aktion Taubblind protest march in Potsdamer Platz, Berlin. A screen displays the composed text also for sighted users.

with it, creating awareness towards this form of communication and the possibilities it offers (see Figure 8.5).

Contrarily to the proliferation of 'rich' audio-visual media on the web, Twitter is an online SNS which has become quite popular in spite of (or perhaps thanks to) its inherent simplicity. Twitter is based almost exclusively on textual content, which can easily be converted to or from other alphabets (and languages), including alphabets designed for hearing and/or sight impaired individuals.

While the Lorm glove was designed for a scenario of personal and ubiquitous usage, the Lorm hand has been developed to be stationary and used by many individuals throughout an event. A glove or wearable technology would have been inadequate in such a case. This resulted in a form better suited to a public installation, one which could be felt and touched, akin to a sculpture or a display for the blind.

Users write the Lorm alphabet signs on the Lorm hand as if they were lorming to another individual, holding the hand shortly to signal the end of each word (a white space character). The Lorm hand is lined with sensors inside to detect the user's touch. When prompted by the user, by holding the Lorm hand's palm for a few seconds, or as the message reaches a 140-character limit, it handles splitting and posting the message onto the Lorm hand Twitter account. An application performs the recognition of Lorm gestures based on sensor data, displays the resulting

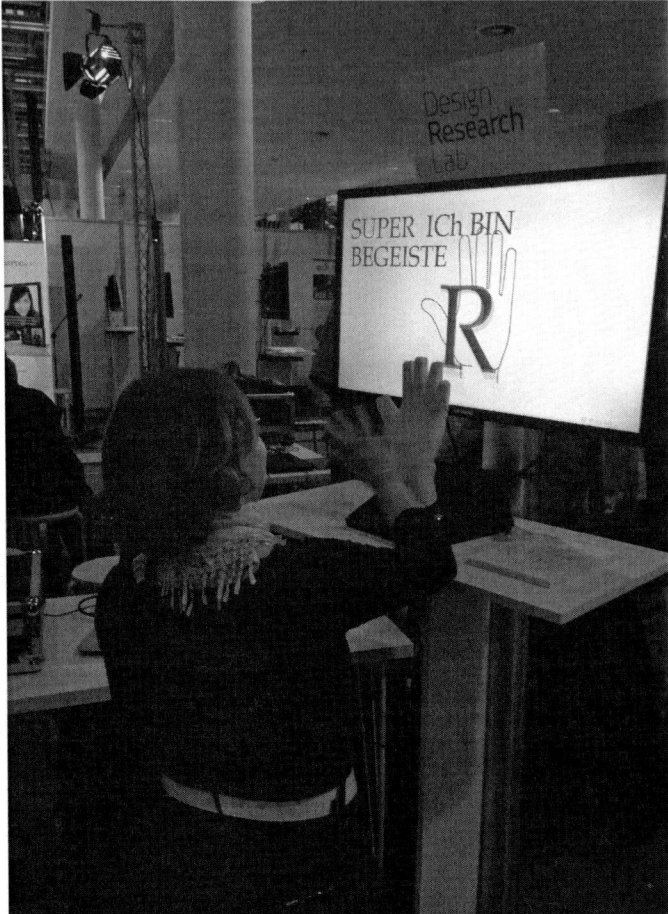

Figure 8.5 A sighted and deaf participant uses the second Lorm hand prototype as a tool for learning and training the Lorm alphabet. Her statement on this picture: 'Super, I am excited!'

message on a screen (especially helpful for non-deaf–blind learners) and handles the posting of messages on the Twitter account @LormHand. The Twitter account is also tied to a Facebook[15] account (www.facebook.com/LormHand), so that messages are posted on both highly popular online social networks.

With this form, appearance and set of functions, the Lorm hand would ideally address the core requirements and basic intention of a protest march, which – in favour of a social or political cause – usually implies physical action (e.g. marching, gathering at a designated spot), auditory elements (e.g. chanting slogans, shouting, singing, artificial or voice-based noise) and visual elements (e.g. banners, posters, flyers).

As an aesthetic form of activism, these may be some of the most popular and often successful elements to formulate and communicate the objectives of a protest. However in a deaf–blind context, such tools do not really exist. Hence, compared to other protest marches and activist assemblies, the Aktion Taubblind appeared to be a rather silent march (see Figure 8.6).[16] Only a few banners and posters were displayed during the march, of which most of them were neither written, nor read by deaf–blind people.

The Lorm hand was a (successful) approach to provide a platform that could be used by all participants (both deaf–blind and sighted/hearing persons). It was a platform to spread and promote their messages, and share them with a bigger group of people – even with those who could not participate in that specific event. And, as a demonstration is usually considered more successful if more people participate, the Lorm hand offered the chance to even expand the protest march beyond the limits of the physical space (Potsdamer Platz) and also extend the time limits through a still ongoing online discourse.

As an interactive installation with a natural shape as its central feature, embodying a concept of accessibility and inclusion, the Lorm hand's notion can be felt both physically and online. As such, it quickly gathered attention, especially in online social networks and related media. Through participatory development, its presence in events as public installation[17] and in the social media, the Lorm hand

Figure 8.6 Moderator at the deaf–blind protest march, wearing white gloves, so the (partly) sighted audience may perceive his gestures more easily

Figures 8.7 and 8.8 A deaf–blind participant tries the Lorm hand in different orientations

has proven itself as a medium for raising awareness towards accessibility issues in new technologies (and the role that technology can play in avoiding isolation) as well as an educational tool to introduce the Lorm alphabet and demystify communication possibilities with deaf–blind individuals (see Figures 8.7 and 8.8).

Disability: A matter of perspective

This case study tackles the issue around the processes of social exclusion and inclusion raised by technology, opening up important questions in regard to the politics of design, research and technology development. One of these is to clarify the positions' design and design research can have in the social sphere and its construction, and thus in the structuring of society. One approach is to more fully integrate disadvantaged, disregarded or marginalised groups through the design process – and in this sense, design also means the determination of decisions, situations and processes or participation.

Design and technology have long become indispensable in broad fields of human ecology. Both are omnipresent in everyday life, and often we do not realise once we become accustomed to and reliant upon them (Goggin & Newell, 2003, p. 3). Both play a fundamental role in developing, understanding and sustaining identities. Both can (even simultaneously) allow or deny access, and so they are often (if not generally) responsible for social and cultural inclusion or exclusion.

Thus design and technology are never socially neutral. And the design processes around understanding and addressing specific user needs, as well as developing innovative technologies, can be described as 'an activity that influences and is influenced by the balancing of interests among different social groups that participate in its process and deal with objects or systems' (Couto & Ribeiro, 2002). Furthermore, technology is never neutral, since 'technological artefacts [. . .] can be used for certain goals but not, or far more difficulty or less effectively, for other goals' (Stanford Encyclopedia of Philosophy, 2013).[18] Technology thus appears to be an exertion of human power,[19] which Hans Jonas describes as a form of action constantly exposed to moral verification (Jonas, 1993).

Assuming that human-made constructions and technologies have influence upon the individual, it becomes comprehensible that technologies 'enforce normalcy'[20] (Davis, 2002). Therefore, they have an effect of 'reproducing an ableist framework, rather than building in, creating and contributing to new modes of living which embrace difference and diversity' (Goggin, 2008, p. 11). In this respect, the 'design perspective' can play a significant role in altering these frameworks and allowing for diversity. Design is especially able to engage with such tasks, since it automatically influences learning as a human activity that is socially situated and mediated through artefacts.

Goggin and Newell (2003, p. 147) have shown how society 'consciously and unconsciously, has built in disability into digital technologies' and how disability is 'constructed in and through technology' (p. 12). In regard to the enabling and disabling practices triggered and represented by technology, the knowledge and perspectives of people with disabilities appear to have a high value of (social, emotional and not least economical) benefit. Both society and industry can benefit if a broad and diverse range of citizens and communities are involved in the process of critical and sustained reflection and development. And in regard to alternative modes of policy exchanges, Goggin and Newell state, that 'such subaltern knowledge can make an important contribution [. . .], and help to shape the emerging social and technological systems that are becoming today's and tomorrow's norms' (p. 80).

Design: Interpreter between object and user

Design can play an important role here in that its artefacts – in the form of products, services or interventions – can create awareness and can motivate alternative patterns of behaviour. As such, design is required to reflect on the scope of its actions and on the responsibility of the designed artefact's possible effects. It is a question of the social responsibility of design and the potential to design social responsibility.

Thus the participatory shift, which can be observed in various fields of research, design and development over the recent years, plays a key role. The principal orientation of participatory design is to integrate different groups of participants in the design process and to thereby create equal roles for the designers and 'non-designers'. These 'non-designers' are potential end-users, employers, public representatives or members from other interest groups. These participants can be subsumed under the concept 'stakeholder', which is to say, every participant possesses a certain, (in)direct interest in the design process, its conception, realisation, implementation or resulting consequences. From the development of questions concerning the generation of ideas and their realisation to the marketing of the products, these participants can be closely integrated in this process in a variety of ways (Sanders, 2013). A more politically oriented variant of participatory design can be found in Pelle Ehn (2001) and Ezio Manzini (2007). Here the focus is on the inclusion of citizens in societal processes as well as the authorisation for independent improvements of living conditions.

In light of the disabling and enabling dimensions of technology, the level of stakeholder involvement will undoubtedly shape the future impact of technology. Especially regarding the 'forces, which construct disablement in the information age' (Sapey, 2000, p. 634). Social media has been broadly defined to refer to 'widely accessible electronic tools that enable anyone to publish and access information, collaborate on a common effort, or build relationships' (Murthy, 2013). Enabling and supporting platforms for activism and participation, it inevitably implies a notion of inclusiveness.

Design: Border between disability and 'normal'

If one assumes that the cultural production of normality is an act of *creation* that is not founded on pure biological predispositions, then design and normality are closely related. Our common understanding of normality is negotiated on a daily basis and therein lies potential for design. Moreover, there are practical references such as, for instance, the extent to which design artefacts represent or distance themselves from clichéd representations of normality.

The conception of 'normal'[21] is often reinforced by design, not only by means of the images produced by advertisements, but also due to the fact that the design itself excludes certain users from using specific services and technologies.

For design research, the question as to how to overcome the established stereotypes of 'disabled' and 'normal' arises. One possible answer to this question is through participatory design. The hypothesis is that a participatory design approach prevents merely reaffirming clichés of 'normal' in design by the mere fact that diverse perspectives of participants are incorporated.

Technology marks the border between disability and normality, and is eventually involved in the cultural production of the participants, as well as in their social, institutional or individual interpretation (see Dederich, 2013). Thus a critical reflection in the development and implementation of technology about common understandings and definitions of 'normal' is needed, especially aiming at empowering viewpoints of people with disabilities themselves (Behrisch & Bieling, 2015). Therefore some reflections for participatory and inclusive technology design and development need to be discussed. Moreover, in the context of information-communication technologies and the related media cultures, a critical perspective is needed. As Goggin and Newell describe, disability is shaped or 'made' in them. (Goggin & Newell, 2003, p. 4). This raises the question of how to define design as a social (relevant) activity and to propose design as a process of social interaction.

Discussion

Goggin and Newell argue that there should be a:

> clear process for the dynamic redefinition of universal service in telecommunications that takes into account the changing sociopolitical spaces of consumers and technology. This means that people with disabilities, as well as all other citizens and consumers, must be able to participate in policy making, research, and knowledge construction on new media.
>
> (Goggin & Newell, 2003, p. xviii)

Ine Gevers claims the margins of society as the 'best laboratories for democratic renewal'. By describing how democracy develops in these margins, she argues that its 'current decline can perhaps partially be attributed to the ever-decreasing visibility of the "others" in our society' (Gevers, Addlahka, & Callon, 2010). Referring to Giorgio Agamben who speaks of a 'post-democratic spectacle society', she raises fundamental questions:

> Which democratic practices still have a right to speak in today's post-political climate? To whom and to what should we listen if we want to restructure [. . .] society in such a way that increasing numbers of new minorities, [. . .] and as yet unfamiliar voices get heard? How do these ideas relate to a society that with its aim of achieving order and perfection seems increasingly to distinguish between citizens and 'other' citizens, with the latter apparently not automatically in a position to claim the rights that the status of citizenship should lend them? How can we bring about a society that doesn't turn its back on its own most fundamental values – diversity, interdependence and asymmetry?

Both the Lorm glove and the Lorm hand function at several cohesive levels – as a design concept for accessibility, as a platform for empowering activism and social movements, as an educational tool, and as an interactive sculpture or public installation representing a cause. The Lorm hand allows deaf–blind users to potentially reach a widespread audience, as messages are posted on two of the most popular online SNS. Additionally, it introduces sighted participants to the Lorm alphabet or prompts them to practise their lorming skill. During exhibitions and presentations, but also through their inherent online presence, both have been raising awareness towards the challenges of deaf–blindness and fostering discussions regarding accessibility of digital media and online communities.

Developed in the context of deaf–blind communication, interaction, activism and empowerment, the collaborations between developers of technologies, their end-users and the devices themselves should play a central role in future investigations. It will be particularly interesting to understand the political implications of modes of collaboration in the processes of development, especially when reflected on how these practices of working together tie into their technological materialisation.

To understand normality as a design playground in which more parties are involved than just the designers is a special point of view that indirectly allows a fundamental reinterpretation of widely anchored social evaluations and understandings of 'normal'.

Outlook

Adopting a design perspective, this case study illustrates how the thematic constellation between disability and social media can be a promising resource to bring about system innovation in which individual interests converge with those of society.

Exploring the opportunities and challenges social media represents for the social inclusion of people with disabilities opens up new opportunities to restore meaning and value to participatory and inclusive approaches as a counterpart to a purely technically driven innovation.

For the future development of social media as a resource for communication, exchange and activism for people with disability, the enabling and disabling practices of technology need to be critically reflected upon in order to avoid replicating and propagating inaccessibility from the physical into the digital world.

The Lorm devices, standing for the possibility of deaf–blind individuals to fight isolation and keep a contact with and knowledge of the world beyond their immediate surroundings, eventually symbolise a potential transition in which disability in its digital incarnations may unfold towards social innovation and sustainability.

Without a doubt technology can provide people who previously existed outside society with means of access to it (Gevers, Addlahka, & Callon, 2010, p. 212). Yet, if one goes beyond the clichéd perceptions as to how 'disabled' or 'non-disabled' people would tend to use certain products and listens instead to what real individuals have to say, then new, unexpected and potentially fairer solutions occasionally arise. It becomes clear that concentrating on 'normality' issues repeatedly requires reflecting upon how much standard roles are thereby implicitly strengthened. It does not necessarily mean that derived concepts contribute to emancipated, inclusive role understanding per se.

This is for sure a critical junction, since it makes the limits of participation clear and also brings the responsibility for the product back to the designers. Dealing with the results of participatory design processes and inclusive design outcomes therefore requires great empathy and reflection as to what can be achieved through the products or services originating in this manner.

Nevertheless a large potential is opened up by bringing together people from a variety of contexts (whether cultural, social or demographic) into the processes of technological and/or social innovation. Not least in order to clarify that the awareness that society is diverse can also be of aid in developing alternative concepts extending far beyond the stereotypical image of so-called norm- or standard-users.

Nevertheless, interrogating our existing and future technologies helps to reflect upon the values and lived social policy (Goggin & Newell, 2003, p. 154), as well as to understand how the associated interpretations of 'normal' could be modified and re-designed. After all, this remains valid not only within a disability context, but for any marginalised group. Thus including the perspectives of people with disabilities in the networked digital society is not only a technological question, but a political one.

Video: The project process and outcome are documented in a short video (3 minutes): https://www.youtube.com/watch?v=TW2FoVVrkEg

Acknowledgements

The project *Speechless* was funded by the BMBF – Bundesministerium für Bildung und Forschung (Federal Ministry of Education and Research). The project *Interaktiv Inklusiv* was supported by the Hochschulwettbewerb (German University Competition), as an initiative within the Wissenschaftsjahr 2014 – Die digitale Gesellschaft (Year of the Sciences 2014 – The digital society).

Notes

1 The Lorm alphabet – as described later in the text – constitutes the main method of communication used by many deaf–blind individuals.

2 The concept 'social' is understood here in a general sense as related to aspects of cohabitation or collective coexistence of humans, their intentional or non-intentional interaction with each other, as well as corresponding organisational patterns.

3 The perspectives described in our previous research are based upon a crucial social challenge, namely, how to deal with diversity in everyday life. A strong characteristic of humans is their diversity. This variety is also reflected in human-made artefacts and can, by implication, also be addressed by looking at the design of such artefacts. The common assumption of a 'normal' user, especially widespread in the fields of marketing, innovation and technological development, stands in contradistinction to diversity and is thus far from reality. We criticise the position that proposes designed artefacts oriented towards the majority as the guiding principle in common design approaches. In turn, we acknowledge diversity, thus discussing the value of including the 'non-majority' (as active partners) in the design and design-research process.

4 We are following a concept of diversity that includes a variety of demographic characteristics, including gender, class, ethnicity or ability amongst others. Different models of diversity have recently been discussed in the field of diversity studies, often aligned with a critical thinking about these social and cultural categories that constitute society. One of their central characteristics is embodied in a commitment, or aim, to social

116   *Tom Bieling et al.*

justice and change, particularly in identifying and critiquing the processes and effects of institutionalised oppression, social inequality or dominant group privileges. As Bessing and Lukoschat (2013) indicate, diversity has increasingly been discussed and shown to contribute to the field of 'innovation'.

5 The team consisted of researchers and doctoral students from the Design Research Lab at Berlin University of the Arts in collaboration with members of two deaf–blind institutions – the *Oberlinhaus* (English: Oberlin House), named after Pastor Johann Friedrich Oberlin (1871), which is an institution focusing on care and education for people with disabilities based in Potsdam-Babelsberg near Berlin; and the ABSV (Allgemeiner Blinden- und Sehbehindertenverein Berlin [English: Public Association of the Blind and Sight Impaired, Berlin]).

6 The world of 'things', including both human and non-human actors and networks.

7 For instance by 'shadowing' daily routines, discussing and co-experiencing attendant challenges.

8 'Lorm' for short.

9 The Austrian poet and philosopher Hieronymus Lorm (Heinrich Landesmann) lost his sight and hearing abilities when he was a teenager. Being familiar with spoken and written language, he later developed this form of tactile signing that was named after him.

10 It has been reported also that when the receiver is not versed in the Lorm alphabet, an alternative method for the sender is to draw each character (as per the Roman alphabet) on the palm of the hand.

11 The Lorm glove, also developed at the Design Research Lab, is a wearable interface/ device. It uses sensitive areas located on the palm of the glove to detect the wearer's touch and thus identify Lorm alphabet signs, composing a message to be wirelessly relayed to a mobile device, such as a smartphone or tablet. Conversely, messages received through the mobile device are wirelessly relayed to the Lorm glove and played back as simulated Lorm alphabet signs through haptic actuators, located on the glove. Thus communication goes both ways and enables the user to both send and receive messages. An early version (functional prototype) is documented in a short video: https://www.youtube.com/watch?v=FLfa9ni7X3I

12 They can be configured or customised for different users/usages.

13 More concrete; the gesture recognition and pattern playback are done by the mobile device. The microcontroller just detects pressure on the sensors and receives messages to activate sensors.

14 English: Mission deaf–blind – Deaf–blind people in isolation (isolated imprisonment). www.aktion-taubblind.de

15 The initial choice fell on Twitter for its popularity, availability and – more importantly – simplicity, as it relies on short, text-based messages.

16 Only the closing rally at Potsdamer Platz included a central speaker stage with sign-language- and other interpreters, translating the speeches to parts of the audience.

17 Different versions of the Lorm hand were publicly exhibited e.g. at the Leben mit Taubblindheit (Living with Deaf–Blindness) Kongress (Potsdam), at the Munich Media Days, at the Sehbehindertentag (German Day of the Deaf–Blind) and at the Zukunfts-kongress (Future Congress) Inklusion 2025.

18 This conceptual connection between technological artefacts, functions and goals makes it hard to maintain that technology is value-neutral (ibid.)

19 German: *Macht*

20 Lennard Davis indicates how the term 'normal' coincides with the birth of statistics and eugenics in the mid nineteenth century, while replacing the former concept of 'ideal' as the regnant paradigm in relation to bodies (Davis, 2005). He further claims that 'the introduction of the concept of normality [. . .] created an imperative to be normal'. An understanding of the built environment as a key actor that privileges certain bodies and excludes others by producing barriers that construct disability (Davis, 2002, p. 31;

Wendell, 1996, p. 55) has established a basis towards a 'shift form the ideology of normalcy to a vision of the body as changeable, unperfectable' (Davis, 2005).
21 Since what is considered 'normal' is relative to cultural practices, definitions and locations in which the social interactions take place, the term appears in quotation marks throughout the chapter.

References

Agichtein, E., Castillo, C., Donato, D., Gionis, A., & Mishne, G. (2008). Finding high-quality content in social media. *WISDOM – Proceedings of the 2008 International Conference on Web Search and Data Mining*, Palo Alto, CA, USA (pp. 183–193).

Behrisch, B., & Bieling, T. (2015). Partizipative und inklusive Mensch-Technik-Interaktion: Technikunterstützung im Rahmen Sozialer Bewegungen. *Lecture at Friedrichshainer Kolloquium 2015: Technikgestaltung – Die Perspektive Behinderung im Kontext der Innovations- und Technikentwicklung*. Institut Mensch, Ethik und Wissenschaft. Berlin.

Bessing, N., & Lukoschat, H. (Ed.). (2013). *Innovation durch Perspektivenvielfalt – Impulse für die industrielle Praxis aus der Gender- und Diversity-Forschung. (Innovation through a diversity of perspectives: Impulses from gender- and diversity studies for the industrial practice)*. Opladen: Verlag Barbara Budrich.

Bieling, T., Gollner, U., & Joost, G. (2012a). Information und Inklusion begreifen. In J. Sieck, & R. Franken-Wendelstorf. *Kultur und Informatik: Aus der Vergangenheit in die Zukunft*. VWH Verlag, Fachverlag für Medientechnik und-Wirtschaft. Bolzenburg. ISBN 3-864880165.

Bieling, T., Gollner, U., & Joost, G. (2012b). Schnittstelle Hand – Kommunikation mit Gefühl: Feeling communication – The hand as an interface. *i-com – Zeitschrift für interaktive und kooperative Medien, August, 11*(2), 32–36; Oldenbourg Wissenschaftsverlag, München. ISSN 1618–162x.

Bieling, T., Goellner, S., & Joost, G. (2013). Design driven diversity – Diversity driven Design. *Proceedings of IASDR 2013–5th International Congress of International Association of Societies of Design Research: Consilience and Innovation in Design, Shibaura Institute of Technology*. Tokyo, Japan. ISBN 978-4-9980776-3-3 C3072.

Bieling, T., Joost, G., & Sametinger, F. (2014a). Die soziale Dimension. In K. Fuhs, D. Brocchi, M. Maxein, & B. Draser (Hg.). *Die Geschichte des nachhaltigen Designs*. VAS. Bad Homburg, (pp. 218–229).

Bieling, T., Sametinger, F., & Joost, G. (2014b). Social dimensions of design research. *Baltic Horizons, 21*(118), 35–40.

Couto, R., & Ribeiro, F. (2002). Projeto em Curso des Design sob o Enfoque do Design em Parceria. Retrieved February 5, 2007, from http://www.puc-rio.br/sobrepuc/depto/dad/lpd/download/designemparceria.rtf

Davis, L. J. (2002). *Bending over backwards: Disability, dismodernism, and other difficult positions*. New York, NY: New York University Press.

Davis, L. J. (2005). The tyranny of normalcy: Diverse ability. *SGI Quarterly*, http://www.sgiquarterly.org/feature2005Jly-2.html, Accessed May 7, 2015.

Dederich, M. (2013). *Philosophie in der Heil- und Sonderpädagogik*. Stuttgart: Kohlhammer.

Ehn, P. (2001). On the collective designer. *Keynote lecture at Cultural Usability Seminar, UIAH Helsinki*, April 2001; as quoted in Diaz-Kommonen (2002). Art, Fact and Artifact Production; UIAH A37, Helsinki (p. 41).

Gevers, I., Addlahka, R., & Callon, M. (2010). *Difference on Display – Diversity in Art, Science and Society*. Rotterdam, The Netherlands: Nai010 Publishers.

Goggin, G. (2008). Innovation and disability. *M/C Journal of Media and Culture, 11*(3). Queensland University of Technology, Australia. Retrieved September 2, 2016, from http://journal.media-culture.org.au/index.php/mcjournal/article/view/56

Goggin, G., & Newell, C. (2003). *Digital disability: The social construction of disability in new media*. Maryland: Rowmann & Littlefield.

Jonas, H. (1993). Warum die Technik ein Gegenstand für die Ethik ist: Fünf Gründe. In H. Lenk & G. Ropohl (Hrsg.), *Technik und Ethik*. Reclam: Stuttgart (pp. 81–91).

Joost, G., & Bieling, T. (2012). Design contra a Normalidade. Traduzido do inglês por Paulo Ortega. in: V!RUS, Sao Carlos, n. 7, Jun. 2012. "ações culturais e meios digitais" NOMADS. USP journal. ISSN 2175–974x. Disponível em [pdf]

Manzini, E. (2007). Design research for sustainable social innovation. In R. Michel. *Design research now*. Birkhäuser. Basel (pp. 233–251).

Margolin, V., & Margolin, S. (2002). A 'social model' of design: Issues of practice and research. *Design Issues, 18*(4), 24–30.

Murthy, D. (2013). *Twitter: Social communication in the Twitter age*. Cambridge: Polity, pp. 7–8.

Sanders, E. (2013). Perspectives on participation in design. In C. Mareis, M. Held, & G. Joost (Hg.) *Wer gestaltet die Gestaltung?* Tagungsband DGTF-Jahrestagung, transcript. Verlag. Bielefeld (pp. 65–79).

Sapey, B. (2000). Disablement in the informational age. *Disability and Society, 15*, 619–636.

Schön, D. (1984). *The reflective practitioner: How professionals think in action*. New York: Basic Books.

Stanford Encyclopedia of Philosophy. (2013). Philosophy of Technology. http://plato.stanford.edu/entries/technology/ [22.04.2015].

9 New media and accessible emergency communications

A United States-based meta analysis

*DeeDee Bennett, Paul M. A. Baker
and Helena Mitchell*

During emergencies and natural disasters, a number of key population segments are disproportionately affected, which is an ongoing problem for planners, first responders, as well as for caregivers of members of these groups. For example, in the United States there are approximately 56.7 million men, women, and children with disabilities that to some degree impact their everyday activities (Brault, 2012). If one expands this population to include children, elderly and aging, other minorities, and those for whom English is a second language, those with low literacy and/or low income are added to vulnerable populations, that number encompasses almost 50 per cent of the population (Kailes & Enders, 2007). This is particularly of concern as researchers have found that a number of critical components (communications, sheltering, evacuations, and planning) do not specifically take into account the needs of people with disabilities (Kailes & Enders, 2007; Mitchell et al., 2011; NCD, 2014). Emergency communications researchers have begun to examine the accessibility and effectiveness of information provided to people with disabilities. A contributing factor is their inability to receive emergency alerts or communications, which would allow them to take protective action. This ranges from more adaptable messages to the use of online and social media platforms. In this context, we use the word 'adaptable' to refer to wearable technologies that may be adapted or personalized for the individual user. This chapter addresses specifically how the role of new media can be incorporated into ensuring that messages are accessible with regards to sociological issues and helpful to people with sensory disabilities.

The term 'emergency communications' typically refers to information dissemination methods that are employed prior to, during, and immediately after emergencies or disasters. Historically this has taken the form of broadcast alerts. The importance of communicating critical information during emergencies has contributed to a growth in the research on this subject. Less studied are effective approaches to protecting vulnerable populations during and after an emergency or disaster. In the past two decades there has been a modest expansion in the enhancement of emergency communications to include accessible emergency alerts and communications. In fact, increasing the accessibility of alerts has become one of

120 *DeeDee Bennett et al.*

the goals of the U.S. government, especially by agencies that are responsible for providing effective emergency alerts to all citizens, including people with disabilities (Executive Order 13407 signed in 2006 and Federal Communications Commission rulemakings from as early as 1996).

As is the case with many public and private sector activities, provision of emergency communications face challenges such as: (a) *technical issues* which impede the ability of first responders to communicate seamlessly with each other during response; (b) *organizational issues* that impede the flow of clear, consistent, and accurate information within and between agencies, corporations and other organizations; and (c) *sociological and cultural issues* that hinder crafting clear messages that make sense to targeted groups, and that will enable effective response (Manoj & Baker, 2007). When disseminating emergency alerts or other emergency messaging, sociological factors can be the most problematic, as they may represent complexities in transmitting information on how to prepare for, take correct protective action, or be able to cope during a heightened emergency situation.

During major emergencies and disasters, emergency communications can help citizens properly prepare, seek shelter, or evacuate, as appropriate. As such, clear, accurate, and understandable emergency messages can help save lives. However, while the message may *reach* a good deal of the population, many messages do not *inform* certain populations because they are inaccessible, or incomprehensible, to the intended recipient. In this case, simple area coverage does not equal effective communications.

Historically, people with disabilities and other socially vulnerable populations have been at an informational disadvantage during disasters, and hence, disproportionately affected (Engelman, et al., 2013). Emergency planning has often neglected to include people with disabilities in the process of preparing citizens for natural or manmade disasters (Bennett, 2010; Gooden, et al., 2009). The National Council on Disability (NCD) (2009) found that publically issued warning messages were not often tailored to people with sensory disabilities. As of 2014, concerns regarding emergency communications for people with disabilities still exist. For example, at least two lawsuits involving emergency planning (in Los Angeles, California, and New York City, New York) have specifically mentioned the inability of emergency management services to properly inform people with disabilities (Kim, 2011; Santora & Weiser, 2013).

Emergency messages have to not only reach, but also provide meaningful information to the intended audiences; the messages also have to be both understood *and* deemed credible by those reached. Message recipients, regardless of vulnerability, heed, and take action, based on whether they recognize the credibility of warning sources (Mileti, 1999). Their decisions influence whether or not they take the proper protective action as a consequence of warning message(s) (Mileti & Peek, 2000). Typically, after receipt of a warning message, individuals follow a process of deciding if they believe the source, and hence the validity of the message. Without access to well-crafted communication, adequate translation, or multiple channels, people with disabilities are less likely to rely on the official disaster warnings (NCD, 2009). For people with disabilities, 'friends, family, neighbors, and coworkers are all important conduits for information dissemination' (NCD, 2009). Receipt of emergency messages in an accessible format, from credible sources, and with information specific to their location, greatly decreases the vulnerability of people with disabilities.

Recently, new media formats (e.g. social media, messaging systems, and user-focused content platforms) have been used as additional modes of providing emergency information enabling almost real-time messaging, two-way communications, and options to improve accessibility, via specifically tailored messages. Alerting authorities have adapted social media as a means to communicate preparedness and warning messages through channels readily used by the general public (Bennett, 2014; Virtual Social Media Working Group (VSMWG), 2013). Social media has been shown to provide people with disabilities an increased independence with regards to general communication and employment (Media Access Australia & Hollier, 2012). Social media, including text, video, captioning, and various other formats, is becoming increasingly relied upon by people with disabilities to get information as a dependable alternative to traditional channels (Baker, et al., 2010; Bertot, et al., 2012; Bricout & Baker, 2010a). Social media is also an important way of leveraging community and social networks for emergency communications and recovery involving persons with disabilities (Bricout, et al., 2013; Bricout & Baker, 2010b). The relative inaccessibility of many social media platforms, still poses a barrier to more widespread adoption (NCD, 2014). However, if social media is able to increase effective communications, then using new media tools for emergency communications may enable people with disabilities to be better prepared and informed, thus increasing the likelihood of taking the proper protective actions to save lives.

Emergencies and emergency communication

A variety of U.S. legislative, regulatory, and policy documents address the importance of providing accessible emergency alerts and communications during disasters. More than a dozen Federal level Executive Orders, statutes, rulemakings, and regulations have been put in place to further the goals of ensuring that emergency alerts and warning are inclusive of people with disabilities. For instance, 'Section 504 of the Rehabilitation Act of 1973, creates broad standards of equal access to government activities and information for individuals with disabilities, which includes content distributed by social media, and establishes general rights to accessible information and communication technologies, which includes [the] social media tool' (Bertot, et al., 2012, p. 32). In 2014, an NCD report detailed solutions to make social media more accessible and provided recommendations on creating accessible features. The United States Congress has also become concerned with access to emergency alert via social media. In July 2014, the U.S. House of Representatives passed the Social Media Emergency Response Bill (HR4263) to establish standards for social media use and to encourage the federal government to communicate with citizens using emergency support technologies.

In response to the increased use of social media by government agencies to deliver services and provide information to the general public, a social media toolkit was developed by the U.S. Department of Labor and the U.S. General Services Administration. Additionally, the Federal Communications Commission (FCC) has advanced webinars, meetings, and discussions with interdisciplinary teams of experts regarding the use of accessible social media tools and content for people with disabilities. The U.S. Department of Justice (DOJ) and the Federal Emergency Management Agency (FEMA) have also helped facilitate the process so that emergency information and alerts are accessible for all citizens, which include people with disabilities.

While the messages sent via traditional broadcast methods provide important, detailed information to households and individuals in the potentially impacted area, they are not interactive in nature. As such, they do not allow the listener on the other end to ask questions, or gain clarification. Furthermore, evidence suggests that there is a decline in use for many of the traditional broadcast channels. Further, in the U.S., a decline in the subscription to dedicated wired telephone lines in households has occurred as people switch to mobile (wireless) phones; from 96 per cent in 1998 to 71 per cent in 2011 (Siebens, 2013).

However, there has been a concurrent increase in the adoption of smart (internet capable) mobile phones. This uptake increase the availability of internet-based platforms, such as websites, social media, and mobile applications, which have become widely used by government agencies, including emergency management agencies to provide important, sometimes critical, information (Bricout & Baker, 2010b). For example emergency management agencies may use websites to present standard information such as how to prepare disaster assistance forms or contact information, as well as links to the social media feeds and mobile apps. Similarly, U.S. public agencies with social media feeds also post information with hypertext links back to their websites. Social media, unlike the other technologies mentioned, provides opportunities for current and frequently updated information to flow in real-time; its use can be quite beneficial in supporting preparedness, response and recovery. Illustrating this, Fraustino and colleagues (2012) highlighted the extent of social media's reach as it relates to disaster situations, and revealed an increase in social media activity during active emergency situations as the public seeks access to timely information from organizations and other users. The opportunity for two-way, interactive communication between organizations and the public is another beneficial aspect of social media that traditional means of communication do not readily provide during emergencies (Bortree & Seltzer, 2009). For example, the unique capacity of two-way communication has assisted in helping locate individuals displaced and notifying authorities of other consequences that arise in the aftermath of disaster events. Some other benefits of social media use during an emergency include the ability to gauge the extent of damage and danger, the ability to extend the reach of communication, the ability to self-mobilize, the ability to maintain a sense of community and seek emotional support, and the ability to provide detailed information for more uncommon needs (Bennett, 2014; Fraustino, et al., 2012).

Social media platforms are increasingly popular among the public and emergency management officials as they offer enhanced means to disseminate and receive warning messages (Bricout & Baker, 2010b, White, et al., 2011), and to aid response and recovery efforts (Bennett, 2014; Mileti, 2010; Mitchell, et al., 2011). One study reported that 74 per cent of States (and 45 per cent of cities) use social media to disseminate emergency information (LaForce, 2011). Social media platforms, which include Facebook, Twitter, and YouTube, have also been used by the public during search and rescue to reconnect with loved ones, and to coordinate resources, volunteers, and donations (Bennett, 2014; Gao, et al., 2011). Globally, the public used social media platforms after the Tohoku earthquake and tsunami 2011, the 2010 Haiti Earthquake, and the Cyclone in Myanmar (Gao, et al., 2011; Mills, et al., 2009; Yates & Paquette, 2011).

In a national, user-needs survey of people with disabilities, the Rehabilitation Engineering Research Centre for Wireless Technology (Wireless RERC) found that use of social media platforms has become increasingly common among people with disabilities as a means to receive and verify public alerts (Wireless RERC, 2010). People with disabilities often obtain information based on their preferred technologies and this has rapidly become standard among the Deaf and hard-of-hearing communities (Mitchell, et al., 2011). Social media platforms, as well as emergency-related mobile software applications are increasingly accessed through the use of wireless, information and communication-based technologies (ICT) such as portable computers, mobile phones, and tablets.

New media and accessibility

The use of these new media internet-based platforms to disseminate emergency messages allows for adaptable, personalizable features (not possible in many of the other current methods) to reach people with disabilities. However, due to the interconnectedness of internet-based platforms and other ICT it is important that accessibility in addition to usability, be considered as key in the design and content placed on each platform.

As social content, data and platforms become more diverse, agencies have a responsibility to ensure these digital services are accessible to all citizens, including people with disabilities. For example, the emerging uses of internet-based platforms to receive and share emergency information concerning the 2007 Southern California Wildfires was remarkable in that activity described in the reports involved primary users (public) with disproportionately lower use by emergency management agencies (Sutton, et al., 2008). In the case of Hurricane Gustav, the report monitored public Twitter use from 8 August through 4 September 2008, finding over 38,373 tweets; the daily average was 3,488 tweets with 14,478 separate users (Palen & Hughes, 2009). According to this same study, an estimated 5.8 per cent of users replied to original and retweeted posts, demonstrating that two-way communication is a public interest during emergency situations (Palen & Hughes, 2009). Social media was used by several emergency management agencies following Hurricane Sandy in 2011.

While the primary consumers of social media in the U.S. are individuals, emergency management agencies are striving to communicate more effectively with the public over multiple new media platforms. Still, regardless of the platform, social media users (74 per cent) expect that emergency management agencies will monitor social media sites and respond within one hour (American Red Cross, 2010). Leaders from both the FCC and FEMA have recognized the importance of using these digital technologies to communicate to the public. David Furth (FCC) (2009) stated, 'one of the challenges we face as a nation is ensuring not only that our technological prowess empowers ALL Americans to lead better and more productive lives, but also that we harness these tools to preserve and protect the lives, property and public safety of ALL citizens by making them universally accessible and usable.' In 2011, Craig Fugate, FEMA administrator stated, 'rather than trying to convince the public to adjust to the way we at FEMA communicate, we must adapt to the way the public communicates.'

Studies have shown disaster communications are increasingly occurring on social media platforms (Fraustino, et al., 2012; NCD, 2014). In 2012 the internet was the third most common way of getting emergency information, with social media and mobile apps tied for fourth place (American Red Cross, 2012). Emergency managers recognize that vulnerable groups – people with disabilities, seniors, and children – may be more reachable via new media platforms. This is especially pertinent, as noted previously given that 50 per cent of the U.S. population may be in need of special attention during emergency events (Kailes & Enders, 2007).

Barriers to the use of new media platforms by people with disabilities fall into several categories: these include lack of skill and familiarity with the media and devices, economic limitations, and a reluctance to learn new technologies. Technological barriers to use include design process shortcomings, inadequate evaluation and feedback mechanisms from target groups, and misplaced deployment priorities (Bricout, et al., 2013). Given that people with disabilities are a heterogeneous group with varying cognitive, communication, social, sensory, and emotional capacities for understanding, delivering effective emergency communications requires an increased sensitivity to the characteristics of this target audience. For the emergency manager to be effective, she/he must generate and disseminate information that not only reaches the users via their preferred channel, but is also comprehensible and actionable by the receivers.

New media platforms can thus serve as viable conduits during emergency situations, as well as providing specific dissemination channels for an emergent community of responders and victims during a specific event (Bricout & Baker, 2010a). Planning for information sharing via social media, and traditional, local community networks, will greatly improve disaster response by cutting across sectors: public, private, and non-profit (Kapucu, 2006). However, during active emergencies, some of these familiar, local social networks may break down or be inaccessible as the individual with a disability is either unable to evacuate, or if evacuated, removed from his/her habitual community. Indeed, communities are a physical example of social networks bounded by identification with a place, group, or interest and a sense of belonging (Bricout & Baker, 2010a). While the community network aspect of social media has been documented to some extent as noted earlier, little research has explored *protective* action decisions made by people with disabilities and how the decision process is affected by which source and channel emergency messages are received (Lindell & Perry, 2012). Sources of information include broadcast news reporters, emergency services officials, and family members, while channels of information include television announcements, radio announcements, and social media (Lindell & Perry, 2004; Mileti, 1999). This suggests another critical need in terms of the developing research and policy agenda.

Strategies for accessible communications

In 2009 the Wireless RERC conducted a survey of 1600 people with disabilities. The results showed that 85 per cent used wireless devices, and 65 per cent used wireless devices every day (Wireless RERC, 2010). In addition, 63 per cent of respondents with disabilities use social media, 31–41 per cent access social media on desktop and laptop platforms, 22 per cent access social media on cellphones, and 25 per cent of the respondents use multiple types of platforms. Social media was used by a small percentage of people with disabilities to receive and verify public alerts, in fact, 22 per cent of people with disabilities had received public alerts via social media, and 16 per cent had verified alerts via social media (Wireless RERC, 2010).

Other researchers conducted a 20-question survey on technology use among U.S.-resident Deaf and hard-of-hearing adults. It indicated that the Deaf community and the general population are more closely aligned than once believed, and that the technology – the prominent use of smartphones and social media – may be leveling the playing field for people with hearing challenges (Maiorana-Basas & Pagliaro, 2014). According to the same survey of 278 Deaf and hard of hearing individuals, 71.6 per cent make use of smartphones and 70.9 per cent make use of personal computers, and, of those percentages, social media, Facebook specifically, was visited by 32.9 per cent of the individuals in the survey (Maiorana-Basas & Pagliaro, 2014).

While officials are mobilizing to better adopt social media for emergency communications, it is important that content be accessible on platforms most commonly used by people with disabilities. This is critical given that people with varying abilities seek out information using social media platforms during emergencies as a means of gaining potentially lifesaving information that they may not have access to through traditional means (Bricout & Baker, 2010b). In short, while being able to access the information is necessary, a more complicated, but essential, objective is that the information be usable (intelligible) over multiple, new media platforms.

Emergency management personnel agree that new media platforms should be an effective mechanism for sharing timely and accurate information during an emergency situation (NCD, 2014). Each year more people become connected to the internet and more people become familiar with and have access to social media.

As social media use continues to rise, it is critical to make new media platforms accessible and easy to use for people worldwide.

Not all new media sites are accessible or usable during an emergency. For example, the current version of Facebook, according to studies, has fewer functional features and reduced usability that is useful to users with disabilities (Bertot, 2014), although Facebook is working towards making their product more accessible. In October 2014, Facebook made an improvement to add captions to videos. Nonetheless, other new media tools are inaccessible to people with disabilities and the accessibility of websites has steadily decreased as website programming become more technologically complex (Bertot, 2014). The current situation creates a concern for people with varying disabilities who need access to emergency alerts and communications over modalities they are most comfortable using.

The U. S. Congress has also become concerned with access to emergency alert via social media. In July 2014, the U.S. House of Representatives passed the Social Media Emergency Response Bill (HR4263) to establish standards for social media use and to encourage the federal government to communicate with citizens using emergency support technologies. New media, specifically social media over the internet, smartphones, laptops, assistive technology, and digital devices has grown and morphed quickly into new services. The accessibility of all these channels of communications, especially for emergency alerts and notifications has not grown as quickly (see Hollier, Chapter 6 this volume). Neither has the associated content on these channels, which would ensure that emergency messages are clear with precise details on how to take proactive actions to avoid life-threatening situations.

Emergency management agencies are often the primary authority providing emergency preparedness, active engagement, and verifiable information when emergencies strike. Therefore their use of new media platforms must have clarity, timeliness, and accessibility features if these agencies are to be recognized as a credible source of information. Additional research is needed to explore ways to increase the efficacy of new media platforms and to ensure the viability of social media–based emergency alerts and communications. Longitudinal studies, data collection on user needs, evidentiary findings, and greater emphasis on inclusive practices regarding emergency alerting would be beneficial to all groups regardless of their abilities.

While the list of recommendations that would provide viable strategies to create accessible emergency communications both in the United States and globally is extensive, there are a few that immediately would be worthy of further research. They include the following:

1   Develop federal (U.S.) programs to encourage research focused on exploring and understanding the factors (such as source and message content) involved in protective action decisions made by people with disabilities; findings could be used to identify effective approaches to enhance the safety of people with disabilities in emergency situations.

2   Sponsor or fund surveys to document the ways in which people with disabilities are using social media during emergencies and disasters. Further investigate if the majority of those who use social media for public safety emergencies expect that first responders are at least monitoring those sites. If this becomes a statistically sound approach, then government agencies must create and provide materials that enforce their ability to serve people with disabilities and language differences.

3   Explore all relevant features of new media. For example, what are the opportunities for, and barriers to, the deployment of two-way communications for emergency alerts and communications? While two-way communications could be useful to both people with disabilities and emergency responders/managers, two-way communications in a new media environment can only be as accessible A) as enabled by the U.S. Congress, federal government rules, and regulations; and B) to the extent that manufacturers incorporate accessibility features into new media emergency alerting capable devices. Positive outcomes would require research and cost benefit analysis of both the long- and short-term consequences and require systematic changes to existing laws and strategies.

4   Technology should be developed using inclusive and participatory design approaches. In previous and ongoing research, not just in the United States but also globally, inclusive and participatory design approaches have been identified as critical to the crafting of more robust, accessible technologies that can be delivered over multiple platforms simultaneously. For this to occur, industry and government should ensure that attention is given to including accessibility solutions for people with disabilities to the greatest extent possible. In efforts to do so, (a) people with disabilities should always be included in the design and development phases of new or changing technologies and services and (b) the accessibility implications of future technologies should become a high-level consideration when planning technology development strategies.

5   Undertake research that supports the inclusion of different languages for emergency alerts and communications. For example, American Sign Language, or ASL, is a distinct language. There are Deaf people who are conversant only in ASL and have difficulty understanding written English. Currently, emergency alert messages are not accessible for those that rely on ASL. This signifies that potentially millions of Americans are not adequately receiving, understanding, and reacting to emergency messages. Moving forward, policy analysts should seek to identify this population so they can have access to emergency alerts. This practice would also extend to the inclusion of other languages.

As accessible alerts are increasingly disseminated over multiple platforms, including new media tools and social media, and engagement by the general population increases, the reach and efficacy of emergency communications will improve. But change will only occur if industry, government, emergency management agencies, and advocacy organizations work together to identify the solutions that will best serve the public, including those with disabilities. Social media and accessible emergency communications can be the door that opens into a more inclusive future for all of us.

References

American Red Cross. (2010). *Social Media in Disasters and Emergencies*. Retrieved from: http://www.redcross.org/wwwfiles/Documents/pdf/other/SocialMediaSlideDeck.pdf

American Red Cross. (2012). *More Americans Using Mobile Apps in Emergencies*. Retrieved on September 14, 2014, from: http://www.redcross.org/news/press-release/More-Americans-Using-Mobile-Apps-in-Emergencies

Baker, P.M.A., Fairchild, A.M., & Pater, J. (2010). E-Accessibility and municipal wifi: Exploring a model for inclusivity and implementation. *International Journal of Information Communication Technologies and Human Development, 2*(2), 52–66.

Bennett, D. (2010). State emergency plans: Assessing the inclusiveness of vulnerable populations. *International Journal of Emergency Management, 7*(1), 110–110.

Bennett, D. (2014). How do emergency managers use social media? *Journal of Emergency Management, 12*(3), 251–256.

Bertot, J.C., Jaeger, P.T., & Hansen, D. (2012). The impact of polices on government social media usage: Issues, challenges, and recommendations. *Government Information Quarterly, 29*(1), 30–40.

Brault, M.W. (2012). Americans with Disabilities: 2010 Household Economic Studies. *Current Population Studies, 70–131, U.S. Census Bureau*. Retrieved from www.census.gov/prod/2012pubs/p70–131.pdf

Bricout, J.C., Agiro, A., & Casiano, A. (2013). Systematic considerations for addressing 'online dead zones' impeding the social engagement of persons with a disability: Policy and practice implications. In Baker, P.M.A., Hanson, J., & Hunsinger, J. (Eds.) *The Unconnected: Social Justice Participation, and Engagement in the Information Society*, 48–57. New York: Peter Lang Publishing Group.

Bricout, J.C., & Baker, P.M.A. (2010a). Deploying Information and Communication Technologies (ICT) to enhance participation in local governance for citizens with disabilities. *International Journal of Information Communication Technologies and Human Development, 2*(2), 34–51.

Bricout, J.C., & Baker, P.M.A. (2010b). Leveraging online social networks for people with disabilities in emergency communications and recovery. *International Journal of Emergency Management, 7*(1), 59–74.

Bortree, D.S., & Seltzer, T. (2009). Dialogic strategies and outcomes: An analysis of environmental advocacy groups' Facebook profiles. *Public Relations Review, 35*(3), 317–319.

Engelman, A.A., Ivey, S.I., Tseng, W., Dahrouge, D., Brune, J., & Neuhauser, L. (2013). Responding to the deaf in disasters: Establishing the need for systematic training for state-level emergency management agencies and community organizations. *BMC Health Services Research, 13*(84).

Fraustino, J.D., Liu, B., & Jin, Y. (2012). Social Media Use during Disasters: A Review of the Knowledge Base and Gaps. *Final Report to Human Factors/Behavioural Sciences Division, Science and Technology Directorate, U.S. Department of Homeland Security*.

College Park, MD: START. Retrieved from http://www.start.umd.edu/sites/default/files/files/publications/START_SocialMediaUseduringDisasters_LitReview.pdf

Fugate, C. (2011). Testimony of Craig Fugate, Administrator, Federal Emergency Management Agency. *Catastrophic preparedness: How ready is FEMA for the next big disaster? US Homeland Security and Government Affairs Committee*, March 17.

Furth, D. (2009). Keynote Address: Accessible Emergency Communications Over Wireless Platforms. *Wireless RERC State of Technology Conference*, Atlanta, Georgia.

Gao, H., Barbier, G., & Goolsby, R. (2011). Harnessing the crowdsourcing power of social media for disaster relief. *IEEE Intelligent Systems*.

Gooden, S., Jones, D., Martin, K.J., & Boyd, M. (2009). Social equity in local emergency management planning. *State & Local Government Review, 41*(1), 1–12.

Kailes, J.I., & Enders, A. (2007). Moving beyond 'special needs' a function-based framework for emergency management and planning. *Journal of Disability Policy Studies, 17*(4), 230–237.

Kapucu, N. (2006). Interagency communication networks during emergencies. *American Review of Public Administration, 36*(2), 207–225.

Kim, V. (2011). Los Angeles' disaster plans discriminate against people with disabilities, judge rules. *Los Angeles Times*. February 11. Retrieved on January 6, 2014 from: http://articles.latimes.com/print/2011/feb/12/local/la-me-disabled-ruling-20110212

LaForce, S. (2011). *Social Media, Emergency Communications and People with Disabilities*. Paper presented at National Emergency Number Association (NENA). 2011 Conference, Minneapolis, MN June 22, 2011.

Lindell, M.K., & Perry, R.W. (2004). *Communicating Environmental Risk to Multiethnic Communities*. Thousand Oaks, CA: Sage Publications.

Lindell, M.K., & Perry, R.W. (2012). The protective action decision model: Theoretical modifications and additional evidence. *Risk Analysis, 32*(4), 616–632.

Maiorana-Basas, M., & Pagliaro, C.M. (2014). Technology use among adults who are deaf and hard of hearing: A national survey. *Journal of Deaf Studies and Deaf Education, 20*(4).

Manoj, B.S., & Baker, A.H. (2007). Communication challenges in emergency response. *Communications of the ACM, 50*(3), 51–53.

Media Access Australia, & Hollier, S. (2012). *SociABILITY: Social media for people with a disability*. Sydney, Australia: Media Access Australia.

Mills, A., Chen, R., Kee, J., & Rao, H.R. (2009). Web 2.0 emergency applications: How useful can Twitter be for emergency response? *Journal of Information Privacy & Security, 5*(3), 3–26.

Mileti, D.S. (1999). *Disasters by Design: A Reassessment of Natural Hazards in the United States*. Washington, DC: Joseph Henry Press.

Mileti, D.S. (2010). Social Media and Public Warnings. *Denver UASI Conference on Shared Strategies for Homeland Security*. Boulder Colorado.

Mileti, D.S., & Peek, L. (2000). The social psychology of public response to warnings of a nuclear power plant accident. *Journal of Hazardous Materials, 75*, 181–194.

Mitchell, H., Bennett, D., & LaForce, S. (2011). Planning for Accessible Emergency Communications: Mobile Technology and Social Media. *In 2nd International AEGIS Conference*. Brussels.

National Council on Disabilities (NCD). (2009). *Effective Emergency Management: Making Improvements for Communities and People with Disabilities*. Washington, DC: National Council on Disabilities.

National Council on Disability (NCD). (2014). *Effective Communications for People with Disabilities: Before, During, and after Emergencies*. Washington, DC: National Council on Disability. May 27.

Palen, L., & Hughes, A.L. (2009). Twitter Adoption and Use in Mass Convergence and Emergency Events. *In Proceedings 6th International Conference on Information Systems for Crisis Response and Management*, Gothenburg, Sweden (ISCRAM 2009).

Santora, M., & Weiser, B. (2013). Court says New York neglected disabled in emergencies. *The New York Times*. November 7. Retrieved from: http://www.nytimes.com/2013/11/08/nyregion/new-yorks-emergency-plans-violate-disabilities-act-judge-says.html?_r=0

Sutton, J., Palen, L., & Shklovski, I. (2008). Backchannels on the Front Lines: Emergent Use of Social Media in the 2007 Southern California Fires. *In Proceedings of 5th Information Systems for Crisis Response and Management Conference* (ISCRAM 2008), Washington, DC, USA, May 4–7.

Siebens, J. (2013). Extended measures of well-being: Living conditions in the United States: 2011. *Household Economic Studies*, U.S. Census Bureau, 70–136.

U.S. Department of Labor, & U.S. General Services Administration. (n.d.). Improving the Accessibility of Social Media. *DigitalGov*. Retrieved from: https://www.digitalgov.gov/resources/improving-the-accessibility-of-social-media-in-government/

Virtual Social Media Working Group (VSMWG), & the DHS First Responders Group. (2013). *Lessons Learned: Social Media and Hurricane Sandy*. Washington, DC: Department of Homeland Security (DHS).

White, J., King-wa, F., & Benson, B. (2011). Social media: An ill-defined phenomenon. *Online Communities and Social Computing: Lecture Notes in Computer Science,* 8029, 422–431.

Wireless RERC. (2010). *SUN: About Wireless Users with Disabilities*. Retrieved from: http://www.wirelessrerc.org/publications/sunspot-latest-findings-from-our-survey-of-user needs/SUNspot_Wireless%20Use%20by%20People%20with%20Disabilities_2010-08-10.doc/view

Yates, D., & Paquette, S. (2011). Emergency knowledge management and social media technologies: A case study of the 2010 Haitian Earthquake. *International Journal of Information Management, 31*(1), 6–13.

Part III

Communications

10 Social media use and mediated sociality among individuals with communication disabilities in the digital age

Meryl Alper and Beth Haller

Introduction

Throughout history, innovations in communication – be it the printed book, electricity or the internet – have offered new opportunities for people to make social connections and express themselves with media (Marvin, 1988; Peters, 1999). While *communication studies* scholars have undertaken most of the research on this topic (for example Baym, 2010), the separate but related field of *communication sciences and disorders* is also concerned with how technologies facilitate interpersonal communication and self-expression, though primarily for the purposes of assessing and treating speech, language and hearing impairments (Plante & Beeson, 2013). Such clinical work expressly involves communication technologies when they fall under the category of 'assistive technology', which the US Assistive Technology Act (2004) defines as 'any item, piece of equipment, or product system, whether acquired commercially, modified, or customized, that is used to increase, maintain, or improve functional capabilities of individuals with disabilities'.

For people unable to or who have significant difficulty producing oral speech, assistive technologies – known as augmentative and alternative communication (AAC) systems – enable individuals to express their needs, wants, feelings and preferences in ways that can be immediately understood by their conversation partners, or what speech–language pathologists refer to as 'functional communication' (Kaiser & Grim, 2006). AAC *augments* other forms of communication (e.g. non-verbal gestures, non-lexical sounds such as laughter) and serves as an *alternative* to talking (Beukelman & Mirenda, 2013). Adults and children might use AAC due to a developmental disability (e.g. autism), an injury or illness (e.g. stroke) or a progressive neurological condition (e.g. multiple sclerosis). AAC technologies span low-tech picture cards with words and symbols to high-tech computers with speech output (also known as speech-generating devices or SGDs) like the one used most famously by British physicist Stephen Hawking.

Over the past five years, smartphones, tablets and apps that together mimic computers used exclusively or primarily as speech aids have made AAC devices on the whole dramatically more accessible, affordable and, some argue, socially acceptable (Haller, Blaser, Jones, & Naidoo, 2016; McNaughton & Light, 2013). While laptops and personal digital assistants have been used as off-the-shelf portable AAC devices for years (Chapple, 2011), today's mobile technologies are comparatively more powerful, compact and have a longer battery life, which is essential for communicating without needing to stop and recharge a device.

Besides apps for AAC, mobile devices also provide other communication benefits. They offer convenient access to a wide range of popular social media apps (e.g. YouTube, Facebook, Twitter) that can connect people with disabilities to one another. Shane et al. (2012, p. 5) write, 'A person may use [a SGD] to have a conversation with a friend; a smartphone to send a text message to a personal care attendant across town; and post a message on Facebook to express delight with or distain [sic] for a sports franchise'. Social media and networked communication technologies give individuals with significant speech and expressive language impairments opportunities to 'increase, maintain, or improve' their own communication in everyday contexts, be they synchronous or asynchronous conversations, face-to-face or from a distance and among others with or without disabilities (Caron & Light, 2016; Light & McNaughton, 2014).

In this chapter, we argue that this cultural convergence between 'mainstream' and 'assistive' technologies (which some argue is an arbitrary distinction; see Hendren, 2013; Pullin, 2009) requires new theoretical approaches for understanding the purpose of AAC devices and a re-examination of the intersections between communication studies and communication sciences. We present an integrated theorization of AAC as transmission, ritual and object. The linear 'transmission model' of communication (Berlo, 1960; Schramm, 1954; Shannon & Weaver, 1949) that underpins clinical and rehabilitative perspectives on AAC is limited. We propose a more expansive notion of AAC that also embraces configurations of communication as 'ritual' (Carey, 1989) and as 'object' (Silverstone, Hirsch, & Morley, 1992), conceptions that originate in media and communication studies.

We advance our theorization through two case studies of communication technology use by individuals with significant communication impairments. We draw on examples from our respective qualitative fieldwork (e.g. see Alper, 2017): one author (Alper) focusing on sociality through shared co-located media experiences, and the other (Haller) focusing on curation on social media platforms. To begin, the following section provides some background on the current state of the provision of multi-purpose computer-based AAC devices by individuals with communication disabilities in the US (where both of the authors work and live).

Background

Third-party funding sources (e.g. Medicare, Medicaid, health insurance) are responsible for the majority of AAC device purchases in the US (Seelman, 1993), with about 2,000–3,000 devices paid for by Medicare each year (Stockton, 2014).

Insurance coverage for SGDs has undergone major shifts over the past two decades and significant upheaval in recent years. In 2001, SGDs became a 'covered benefit' under Medicare and considered 'durable medical equipment', a category that also includes wheelchairs, iron lungs and hospital beds used at home. This expansion of coverage came with restrictions though. If the AAC device could also serve the functions of a personal computer (e.g. email, texting, web browsing), then it was not covered through Medicare.

To comply with the restrictions, device manufacturers automatically 'locked' these communication features in insurance-covered SGDs. Once the AAC user owned the device, he or she could 'unlock' the additional functionality, but only by paying a fee to the manufacturers (Tobii DynaVox, 2014). This system allowed for greater autonomy by AAC users, but it also inherently privileged those individuals and their families who could afford to incur the out-of-pocket costs for full communication functionality (Abbott & McBride, 2014).

A sudden revision to the SGD policy of the Centers for Medicare and Medicaid Services (CMS) in February 2014 had people with communication disabilities worried about their future access to these non-speech modes of communication (Bardach, 2014). The CMS stated that they would no longer approve reimbursement for new or upgraded AAC devices on which non-AAC functions were ever possible (Center for Medicare Advocacy, 2014). The change severely restricted the ways that individuals like AAC user and researcher Michael B. Williams maintain their ties to society. Williams noted that while he had spent decades 'trying to build interpersonal relationships through face-to-face communication', human connections are increasingly remotely mediated. Said Williams:

> I use the Internet every day to do research, read news, check in with friends and family via various social networking sites, video chat once a week with my daughter at college and shop online for a myriad of products and services. [. . .] It is vitally important these tools and technologies are available to all persons with complex communication needs.
>
> (quoted in Shane et al., 2012, p. 4)

Non-profit organization United Cerebral Palsy also weighed in on misperceptions of social media as trivial, explaining how devastating the change in CMS policy could be for people with communication disabilities: 'To them, it's not a toy; it's a lifeline and it's not frivolous' (quoted in Stockton, 2014, para. 25). In effect, the proposed Medicare changes would freeze AAC devices in time, out of step with technological, social and cultural shifts of the past two decades.

Following concerted advocacy efforts from the American Speech–Language–Hearing Association, AAC users and other stakeholders, the CMS not only rescinded the policy change in late 2014 (Duggirala, 2014), but also expanded coverage rules in July 2015 (Wilson, Kaiser, & Simpson, 2015). In a major departure, Medicare would now cover SGDs that connect to the phone and the internet, allowing users to update their own software and to communicate remotely via written or voice messages (provided they pay on their own for the necessary tele-communication services).

While the change in CMS policy eliminates the need for unlocking fees, it is still restrictive in a number of ways. First, coverage is limited to computers that primarily function to generate speech and only secondarily to enable non-speech communication (Satterfield, 2015). In other words, Medicare does not cover tablet computers such as iPads for use as SGDs, though they will cover AAC apps that allow an iPad to function as an SGD. Medicare's stated reason is that tablets 'are useful in the absence of an illness or injury' and thus cannot be classified as 'durable medical equipment' (Wilson, Kaiser, & Simpson, 2015). Second, the CMS policy privileges audible/verbal speech, email, text and phone messages over other forms of communication (e.g. visual communication). Medicare will not cover 'hardware or software used to create documents and spreadsheets or play games or music, and [. . .] video communications or conferencing' (Wilson, Kaiser, & Simpson, 2015).

Whether or not Medicare should pay for these communication technologies is up for debate. But as we illustrate in the next section, such continued restrictions and narrow definitions of communication remain inherently out-of-touch with the ways in which individuals with significant speaking impairments engage socially with software (e.g. iTunes) and social media (e.g. Pinterest) in their daily lives, and how they do so through off-the-shelf mobile devices.

CASE STUDIES

iTunes

When I (Meryl) first entered the home of Nash[1] (a three-year-old, non-speaking, non-ambulatory, upper-middle class white boy with cerebral palsy), loud funk music was playing from surround sound speakers in his living room. Rachel, the speech–language pathologist whom I was shadowing in her AAC device consultations with families, explained that Nash's mom, Taylor, was a musician, and that she and her husband, Todd, had been playing music to Nash since he was a baby. As Taylor fed Nash through his feeding tube, she bobbed to the music with him on her lap. Todd commented that Nash was more adult than kid-like in his musical preferences, noting, 'He's not typical – I mean, we listen to Miles Davis together'. In terms of atypicality, Todd was not referring to Nash's physical development, which caused him to use a wheelchair and require round-the-clock attendance, but rather his musical tastes.

Nash loved music so much so that his iPad (purchased out-of-pocket by his parents) not only had the AAC app Proloquo2Go installed, but also held a vast iTunes library of mp3s. During another visit I made to Nash's house, Rachel and Taylor reorganized a stored set of phrases in the Proloquo2Go app that allowed Nash to request specific musical artists (e.g. Bill Withers, Aretha Franklin) from iTunes. Though Nash could not use Proloquo2Go to directly trigger the playing of music in iTunes, he could use the app to ask another person to select the song of his choice. The songs that Nash chose were an important way for him to speak on his own behalf. Nash's daily communication with Proloquo2Go and his frequent expression through his iTunes music catalogue were intertwined on his iPad and his family's shared iTunes account.

This overlap was also a source of tension between Nash's family and his school. After an initial home visit, my second encounter with Taylor was a month later at a local assistive technology conference. During a Q&A session with parents of children using AAC devices, Taylor raised her hand and asked the panelists for some advice. She said that she wanted to upgrade Nash's iPad from a nearly-obsolete first-generation one to a third-generation one, but wondered about the pros and cons of asking the school to provide one for Nash as part of his individualized education plan (IEP) versus maintaining family ownership. She wanted to ensure that Nash retained access to his music, but was concerned that there might be issues with having two iTunes accounts (home and school) for downloading media and apps on the same device. In addition, Taylor said, 'His music has swear words on it', not something that school would likely consider appropriate. All of the parents on the panel agreed that Taylor should go ahead and make the purchase. 'The ideal is if you own it', said one mother, but 'it has to be written into the IEP'.

Using the social, cultural and economic resources at her disposal (a privilege that not all parents of children with disabilities share), Taylor was able to advocate on Nash's behalf for him to use the family-owned iPad in school. A few months later, towards the end of another consultation visit that Rachel and I made to Nash and his family, Taylor asked Nash to choose an activity he'd like to do. He raised his right arm to indicate, 'yes', when Taylor suggested, 'have a dance party', a favorite family routine. Seeing Todd working on a computer out of the corner of her eye, Taylor called him over. He playfully evaded until he got up from his office chair. 'See, Nash, the power of communication!' Taylor said to her son, with a wink towards Rachel and me.

Todd selected a song from the iPod hooked up to the living room speakers and *Jump in the Line (Shake, Señora)* by Harry Belafonte burst from the walls. He scooped Nash up into his arms, tossed him into the air with dangling feet and twirled his dance partner around. Nash grinned big and smiled even wider when Todd stomped in time with the calypso beat. Taylor, turning to Rachel and I, remarked that she was glad that Nash had a way to ask for dance parties and ready access to music for dancing. 'He's learning that if you ask for what you want', Taylor said, 'all of a sudden you can do something awesome'. Nash's affinity for music was deeply linked to his identity and his familial bonds. Beyond the Proloquo2Go AAC app, the personally curated digital library of music on his iPad and on the family iTunes account allowed him to express himself and expanded his communication options with his social partners.

Pinterest

Assisting those with the communication disability aphasia now involves much new technology, as well as social media. Aphasia is rarely discussed but actually quite prevalent as a communication disability that comes from a stroke or traumatic brain injury. 'Nationally, more than one million Americans are living with aphasia', said Denise McCall, program director for the Snyder Center for Aphasia Life Enhancement (SCALE) in Baltimore. 'Aphasia is more prevalent than Parkinson's disease, cerebral palsy or muscular dystrophy, yet public surveys show that only one in 100 people know about aphasia' (see Code et al., 2001; McCall, 2013a). SCALE is one of eight independent aphasia centers in the US (Elman, 2011) that addresses the ongoing needs for people with aphasia who are no longer eligible for rehabilitation, but struggle to engage with daily life because of their communication impairments.

I (Beth) observed programs at SCALE multiple times to see their innovative use of social media for people with aphasia. McCall said that because most people with aphasia are over 50 years old, they are looking for ways to continue to communicate with their younger family members, who sometimes don't know how to maintain a relationship when verbal speech is gone or impaired (B. Haller, personal communication, November 25, 2014). She added that individuals with aphasia need to advocate for themselves in new ways. Besides courses in photography, art and gardening, SCALE offers classes on how to use Pinterest, Skype, Facebook, Twitter and YouTube with the intention to 'empower individuals with aphasia to advocate and educate' (McCall, 2013b).

Founded in 2008, Pinterest is a web and mobile application for the creation and sharing of visual bookmarks or 'pins', on personalized Pinterest pages or 'boards'. The way Pinterest is used is one of the more innovative ways SCALE supports communication instruction for individuals with aphasia. McCall, who is a speech–language pathologist, said Pinterest is particularly useful for people with aphasia because some studies show they can process realistic pictures much better than icons or drawings (Rose, Worrall, Hickson, & Hoffmann, 2011). Photos on Pinterest stimulate the brains of individuals with aphasia for conversation prompts, and the individuals are in control of what prompts they use and how they decide to use the photos to communicate. This is in contrast with a medical professional imposing his or her ideas on the individuals with aphasia. In addition, Pinterest allows individuals with aphasia to organize their thoughts around themes, which enhances their ability to build communication structures by themselves, McCall explained (B. Haller, personal communication, November 25, 2014).

Pinterest does not get much attention from researchers as a social media platform compared to Facebook and Twitter (Chang, Kumar, Gilbert, & Terveen, 2014), but it is still used by many people, especially women. The Pew Research Center's Internet Project reports that the percentage of online adults using Pinterest increased from 15% in 2012 to 21% in 2013 (Duggan & Smith, 2013). It has become a gendered social media space, with women four times more likely to use Pinterest than men (Duggan & Smith, 2013). Demographically, Pinterest is also used much more by white online adults: 18% of whites use the site, compared to 8% of blacks and 10% of Latinos (Delo, 2013). However, these national statistics do not take regional demographics into account. In the city of Baltimore, for example, about 63% of residents are black (US Census Bureau, 2010).

On one visit to SCALE, I brought several international visitors who were interested in how social media can be used to empower people with disabilities, as other researchers have also examined (e.g. Dobbs, 2009; Shpigelman & Gill, 2014). Individuals with aphasia introduced themselves in various ways, some using audio prompts on an iPad and several using Pinterest pages that were projected on a screen. Myra's Pinterest page was an in-depth introduction to her interests. Myra is an over-50 black stroke survivor; the stroke affected her vocal cords, which no longer allow her to make a sound. Myra used her Pinterest page to introduce herself to me and the international visitors through her curated images and captions. Of her 30 pins, the first 10 were about SCALE activities, her family, her dog, but the other 20 pins were about her love of Westerns, both films and TV shows, with several pins about the actor Rory Calhoun, who starred in film Westerns in the 1950s and 1960s. What was so powerful about her Pinterest introduction was that if we had interacted with Myra verbally, it is unlikely that we would have learned about her interest in Westerns. In a verbal conversation, we might have only learned the information in the first 10 pins. This image-based curation on Pinterest of what interested Myra gave everyone meeting her in-depth information and a glimpse into her real passions.

SCALE has its own group Pinterest page, with 29 individuals with aphasia using the social media platform. The number of images pinned range from 1 to 82, with three women, all black, having pinned the most. Other SCALE members revealed their fandom for Michelle Obama or love of TV game shows and stylish women's hats. McCall said some SCALE members use Pinterest for communication in the community, such as pointing to a picture of food they want order in a restaurant (B. Haller, personal communication, November 25, 2014). Other SCALE members have bonded with their spouses by collaborating on Pinterest pages about shared interests or past travel. McCall explained that many times their families also have newfound respect for the individuals with aphasia when they illustrate their proficiency with a range of social media apps and then use them to communicate (B. Haller, personal communication, November 25, 2014).

Pinterest is also uniquely useful for individuals with aphasia, McCall said, because, in addition to a communication disability, someone who has had a stroke may have an impairment in one or both of his or her hands, making typing difficult (B. Haller, personal communication, November 25, 2014). Because Pinterest is image-based and typing captions for pictures is optional, it is an excellent platform for some stroke survivors. Government programs, such as Medicare, and many speech–language pathologists are clearly unaware of how the curation function available on social media like Pinterest serves to empower people with communication disabilities, as well as how their curation of images is a form of communication with their family members, friends and community.

Discussion

The examples of iTunes and Pinterest as personally meaningful communication technologies for individuals with significant speech impairments suggest the need for broader interpretations of what constitutes 'functional communication' and what determines Medicare coverage. While the early focus of AAC technology in the 1970s and 1980s was on synchronous face-to-face interactions (Shane et al., 2012), interpersonal communication has broadened in subsequent decades to include more networked and remote forms (Baym, Zhang, & Lin, 2004). Conversely, all communication technologies used by individuals with and without disabilities might be rethought as existing on a spectrum between augmentation and alternatives to oral speech (Alper, in press), reflecting the idea that all technologies are 'assistive' in some manner (Hendren, 2013).

Government policies about assistive technology have long had problems that lead to discrimination against people with disabilities. Seelman (1993), for example, argues for more equitable policies because they will lead to empowerment, independence and community inclusion for disabled people. Medicare's insistence that communication technologies like those used by Nash and Myra to produce digital or synthetic speech should only secondarily be capable of that function is grounded in a medical model of disability. This view inaccurately frames disability as something to be cured in the individual (Linton, 1998), leading to the conclusion that communication technologies should remedy breakdowns in communication by fixing the 'broken' person with impaired speech. Engelke (2013) contends that the very term 'AAC user' inherently places more emphasis on the speaker and their sending of unambiguous messages and less so on the listener and their role in the social co-construction of meaning.

Recent critical work exploring the intersection of communication studies and communication sciences illustrates how what are seen as 'natural' forms of communication and expression are socially constructed (Axel, 2006; Mills, 2009; Sterne, 2003). With respect to AAC, clinicians generally guide individuals with significant speech impairments in how to use AAC devices to meet the daily communication needs that they would otherwise have met through 'natural' communication methods (i.e. oral speech) (Beukelman, 1991). By this definition, even though social media is embedded in all aspects of daily life, it is considered 'unnatural'.

At the core of the debate over what counts as legitimate, mediated communication by individuals with communication disabilities are three different theories of communication, each with their own complex origins and legacies that is beyond the scope of this chapter. First, restricting communication technology use by individuals with communication disabilities to 'functional' purposes reflects the transmission or 'sender–receiver' model of communication. This model, developed at Bell Labs by Shannon and Weaver (1949) in their work on telephony, has had a far-reaching influence not only on speech–language pathology, but also on cybernetics, linguistics and modern communication theory (Axel, 2006). This model characterizes a 'successful' communication act as one in which a message is transferred from point A to point B through channel C with its singular meaning intact. From this perspective, language and information are quantifiable in terms of amount and frequency, which speech–language pathologists can then measure.

However, as communication theorist James Carey (1989) pointed out in his landmark essay *A cultural approach to communication,* the transmission model of communication is limited in that it does not take into account how social and cultural dynamics shape the meaning of messages, or what Carey termed a 'ritual view of communication' (p. 15). Drawing on the work of anthropologists Clifford Geertz (1973), Carey (1989, p. 23) wrote that 'communication is a symbolic process whereby reality is produced, maintained, repaired, and transformed'. Quantitative measures of communication do not fully capture whether or not a communicative act was a success. For example, the number of Facebook 'likes' on a post cannot tell us what a Facebook like signifies to each person who clicked on the like icon. From this perspective, all media that augment and provide an alternative to oral speech – from AAC software to social networking sites – are in some way made meaningful through this interpretive process. As long as AAC is seen primarily as a tool for the transparent transmission of messages, there is a missed opportunity to support more creative, multimodal expressions among individuals with communication disabilities through media and communication technologies (Pullin, 2009).

In addition to the transmission and ritual view of communication, focusing respectively on effects and meanings, a third theory – domestication (Silverstone, Hirsch, & Morley, 1992) – also underlies part of the conceptual split over AAC devices. Domestication theory posits that since media and communication technologies are material objects with a physical presence, they develop their own 'biographies' as they accompany individuals throughout their lives. People with communication disabilities grow attached to (or come to loathe) particular media platforms and the specific AAC devices they use (whether they are owned, rented or borrowed). The proposed changes to Medicare policies do not take into account that mobile technologies for communication are themselves expressive and are not interchangeable with traditional SGDs.

Conclusion

Adults and children with significant speech and expressive language impairments– across race, ethnicity, class, gender, sexuality and nationality – are adapting a variety of social media and new media platforms as ways to communicate in innovative ways, from creating an iTunes playlist to curating an array of photos on Pinterest. Their transformational use of new communication technologies and social media educates society about broader definitions of what human communication might truly be. Assistive technology policies denying access or making access to social media very difficult for people with significant speech impairments restricts their personal relationships and societal participation and, in turn, also denies society the opportunity to learn from those who engage in communication in unique ways. People with communication disabilities can be leaders in showing how new media could be used in a myriad of unexpected ways that end up benefitting society broadly, not just individuals with significant speech impairments. Validating the countless ways adults and children with communication disabilities use media and technology socially everyday requires an integrated theorization of AAC that takes into account understandings of communication as transmission, ritual and object.

Note

1 Names of children with communication disabilities, names of their parents and therapists and the names of adult individuals with aphasia have been changed to protect their privacy.

References

Abbott, M.A., & McBride, D. (2014). AAC decision-making and mobile technology: Points to ponder. *Perspectives on Augmentative and Alternative Communication, 23,* 104–111.

Alper, M. (in press). When face-to-face is screen-to-screen: Reconsidering mobile media as communication augmentations and alternatives. In K. Ellis, G. Goggin, & B. Haller (Eds.), *Routledge companion to disability and media.* London: Routledge.

Alper, M. (2017). *Giving voice: Mobile communication, disability, and inequality.* Cambridge, MA: MIT Press.

Axel, B.K. (2006). Anthropology and the new technologies of communication. *Cultural Anthropology, 21*(3), 354–384.

Bardach, L.G. (2014). Medicare rules leave patients speechless. *The ASHA Leader, 19,* 30–31.

Baym, N. (2010). *Personal connections in the digital age.* Cambridge and Malden, MA: Polity.

Baym, N., Zhang, Y., & Lin, M. C. (2004). Social interactions across media: Interpersonal communication on the internet, telephone and face-to-face. *New Media & Society*, *6*(3), 299–318.

Berlo, D. K. (1960). *The process of communication: An introduction to theory and practice.* New York: Holt, Rinehart & Winston.

Beukelman, D. (1991). Magic and cost of communicative competence. *Augmentative and Alternative Communication*, *7*(1), 2–10.

Beukelman, D., & Mirenda, P. (2013). *Augmentative and alternative communication: Supporting children and adults with complex communication needs* (4th ed.). Baltimore, MD: Brookes Publishing.

Carey, J. W. (1989). *Communication as culture: Essays on media and society.* New York: Routledge.

Caron, J., & Light, J. (2016). Social media has opened a world of 'open communication': Experiences of adults with cerebral palsy who use augmentative and alternative communication and social media. *Augmentative and Alternative Communication, 32*(1), 25–40.

Center for Medicare Advocacy. (2014, November 19). Medicare's reluctance to embrace technology: Effects on the coverage of speech generating devices. Retrieved from http://www.medicareadvocacy.org/medicares-reluctance-to-embrace-technology-effects-on-the-coverage-of-speech-generating-devices/.

Chang, S., Kumar, V., Gilbert, E., & Terveen, L. (2014). Specialization, homophily, and gender in a social curation site: Findings from Pinterest. In *Proceedings of ACM Conference on Computer-Supported Cooperative Work and Social Computing (CSCW)* (pp. 674–686). New York: ACM.

Chapple, D. (2011). The evolution of augmentative communication and the importance of alternate access. *Perspectives on Augmentative and Alternative Communication, 20*(1), 34–37.

Clifford Geertz, G. (1973). *The interpretation of cultures.* New York: Basic Books.

Code, C., Mackie, N. S., Armstrong, E., Stiegler, L., Armstrong, J., Bushby, E., . . . Webber, A. (2001). The public awareness of aphasia: An international survey. *International Journal of Language & Communication Disorders*, *36*, 1–6.

Delo, C. (2013, February 14). Pew study: Blacks over-index on Twitter; whites on Pinterest. *Advertising Age*. Retrieved from http://adage.com/article/digital/pew-study-blacks-index-twitter-whites-pinterest/239810/.

Dobbs, J. (2009, August). Why Facebook matters. *New Mobility*. Retrieved from http://www.newmobility.com/2009/08/why-does-facebook-matter/.

Duggan, M., & Smith, A. (2013). Social media update 2013. *Pew Research Center's Internet Project*. Retrieved from http://www.pewinternet.org/2013/12/30/social-media-update-2013/.

Duggirala, S. (2014, November 6). Speech generating devices. *Centers for Medicare and Medicaid Coverage*. Retrieved from http://www.cms.gov/medicare-coverage-database/details/medicare-coverage-document-details.aspx?MCDId=26.

Elman, R. (2011, June 15). A brief history of aphasia centers. *Aphasia Corner* [Blog]. Retrieved from http://aphasiacorner.com/blog/experts-talk/a-brief-history-of-aphasia-centers-1227.

Engelke, C. R. (2013). *Technically speaking: On the structure and experience of interaction involving augmentative alternative communications* (Unpublished dissertation). UCLA: Los Angeles, CA.

Haller, B., Blaser, A., Jones, C. T., & Naidoo, V. (2016). iTechnology as cure or iTechnology as empowerment: What do North American news media report? *Disability Studies Quarterly, 36*(1). Retrieved from http://dsq-sds.org/article/view/3857.

Hendren, S. (2013, September 20). All technology is assistive technology. *Medium*. Retrieved from https://medium.com/thoughtful-design/a8b9a581eb62/.

Kaiser, A., & Grim, J. (2006). Teaching functional communication skills. In M. E. Snell & F. Brown (Eds.), *Instruction of students with severe disabilities* (6th ed., pp. 447–488). Upper Saddle River, NJ: Pearson.

Light, J., & McNaughton, D. (2014). Communicative competence for individuals who require augmentative and alternative communication: A new definition for a new era of communication? *Augmentative and Alternative Communication, 30*(1), 1–18.

Linton, S. (1998). *Claiming disability: Knowledge and identity*. New York: NYU Press.

Marvin, C. (1988). *When old technologies were new*. New York: Oxford University Press.

McCall, D. (2013a). Giving aphasia a voice in Baltimore. *ASHA Sphere* [Blog]. Retrieved from http://blog.asha.org/2013/06/27/giving-aphasia-a-voice-in-baltimore/.

McCall, D. (2013b). *Aphasia, the internet, & social media: Powerful tools for advocacy, education, & community-building*. Conference presentation at ASHA Convention, Chicago.

McNaughton, D., & Light, J. (2013). The iPad and mobile technology revolution: Benefits and challenges for individuals who require augmentative and alternative communication. *Augmentative and Alternative Communication, 29*, 107–116.

Mills, M. (2009). When mobile communication technologies were new. *Endeavour, 33*, 140–146.

Peters, J. D. (1999). *Speaking into the air: A history of the idea of communication*. Chicago, IL: University of Chicago Press.

Plante, E. M., & Beeson, P. M. (2013). *Communication and communication disorders: A clinical introduction* (4th ed.). Boston, MA: Pearson.

Pullin, G. (2009). *Design meets disability*. Cambridge, MA: MIT Press.

Rose, T. A., Worrall, L. E., Hickson, L. M., & Hoffmann, T. C. (2011). Exploring the use of graphics in written health information for people with aphasia. *Aphasiology, 25*(12), 1579–1599.

Satterfield, L. (2015). The latest on Medicare coverage of SGDs. *The ASHA Leader, 20*, 28–29.

SCALE Baltimore. (2014, November 19). 68 boards. [Pinterest page.] Retrieved from https://www.pinterest.com/scalebaltimore/.

Schramm, W. (1954). *How communication works: The process and effects of mass communication*. Urbana, IL: University of Illinois Press.

Seelman, K. (1993). Assistive technology policy: A road to independence for individuals with disabilities. *Journal of Social Issues, 29*(2), 115–136.

Shane, H. C., Blackstone, S., Vanderheiden, G., Williams, M., & DeRuyter, F. (2012). Using AAC technology to access the world. *Assistive Technology: The Official Journal of RESNA, 24*(1), 3–13.

Shannon, C. E., & Weaver, W. (1949). *The mathematical theory of communication*. Urbana, IL: University of Illinois Press.

Shpigelman, C. N., & Gill, C. J. (2014). Facebook use by persons with disabilities. *Journal of Computer-Mediated Communication, 19*, 610–624.

Silverstone, R., Hirsch, E., & Morley, D. (1992). Information and communication technologies and the moral economy of the household. In R. Silverstone & E. Hirsch (Eds.), *Consuming technologies: Media and information in domestic spaces* (pp. 15–31). London: Routledge.

Sterne, J. (2003). *The audible past: Cultural origins of sound reproduction*. Durham, NC: Duke University Press.

Stockton, H. (2014, November 16). A silent community speaks out about communications technology. *Public Source*. Retrieved from http://publicsource.org/investigations/silent-community-speaks-out-about-communications-technology.

Tobii Dynavox. (2014). Funding. [Website]. Retrieved from http://www.tobiidynavox.com/funding/.

US Assistive Technology Act of 2004, Pub. L. No. 108–364 (2004).

US Census Bureau. (2010). The black population: 2010. Retrieved from http://www.census.gov/prod/cen2010/briefs/c2010br-06.pdf.

Wilson, L., Kaiser, J., & Simpson, C. (2015, July 29). Final scope of benefit NCD: Speech generating devices. *Centers for Medicare & Medicaid Services*. Retrieved from https://www.cms.gov/medicare-coverage-database/details/medicare-coverage-document-details.aspx?MCDId=26&TimeFrame=7&DocType=All&bc=AgAAYAAAAAAAA%3D%3D&.

11 #Socialconversations

Disability representation
and audio description on
Marvel's *Daredevil*

Katie Ellis

Introduction: Making sense of the world through television, social media and disability

Writing in 1978, television scholars John Hartley and John Fiske argued television was 'rather like the language we speak: taken for granted, but both complex and vital to an understanding of the way human beings have created their world' (Fiske, 2003, p. 16). Disability theorists likewise recognise disability as a by-product of the way human beings have created their world (Ellis & Kent, 2011; Finkelstein, 1981; Mitchell & Snyder, 2000; Oliver, 1996). Harrington et al. identify social media, and particularly Twitter, as providing an opportunity for researchers to understand how 'people make sense of the world' (Harrington, Highfield, & Bruns, 2013, p. 406). This chapter takes these observations about television, disability and social media as a starting point to explore the 'social conversations' (Nielsen, 2014) about disability occurring on social media regarding television representations and accessibility, focusing in particular on the original video on demand (VOD) Netflix series *Daredevil*. *Daredevil* is an adaptation of the Marvel comic of the same name. Set in the Marvel universe and centred on vision impaired lawyer by day/superhero–vigilante by night Matt Murdock, the social media activism prompted by the representation of disability has achieved significant results for the accessibility of television to people with disability.

Matt Murdock/Daredevil lost his vision during a chemical spill as a child. Without vision and with the training of his vision impaired mentor Stick, Matt developed his other senses and began navigating the world in a different way. Encouraged by his father to use his intelligence rather than fight, Matt became a lawyer. However, after witnessing the moral corruption of corporations while interning at a large law firm and hearing the cries of people in trouble in his neighbourhood of Hell's Kitchen, Matt turns vigilante, not to save the world like other Marvel superheroes but to 'keep his corner clean' (Vejvoda, 2015).

Daredevil is a significant television show in the context of disability inclusion – for both its representation of disability and for becoming the first show on Netflix to be offered with audio description. I offer analysis of the Disability Visibility Project's (DVP) live tweetup around the *#DaredevilDVP* when the episodes were released on Netflix. The chapter also draws on the activism of the Accessible

Netflix Project (ANP) who successfully lobbied Netflix to introduce audio description across its catalogue and on *Daredevil* in particular.

In my book *Disability and Popular Culture* (Ellis, 2015a) I argued online discussions of television programming – via social media, popular blogs and sponsored internet forums – give people with disability the opportunity to 'narratise the society they actually want' (p. 82). As I argue in this chapter, the narratisation that has taken place focuses on both representations of disability and on the opportunity to access television via alternative modes such as closed captions and audio description. It is a collaborative narratisation and encompasses production, consumption and design.

Collaborative media

Jonas Löwgren and Bo Reimer (2013) identify collaboration as a defining feature of social media. Media that allows people to 'collaborate on messages, content [and] meaning' (p. 4) has fundamentally changed communication. People formerly known as the audience now occupy production roles as part of their consumption practices. Accessibility, creativity and, potentially, global cooperation are key features of both the media and the media practices people employ in a collaborative media environment (p. 14). While a number of theorists argue that social (or collaborative) media blur the boundary between producer and consumer (Bruns & Jacobs, 2006), Löwgren and Reimer maintain that this distinction continues to be useful, particularly because collaborative media opens up a possibility for people to both produce media texts and participate in the 'design of the infrastructure' (p. 18) which distributes them. Increasingly, collaborative media services recognise that people seek to make modifications which enable a more personalised experience (p. 18). As a result, both amateurs and professionals engage in a simultaneous redesign of the system.

New forms of television are a key site for the study of collaborative media. This is due to two reasons. First, with the advent of user-generated content such as YouTube, new forms of on-demand television platforms, the increasing importance of social media 'overflow' (Gray, 2008) and viewer 'teleparticipation' (Ross, 2009), the amount of relevant audio-visual material is growing exponentially. Second, as Löwgren and Reimer (2013) argue, these new forms 'facilitate the tribal joining of forces' (p. 99). While the earlier comments relate to use of collaborative media in general, they take on specific meaning when discussing their use in the disability arena. The DVP and the ANP have both contributed to the amount of available material and have facilitated the creation of communities of people with disabilities advocating for television accessibility and better disability representations.

The second screen and transmedia paratexts

Television has stopped being an experience between viewer and show (Nielsen, 2014) and now encompasses 'real time conversations' with disparate people via social media (Hsia, 2010). This social media engagement is often described as the 'second screen' – TV viewing is no longer restricted to a single screen. This increasing interaction and engagement with social media as a component of television viewing has also affected programme development and provides the opportunity to have social conversations (Nielsen, 2014).

Television exists in a transmedia environment where viewers gain entry to a narrative world from a number of different points including the television text itself, official and unofficial social media discussion, source texts (including books, comics or cinema), merchandising (such as toys) and fanfiction. Each iteration of the text makes a unique contribution to our understanding of it. Henry Jenkin's (2006) observations about transmedia storytelling are useful to understanding VOD as collaborative media, particularly in terms of disability access and representation. Jenkins describes consumers as 'hunters and gatherers', tracking down information about stories across multiple media channels, collaborating with one another to ensure a 'richer entertainment experience' (p. 21). Jenkins explains this new aesthetic and textual experience, and calls on consumers to participate in 'knowledge communities'.

Knowledge communities or spaces

French cyber theorist Pierre Lévy (1997) also emphasises the importance of collaboration in his utopian vision of the ways the computerisation of society will 'promote the construction of intelligent communities in which our social and cognitive potential can be mutually developed and enhanced' (p. 17). Knowledge spaces are central to his vision of a collaborative exchange amongst and between diverse people with different levels of knowledge, information, skills – and ignorance. For Lévy, the more people who become connected to the knowledge space and engage in a collaborative collective intelligence to participate in the sharing of information, the more we can come to learn. These online knowledge spaces hold particular significance to both representations of disability and a broader social understanding of disability inclusion because users come together to discuss and debate both the definition of disability and people's personal experiences of it (Ellis, 2014c). Television and popular culture provide an accessible space for these discussions to take place.

Video on demand as collaborative media

VOD systems allow users to access audio-visual content whenever they want to rather than being forced to view programmes during an allotted broadcast schedule. Programmes can be watched in real time or downloaded to view later. Content is typically watched on a television or computer screen. Some services such as catch up television are free to use and rely on advertising for revenue; others such as Netflix adopt a subscriber model where users pay a fee to gain access to a wide selection of video content. Subscription VOD services have caused a major shift in the ways television is used and consumed.

The three principles Löwgren and Reimer (2013) identify as central to collaborative media – production, consumption and design – feature heavily in VOD functionality and use. Social media conversations about television, in the context of transmedia storytelling, form part of the production arm by allowing another entry point to the complete story world while also demonstrating a simultaneously active and creative form of television consumption. Additionally, the impacts audiences have had on the design of VOD, particularly disabled audiences advocating for accessibility, correspond to a collaborative media ethos of influencing design and personalising the viewing experience. This is certainly true for VOD which typically creates personalised recommendations for future viewing based on what a user has watched before.

Disability television research – from content analysis to accessibility

Disability theorists have frequently turned their attention toward the study of television and in particular how representations could negatively impact the lived experience of people with disability (Barnes, 1992; Cumberbatch & Negrine, 1992). Lingling Zhang and Beth Haller's (2013) observations that disability media theorists have, for the last 30 years, relied on content analysis to reveal 'problematic media representations of people with disabilities and their issues' (p. 321) certainly applies to television. However, as television has become increasingly integrated with online media, theorists have identified online social conversations (Ellis, 2014a, 2014c, 2015a; Quinlan & Bates, 2008; Quinlan & Bates, 2009; Rodan, Ellis, & Lebeck, 2014) and alternative modes of access (Ellis, 2014b; Jaeger, 2012) as new areas of concern.

For example, theorists Quinlan and Bates offer two studies of blogger discourse surrounding popular television shows, including *Dancing with the Stars* (2008) and *The bionic woman* (2009). A 2008 investigation of *Dancing with the stars* found audiences were concerned with three aspects related to Heather Mills's performance and lived experience of disability – her status as a 'supercrip', whether she was 'taking advantage of the sick role', and the overt sexualisation of her disabled body. Their analysis showed people struggled to move beyond stereotypes. Furthermore, their 2009 investigation of *The bionic Woman* added an important insight to the theorisation of disability, television and social media discussion – representation and interpretation of disability change alongside social change. My own 2014 investigation into *Game of Thrones* found audiences with disabilities were active, engaged and knowledgeable about historical representations of disability on television and the ways the *Game of Thrones*'s character Tyrion Lannister challenged these. Significantly, this research identified access as a key concern of disabled television audiences. Some audience members focused on access to television itself and particularly the absence of closed captions on first airings of *Game of Thrones* in Australia (Miles, 2013; Stombat, 2013).

Alongside the content of television representation, television accessibility is emerging as a site of social disablement (Ellcessor, 2011; Ellis & Kent, 2011; Goggin & Newell, 2003; Jaeger, 2012). As Goggin and Newell (2003) observe, 'for many people with disabilities [television] has been difficult to see or hear, [and] impossible to watch or listen to, absent cultural technology' (p. 90). Accessible features such as captions to communicate important audio information and audio description to communicate visual information for people with hearing and vision impairments respectively mitigate this. However, despite the potential for change afforded by digitisation (Ellis, 2014b; Goggin & Newell, 2003), new forms of television such as VOD have followed the 'familiar' trajectory of implementing an inaccessible technology attempting to retrofit access only when mandated to by law (Ellcessor, 2011; Ellis, 2015b)

Accessing television/ accessible television

While a 2013 survey into the use of television by 341 Australians with disability found only 71 watched television online (see Ellis, 2015b), ongoing research suggests this form of viewing is becoming increasingly important to this group, particularly as they seek accessibility (Ellis, 2014a, 2015b). Subscription VOD is quickly replacing broadcast television as the preferred mode for viewing television (Sifferlin, 2015). Popular rhetoric and research alike situate this form of viewing as more *accessible* than broadcast television. For example, a Screen Australia (2014) study described VOD as being 'for everyone' and 'accessible to everyone with an internet connection' (p. 2). However, none of the Australian VOD providers – Netflix Australia, STAN, Presto and Foxtel Play – have accessibility policies for people with disabilities despite these sites being otherwise characterised by an ethos of a personalised viewing experience.

Netflix

Subscription VOD provider Netflix is often described as bringing about a fundamental shift in television (Barr, 2011; Lotz, 2007; Morsillo & Barr, 2013). Netflix members subscribe to the platform for a weekly fee to watch as much as they want, anytime they want, from any internet-enabled device. While Netflix began as a DVD service before becoming an online streaming service, it has evolved to now produce original programming.

Netflix has been the target of a number of activist interventions of audiences with disabilities seeking a more accessible television experience (Ellis, 2015b). For example, when Netflix screened *The Wizard of Oz* without captions as part of seventy-fifth anniversary celebrations of the film's release, it was heavily criticised by Deaf activists who noted that captioned DVD and broadcast versions of the film were widely available (Ellis & Kent, 2011). Deaf activists continued their campaign against Netflix's lack of captions through the courts. Following their successful *Americas with Disabilities* (ADA) Act complaint, Netflix agreed to caption 100% of its catalogue (Mullin, 2012). However, a Federal court of appeals subsequently found Netflix did not have to comply with the ADA because it was not connected to 'any physical place' (Hattem, 2015).

These battles in court and in the media – and increasingly in social media – go beyond the provision of accessible VOD for people with disabilities; they force governments, legislators and corporations to reflect on whether the internet, the biggest communications shift in recent history, constitutes a place of public accommodation. As the internet becomes increasingly vital to all forms of participation in life – from education to employment to leisure – it must be made accessible to the whole population, including people with disabilities who are already disproportionally marginalised in social life (Jaeger, 2015).

Disability *Daredevil*

Immediately after it was made available on Netflix, audiences initiated social conversations about disability on blogs and in social media using the *Daredevil* narrative. Whereas some argued the narrative fell back on stigmatising one-dimensional stereotypes, others celebrated perceived new directions in disability representation. Elsa Henry, a vision impaired blogger, argues Matt Murdock's relationship to his disabled body and accessible devices such as his white cane is 'fraught':

> Matt Murdock neither behaves like a blind person (he does not kiss like a blind person, he does not do parkour like a blind person, and nor does he treat his white cane like a blind person) but he also doesn't treat his body like a disabled body. A white cane is not just a tool, though it is the most useful tool in my arsenal, but it is also an extension of one's body.
>
> (Henry, 2015)

By comparison, David Perry found 'a lot to like' in *Daredevil's* everyday portrayal of blindness:

> Murdock negotiates space using touch. His electronic devices – phone, alarm clock – talk to him. He frequently has conversations in which his sighted interlocutors catch themselves using visual cues (nods, shrugs, etc.) and then redirect.
>
> (Perry, 2015)

Although Matt frequently 'tosses his cane in an alleyway' (Henry, 2015), a number of assistive devices Matt uses to navigate his day – for example a braille display, talking alarm clock and voice-over enabled mobile phone – are emphasised for their importance in enabling Matt to maintain employment and relationships. People he comes in contact with also continually engage in visual forms of body language communication such as the real estate agent who ends up curtseying because she does not know how to greet him; people also nod and shrug. While Matt misses these cues, he relies on other heightened senses such as hearing – a good example is when he hears Karen's heartbeat and knows she is telling the truth about not murdering her colleague despite the evidence against her.

This concept of heightened senses and verisimilitude to the actual experience of blindness was also discussed online, by both scientists and people with disabilities:

While *Daredevil* may seem like just another high-flying superhero epic, there's at least a sliver of truth to the notion that blind people develop heightened adeptness with their other senses as compared to those who can see. According to research into blindness and the senses, Marvel's superhero isn't quite plucked from the real world, but he can teach us a thing or two about how blind people adapt to a world without sight.

(Keller, 2015)

Keller (2015) goes on to explain a number of research projects and anecdotal statements that illustrate the ways people with and *without* vision impairment rely on echoes to navigate space, and ultimately argues that when it comes to tactile, audio and sensory advantages 'it's the same principle that governs any muscle in the human body: the more you use it, the better'. Ultimately, for Keller, while *Daredevil* gets some things right, it exaggerates others.

#Daredevil: Social conversations about disability in a transmedia tweetup

In anticipation of the release of *Daredevil* on Netflix, Alice Wong of the DVP organised a live tweetup of the first episodes and invited interested viewers to contribute to the conversation using the hashtag #DaredevilDVP. Following the tweetup, Wong created a Storify visualisation of tweets and identified the dominant themes as 'the lack of audio description and disability representation' (Wong, 2015). Wong's Storify documents a dynamic conversation between 10 people totalling 130 tweets. Analysis of these tweets identified the following key themes:

Anticipation/ excitement
Audio description campaign
Calls to further social media conversations
Disability comedy
Disability narrative
Disability stereotype
Discussion of narrative
Foggy as assistance
Intertextual reference
Marginalisation of others
Marvel reference
Religion
Superpowers/heightened senses/awareness
Visualisation of story

As Figure 11.1 shows, tweeters overwhelmingly focused their discussion on the narrative in a general sense. However, this was largely through a disability lens. For example, a robust discussion around the character of Foggy as a form of assistance aid for Matt to navigate the world emerged, with some seeing him as

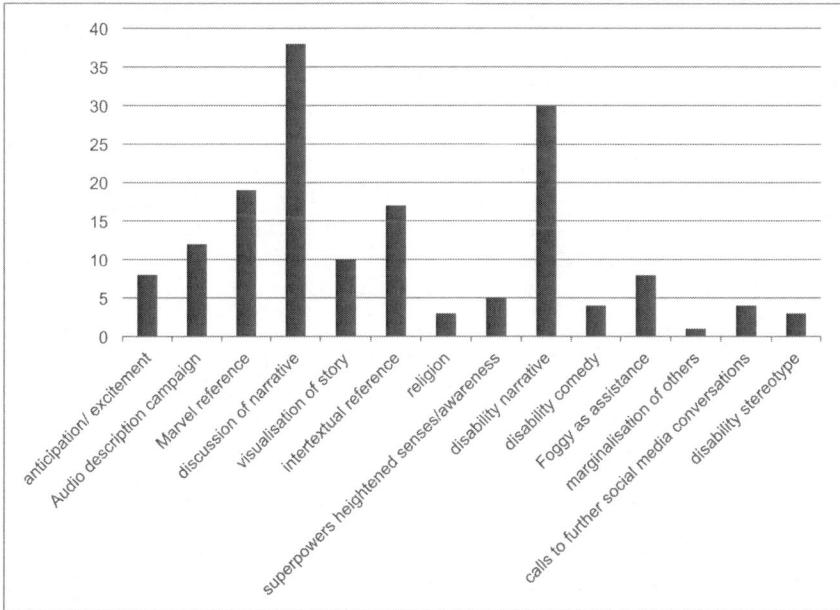

Figure 11.1 Content analysis of #DaredevilDVP

helpful, others patronising and one tweeter even suggested he was just a 'jerky friend' (Rebecca Cokley tweet on Wong, 2015). In any case, the discussion raised interesting insights around the notion of interdependence.

A small discussion about disability stereotypes took place in response to the scene where Matt feels Claire's face and admits to missing the sky:

> Are you kidding me?! Stupid blindness stereotype! I don't want to touch people's greasy, pimple-covered faces!
>
> (Dayin Washington tweet on Wong, 2015)

> "Give anything to see the sky again." A very old trope, but it feels earned.
>
> (Andrew Pulrang tweet on Wong, 2015)

> I like the sky reference – it actually makes sense.
>
> (Lead On Update tweet on Wong, 2015)

Viewers predicted the focus on blindness would fade in later episodes:

> Getting a lot of blind stuff out of the way fast. Does that mean they won't talk about it much hereafter?
>
> (Andrew Pulrang tweet on Wong, 2015)

Let's hope that was a one-off, to placate the non-blind folks!!

(Alice Wong tweet on Wong, 2015)

Similarly, the way the story was visualised was of interest during the tweetup. This feature of *Daredevil* has received broad critical acclaim, as Amy Chambers of the *Science and Entertainment Laboratory* observes:

> Moving image media – including television, cinema, and video games – are multi-sensory and do not simply rely upon the visual as a mode of storytelling. The producers of *Daredevil* had to produce a non-visual experience by developing a visual tone and texture that communicates Murdock's enhanced allocentric sense.

(Chambers, 2015)

Throughout her article, Chambers raises a number of relevant points about the ways people with different impairments access moving images and, by extension, the importance of providing different points of access. Tweeters picked up on this topic through their discussions about Netflix's visualisation of the Marvel universe from opening credits, lighting and particularly from Matt's point of view and understated *mise-en-scène* compared to previous iterations:

> Like how Karen's image is reflected in his glasses and how her image is fuzzy when Matt's looking at her.

(Alice Wong tweet on Wong, 2015)

> Marvel on Netflix is much darker tone!

(Jihan Abbas tweet on Wong, 2015)

While Wong is correct that discussions of disability representation was a key theme and the lack of audio description clearly a problem, the people participating in the social conversations also contributed their transmedia knowledge of the story by offering insights regarding both the wider Marvel universe and the influence certain actor's previous body of work had on their interpretation of the show:

> Looking forward to the introduction of the employer, Kingpin, played by Vincent D'Onofrio.

(Alice Wong tweet on Wong, 2015)

Transmedia allows viewers to enter into a narrative world at many different points and together, through knowledge spaces such as Twitter and Storify, to collate information to enhance their experience:

> I love the understanding that the events of avengers cause profits for both the good and the bad.

(Lead On Update tweet on Wong, 2015)

Rebuilding? The Incident? Marvel backstory, yes? Nicely done. Sort of doesn't matter that I don't know all about it.

(Andrew Purlang tweet on Wong, 2015)

However, tweeters were conflicted that a portion of the disability community were unable to fully experience the show with them, ironically people with the same vision impairment as *Daredevil's* protagonist Matt Murdock:

Out of all the times for *@Netflix* to improve their accessibility, they don't w/ premiere of *#Daredevil* Thoughts?

(Alice Wong tweet on Wong, 2015)

I am feeling a little twinge of guilt/anger that our blind friends do not have full enjoyment of this w/o audio description.

(Alice Wong tweet on Wong, 2015)

they translated it to 3 other languages and [cc] and no audio descriptions. Wtf?!

(Amanda Koski tweet on Wong, 2015)

The Accessible Netflix Project (ANP)

Robert Kingett initiated the ANP in 2013 to encourage Netflix and other VOD providers to introduce audio description on their platforms. They describe their mission as:

1   To provide accessible software and interface to Netflix users
2   To implement and ensure future accessibility practices and consideration
3   To ensure that relatively all types of disability are taken into careful consideration at all times.

(Kingett, 2014)

The group traverses a number of social media platforms, including Facebook, Twitter, YouTube and the ANP official website, which acts as a clearing house for discussions. The group set three targets to meet:

1   Provide a screen reader friendly experience to all Netflix functions on the PC and mobile devices with all screen readers.
2   Provide an easily navigable interface for the mobility impaired using adaptive technology.
3   Provide easy access to audio described content for the blind and the visually impaired on streaming services as well as DVD selection currently and in the future.

Following intense advocacy, and particularly around the original Netflix programme *Daredevil*, the ANP achieved their third mission as Netflix announced 'we're expanding our accessibility options by adding audio description on select titles, beginning today with our new critically acclaimed series, Marvel's *Daredevil*' (Wright, 2015). Netflix operations manager Tracy Wright explained viewers could 'choose audio narration just like choosing the soundtrack in a different language'. Previously Netflix had informed the ANP they had 'no immediate plans to add audio description to our service' (Kingett, 2014).

While the ANP has been advocating this since 2013, the announcement that Netflix, together with Marvel, would be producing *Daredevil* gave the community a clear focus and example through which to explain why audio description was so important:

> *Daredevil* is a hero loved by all, including blind comic book fans. Since we could not find any definitive answer online could you elaborate on plans, if any, about adding audio description to the show so that blind and sighted can enjoy the heroics together?
>
> (Hannah cited on Katie, 2014)

When *Daredevil* debuted without audio description, the ANP gained momentum and recruited a number of important allies, including the webmaster of Man Without Fear who agreed audio description on the Netflix series was 'a great idea' (Daredevil, 2014). It took only five days of media and social media focus on the importance of audio description for Netflix to agree to alter their design. Kingett reflects on the importance of social media to disability inclusion:

> People will remember the Accessible Netflix Project as the one that started it all – global accessibility and global audio description. I see both common on streaming platforms soon. I see it happening now more than ever. I see it happening because, one, there isn't an excuse anymore and two, because someone will make it happen with the power of an email, tweet or some other form of the written word.
>
> (Kingett, 2015)

Conclusion

Kingett recognises the importance of social media disability advocacy in a collaborative media environment. This chapter has approached the topic of disability, television and social media from the perspective of collaborative media using social conversations occurring around the Netflix production *Daredevil*. *Daredevil* as a transmedia text illustrates the ways accessibility, creativity and potentially global cooperation can benefit people with disabilities.

Other chapters in this collection have identified Twitter as an important social media channel of communication for people with disabilities for a diverse range of reasons, from disaster communications (Bennett et al., Chapter 9), to advocacy (see Xu et al., Chapter 23 and Ryan & Julian Chapter 3), to engaging the disability community in interactive transmedia quests for social change (Burke &

Crow, Chapter 5). In the context of second screen engagement with television, the DVP live tweetup of the first episode of *Daredevil* provides 'empirical evidence' of how people interpret the world and also illustrates the ways people engage in knowledge spaces to both produce and consume a 'richer entertainment experience' (Harrington, Highfield, & Bruns, 2013).

The conversations occurring around the #DaredevilDVP shows the ways viewers with varying degrees of knowledge about topics such as the lived experience of disability come together to assist one another in the process of meaning making and, further, to identify associated points of disablement. While a television series with a disabled protagonist was celebrated, the inaccessibility of the show itself to people with the same impairment was emphatically discussed, with further calls to action. These calls to action, along with the activities of the ANP, successfully changed the way Netflix delivered television to its vision impaired audience. While Netflix embraces an ethos of personalisation and encourages second screen consumption through Twitter for example, the VOD has resisted implementing accessibility features for its disabled audience (Ellis, 2015b).

Changes in the way we access television has fundamentally changed television (Ellis & Goggin, 2015; Gray, 2008; Napoli, 2011; Sepinwall, 2012). Digital modes of access such as VOD – in combination with access to the views of other fans through online wikis and forums – have seen television characters and modes of delivery evolve and change in unprecedented ways. It is no accident that these communities are held together via collaboration. Collaborative media is characterised by an environment where people formerly known as the audience participate in production, consumption and design practices. Increasingly, television texts have become transmedia texts where viewers gain entry to the narrative worlds from many different points. This chapter argues that transmedia and collaboration are effective ways for viewers with disabilities to engage in a wider social conversation about disability inclusion beyond the television screen.

Acknowledgements

Research for this chapter was supported by grants from the Australia Research Council Discovery Early Career Researcher award (DE130101712) and the Australian Communications Consumer Action Network (2015048).

References

Barnes, C. (1992). Disabling imagery and the media: An exploration of the principles for media representations of disabled people. Retrieved from http://www.leeds.ac.uk/disability-studies/archiveuk/Barnes/disabling%20imagery.pdf Retrieved from http://www.leeds.ac.uk/disability-studies/archiveuk/Barnes/disabling%20imagery.pdf

Barr, T. (2011). Television's newcomers: Netflix, Apple, Google and Facebook. *Telecommunications Journal Australia, 61*(4), 60.61–60.10. Retrieved from http://tja.org.au

Bruns, A., & Jacobs, J. (2006). *Use of Blogs*. New York: Peter Lang.

Chambers, A. (2015, 20 April). You're blind, but you see so much: Netflix's Daredevil and blindness. Retrieved from http://thescienceandentertainmentlab.com/daredevil/

Cumberbatch, G., & Negrine, R. (1992). *Images of Disability on Television*. London: Routledge.

Daredevil. (2014, 6 July). @manwithoutfear. Retrieved from https://twitter.com/man withoutfear/status/485904399038836736

Ellcessor, E. (2011). Captions on, off on TV, online: Accessibility and search engine optimization in online closed captioning. *Television & New Media, Published Online before Print*. Retrieved from http://tvn.sagepub.com/content/early/2011/2010/2024/152747641 1425251.abstract?patientinform-links=yes&legid=sptvn;1527476411425251v1527476 411425251

Ellis, K. (2014a). Cripples, bastards and broken things: Disability in game of thrones. *Media Culture, 17*(5). Retrieved from http://journal.media-culture.org.au/index.php/ mcjournal/article/viewArticle/895. Retrieved from http://journal.media-culture.org.au/ index.php/mcjournal/article/viewArticle/895

Ellis, K. (2014b). Digital television flexibility: A survey of Australians with disability (Report). *Media International Australia Incorporating Culture and Policy,* (150), 96.

Ellis, K. (2014c). The voice Australia (2012): Disability, social media and collective intelligence. *Continuum, 28*(4), 482–494. doi:10.1080/10304312.2014.907874

Ellis, K. (2015a). *Disability and Popular Culture: Focusing Passion, Creating Community and Expressing Defiance*. Surrey: Ashgate.

Ellis, K. (2015b). Netflix closed captions offer an accessible model for the streaming video industry, but what about audio description? *Communication, Politics & Culture, 47*(3) 3–20.

Ellis, K., & Goggin, G. (2015). *Disability and the Media*. New York: Palgrave Macmillan.

Ellis, K., & Kent, M. (2011). *Disability and New Media*. New York: Routledge.

Finkelstein, V. (1981). Disability and the helper/helped relationship: A historical view. *Disability Archive UK*. Retrieved from http://www.leeds.ac.uk/disability-studies/archiveuk/ finkelstein/Helper-Helped%20Relationship.pdf

Fiske, J. (2003). *Reading Television / John Fiske, John Hartley* (2nd ed./with a new foreword by John Hartley. ed.). London: Routledge.

Goggin, G., & Newell, C. (2003). *Digital Disability: The Social Construction of Disability in New Media*. Lanham: Rowman and Littlefield Publishers Inc.

Gray, J. (2008). *Television Entertainment*. New York: Routledge.

Harrington, S., Highfield, T., & Bruns, A. (2013). More than a backchannel: Twitter and television. *Participations: Journal of Audience & Reception Studies, 10*(1), 405–409.

Hattem, J. (2015, 3 April). Court: Netflix doesn't have to comply with disability law. Retrieved from http://thehill.com/policy/technology/237829-court-netflix-doesnt-have-to-comply-with-disability-law

Henry, E. (2015, 1 May). Daredevil and disability politics. Retrieved from http://herstoryarc. com/2015/05/01/daredevil-and-disability-politics-2/

Hsia, L. (2010, 2 December). How social media is changing the business of television. Retrieved from http://mashable.com/2010/12/10/social-media-business-tv/#SLf7o Hc3Caqa

Jaeger, P. (2012). *Disability and the Internet: Confronting a Digital Divide*. Boulder, London: Lynne Rienner Publishers.

Jaeger, P. (2015). Disability, human rights, and social justice: The ongoing struggle for online accessibility and equality. *First Monday, 20*(9). Retrieved from http://firstmonday. org/ojs/index.php/fm/article/view/6164/4898

Jenkins, H. (2006). *Convergence Culture: Where Old and New Media Collide*. New York: New York University Press.

Katie. (2014, 6 July). Advocating for audio description on Netflix's Daredevil series. Retrieved from https://netflixproject.wordpress.com/tag/daredevil/

Keller, J. (2015, 15 April). What Daredevil gets (Kinda) right about blindness and heightened senses. Retrieved from http://nymag.com/scienceofus/2015/04/what-daredevil-gets-right-about-being-blind.html#

Kingett, R. (2014). The accessible Netflix project advocates taking steps to ensure Netflix accessibility for everyone. Retrieved from http://netflixproject.wordpress.com/

Kingett, R. (2015, 1 June). "Daredevil", audio description and the accessible Netflix project. Retrieved from https://usodep.blogs.govdelivery.com/2015/06/01/daredevil-audio-description-and-the-accessible-netflix-project/

Lévy, P. (1997). *Collective Intelligence: Mankind's Emerging World in Cyberspace* (R. Bononno, Trans.). New York and London: Plenum Press.

Lotz, A. D. (2007). *The Television Will be Revolutionized.* New York: New York University Press.

Löwgren, J. A., & Reimer, B. (2013). *Collaborative Media: Production, Consumption, and Design Interventions.* Cambridge, MA, USA: The MIT Press.

Miles, C. (2013). Facebook post. Retrieved from https://www.facebook.com/FOXTEL/posts/10152863155815074

Mitchell, D., & Snyder, S. (2000). *Narrative Prosthesis: Disability and the Dependencies of Discourse.* Ann Arbor: The University of Michigan Press.

Morsillo, R., & Barr, T. (2013). Innovation or Disruption? The national broadband network comes to Australian TV. *International Journal of Digital Television, 4*(3), 239–260.

Mullin, J. (2012, 11 October). Netflix settles with deaf-rights group, agrees to caption all videos by 2014. Retrieved from http://arstechnica.com/tech-policy/2012/10/netflix-settles-with-deaf-rights-group-agrees-to-caption-all-videos-by-2014/

Napoli, P. M. (2011). *Audience Evolution: New Technologies and the Transformation of Media Audiences / Philip M. Napoli.* New York: Columbia University Press.

Nielsen. (2014, 4 August). Living social: How second screens are helping TV make fans. Retrieved from http://www.nielsen.com/us/en/insights/news/2014/living-social-how-second-screens-are-helping-tv-make-fans.html

Oliver, M. (1996). *Understanding Disability: From Theory to Practice.* Houndsmill, Basingstoke: Macmillan.

Perry, D. (2015, 20 April). How well does 'Daredevil' handle disability issues? Retrieved from http://www.vice.com/read/how-well-does-daredevil-handle-disability-issues-320

Quinlan, M. M., & Bates, B. R. (2008). Dances and discourses of (Dis)ability: Heather Mills's embodiment of disability on dancing with the stars. *Text and Performance Quarterly, 28*(1–2), 64–80.

Quinlan, M. M., & Bates, B. R. (2009). Bionic woman (2007): Gender, disability and cyborgs. *Journal of Research in Special Educational Needs, 9*(1), 48–58. doi:10.1111/j.1471-3802.2009.01115.x

Rodan, D., Ellis, K., & Lebeck, P. (2014). *Disability, Obesity and Ageing: Popular Media Identifications.* Surrey: Ashgate.

Ross, S. (2009). *Beyond the Box: Television and the Internet.* Hoboken, NJ: Whiley-Blackwell.

Screen Australia. (2014). Online and on Demand: Trends in Australian online video use. Retrieved from https://www.screenaustralia.gov.au/getmedia/d61a7c4b-3abf-444c-9367-aa8dc8b1b8f6/OnlineOnDemand_2014.pdf

Sepinwall, A. (2012). *The Revolution Was Televised: The Cops, Crooks, Slingers and Slayers Who Changed TV Drama Forever.* Austin, TX: Touchstone.

Sifferlin, A. (2015, 11 March). Americans are watching more streaming video and less live TV. Retrieved from http://time.com/3740865/more-americans-streaming-television/

Stombat. (2013, 16 April). No closed captions on new programs. Retrieved from http://crowdsupport.telstra.com.au/t5/Foxtel/No-closed-captions-on-new-programs/td-p/148074

Vejvoda, J. (2015, 29 September). Drew Goddard on how he would've made the sinister six movie and comparisons to suicide squad. Retrieved from http://au.ign.com/articles/2015/09/29/drew-goddard-on-how-he-wouldve-made-the-sinister-six-movie-and-comparisons-to-suicide-squad?%20hub%20page&utm_content=1

Wong, A. (2015). #Daredevil & disability: #DaredevilDVP. Retrieved from https://storify.com/SFdirewolf/daredevil-and-disability#publicize

Wright, T. (2015, 14 April). Netflix begins audio description for visually impaired. Retrieved from http://blog.netflix.com/2015/04/netflix-begins-audio-description-for.html

Zhang, L., & Haller, B. (2013). Consuming image: How mass media impact the identity of people with disabilities. *Communication Quarterly, 61*(3), 319–334. doi:10.1080/01463373.2013.776988

12 Articulating vulnerability and interdependence in networked social space

Brian Goldfarb and John E. Armenta

In this chapter we explore some resonances and connections among particular uses of social media in the US alongside cultural understandings and experiences of interdependency, vulnerability and disability. Following lines of thought in recent disability scholarship that draw from feminist ethics of care and dependency theory, we consider how certain uses of social media might contribute to the formation of an ethics of vulnerability and reshape cultural understanding of interdependency. By foregrounding the role of connection in human agency rather than the liberal ideal of individual autonomy, these theoretical perspectives prompt us to seek alternatives for understanding and responding to diversity in embodiment and ability. In response to this provocation, we consider how social media can provide a unique arena for envisioning and enacting modes of connection that embrace shared and incommensurate dynamics of dependency and vulnerability. If vulnerability often takes on negative connotations within discussions of disability and illness, an important dimension of this chapter draws upon theoretical discussions that position it as a necessary and productive force rather than a condition to be minimised. Vulnerability, in important ways, underwrites all social relations, and is inextricably entwined with violence and injustice, but also with care and empathy. Our analysis provides us with a lens for examining two examples of social media practices that we see as fostering imaginative collective engagements with disablement.

What follows is a consideration of articulations of vulnerability, care and interdependence in two examples of social media forms and practices – AmputeeOT, a vlog and Facebook page that serve as forums for convergence of amputee experience across diverse perspectives and positions; and POS REP, an app developed to enable connection and mutual support between US military veterans, particularly with regard to the effects of widespread post-traumatic stress disorder (PTSD) and mental health issues that are linked to high suicide rates. These examples offer possibilities for noting distinct creative approaches that bridge online and embodied practices of care – ones that openly embrace unequal relations, acknowledge unstable positions of support and dependency and belie binary positions of abled/disabled.

Interdependency and the social model of disability

The social model of disability implies not only that disability is constructed or experienced in relation to social, cultural and built barriers, but also that disablement is enacted upon and experienced by people in a range of roles beyond those labelled disabled. That disability itself has become an increasingly significant analytic framework in disability studies. The emergent sociality of networked culture presents an important context for this critical concern with the intersubjective nature of disability. Goggin and Newell (2006) point to this nexus, noting that there is 'a growing recognition of the balance between dependence and independence – and that all in society are engaged in understanding their interdependence and connectedness, something in which the shaping of ICTs [Information and Communication Technology] is offering innovative ways to understand such new social forms' (pp. 309–310).

More than an argument about our (inter)dependence, these innovative ways of understanding it involve experimentation with how we structure and enact mutual care. This includes exploration of diverse arrangements that creatively bridge domestic and institutional space and the legitimation of forms of expertise that challenge boundaries between clinical and pedestrian knowledge and experience. We are interested in social media practices that are a crucible for spawning what artists and disability theorists McArthur and Zavitsanos (2013) call 'new models of conviviality'. These are modes of structuring and conveying care that evade characterisation as exchange, and require that participants recognise and manage shared and disparate experiences of precariousness and vulnerability. Fashioning them involves openness to concealed dependencies and the unmarked infrastructures that allow the 'able-bodied' to pass as autonomous. Invoking Kittay's term for undoing the category of non-disabled people, McArthur and Zavisanos ask, 'What are the possibilities of (inter)dependency for the "temporarily abled"?' (p. 127). One place to grasp these potentialities is in the emerging discursive configurations and reorganisations of care facilitated by online interactions that bridge family, close friends and intimate strangers to recast our responsibility and concern for others.

In the examples of social media that we discuss, we are interested in how relations around vulnerability are represented or performed, and how they are redistributed. Moreover, we are concerned with how they can contribute to the public sanctioning of empathy. Crucial here is the movement of forms of care and responsibility for others across social arenas and physical space. Uneven dynamics of interdependency that traditionally have been forged and embraced in personal, intimate and domestic relationships can be seen to migrate into public space, consciousness and participatory practice. Sharing knowledge and the coordination of activity and support contribute to inventive configurations of interpersonal care that emerge from familial or personal relations to bridge intimate and public discourse. Anthropologists and disability activists Rapp and Ginsburg provide a provocative account of how counter-normative forms of sociality and attitudes toward embodied differences develop within families, friends and other intimate constellations living with disability. They observe that important dimensions of public discourse on disability are being recast as these intimate experiences of disability find their way into public consciousness. In this respect, they suggest we can productively understand shifts in moral stances toward disability in secular civil society as forms of kinship writ large (Rapp & Ginsburg, 2001). While their work does not focus explicitly on the role of social media, there is little doubt that networked and mobile media have provided expanded opportunities for the transfer and translation of these attitudes and practices into public consciousness.

The movement of forms of care and responsibility between pubic and personal realms is paralleled by increasing permeability of the boundaries between professional/clinical and lay knowledge of care practices. Within the US context, the formation of lay expertise associated with the women's movement and later AIDS activism (Epstein, 1996) provides a notable instance of redistribution of dependency and vulnerability. The centrality of self-advocacy and deinstitutionalisation within the US and UK disability rights movement from the early 1970s has provided a strong framework for permeability of professional and personal care practices (Shapiro, 1993). In the first decades of public use of the internet, email and listservs contributed significantly to this development by placing professional and institutional knowledge within reach of informal caregivers. At the same time internet platforms provided a medium for expressing the importance of tacit knowledge and embodied experience. These earlier uses of the internet as a vector for the formation of lay-experts in arenas of health and disability provide a basis for considering innovative uses of social media to constitute relationships of interdependency and mutual care.

If so much activity on social media platforms reproduces dominant modes of sociality, there are also noteworthy appropriations of these platforms as conduits of public intimacies where performance of vulnerabilities and enactment of care challenge us to look beyond fixed roles of carer/caree and abled/disabled. The affordances of social media invite integration of forms of online and off connection. They present distinct opportunities for transforming interpersonal relations through a proliferation of mechanisms for encountering others, establishing connection, transmitting advice and experience, and coordinating activities. More flexible participatory software capabilities loosely framed as Web 2.0 alongside the profusion of mobile devices has invited people to rethink and play with the spatial-temporal terms of sociality.

Balancing autonomy and interdependency

Our examination of AmputeeOT and POS REP centres on how they articulate concerns with agency and autonomy within disability rights as well as disability studies. Scholarly and activist concern with how new media reshape access to participation in cultural, economic and political institutions is guided by an interest in minimising concrete disparities in individual agency and autonomy. However, while championing individual autonomy, this framework leaves intact (and might inadvertently reinforce) the fear and denigration of states of dependency that constitute an underlying ideological force in ableist social relations. Shifting the terms of discussion need not diminish the continued significance of stances on technological innovation linked to core agendas of the disability rights movement, e.g. advocacy for 'independent living' and rights-based legislative mandates for inclusion and accommodation.

The critical turn to balancing autonomy and dependency allows us to situate struggles for independent living and equal rights as indispensable but limited frames for confronting ableism. Beyond removing material and institutional barriers affecting disabled individuals, these efforts have and continue to reshape perceptions of diversity of ability. Critical approaches to interdependence also call on us to destigmatise dependency itself, by establishing ethical frameworks that acknowledge, value and provide tools for dealing with the multiple forms of non-equivalence that structure manifold aspects of human relations. Feminist ethicists of care established this agenda centrally in relation to concerns with pedagogical and caring relationships. Rather than ameliorating or compensating for inequity, they asserted the need for recasting understanding of human value, diversity and connection (Gilligan, 1982; Noddings, 1984). Contemporary feminist ethicists have articulated these arguments to disability studies, offering a theoretical/philosophical basis for shifting concern away from individual deficits or needs (Kittay & Feder, 2002; Fineman, 2008; Turner, 2006). Putting this in the context of digital technology, Moser (2006) insists that '[t]he issue . . . is not first and foremost whether new, digital, ICT-based technologies will revolutionize the lives and situation of disabled people, but rather whether they will revolutionize the way we conceive of and make distinctions between abled and disabled people in the first instance' (p. 389). This core binary distinction (abled/disabled) of ableist culture is maintained through a widespread disavowal of our shared experience of dependency, and the multiple dimensions of how human corporeality itself is entwined with vulnerability.

Feminist care ethicists critique prevailing equity-based moral frameworks, by offering critical approaches to dependency that underscore how nearly all of us occupy fluctuating roles of caring and being cared for at different points in our lives (Fineman, 2008; Kittay, 1999; Kittay & Feder, 2002; Turner, 2006). Examining cases of people with extreme and unavoidable dependency (and their carers), these scholars articulate the need for a disability ethics that questions the limits of how human value is understood on the most basic level. A cornerstone of such an ethics is the recognition that vulnerability conditions the very possibility of social connections that are intertwined with fundamental ideas of humanness and human rights. While offering ways of thinking about human value apart from norms of ability and measures of productive contribution or need, they insist on the urgency of radically redistributing responsibility and support for care from domestic to public spheres across local and global arenas.

Vulnerability and dependency are not only widely shared, but they are what make us human. While we are not equally vulnerable, the fact of universal vulnerability makes unstable the boundaries between any notion of health and un-health, and between ability and disability (Shildrick, 2000). Conscious recognition of how the character and degree of our respective vulnerabilities change dramatically across time and context allows us to understand and respond to interdependency in new ways. Disability can be reconceived as a tangle within social fabric that we negotiate intimately and relationally through constellations of interdependence across private and public spaces and activities. Extending a principle from feminist ethics of care, an ethics of vulnerability shifts our focus from issues of equity among individuals to the challenge of fashioning social relations that facilitate caring responses to vulnerability and ethical distribution of responsibility.

Against prevailing negative connotations of vulnerability as a condition to be minimised, scholars including Butler (2004), Fineman (2008) and Gilson (2011) have theorised a nuanced understanding of vulnerability as a productive force. Vulnerability, they contend, is fundamental insofar as it necessitates and enables all social relations, allowing for violence and injustice, but also for solidarity, empathy and care across intimate and public encounters. Gilson (2011) argues that '[v]ulnerability is a basic kind of openness to being affected and affecting in both positive and negative ways, which can take diverse forms in different social situations' (p. 310). Engaging this expanded understanding of vulnerability, we turn to our two case studies to ask this question: how the development of networked culture and, more particularly, the proliferation of social media have enabled a consciousness of interdependency and facilitated social practices that trouble distinctions of abled/disabled?

AmputeeOT, v-blogging across the therapeutic divide

Contemporary social media use is characterised by a rich interaction between online discourse and everyday, embodied experience. The ever-expanding interpenetration of offline and online activity eclipses the initial phantasm of an alternate cyber-world of free-floating identities. Accounts of people falsely representing themselves as disabled or infirmed were highlighted as exemplars of this phenomena, and served as platform for considering the ethical challenges posed by networked culture (Stone, 1991; Turkle, 1984). This discourse developed within an online culture in which it was still possible to imagine the largely independent realms of online and offline sociality, one that was far less integrated with face-to-face interaction than today's social media. Putting aside the spectre of wholly fictionalised personalities, contemporary social media practices provide an arena for users to perform more quotidian forms of shifting or composite identities by offering a space to articulate distinct and overlapping roles, interleaving intimate and public experiences, and traversing lay and professional knowledge.

Christina Stephens's video blog, AmputeeOT (Stephens, 2013), offers an instructive articulation of this potential for social media users to traverse roles, identities and knowledge domains. Stephens is an occupational and rehabilitative therapist affiliated with the occupational therapy program at Washington University in St. Louis, Missouri, where she divides her time between clinical and research practice. Within the US context, occupational therapy involves work that articulates clinical settings with the patient's home and place of work, with its focus on helping patients overcome impairment in relation to life contexts and goals. Stephens's relation to her profession took on new dimensions when, just three years into her professional career as an OT, her left foot and ankle were crushed in an accident. While fixing her brakes, the car fell off the jack, landing on her leg. This transformative event prompted Stephens to create a weekly video blog about adapting to and embracing life as an amputee, featured on a YouTube channel and Facebook. In the vlog's first instalments (2013, February 22) Stephens directly addresses the camera, talking about her decision to undergo a below-the-knee amputation. They feature graphic segments in which she redresses her wound, examining the condition of her leg and discussing treatment options. In these first episodes she discusses her unique position as someone who can approach both sides of the caring process, offering a blend of professional clinical knowledge and experience as a (soon-to-be) amputee.

Stephens's ability to straddle these two perspectives is part of what makes her vlog a provocative case for thinking through how social media can creatively unsettle boundaries between abled and disabled identity. More than combining or balancing the two perspectives, Stephens embodies these simultaneous roles in a manner that undermines normative apprehension of vulnerability and how it is entwined with care. Her clinical expertise is productively infused with the experience of precariousness; her life as an amputee is inflected by an orientation to mutual care that draws from her professional knowledge and practice.

Early segments of AmputeeOT provide a chronicle of the psychic and physical processes of preparing for amputation, undergoing surgery and recovery. Intimately engaging with this transition underscores the insecurity of normative ability and embodiment. Viewers are confronted with graphic representations, frank deliberation and reflections that convey Stephens's journey across the boundary from full-bodied to amputee. The viewer comments for these segments clearly demonstrate how her narrative elicits a keen sense of vulnerability among the vlog's visitors/followers. Many express empathic concerns about the experience of extreme pain and fear. Others remark on Stephens's strength and courage. As might be expected, a unifying, underlying frame for understanding the experience of adapting to amputation is negotiating loss. But for Stephens, life as an amputee is not simply about trying to regain lost abilities; she highlights how her amputation has led her to meet people and do things that she would never have if she had not injured her leg.

Stephens's pursuit of the unforeseen possibilities of her difference in embodiment is wedded to a DIY spirit that moves from the practical to the fanciful. This spirit is pronounced in an instalment that presents a time-lapse recording of Stephens fashioning a prosthetic leg entirely out of Lego that went viral, received nearly two million views on YouTube and garnered her television interviews and extensive media attention (see Figure 12.1). The broad appeal of the video is in how her Lego project fuses vulnerability and capacity. This is something that is evident in the overall appeal of her vlog – openness and possibilities of precariousness form the basis of new ways of communicating, connecting and experiencing life. Opening up creative ways of thinking about the experiences and activities of amputees and people with congenital limb differences, AmputeeOT has become a hub of interaction for a wider range of people with close and peripheral interest in rethinking ability and embodiment. These include prosthetists and other clinical professionals, designers,

Figure 12.1 Video still from *AmputeeOT: My Legoleg*, 2013, June 12

family, friends, devotees as well as others whose comments and queries reveal curiosity formed in the vacuum created by social anxieties around differences in corporeality.

AmputeeOT's constitution of an audience/constituency around heterogeneous connections to conditions of vulnerably provokes consideration of how social media offers distinct possibilities for reconceiving care and interdependence. While key examples examined in scholarship on feminist care ethics have mainly centred on interdependency within domestic life, AmputeeOT provides an opportunity for thinking about how social media can provide a platform for enacting care ethics in ways that bridge familial and professional as well as domestic and public arenas.

Perhaps central to this affordance of social media is the heightened role of aesthetic and affective dimensions of experience as the basis of social exchange and connection. Many AmputeeOT videos are formulated around 'how to' topics such as caring for a residual limb, cleaning a prosthetic limb socket, and doing various activities with or without a prosthetic (driving, bicycling, getting dressed, swimming, cleaning the house). There are also segments dedicated to less 'useful' topics such as tattooing on residual limbs. Stevens dedicates other episodes to introducing new devices, prosthetic technology or amputee fashion. Prosthetic options are considered in terms of a range of functions including fashion, mobility and comfort. They are repurposed as cavities for storing things or as weapons for jousting. But even the most practical themes are addressed in ways that stress the unique aesthetic and interpersonal experiences of living with an amputation (see Figure 12.2). Walking is never bare walking, but an activity attached to a full life populated by endless options and creative choices. How one makes one's life as an amputee

Figure 12.2 Video still from *AmputeeOT: We screwed ourselves together,* 2013, September 16

is framed as a process of engaging personal interests and expanding experience, rather than modes of accommodating lack. Prosthetics are more than replacements, and adapting to limb loss is a generative process.

Throughout AmputeeOT, there is a focus on the creative and innovative ways that people who are amputees perform everyday activities. Two videos playfully reflect on this. *Why being an amputee is AWESOME!* (2014, July 17) features a host of Stephens's amputee friends clowning around with prosthetics and affirming the ways in which amputees engage their particular physicality. *Things amputees do that'd be weird if fully-limbed people did them* (2014, August 5) presents the flipside of this. It features Stephens's full-bodied husband attempting to perform a range of amputee abilities. The absurdity and failure of these attempts playfully articulates a sort of full-bodied disablement.

We can read these videos together as performing the concept of 'misfit' described by Garland-Thomson (2011). She uses the term 'misfit' to describe how particular experiences of disability are situated in space and time where 'lack of fit' to the physical and social context lays bare our vulnerability and dependency. A misfit, then, refers to a circumstance or process in which embodiment brushes up against environment. Garland-Thomson invokes this framework to break down fixed and generic conceptions of disabled identity or the disabled body. Misfitting, like vulnerability and dependency, is a universal dimension of human experience. It is also a generative situation – it can initiate shifts in ethical understanding, open new analytic perspectives and can lead to new skills and innovative modes of responding to changing environments (Garland-Thomson, 2011). This generative capacity of a misfit is predicated on the productive openness and connection that vulnerability affords.

For reasons that might seem natural, fit and misfit are key recurring themes in AmputeeOT. Fit is a concern that comes up in many ways for new amputees – challenges of fit between a residual limb and a prosthesis; attending to the perspiration generated in a socket; the variety of mechanisms for adhering 'meat' to carbon fibre; fitting a prosthesis to high heels etc. Misfit also takes on a social and cultural valence for AmputeeOT. There is the misfit between things people say to amputees and how they feel and also the fit and misfit among amputees and devotees (people with a sexual preference for amputees). Stephens dedicates an episode to the complexity of her feelings about this. This variegated attention to how thing fit and do not is arguably one of the appeals of Stephens's vlog for an audience that extends beyond users of prostheses, their families, friends and clinicians.

In the following we turn our attention to the social media smartphone app POS REP that, like AmputeeOT, focuses on transition and adaptation to changes in ability. But POS REP is distinct in so far as it addresses a community whose implication in broader social anxiety around disablement produces experiences of vulnerability that potentially link those who are affected by very different forms of impairment (and aims to include those who do not identify as disabled). The app responds to needs for mutual care with attention to the particular ways that vulnerability is experienced spatially and temporally.

POS REP: Mediating veteran's vulnerability in public space

POS REP is a proximity-based smartphone social media app that is not explicitly designated as a forum for discussion of disability and vulnerability, however, the social space that it establishes is designed to produce the conditions which make such discussion more likely among veterans of US military service. We suggest that this is of particular significance given the prominent role that veterans have played in the history of US disability activism (Fleischer & Zames, 2012; Goodley, 2011). The situation of veterans continues to be central to contemporary discussions of disability within the US, especially as it responds to the increase in diagnoses of PTSD and traumatic brain injury (TBI) among returning veterans of recent wars in the Middle East and Central Asia. Our discussion of this app is focused on how the particular concerns that guided its design reflect insights into the potential for networked and mobile media to address uniquely vulnerable groups or communities. An important dimension of this analysis hinges on the observation that while opposing categories of abled/disabled are inscribed and maintained discursively and through diverse institutions, certain social groups experience elevated ambiguity with respect to this boundary. As POS REP is too new to reasonably assess the success of its implementation, our analysis engages the discourse of the designers and responses of early testers/adopters.

Anthony Allman and Jake Wood conceived and began development of POS REP after the suicide of Wood's friend and fellow Iraq War veteran Clay Hunt. POS REP is designed to address the problem of veteran suicides, which is estimated at 22 per day. Young male veterans are over four times more likely to die by suicide than their non-veteran peers (Gibbons, Brown, Hendricks & Hur, 2012). While suicide itself is not a disability, it is generally the result of living with untreated disabilities, especially mental disabilities (Tanielian & Jaycox, 2008). Military veterans have long held an important and sometimes problematic position in disability scholarship, advocacy/activism and medical research (Gerber, 2000). Being a highly visible demographic with an elevated incidence of disability, veterans' disablement carries political resonance inflecting the ways civilian populations understand war. Of course not all veterans are disabled, but veteran status often implies disability even if no disability is present or acknowledged. Growing public awareness of increased incidence of PTSD has reinforced this association (Wool, 2015). Arguably, cognitive and psychological disabilities convey a greater measure of stigma and social anxiety for veterans when compared with amputees and those with other physical disabilities. Veterans with PTSD are often portrayed as unpredictable and violent in popular media, and are sometimes accused of malingering by fellow soldiers (Hautzinger & Scandlyn, 2013).

The app's name, POS REP, is military shorthand for 'position report', used to inform other units of one's geographic position. This use of military jargon populates the app. POS REP's overall design, organisation and functionality engages modes of spatial and temporal regimentation of sociality familiar to military veterans. The app uses a smartphone's geo-location features to let users establish a variety of forms of contact with other nearby veterans. Wherever the user is, the RADAR function orients them to nearby veterans and veteran-specific resources within 50km (see Figure 12.3). FLARES allow users to share veterans-only events, alert them to personal crisis/needs or invite them to group opportunities/activities. And a real-time instant messaging feature allows group chatter within a close periphery. SQUADS helps veterans maintain connections across distance with members of their former military units. Finally, the SRB component allows users to view service records and badges, and is securely integrated with systems such as id.me to ensure the validity of users' identity and veteran status.

A unique aspect of POS REP's design is that it leverages social media technology to address the distinct opportunities for and values of various spatially and temporally situated relationships. Social media platforms often serve as a substitute for physical or proximal interactions. POS REP instead is framed as a platform to encourage and enable the movement between networked and face-to-face interactions. And this is conceived in relation to the affordance networked media can offer for discretion, security and confidentiality as important basis for mutual care. According to Allman, the idea behind POS REP is more than creating a social network: 'This is a social networking app, but primarily it is a health care app. The social network *is* the health care' (personal communication, February, 2014). Allman states that veterans meeting other veterans will assist in creating meaningful social networks based in shared experience that are essential for the management of PTSD, major depressive disorders and general feelings of isolation – all among the leading causes of suicide (Charuvastra & Cloitre, 2008).

The experiences of veterans after combat can be understood as an ontological transformation rather than pathology (Wool, 2015). We should examine their new senses of self and their relationships to their bodies, other people and their

Figure 12.3 Screen shot from pos-rep.com, POS REP, 2014

environment rather than how they might be 'damaged'. Part of veterans' ontological transformation is a new relationship to disability (physical, mental, unknown), whether experienced personally, apprehended empathically in relation to other veterans, or as implied through broader cultural perceptions of all veterans. Learning how to be a veteran entails adapting to this relationship with disability. Existing social networking platforms might contribute to establishing informal connections, but there are important reasons that a dedicated app can be more suited to the needs of veterans transitioning to civilian life and a transformed relationship to disability. Many veterans may not want to be public about their disabilities, especially PTSD, given its stigma. Others choose to be open about their disabilities regardless or even because of the stigma (Corrigan & Watson, 2002). Suicide ideation, too, is often concealed due to feelings of shame and fear of social repercussions. This negotiation of publicness, disability disclosure and vulnerability is an underlying concern that was central to the development of POS REP.

Allman's framing of the social network as healthcare invokes our earlier discussion of productive frameworks for engaging vulnerability and establishing interdependence. POS REP draws on the affective resonance of bonds created within the organisational structures of military service to encourage veterans to make connections within civilian space. The close-knit ties and interdependence found in military units has long been known to foster combat effectiveness, but the loss of these ties can leave veterans with a sudden interruption in social connection that can handicap their re-integration into civilian life (Braswell & Kushner, 2010). Lacking the network of close ties and facing problems of dealing with (for example) PTSD in the civilian world, a veteran may lack self-confidence and emotional resources required to face their problems. Veterans service organisations (VSOs) such as the American Legion and Veterans of Foreign Wars (VFW) have attempted to re-create these close ties through the establishment of 'halls' where members gather for meetings, parties or just meet for a drink. But traditional VSOs have not attracted substantial numbers of veterans from recent wars.

POS REP works by allowing veterans to make any space an ad hoc VSO hall rather than taking the halls of VSOs and putting them online. In their aims to create 'mobile veterans' halls', POS REP designers were faced with the importance of secure and confidential connections and therefore prioritised the challenges of making an app that could verify membership in the community of veterans. Veterans who initially tested the app wanted verification that other users were also veterans. Importantly, the hurdle of addressing this need provided a central insight into what the app could offer. Defining the community became the primary focus of the POS REP developers. If the insistence on 'verified users' might suggest a distrust of civilians, it is probably more productive to frame it in terms of how it builds upon trust in other veterans. This affordance of the app establishes a safe space, and signals the ability to be vulnerable.

The verified user function of POS REP shows that there is still a concern about people falsifying identity in networked and online spaces while attempting to mimic the membership requirements of the VSOs. Here, the design of POS REP as a circumscribed social media platform directly confronts the spectre of fictional identity raised by early theorists of the internet community discussed earlier. What has made VSOs successful historically has been bringing veterans into the same place at the same time. When a veteran enters a Legion or VFW hall, membership requirements assure them that everyone there is also a veteran.

This creates a space for informal discussions and frank conversations about wartime experiences and their effects on civilian life. These conversations can help teach veterans that emotional problems they face are also faced by others, thus normalising experiences of mental disability at least within the community of veterans. But these conversations only happen under specific circumstances – when veterans share the same space and are surrounded only by other veterans. Being *beside* other veterans is important for these conversations to happen. While the position of *beside* creates opportunities for vulnerability, it is a shared vulnerability that creates spaces for interdependence (Sedgwick, 2003). This does not mean that shared veteran status creates an even playing field – there will always be hierarchies and differences, but these are unsettled, constantly shifting and do not map onto previous hierarchies of the former military life. What POS REP does is enable users to create their own spaces that allow interdependence to emerge from shared vulnerabilities.

Communication amongst veterans creates a network of experiential knowledge in how to become a veteran. This network provides access to varied responses to life as a veteran and its entanglement with visible and invisible disability and social displacement. It also facilitates sharing hard-earned insights into navigating systems of social support including the byzantine workings of the Department of Veterans Affairs (DVA), something that cannot be transferred through a DVA pamphlet, website or the pre-separation briefing required of all soldiers. In creating proximate and immediate social networks, POS REP offers local knowledge of available services (official and not) that expand far beyond those of a national DVA database. Most importantly, the proximity and immediacy of these connections are what matters in moments of personal crisis, especially suicide ideation.

Conclusion

Drawing upon feminist care ethics and dependency theory, our analysis of these examples offered a conceptual basis for thinking through the intersections of social media and disability that complement approaches concerned with access and accommodation. A guiding concern of our inquiry, drawn from these philosophical projects, is that ableist culture and its dominant ethical perspectives are characterised by the disavowal of the fundamental precariousness of life. This refusal and stigmatising of vulnerability is coupled with an idealisation of autonomy and social equity that eclipses recognition of the predominantly unequal and (inter) dependent nature of social relationships. The fetishistic projection of vulnerability and dependency onto particular forms of embodiment underlies the binary categories of able-bodied/disabled that structure ableism. An ethics of vulnerability entails an engagement with vulnerability as constitutive of human life and sociality – both as a threatening and productive force – and calls for the envisioning practices that attend to diversity and instable distribution of ability, health and need. Our examination of examples of social media uses and forms focused on how they might contribute to cultural recognition of interdependency, act as a vector for new configurations of care, destabilise the division of abled/disabled and condition ethical responses to experiences of vulnerability. AmputeeOT and POS REP act in accordance with this ethic of care and ethics of vulnerability in their own distinct ways.

In AmputeeOT, Stephens embraces the vulnerabilities that accompanies adaptation to limb loss or congenital limb anomalies and investigates them as sites of productive opportunity. This recasting of vulnerability is addressed to amputees as well as full-bodied visitors to her vlog. Her direct engagement with the transitional experience of amputation offers a point of entry for full-bodied consideration of the instability of their embodiment. Often addressing comments or topics in her videos to 'full-limbed' viewers, she unsettles assumptions about normative ability. Thematically, her videos and accompanying discussion frame the experiences of limb differences as domains of creative rethinking about ability, lifestyle and relationships. Confronting the 'lack of fit' that shapes amputee's experience of vulnerability, AmputeeOT imagines prostheses as devises of wonder – probed for diverse forms of utility and aesthetic intervention, and not centrally as replacements.

POS REP also confronts the misfit experience of social dislocation in veterans' transition to civilian life. The increased prevalence of invisible disability such as PTSD within veteran populations has contributed to the incidence of suicide, and further implicated all veterans in disability identity. Within this context, an important aspect of what POS REP accomplishes is to mediate experiences of vulnerability by providing tools for navigating the public space and establish a connection within an empathetic community. Enabling a certain level of security for its users by ensuring veterans-only meet-ups outside of established VSOs, POS REP creates more opportunities for shared vulnerability and mutual care between veterans. Rather than substituting for physical encounters, the POS REP app creates opportunities for and encourages face-to-face meetings between veterans. Ensuring that users are verified veterans, the app helps users feel safer as they negotiate their publicness about disability.

Both AmputeeOT and POS REP provide platforms for envisioning and performing arrangements of care in expansive terms. AmputeeOT folds together Stephens's clinical/research expertise in occupational therapy with tacit knowledge and affective experience generated in her interactions with other amputees and people with limb anomalies. The open-ended sense of care that AmputeeOT spans is generated by slipping seamlessly between concerns as diverse as the technical aspects of prosthetic devices, some fashion opportunities, the language people use to describe residual limbs and the relationship of amputees to devotees. POS REP's designers' conception of their app as a form of 'healthcare' is predicated on the notion that intervention in PTSD and suicide prevention begins with establishing safe social connections. The resulting approach is a form of social network that facilitates interaction around shared experiences and needs while acknowledging the reality of veterans' potential isolation in public. For this reason, POS REP's use of social media is conceived to enable diverse possibilities situated and immediate forms of embodied connection.

References

Braswell, H., & Kushner, H. (2010). Suicide, social integration, and masculinity in the U.S. military. *Social Science & Medicine, 74*(4), 530–536.

Butler, J. (2004). *Precarious life: The power of mourning and violence.* New York: Verso.

Charuvastra, A., & Cloitre, M. (2008). Social bonds and posttraumatic stress disorder. *Annual Review of Psychology, 59*, 301–328.

Corrigan, P. W., & Watson, A. C. (2002). The paradox of self-stigma and mental illness. *Clinical Psychology: Science and Practice, 9*(1), 35–53.

Epstein, S. (1996). *Impure science: AIDS, activism, and the politics of knowledge.* Berkeley: University of California Press.

Fineman, M. (2008). The vulnerable subject: Anchoring equality in the human condition. *Yale Journal of Law and Feminism, 20*(1), 1–23.

Fleischer, D. Z., & Zames, F. (2012). *The disability rights movement: From charity to confrontation.* Philadelphia: Temple University Press.

Garland-Thomson, R. (2011). Misfits: A feminist materialist disability concept. *Hypatia: A Journal of Feminist Philosophy, 26*(3), 591–609.

Gerber, D. A. (Ed.). (2000). *Disabled veterans in history*. Ann Arbor: University of Michigan Press.

Gibbons, R., Brown, D., Hendricks, C., & Hur, K. (2012). Is the rate of suicide among veterans elevated? *American Journal of Public Health, 102*(S1), S17–S19.

Gilligan, C. (1982). *In a different voice*. Cambridge: Harvard University Press.

Gilson, E. (2011). Vulnerability, ignorance, and oppression. *Hypatia: A Journal of Feminist Philosophy, 26*(2), 308–332.

Goggin, G., & Newell, C. (2006). Disability, identity, and interdependence: ICTs and new social forms. *Information, Communication & Society, 9*(3), 309–311.

Goodley, D. (2011). *Disability studies: An interdisciplinary introduction*. London: SAGE Publication.

Hautzinger, S., & Scandlyn, J. (2013). *Beyond post-traumatic stress: Homefront struggles with the war on terror*. Walnut Creek: Left Coast Press.

Kittay, E. F. (1999). *Love's labor: Essays on women, equality and dependency*. New York: Routledge Press.

Kittay, E. F., & Feder, E. (Eds.). (2002). *The subject of care: Feminist perspectives on dependency*. Lanham, MD: Rowman and Littlefield Publishers.

McArthur, P., & Zavitsanos, C. (2013). Other forms of conviviality: The best and least of which is our daily care and the host of which is our collaborative work. *Women & Performance, 23*(1), 126–113.

Moser, I. (2006). Disability and the promises of technology: Technology, subjectivity and embodiment within an order of the normal. *Information, Communication & Society, 9*(3), 373–395.

Noddings, N. (1984). *Caring: A feminine approach to ethics and moral education*. Berkeley: University of California Press.

POS REP. (2014). POS REP (Version 1.1) [Mobile App]. Retrieved from: http://pos-rep.com/about/

Rapp, R., & Ginsburg, F. (2001). Enabling disability: Rewriting kinship, reimagining citizenship. *Public Culture, 13*(3), 533–556.

Sedgwick, E. K. (2003). *Touching feeling: Affect, pedagogy, performativity*. Durham: Duke University Press.

Shapiro, J. P. (1993). *No pity: People with disabilities forging a new civil rights movement*. New York: Times Books.

Shildrick, M. (2000). Becoming vulnerable: Contagious encounters and the ethics of risk. *Journal of Medical Humanities, 21*(4), 215–227.

Stephens, C. (2013, February – Present). AmputeeOT [Video blog]. Retrieved from https://www.youtube.com/user/AmputeeOT

Stone, A. R. (1991). Will the real body please stand up? Boundary stories about virtual cultures. In M. Benedikt (Ed.), *Cyberspace: First steps* (pp. 81–118). Cambridge: MIT Press.

Tanielian, T. L., & Jaycox, L. (Eds.). (2008). *Invisible wounds of war: Psychological and cognitive injuries, their consequences, and services to assist recovery*. Santa Monica, CA: RAND.

Turkle, S. (1984). *The second self: Computers and the human spirit*. Cambridge: MIT Press.

Turner, B. (2006). *Vulnerability and human rights*. University Park: Penn State University Press.

Wool, Z. H. (2015). *After war: The weight of life at Walter Reed*. Durham: uke University Press.

13 Social media and disability inclusion

Critical reflections of a Zimbabwean activist

Kudzai Shava

A personal beginning

17 October 2014: Here in Zimbabwe, it is quite difficult for us to access a lot of reading materials, particularly those that require subscription for access such as journal articles. Is [the article you suggest reading] a kind of resource you can email me as an attachment? If not, then I may not be able to access it. This is why it is so vital for us here in the Global South to collaborate with colleagues like you in the Global North where reading materials and other knowledge forms can be easily accessed.

1 November 2014: A devastating rainstorm ripped through the area I live in on Tuesday evening, destroying most houses including mine. I have lost most of my belongings which include my Braille printer, my computer, scanner and Braille and electronic reading materials, among other personal things. We were all moved to safety and were put up in classrooms at a school in the centre of town where we spent the night and on Wednesday, one of my friends took me in to live with his family, where I am now. I am utterly devastated and still in great shock. . . . Presently, the only information that I can retrieve is only through the emails I wrote you and the responses I got from you. With [my friend's] assistance I am determined to work on my book chapter (albeit using his computer which does not have a screen reader) which means he has to be helping with a little bit of proofreading.

8 December 2014: We have not had electricity for more than three weeks here where I am living with friends. I have to travel to a town 45 kilometres away to access the internet and it is very costly to get transport – hiring a taxi to and from the town where there is electricity. I therefore have resorted to coming here to the internet cafe twice per week – Monday and Friday. I have made significant progress on the chapter and will be sending you the draft for your help and input before I finalise it. I will try to send it this week, probably by Wednesday. I will have to travel to come here.

21 October 2015: As I said the other day, it is really difficult here but I am determined to finish this chapter. I had to request for a couple of days (Thursday and Friday) to be off from work and travelled 280km to come to Harare, the capital city, where there is slightly better access to electricity, so that I can finish this chapter.

9 November 2015: It is increasingly difficult to communicate with you through email as we are going through a hell of a time with electricity outages and no or limited internet connectivity where I live.

The editors of this collection, Katie Ellis and Mike Kent asked me to include these emails as a prequel to this chapter because they document my experiences as a person with vision impairment relying on assistive technology to undertake my work. They also parallel the plight of people with disabilities in Zimbabwe as they are denied access to information communications technology (ICT) despite the government having ratified the United Nations *Convention on the Rights of Persons with Disabilities* (CRPD) in 2013. Zimbabwe is beset with endemic problems related to poor access to information for all citizens, essential service infrastructure failures, and information technologies that are sparse. For a disabled person, these challenges are magnified!

This chapter encapsulates my reflections as a disability activist in Zimbabwe on the liberating potential of social media, but also raises a number of questions which need to be addressed. While social media represents great potential to people with disabilities in Zimbabwe, we must ask this question: to what extent has this group been able to embrace any new social media forms and advance disability inclusion? While some disability theorists note the potential for social media to address this marginalisation (see Alper & Haller, Chapter 10 this volume), others emphasise the potential for further exclusion (see Ellis & Kent, Chapter 1 and Hollier, Chapter 6 this volume). Throughout this chapter I argue that the characteristics of social media – participation, openness, conversation, community, and connectedness – are the very principles that disability social inclusion is built on. Blogs also play an important role in raising awareness of how social media can influence and improve lives for those with a disability However, this social inclusion cannot be realised when ICT is unavailable, inaccessible, and unaffordable.

The chapter proceeds from John Naisbitt's (1982) observation that 'the new source of power is not money in the hands of a few, but information in the hands of many' (p. 7). The advent of social media and its evident global proliferation embodies Nasbitt's prediction – no other communication platform allows the ordinary individual to generate and disseminate, at times almost instantaneously, one's ideas, thoughts, viewpoints, and information to a wide and diversified audience as social media does. Indeed, no other communication platform has the ability to put information, and ultimately power, in the hands of many as social media. However, it is important to see where this places Zimbabwean disabled people.

People with disability in Zimbabwe

Estimating the extent of people with disabilities living in Zimbabwe is unreliable. Much depends upon what is considered a disability, hence the figures are dynamic (Choruma, 2006; Mugumbate & Nyoni, 2013; Viriri & Makurumidze, 2014). As Mugumbate and Mtetwa (2014) note: 'Disability is a highly contested concept varying in definition, understanding and interpretation within and across cultural boundaries' (p. 145). This section of the population is estimated to be approximately three million (Viriri & Makurumidze, 2014), with 70% living in rural areas, and around 300,000 being HIV positive (Chakuchichi, Chitura & Gandari, 2011).

Precise statistics aside, what is clear is that from pre-colonial Zimbabwe to date, disabled people have been marginalised and treated as second-class citizens, deemed passive, economically unproductive, and a burden on the community (Chataika, 2007; Mandipa & Manyatera, 2014; Mpofu, 2000; Mutepfa, Mpofu & Chataika, 2007; Viriri & Makurumidze, 2014). An indigenous Zimbabwean conception of disability equates disability with inability and considers a disabled person as the borderline between a human being and an animal (Chataika, 2007; Choruma, 2006; Devlieger, 1998). As a result, disabled people have, for a long time, been perceived by society as lacking clear social role functions. As Eide, Khupe and Mannan, (2014) argue:

> Even during these modern times indigenous people still use culture to justify discrimination against persons with disabilities. In Zimbabwe, cultural reasons are often used successfully as convenient tools to oppress persons with disability and deny their rights. Although there have been nominal positive change as a result of campaigns to stop certain cultural practices that sustain discrimination against disabled persons, some oppressive aspects of culture are still intact.
>
> (p. 79)

Disabled Zimbabweans – income, employment, and quality of life

Statistically, disabled Zimbabweans are more likely to be unemployed, illiterate, have less formal education, have less access to support networks, and have less disposable social capital. In addition, tolerance of people with disabilities has also tended to diminish sharply during periods of economic hardship (Choruma, 2006). This lack of income security results in financial hardship, meaning disabled people and their families 'live in rented squalid, crowded and unclean conditions' with limited access to reliable electricity and therefore, specifically in the context of this chapter, reduced access to ICT and social media (Moyo & Nkomo, 2014, p. 900).

Despite this bleak situation, studies show that disabled people have a higher rate of *self-employment* than people without disabilities. Many of the barriers to self-employment are faced by people with disabilities and non-disabled people alike. However, despite this, the overall economic situation, and therefore quality of life, of the majority of disabled Zimbabweans is poor. Somewhat paradoxically, while disabled Zimbabweans spearheaded many of the disability rights changes in Africa – it was the first country to adopt disability-related legislation (Manatsa, 2015, p. 25) – today, Moyo suggests that 'the quality of life of PWDs [sic] in Zimbabwe has never taken off the ground as compared to other countries' (Moyo & Nkomo, 2014, p. 901). This reduced quality of life is also apparent in the reduced access to ICT and, significantly, social media.

While social media has been recognised for empowering people with disability (see Broadband Commission for Digital Development et al., 2013; Chadwick,Wesson & Fullwood 2013; Chari, 2013; Ellis & Goggin 2015; Haller,

Dorries & Rahn, 2006; Tollefsen et al., 2010; Viluckiene, 2015), the situation in Zimbabwe is not so straightforward. Unavailability, inaccessibility, and unaffordability of ICT as well as costly internet connectivity in Zimbabwe are major hindrances in an already stressed economic climate characterised by a frighteningly rapid decline. As a number of disability theorists observe, for disabled people, particularly in the global south, the need for survival takes precedence over everything else (Choruma, 2006; Stone, 1999):

The United Nations Convention on The Rights of People with Disability (CRPD): Its impact on disabled Zimbabweans

The availability of social media for disabled Zimbabweans cannot be conceived outside the framework of the United Nations CRPD. The CRPD constitutes a commitment of the international community to the inclusion of the disability perspective and persons with disabilities in all aspects of development. Not only does it hold great potential for the equalisation of opportunities for people with disabilities, it provides a roadmap to disability inclusion and for the removal of the multifaceted barriers that perpetuate disability exclusion in all aspects of life. Zimbabwe acceded to the CRPD on 23 September 2013 (United Nations, 2015).

However, as some commentators observe, 'the optimism surrounding the CRPD in particular may have a bleak flipside, that is, the celebration of good policies with no effect on the lives of persons with disabilities, in particular in poor contexts where the gap between policy and reality is most pronounced (Eide, Khupe & Mannan, 2014, p. 78). This is particularly so given that Zimbabweans are ignorant of the legislation and policies due to limited exposure to, and education on, these instruments (Choruma, 2006, p. 11).

Article 9 of the CRPD refers to 'Accessibility' and places obligations on the state to enable people with disabilities to live independently and participate fully in all aspects of life:

> States Parties shall take appropriate measures to ensure to persons with disabilities access, on an equal basis with others, to the physical environment, to transportation, to information and communications, including information and communications technologies and systems, and to other facilities and services open or provided to the public, both in urban and in rural areas.

The Convention further calls on States to promote other appropriate forms of assistance and support to persons with disabilities to ensure their access to information; promote access for persons with disabilities to new information and communications technologies and systems, including the internet; and promote the design, development, production, and distribution of accessible information and communications technologies and systems at an early stage, so that these technologies and systems become accessible at minimum cost.

ICT access in Zimbabwe: Availability, accessibility, and ability

However, despite this seeming willingness to accept the ideas behind CRPD, the state parties' level of CRPD ICT availability, accessibility, and affordability compliance by countries in the global south is, at best, far below the levels of the countries in the global north and, at worst, non-existent. While these are issues for all Zimbabweans, for those already marginalised by disability and reduced income, the issues become magnified.

With regards to availability, the low CRPD ICT compliance rate of 30% for low-per-capita income countries and 83% for high-per-capita income countries (Broadband Commission for Digital Development et al., 2013) suggests a low availability of social media in the global south; ICT is a critical enabler of social media. The report on *The high-level meeting on disability and development* of the 68th session of the United Nations General Assembly (2013) notes that the use of ICTs is deeply woven into the fabric of society and has become a crucial element of any personal development/empowerment as well as an institutional framework for inclusive social progress and economic growth. In addition, it further observes that even with this positive force of transformation, key challenges should be addressed if persons with disabilities are to fully benefit from the use of ICTs.

Accessibility is also an issue. The unstable and mono-political scene in Zimbabwe means that information to the general public is severely restricted which, according to some lawyers, suggests that 'access to information is not seen as a right but a privilege that government officials dispense at will' (African Network of Constitutional Lawyers, 2012, p. 5). This means that not only disabled people, but for Zimbabweans generally, there is a lack of awareness 'of their right to access information and the procedure of requesting information from government departments.' As the Magamba Network observed in 2014:

> Zimbabwe finds itself in an interesting space. On the one hand expression is still not free and the media space is polarised. On the other hand we see the rapid expansion of the Internet access across the country and the fact that Zimbabwe has the second highest mobile broadband penetration in Africa.
>
> (p. 2)

Finally, improved ICT access in Zimbabwe is also characterised by affordability aspects, including not only monetary constraints, but also location and even gender. Although the cost of phones and browsing fees continue to exclude the poor, Chiweshe (2011) argues that 'cyberspace has become an important political space in urban Zimbabwe however the majority of people are resident in the rural areas. Rural areas have serious challenges including network coverage and lack of electricity.'

Social media and disability in Zimbabwe

When ICTs are available, accessible, and affordable, they significantly improve the Zimbabwean disabled population's access to all aspects of society and development, thereby enabling and accelerating their social and economic inclusion (Chakuchichi, Chitura & Gandari, 2011; Magamba Network, 2014). This is particularly the case when using ICT to access social media sites. According to Hollier (2012), the ascendancy of social media as a quintessential mode of communication is evidenced by its rapid growth, a shift toward using social media on mobile devices, the emergence of new accessibility options, an increasing reliance on social media to communicate and achieve everyday tasks, and international shifts towards seeing social media as a democratic tool with strong potential for social inclusion. These ideas relate to the aforementioned characteristics of social media – participation, openness, conversation, community, and connectedness – which are discussed in a later section. Harnessing the full potential of social media would result in immense economic, social, and political benefits for disabled people in Zimbabwe.

Participation and openness – disability inclusion

The hallmark of disability inclusion is participation. The blurring of the line between the media and the audiences provides ample opportunity for people with disabilities to leverage the potential of social media through providing contributions and feedback on disability issues and the need for holistic disability inclusion in all spheres of life (see Ellis, Chapter 11 this volume). This openness that is a distinct feature of social media is also a barometer of disability inclusion. In addition to being open to feedback and participation, most social media services encourage voting, comments, and the sharing of information.

Conversation, connectedness, and community

Conversation is another crucial characteristic of both social media and disability advocacy. Conversation already plays a primary role amongst disabled people, their families and friends as the *Gallup Poll of 2012* indicates:

> Zimbabwe's restrictive media environment and limited access to media devices in many places help explain the importance of word-of-mouth as a source of news and information. Just over 7 in 10 Zimbabweans (71.9%) say they get news from friends or family at least weekly.
>
> (Gallup, 2012, p. 1)

Harnessing social media for a reciprocal conversation allows advocates to engage in constructive conversations on disability inclusion. Social media presents itself as a communication platform with great potential for sharing disability viewpoints, ideas, challenges, and aspirations. Most kinds of social media thrive on their connectedness, making use of links to other sites, resources, and people. This characteristic of community is central to disability inclusion. Disability activists such as Abraham Mateta and Edmore Masendeke embrace social media's ability to allow communities to form quickly and communicate effectively around common interests (see Haller et al., 2006; Magamba Network, 2014). Social media offers great scope for the advancement of disability as a shared common interest in Zimbabwe. It allows people with disabilities to make strategic use of links to other sites, resources, and people (Ellis, 2014; Haller et al., 2006).

The use of blogs to promote disability issues

As other chapters in this volume illustrate, blogs remain a popular form of social media amongst the disability community (see Ryan & Julian, Chapter 3; Bundon, Chapter 18; and Masschelein & Van Goidsenhoven, Chapter 19 this volume). Two examples of blogs established by Zimbabwean disability activists for the purposes of enlightening the public about disability rights are mukoma-a.blogspot. com and http://disabilityzimbabwe.blogspot.com.au. Abraham Mateta runs a blog with dedicated disability content and a raunchy analysis:

> One of the serious challenges which we have in Zimbabwe is that of negative attitudes against persons with disabilities. It is however, not necessarily Zimbabwean to be anti-disability as we have a lot of Shona and Ndebele proverbs warning against such behaviour. The main root of disability discrimination and underdevelopment is lack of information. It is therefore instructive for any strategist to take advantage of the new position of madam Mupfumira to ensure that she influences the dissemination of disability awareness. The state papers and broadcasters in particular must be obliged to give more space to regular and acceptable disability content. Zimbabwean disability rights activists would benefit from remembering that Article 8 of the UN Convention on the Rights of Persons with disabilities (CRPD) to which Zimbabwe is party, requires state parties to raise awareness on disability issues.
>
> (Mateta, 2015)

Meanwhile Edmore Masendeke runs a Twitter site with 261 followers. Edmore is the Founder/Executive Director of Endless Possibilities, an economist at the Reserve Bank of Zimbabwe, a poet, and blogger of disability issues. Edmore has used Twitter to link up with his blogger site http://disabilityzimbabwe.blogspot.com.au/ titled: *The diary of a disability advocate, alive, able, active* where he has posted essays about disability socio-political issues such as the quintessential essay; *Able-bodied people only: The nexus between race discrimination* (Masendeke, 2015b):

> Prejudice is embedded in the walls of our cities. Admittedly disabled people, being ten per cent of the population, are a minority constituency but then modern society and the very essence of democracy ensures that even minorities are given equal opportunities and access to facilities and benefits. Everybody deserves equal access to everything that our cities have to offer and all our

societies should, from now on, design, renovate and build our cities in ways that allow accessibility to everyone, most notably the disabled among us. In the words of Mahatma Ghandi, 'A Nation's greatness is measured by how it treats its weakest members'.

(Masendeke, 22 October 2015b)

And this extract from 'What makes people with disabilities invisible?' (Masendeke, 2015a):

Let me end this post by asking you to interrogate yourself. Ask yourself whether you see persons with disabilities as equals or lesser beings as reflected in your attitudes and actions. Also ask yourself if you believe that discrimination against persons with disabilities is something that you regard to be socially unacceptable behaviour as reflected in your attitudes and actions. Finally, ask yourself whether you have attitudes and behaviours that you would like to change or adopt in your life as a statement to say I see persons with disabilities as equals and discrimination against persons with disabilities is something that I regard to be socially unacceptable behaviour.

(Masendeke, 14 August 2015a)

These blogs and Facebook pages project a significantly different image of disability than the one offered by the media in Zimbabwe. Stereotyped assumptions about people with impairments are predominantly based on superstition, myths, and beliefs. These are inherent to our culture and persist partly because they are constantly reproduced through the communications media (see Barnes, 1991). The media has focused on portraying disability as impairment through the influence of the medical model of disability which perceives disabled people's inability to interact in 'normal' daily life is a direct result of their physical, sensory, and/ or mental impairments. The reduced availability of social media to disabled people in Zimbabwe further diminishes the capacity of this group to use their disability advocacy competencies in fostering disability inclusion. Choruma sharply criticises the consequences of this problem:

there is lack of information about disabilities in Zimbabwe; outdated disability policies continue to influence decision making processes such as underfunding and purposefully making the national body of the disabled people invisible or dysfunctional and fragmented.

(Choruma, cited in Moyo & Nkomo, 2014, p. 901)

Indeed, it is argued here that the aforementioned three main barriers to ICT access – availability, accessibility, and affordability – also resonate when discussing social media access.

Social media access in Zimbabwe: Availability, accessibility and affordability

Availability of social media

In Zimbabwe, the majority of the approximately three million people with disabilities are largely excluded from using ICTs and their myriad of applications and services, particularly social media sites. This can have ramifications in many areas, including in education, political life, cultural activities, e-government, or e-health to cite a few examples (African Network of Constitutional Lawyers, 2012; Chakuchichi, Chitura & Gandari, 2011; Mugumbate & Mtetwa, 2014). The *ICT Opportunity for an Inclusive Development Framework* (Broadband Commission for Digital Development et al., 2013) notes that being excluded from these ICT-enabled applications such as social media sites implies being shut out not only from the information society, but also from accessing essential public services, as well as from the opportunity of living an independent life.

Accessibility of social media: The use of assistive technologies

Allied to the limited availability of the internet and social media is the issue of accessible assistive technologies. For people with disabilities, screen readers, speech recognition, video communication (for sign language communication and video relay interpretation), voice to text services (open and closed captioning, both real-time and embedded) and visual assistance (Chakuchichi et al., 2011) actually make ICTs – and specifically social media sites and apps – useable for people with disability. Where these accessible features are not embedded into the computers, people with disabilities have to go to extra lengths to acquire these technologies, a tall order in Zimbabwe considering per capita income constraints.

The lack of policies which would foster widespread availability of accessible ICTs is also a seemingly perennial impediment which disabled Zimbabweans have to grapple with. It appears that there is no sufficient political will on the part of the government to put in place such legislative mechanisms which would ensure that appropriate ICTs and assistive technologies are available to disabled people in order for them to ordinarily access social media (Choruma, 2006; Moyo, 2015; Mpofu & Shumba, 2013; Mugumbate & Nyoni, 2013). As Thandeka Moyo, writing for *The Chronicle*, puts it, 'in low-income countries, including Zimbabwe, there is inadequate information on disability, translating to limited information on which to base advocacy, policy development and effective resource mobilisation and utilisation' (Moyo, 2015).

Furthermore, assistive technologies or embedded accessibility features in commodity products might still remain unused as there is a lack of experts and rehabilitation professionals trained in the use of these technologies and features. Basic mobile phones have proved invaluable in providing a means of on-demand communication for users with disabilities through both SMS and voice calls (African Network of Constitutional Lawyers, 2012; Gallup, 2012; Chiweshe, 2011). They have evidently had the greatest impact on independent living for them, but this is as far as it goes. Most disabled people, including those in rural Zimbabwe, own just very simple mobile phones which only enable them to make calls and text messages – they do not facilitate easy social media access.

At a more sophisticated level, smartphones address the unique sensory, physical, and cognitive needs of customers with disabilities (Broadband Commission for Digital Development et al., 2013). Customers can enjoy open or closed-captioned multimedia content and use face-to-face video chat applications or dedicated video relay services to communicate via sign language. They are also able to access content non-visually – through screen-reading applications and customised alert settings using a combination of audible, visual, and vibration alerts – and take advantage of voice-commands, adjustable font sizes, predictive text, and a range of other innovative features, accessories, and third-party applications.

By providing access to a wide array of computing functions, smartphones also exhibit social media capability and its attendant advantages of promoting the inclusion of persons with disabilities in healthcare, primary and secondary education, tertiary, professional and lifelong learning, employment, and government services (Broadband Commission for Digital Development et al., 2013; Mukundu, 2006). However, only a few disabled people can afford these smartphones, given that most of them are vulnerable and are the poorest of the poor.

Affordability of social media

This unaffordability of ICTs and assistive technologies as key 'enablers' and 'facilitators' of social media can be understood from the perspective of the narrative that poverty is both the cause and consequence of disability (Choruma, 2006; Stone, 1999). For disabled persons in Zimbabwe, and indeed in many other low-income countries, their 'hierarchy of needs' logically places their survival above all else, not least above communication devices and social media. The prohibitive cost of assistive technologies, which is comprised of the cost of the technology as well as the cost of assistive technology assessment, training, and support services, is still a significant barrier that prevents persons with disabilities from fully accessing healthcare, education, and employment – or, put another way, living independently.

Challenges for the future?

This chapter sought to highlight the fact that despite the proliferation and the ubiquitous impact of social media in accelerating social, economic, and political development, the unavailability, inaccessibility and unaffordability of ICT devices, which are critical enablers of social media, only serve to hinder the participation of the socially and economically marginalised Zimbabwean disabled people in the optimum utilisation of social media.

My personal experience of losing my assistive devices, ICTs, and resource materials in a flood, coupled with the high financial costs of accessing ICTs hundreds of kilometres from my home, to ultimately being unable to communicate with the editors of this book via email, were documented at the beginning of this chapter. These show that, for disabled people, access to social media in Zimbabwe relies on a complex mix of availability, accessibility, and affordability.

Despite the gains made by individual disabled bloggers such as Abraham Mateta and Edmore Masendeke, the potential and impact of social media in ensuring access to economic and social activities, and in promoting the inclusion of persons with disabilities in healthcare, education, employment, and government services, is regrettably diminished when ICT is unavailable, inaccessible, and unaffordable. Much depends upon the Zimbabwean government's commitment to implement legislative reform that is congruent with the CRPD and to rollout a social policy action plan (Mugumbate & Nyoni, 2013). Chakuchichi et al. (2011) have noted the necessity for routine information presentation and mass campaigns on the part of service providers and the disability rights movement. Information is the staple of freedom, and ICTs, particularly in the form of social media, are essential for growing a diverse Zimbabwean culture that values information dissemination and dialogue.

References

African Network of Constitutional Lawyers. (2012). *National study on access to information in Zimbabwe*. Cape Town, SA: African Network of Constitutional Lawyers.
Barnes, C. (1991). Discrimination: Disabled people and the media. *Contact*, 70 Winter, 45–48.
Broadband Commission for Digital Development, G3ict, IDA, ITU, Microsoft, the Telecentre.org Foundation or UNESCO. (2013). *The ICT opportunity for a disability-inclusive development framework: Synthesis report of the high level meeting on disability and development of the 68th session of the United Nations General Assembly*. September 2013. Retrieved from https://www.itu.int/en/action/accessibility/Documents/The%20 ICT%20Opportunity%20for%20a%20Disability_Inclusive%20Development%20 Framework.pdf
Chadwick, D., Wesson, C., & Fullwood, C. (2013). Internet access by people with intellectual disabilities: Inequalities and opportunities *Future Internet*, 5, 376–397.
Chakuchichi, D., Chitura, M., & Gandari, E. (2011). Mitigating the impact of HIV & AIDS on people with disabilities through equitable information dissemination, Zimbabwe. *International Journal of Open & Distance Learning*, 1(1), 18–24.
Chari, T. (2013). New communication technologies and journalism ethics in Zimbabwe: Practices and malpractices. *Online Journal of Communication and Media Technologies*, 3(2) April, 112–136.
Chataika, T. (2007). *Inclusion of disabled students in higher education in Zimbabwe: From idealism to reality*. Unpublished Thesis. University of Sheffield, UK.
Chiweshe, M. (2011). *Social networks as antirevolutionary forces: Facebook and political apathy among youth in urban Harare, Zimbabwe*. Chinhoyi, Zimbabwe: Centre for Development Studies, Chinhoyi University of Technology.
Choruma, T. (2006). *The forgotten tribe: People with disabilities in Zimbabwe*. Progressio Report, London: Catholic Institute of International Relations.
Devlieger, P. J. (1998). Physical "disability" in Bantu languages: Understanding the relativity of classification and meaning. *International Journal of Rehabilitation Research*, 21, 51–62.

Eide, A. H., Khupe, W., & Mannan, H. (2014). Development process in Africa: Poverty, politics and indigenous knowledge. *African Journal of Disability*, 3(2).

Ellis, K. (2014). The voice Australia (2012): Disability, social media and collective intelligence. *Continuum: Journal of Media & Cultural Studies*, 28(4), 482–494.

Ellis, K., & Goggin, G. (2015). *Disability and the media*. London, United Kingdom: Palgrave Macmillian.

Gallup. (2012). *Zimbabwe media use 2012*. Washington, DC, USA: Broadcasting Board of Governors.

Haller, B., Dorries, B., & Rahn, J. (2006). Media labelling versus the US disability community identity: A study of shifting cultural language. *Disability and Society*, 21(1), 61–75.

Hollier, S. (2012). *Sociability: Social media for people with disability report*. Sydney: Media Access Australia.

Magamba Network. (2014). *Hashtags & freedom: A report on new media, citizen journalism & technology in Zimbabwe and beyond*. Harare, Zimbabwe: Magamba Network and Free Press.

Manatsa, P. (2015). Are disability laws in Zimbabwe compatible with the provisions of the United Nations Convention on the Rights of Persons with Disabilities (CRPD)? *International Journal of Humanities and Social Science Invention*, 4(4), 25–34.

Mandipa, E., & Manyatera, G. (2014). Zimbabwe. *African disability rights yearbook, 2014*(2), 287–306.

Masendeke, E. (2015a, August 14). What makes people with disabilties invisible? *The Diary of a Disability Advocacte, Alive, Able, Active*. Retrieved from http://disabilityzimbabwe.blogspot.com.au/2015/08/what-makes-people-with-disabilities.html

Masendeke, E. (2015b, October 22). Able-bodied people only: The nexus between race discrimination. *The Diary of a Disability Advocacte, Alive, Able, Active*. Retrieved from http://disabilityzimbabwe.blogspot.com.au/2015/10/able-bodied-people-only-nexus-between.html?spref=tw

Mateta, A. (2015, July 28). Disability rights with Abraham. [Blog]. *Hail Madam Mupfumira*. Retrieved from http://mukoma-a.blogspot.com.au/search?updated-min=2015–01–01T00:00:00–08:00&updated-max=2016–01–01T00:00:00–08:00&max-results=6

Moyo, T. (2015, March 18). 900K Zimbabweans disabled: Survey. *The Chronicle*. Retrieved from http://www.chronicle.co.zw/900k-zimbabweans-disabled-survey/

Moyo, W., & Nkomo, T. (2014). A comparative analysis of the effectiveness of organisations of people with disabilities and organisations for people with disabilities in advocacy and outreach. *Scholars Journal of Arts, Humanities and Social Sciences*, 2(6A), 900–908.

Mpofu, E. (2000). Rehabilitation in international perspective: A Zimbabwean experience. *Disability and Rehabilitation*, 23, 481–489.

Mpofu, J., & Shumba, A. (2013). Disabilities and entrepreneurship in Makonde rural community in Zimbabwe. *Studies of Tribes and Tribunals*, 11(2), 135–144.

Mugumbate, J., & Mtetwa, E. (2014). People with disabilities in Zimbabwe. In A. Nyanguru & C. Nyoni (Eds.). *Promoting social work for Zimbabwe's development* (p. 143). Bindura Town: Bindura University Press.

Mugumbate, J., & Nyoni, C. (2013). Disability in Zimbabwe under the new constitution: Demands and gains of people with disabilities. *Southern Peace Review Journal*, 2(2) September, 178–195.

Mukundu, R. (2006). *Zimbabwe research findings and conclusions*. African Media Development Initiative, London: BBC World Service Trust.

Mutepfa, M. M., Mpofu, E., & Chataika, T. (2007). Inclusive education practices in Zimbabwe: Curriculum, family and policy issues. *Childhood Education*, 83, 342–346.

188   *Kudzai Shava*

Naisbitt, J. (1982). *Megatrends: Ten new directions transforming our lives*. New York, NY: Warner Books.
Stone, E. (1999). *Disability and development: Learning from action and research on disability in the majority world*. Leeds: Disability Press.
Tollefsen, M., Øystein D., Berg, M., & Nordby, R. (2010). *Connected! A paper about the disabled and the use of social media*. Translation (from Norwegian): Catherine Kalvenes. Retrieved from http://www.medialt.no/pub/info_pdf/status_social_media_2010_english.pdf
United Nations. (2015). United nations treaty collection: Chapter IV human rights, 15. *Convention on the Rights of Persons with Disabilities*. Retrieved from https://treaties.un.org/Pages/ViewDetails.aspx?src=TREATY&mtdsg_no=iv-15&chapter=4&lang=en
Viluckiene, J. (2015). The relationship between online social networking and offline social participation among people with disability in Lithuania. *Procedia – Social and Behavioral Sciences*, 185 May, 453–459.
Viriri, P., & Makurumidze, S. (2014). Engagement of disabled people in entrepreneurship programmes in Zimbabwe. *Journal of Small Business and Entrepreneurship Development*, 2(1), 1–30.

Part IV
Education

14 Opportunities for eLearning, social media and disability

Mike Kent

Introduction

This chapter looks at the potential for social media, and specifically Facebook, to be used to provide greater accessibility for people with disabilities to online or eLearning, particularly in a tertiary environment. It begins by providing a brief overview of the developing area of eLearning and its potential appeal and utility for people with disabilities. It will then look at the potential for social media and specifically the social networking site Facebook – how it could play an effective role in an online tertiary learning environment, both as an important social space and also as an effective tool in the formal learning and teaching process. The final section of this chapter will then look at a specific case study regarding students with disabilities who were studying fully online through Open Universities Australia (OUA). The students were surveyed to determine the accessibility of different online platforms they used in their learning and teaching, and specifically to compare the largest of the formal online learning management systems, Blackboard, with Facebook. It was found that, in addition to the latter being more accessible to these students with disabilities than Blackboard overall, this was also the case in seven of the eight broad impairment categories that the survey explored. The chapter then concludes with a brief discussion of the implications of the findings for the development of accessible online learning environments for people with disabilities.

eLearning and higher education: An overview

Using the internet as a tool for higher education has been around almost as long as the world wide web itself, with recorded lectures being placed online since the late 1990s (Williams, 2006) and the Blackboard learning management system launching in 1997. Over the last 15 years in particular this area has undergone rapid growth relative to the rest of the higher education sector (Allen & Seaman, 2014; Sugar, Martindale, & Crawley, 2007; Waits & Lewis, 2003). Allen and Seaman (2014) observed that in 2012 more than one in three students in the United States were studying at least one class online. eLearning can involve students studying fully online away from campus or in a blended environment where elements of learning take place in a more traditional classroom or lecture theatre environment while other elements occur online. eLearning can take place using dedicated learning management systems, such as Blackboard or Moodle; web-based lecture systems, such as Lectopia or Echo 360, and, more recently, massive open online courses (MOOCs) such as edX and Coursera. It can also utilise other online platforms, particularly from social media sites such as YouTube, Facebook and Twitter.

People with disabilities, higher education and eLearning

People with disabilities have been, and continue to be, under-represented in higher education. While people with disabilities in Australia are approximately 18.5 per cent of the population (Australia Bureau of Statistics, 2013), Sachs and Schreuer (2011) estimated the number of students with disabilities studying in higher educa-tion at between 8 per cent and 14 per cent in both the United States and the United Kingdom. Specifically in Australia this number has been reported as being as low as 4 per cent (Ellis, 2011). However, Madaus, Banerjee and Merchant (2011) have observed that the numbers of students with disabilities enrolling in higher educa-tion is increasing, and Fichten et al. (2009) note the role of eLearning services in promoting inclusion for this group in this environment.

Many of the eLearning tools that are used to support this form of learning and teaching were originally designed to assist students with disabilities (Williams, 2006). There are a number of advantages to studying online for students with disabilities. These advantages revolve around three areas: accessibility, flexibil-ity and disclosure (see Kent, 2015a). Both Dobransky and Hargittai (2006) and Guo, Bricout and Huang (2005) detailed how eLearning can reduce the barriers normally faced in the physical university environment for students with disabili-ties, and increase their independence and self-determination. Difficult-to-access lecture theatres and laboratories can be avoided, as can potentially inaccessible commutes to and from a physical campus – even library services can be accessed from a student's home. As Leaver (2014) found, social aspects of campus life can also be reinterpreted online.

Similarly, students who might have fluctuating impacts from a range of different impairments, or who might require more time to spend on different activities can also manage their learning at their own pace. Recorded lectures and asynchronous online tutorial discussions can be accessed when convenient for the student and group discussions can be managed via discussion boards and emails (see Heijstra & Rafnsdottir, 2010).

Finally, students have a lot more control over the disclosure of their disability. Both Roberts, Crittenden and Crittenden (2011) and Sachs and Schreuer (2011) observed the value placed in this by students, with many prepared to forgo access to inaccessible online materials rather than disclose that they had a disability. This control extends to both the faculty and also to fellow students.

While there can be seen to be many advantages to online learning for students with disabilities, there are also potential pitfalls. Online spaces for teaching and learning can be constructed in a way that is not accessible. Kelly (2009) and Van de Bunt-Kokhuis and Bolger (2009) identified online content that was inaccessible for many students with disabilities. Some documents were formatted in a way that prevents access through assistive technology such as screen readers or Braille tablets, videos were uploaded without captions or audio files were presented with no written transcript. The actual learning environments themselves, such as online chatrooms, were also sometimes constructed in ways that made them inaccessible to some students (Van de Bunt-Kokhuis & Bolger, 2009). This inaccessibility is rarely a deliberate feature, but rather a side effect of a lack of thought around accessibility in this type of environment (see McRae, Chapter 16 this volume). It can extend beyond the formal learning and teaching platforms and can, in some circumstances, start to make aspects of a university's physical campus and social life less accessible (see Ellis & Kent, 2014).

This lack of awareness and corresponding lack of accessibility is compounded by the relative invisibility of students with disabilities in an eLearning environment. Students studying fully online might not meet their lecturers face to face until their graduation ceremony. The reluctance of students to disclose their disability – as identified by Roberts, Crittenden and Crittenden (2011) – serves to mask their existence, and this is exacerbated by the reluctance from students to ask for help when content is provided in an inaccessible way. This invisibility only increases the importance of questions about accessibility in this environment.

Social media, Facebook and eLearning

Universities are increasingly making use of social media platforms – both informally by staff and students and also as a dedicated place for official communications, learning and teaching. These can include Facebook, Twitter, Skype, YouTube and other online networks and web 2.0 applications (see Baran, 2010; Kent & Leaver, 2014; Tay & Allen, 2011). Facebook in particular has been explored as a place for both informal and formal interaction. Facebook offers a number of potential advantages as a place for learning and teaching (see also Collinson & Barden, Chapter 17 this volume). It provides a platform that students can access more readily and is already integrated with their lives, promotes a place where learning communities can be developed, and offers significant advantages over traditional learning management systems such as Blackboard. It therefore has the potential to transform the way that learning occurs.

Grey, Lucas and Kennedy (2010) noted that Facebook is easier to use than more traditional learning management systems. A number of researchers have noted Facebook's value as a place where students can come together to collaborate and form learning communities (Cluett, 2010; Ellison, Steinfield, & Lampe, 2007; Grey, Lucas, & Kennedy, 2010), particularly for a geographically-dispersed student body (Bateman & Willems, 2012). Students accessed Facebook more often than traditional learning management systems (Bateman & Willems, 2012) and the level of online student activity is significantly increased (Kent 2013; Schroeder & Greenbowe, 2009). Mazman and Usluel (2010) found that Facebook provides greater opportunity for personal communications and personal profiles than a traditional learning management system. By comparison Gao, Zhang and Franklin (2013) noted that the threaded discussion forums used in Blackboard and Moodle are not well suited to fostering effective online discussions.

McLaughlin and Lee (2010) observed of Facebook that 'Used appropriately, these tools can shift control to the learner, through promoting learner agency, autonomy and engagement in social networks that straddle multiple real and virtual learning spaces independent of physical, geographic, institutional and organisational boundaries' (p. 28). This is supported by Kayri and Çakir (2010) who found that, with the use of Facebook, learning was increasingly shaped by students – they also started to develop lesson materials. Similarly, my own research has found that Facebook facilitated an environment that encouraged both students and teaching staff to share resources, with students linking to material they found related to the topics being studied online and leading the discussion around them (Kent, 2013). In addition, other social media has been found to play an effective role as a platform for online learning and teaching, with Tade and Ondrey (2015) noting the value of YouTube in this context and Cheung, Chiu and Lee (2011), Kassens-Noor (2012) and Leaver (2012) all exploring the value of Twitter particularly as an informal learning tool.

However, there are also a number of criticisms of the use of social media as a formal learning and teaching space. A number of scholars have pointed to Facebook in particular as something that should be seen as a student-only space and one where students might resent the intrusion of teaching staff into what they might see as their private space (Best, Hajzler, Pancini, & Tout, 2011; Grey, Lucas, & Kennedy, 2010; Teclehaimanot & Hickman, 2011). Others have pointed to boundary and privacy problems for both staff and students that this platform potentially opens up (Raynes-Goldie & Lloyd, 2014). Further, there are issues regarding allowing a for-profit commercial enterprise to both have access to an essentially private learning conversation and to make money through its advertising from the delivery of higher education in this way (Croeser, 2014; Raynes-Goldie, 2012). While taking these objections and concerns into account, it may be that, following Palloff and Pratt (2009), 'The positive aspects of using these forms of technology, however, may outweigh the negatives' (p. 4).

Given these potential benefits for social media to be used as a platform for learning and teaching, questions of the accessibility of these platforms in this context need to be raised. For example, in 2010 Blackboard was awarded a non-visual accessibility gold certification by the National Federation of the Blind in the United States – the use of this platform will be discussed in more length, particularly in the context of it being able to be seen as a form of social media in its own right by Leanne McRae in Chapter 16 of this volume. This accreditation sets an important benchmark for accessibility in eLearning, particularly in the context of an area that has increasingly come under the focus of legislation to ensure access to learning technology for people with disabilities (Wentz, Jaeger, & Lazer, 2011). Scott Hollier also explores closely the accessibility of social media platforms and in particular the way that access to Facebook and other social media sites have improved over time (see Chapter 6 of this volume).

The following section in this chapter will look at the results of a comparative study on the accessibility of Blackboard and Facebook when used in an online learning and teaching environment. The study looks at students with disabilities in general and also the impact on specific types of impairments for students studying online.

The study: Access and barriers to online education for people with disabilities

This study explored the accessibility of different online platforms used in online learning and teaching by students with disabilities studying in higher education at OUA. OUA is an organisation that brings together online teaching from 15 different institutions under the OUA banner. In 2014, when this study was conducted, there were 42,898 students enrolled through the institution. Of these, 2,925 identified as having a disability and 1,480 had registered for disability support. This group was emailed an invitation to participate in a survey that explored issues of disclosure, accommodation and accessibility in relation to the online learning and teaching platforms used by the various teaching institutions (for full details of this study see Kent, 2016). A total of 226 students responded to this invitation. OUA asks students to identify as having one of eight different categories of impairment when they enrol – mental illness, medical, mobility, hearing, learning, vision, acquired brain impairment and intellectual disability. This study asked students to nominate their type of disability or disabilities into these categories. This allowed for the impact of different impairments to the access of online platforms to be more closely observed.

The survey produced some notable findings, including the high proportion of students who identified as having a mental illness (see Kent, 2015b) and the relatively low level of students with a learning disability (see Table 14.1), a category that has previously been reported as the largest disability type enrolling in higher education (Sparks & Lovett, 2013).

The study also looked specifically at the accessibility of a number of online platforms. When students were asked overall if they had any problems accessing

Table 14.1 Occurrence of different impairment types in students in eLearning

Impairment classification	Response count	Response percentage
Mental illness	149	44.9%
Medical	130	39.2%
Mobility	84	25.3%
Hearing	34	10.2%
Learning	29	8.7%
Vision	24	7.2%
Acquired brain impairment	15	4.5%
Intellectual disability	6	1.8%
Other	64	

online content for their studies, a relatively low percentage of students, 17.9 per cent, indicated that they had. However, when presented with a list of specific online platforms used in learning and teaching, nearly one in three users overall, 32.8 per cent, indicated that they had some problem with access (see Table 14.2).

It is disappointing to see that the two most used platforms, Blackboard and University websites, were simultaneously the most likely to cause problems for accessibility, and that they were also platforms which were provided and maintained by the universities utilising them. It is equally disappointing to see the highly used online lecture system Echo 360 rounding out the top three in terms of accessibility problems. By contrast, social media platforms used in learning and teaching at OUA such as YouTube, Facebook and Twitter were far more likely to be accessible.

When the results are broken down by the different impairment categories in the survey, and when looking specifically at a comparison of Blackboard and Facebook, this contrast in accessibility was consistent across seven of the eight impairment categories, with only the sparsely sampled intellectual impairment group finding more problems accessing Facebook compared with Blackboard (see tables 14.3 through 14.10).

Table 14.2 Accessibility of different online platforms used in eLearning

Platform	No problem	Minor problems	Major problems	Unusable	Percentage problems	Percentage used
Blackboard	68	51	12	1	43.0%	82%
University websites	78	42	17	1	39.5%	86%
Echo 360 / Echo Centre	39	28	8	2	26.4%	47%
PDFs	81	27	6	1	25.8%	71%
YouTube	78	14	6	1	15.4%	61%
Facebook	63	13	3	1	12.3%	50%
Moodle	26	13	1	0	10.1%	25%
Lectopia	18	7	5	0	8.9%	19%
Blogger	21	6	1	0	5.3%	17%
WordPress	27	4	1	0	3.8%	20%
Twitter	37	3	1	1	3.7%	26%
Prezi	20	2	1	1	3.0%	15%
WebCT	12	1	2	0	2.3%	9%
Slideshare	15	0	2	0	1.5%	11%

Table 14.3 Accessibility of Blackboard and Facebook for students with mental illness

Platform	No problem	Minor problems	Major problems	Unusable	Percentage problems
Blackboard	32	20	5	1	45%
Facebook	32	4	1	1	16%

Table 14.4 Accessibility of Blackboard and Facebook for students with a medical disability

Platform	No problem	Minor problems	Major problems	Unusable	Percentage problems
Blackboard	23	18	8	0	54%
Facebook	21	6	3	1	32%

Table 14.5 Accessibility of Blackboard and Facebook for students with a mobility impairment

Platform	No problem	Minor problems	Major problems	Unusable	Percentage problems
Blackboard	16	11	3	0	47%
Facebook	12	3	2	1	33%

Table 14.6 Accessibility of Blackboard and Facebook for students with a hearing impairment

Platform	No problem	Minor problems	Major problems	Unusable	Percentage problems
Blackboard	10	3	2	0	33%
Facebook	10	2	0	0	17%

Table 14.7 Accessibility of Blackboard and Facebook for students with a learning disability

Platform	No problem	Minor problems	Major problems	Unusable	Percentage problems
Blackboard	4	8	0	0	33%
Facebook	9	1	0	0	10%

Table 14.8 Accessibility of Blackboard and Facebook for students with a vision impairment

Platform	No problem	Minor problems	Major problems	Unusable	Percentage problems
Blackboard	6	6	2	0	57%
Facebook	9	1	0	0	10%

Table 14.9 Accessibility of Blackboard and Facebook for students with an acquired brain impairment

Platform	No problem	Minor problems	Major problems	Unusable	Percentage problems
Blackboard	6	2	1	0	33%
Facebook	6	2	0	0	25%

Table 14.10 Accessibility of Blackboard and Facebook for students with an intellectual disability

Platform	No problem	Minor problems	Major problems	Unusable	Percentage problems
Blackboard	1	1	0	0	50%
Facebook	3	2	0	0	40%

Discussion and conclusion

From these results it would seem that there are problems with Facebook when used by these students as a learning and teaching platform – it was found to be unusable by at least one respondent to the survey and presented major problems for a number of others. Using Facebook as a reliable teaching and learning tool would therefore need to be carefully considered. Disappointingly, the major problems were found in the three largest impairment categories. However, having made this observation, Facebook was seen to be overwhelmingly more accessible than Blackboard. Blackboard presented major problems to accessibility for students in six of the eight categories, and despite its gold certification, still presented a problem for more than half the users with a vision impairment.

It would seem from these results that – from the point of accessibility – Facebook would be a better platform to use for students with disabilities than Blackboard *and* would be able to provide the added engagement and functionality observed earlier. However, there are a number of additional cautions to consider and areas for research to explore.

While Facebook would seem to help with the accessibility issues that students with disability face in eLearning, there may be issues around flexibility. If student conversations grow in intensity – and, through the greater integration of Facebook into people's lives, also in immediacy – this may start to impinge on the flexibility of students to choose when to participate. This is another theme further explored by McRae in Chapter 16. By contrast, for others this flexibility/integration may enhance its use – for example the ability to access Facebook through mobile phones or smartwatches at a time that is convenient.

The other area of concern would be around disclosure. While it is possible to separate the private and friendship aspects of Facebook from learning and teaching (see Allen, 2012; Kent, 2014), this creates an added area of overlap and ambiguity when it comes to students' ability to choose if they want to disclose their disability to their peers and teachers.

Despite these concerns, it may be that, following Palloff and Pratt (2009), the benefits may outweigh the risks. Social media is effective because it engages students in an online venue where they already have literacy and familiarity – where they don't need to learn how to use the platform before they start learning. For students with disability – for whom access to a new platform will often require additional learning in order to develop a working familiarity – this affordance is enhanced.

This chapter has demonstrated the potential for social media, and Facebook in particular to be an effective tool in eLearning, and one that is more accessible than traditional learning management systems for students with disability. These students are already offered a number of advantages through studying online, and the use of social media in this context can be seen to further enhance these possibilities.

Acknowledgements

The author would like to thank all the students who took the time to participate in this research. The interview phase of this research was conducted with funding from the National Centre for Student Equity in Higher Education [https://www.ncsehe.edu.au] and the Australian Commonwealth Government.

References

Allen, I. E., & Seaman, J. (2014). *Grade change tracking online education in the United States*. Babson Park, MA: Babson Survey Research Group and Quahog Research Group.

Allen, M. (2012). An education in Facebook. *Digital Culture and Education, 4*(3). Retrieved from http://www.digitalcultureandeducation.com/cms/wp-content/uploads/2012/12/dce1077_allen_2012.pdf

Australian Bureau of Statistics. (2013). *Disability, ageing and carers, Australia: Summary of findings*. 4430.0. Canberra: Australian Government. Retrieved from http://www.abs.gov.au/ausstats/abs@.nsf/Lookup/3A5561E876CDAC73CA257C210011AB9B?opendocument

Baran, B. (2010). Facebook as a formal instruction environment. *British Journal of Education Technology, 41*(6). Retrieved from http://dx.doi/10.1111/j.1467-8535.2010.01115.x

Bateman, D., & Willems, J. (2012). Chapter 5 facing off: Facebook and higher education. In L. A. Wankel & C. Wankel (Eds.), *Misbehavior online in higher education: Cutting-edge technologies in higher education* (vol. 5) (pp. 53–79). Emerald Group Publishing Limited. Retrieved from http://dx.doi/10.1108/S2044-9968(2012)0000005007

Best, G., Hajzler, D., Pancini, G., & Tout, D. (2011). Being 'dumped' from Facebook: Negotiating issues of boundaries and identity in an online social networking space. *Journal of Peer Learning, 4*(1), 24–36. Retrieved from http://ro.uow.edu.au/ajpl/vol4/iss1/5

Cheung, C. M. K., Chiu, P. Y., & Lee, M. K. O. (2011). Online social networks: Why do students use Facebook. *Computers in Human Behavior, 27*(4), 1337–1343. Retrieved from http://dx.doi/10.1016/j.chb.2010.07.028

Cluett, L. (2010). Online social networking for outreach, engagement and community: The UWA student's Facebook page. *Educating for Sustainability: Proceedings of the 19th Annual Teaching Learning Forum, 28*–29 January. Perth, WA: Edith Cowan University. Retrieved from http://otl.curtin.edu.au/professional_development/conferences/tlf/tlf2010/refereed/cluett.html

Croeser, S. (2014). Changing Facebook's architecture. In M. Kent & T. Leaver (Eds.), *An education in Facebook: Higher education and the world's largest social network* (pp. 185–195). New York, NY: Routledge.

Dobransky, K., & Hargittai, E. (2006). The disability divide in internet access and use. *Information Communication and Society, 9*(3), 309–311.

Ellis, K. (2011). Embracing learners with disability: Web 2.0, access and insight. *Telecommunications Journal of Australia, 61*(2), 30.1–30.2.

Ellis, K., & Kent, M. (2014). Facebook, disability and higher education: Accessing the digital campus. In M. Kent & T. Leaver (Eds.), *An education in Facebook: Higher education and the world's largest social network* (pp. 196–204). New York, NY: Routledge.

Ellison, B., Steinfield, C., & Lampe, C. (2007). The benefits of Facebook 'friends': Social capital and college students' use of online social networking sites. *Journal of Computer-Mediated Communication, 12*(4), 1143–1168. Retrieved from http://dx.doi/10.1111/j. 1083-6101.2007.00367.x

Fichten, C. S., Ferraro, V., Asuncion, J. V., Chwojka, C., Barile, M., Nguyen, M. N., Klomp, R., & Wolforth, J. (2009). Disabilities and e-Learning problems and solutions: An exploratory study. *Educational Technology & Society, 12*(4), 241–256. Retrieved from http://www.adaptech.org/cfichten/abDisabilitiesAndE-LearningProblems.pdf

Gao, F., Zhang, T., & Franklin, T. (2013). Designing asynchronous online discussion environments: Recent progress and possible future directions. *British Journal of Educational Technology, 44*(3), 469–483. Retrieved from http://dx.doi/10.1111/j.1467-8535. 2012.01330.x

Grey, K., Lucas, A., & Kennedy, G. (2010). Medical students' use of Facebook to support learning: Insights from four case studies. *Medical Teacher, 32*(12), 971–976. Retrieved from http://dx.doi/10.3109/01421590903394579

Guo, B., Bricout, J. C. & Huang, J. (2005). A common open space or a digital divide? A social model perspective on the online disability community in China. Disability & Society, 20(1), January, 49–66

Heijstra, T. M., & Rafnsdottir, G. L. (2010). The internet and academics' workload and work family balance. *Internet and Higher Education, 13*, 158–163.

Kassens-Noor, E. (2012). Twitter as a teaching practice to enhance active and informal learning in higher education: The case of sustainable Tweets. *Active Learning in Higher Education, 13*(1), 9–21.

Kayri, M., & Çakir, Ö. (2010). An applied study on educational use of Facebook as a Web 2.0 tool: The sample lesson of computer networks and communication. *International Journal of Computer Science & Information Technology, 2*(4), August. Retrieved from http://dx.doi/10.5121/ijcsit.2010.2405

Kelly, S. M. (2009). Distance learning: How accessible are online educational tools. *Paper Presented at the Equal Access to Software and Information Webinar*, February, Lake Forrest, California.

Kent, M. (2013). Changing the conversation: Facebook as a venue for online class discussion in higher education. *Journal of Online Teaching and Learning, 9*(4), December. Retrieved from http://jolt.merlot.org/vol9no4/kent_1213.pdf

Kent, M. (2014). What's on your mind? Facebook as a forum for teaching and learning in higher education. In M. Kent & T. Leaver (Eds.), *An education in Facebook: Higher education and the world's largest social network* (pp. 53–60). New York, NY: Routledge.

Kent, M. (2015a). Disability and eLearning: Opportunities and barriers. *Disability Studies Quarterly, 35*(1). Retrieved from http://dsq-sds.org/article/view/3815/3830

Kent, M. (2015b). Disability, mental illness, and eLearning: Invisible behind the screen? *Journal of Interactive Technology and Pedagogy, 8.*

Kent, M. (2016). *Access and barriers to online education for people with disabilities.* Perth, WA: National Centre for Student Equity in Higher Education. Retrieved from https:// www.ncsehe.edu.au/wp-content/uploads/2016/05/Access-and-Barriers-to-Online-Education-for-People-with-Disabilities.pdf

Kent, M., & Leaver, T. (2014). *An education in Facebook: Higher education and the world's largest social network.* New York, NY: Routledge.

Leaver, T. (2012). Twittering informal learning ad student engagement in first year units. In A. Herrington, J. Schrape & K Singh (Eds.), *Engaging students with learning technology* (pp. 97–110). Perth, WA: Curtin University.

Leaver, T. (2014). Facebook student engagement and the 'Uni Coffee Shop' group. In M. Kent & T. Leaver (Eds.), *An education in Facebook: Higher education and the world's largest social network* (pp. 121–131). New York, NY: Routledge.

Madaus, J. W., Banerjee, M., & Merchant, D. (2011). Transition to postsecondary education. In J. M. Kauffman & D. P. Hallahan (Eds.), *Handbook of special education* (pp. 571–583). New York, NY: Routledge.

Mazman, S. G., & Usluel, Y. K. (2010). Modeling educational usage of Facebook. *Computers and Education, 55*(2), 444–453. Retrieved from http://dx.doi/10.1016/j.compedu.2010.02.008

McLaughlin, C., & Lee, M. J. W. (2010). Personalised and self-regulated learning in the Web 2.0 era: International exemplars of innovative pedagogy using social software. *Australasian Journal of Educational Technology, 26*(1), 28–43. Retrieved from http://www.ascilite.org.au/ajet/ajet26/mcloughlin.pdf

Palloff, R. M., & Pratt, K. (2009). Web 2.0 technologies and community building online. *Paper Presented at the 25th Annual Conference on Distance Teaching & Learning: Madison,* Wisconsin, 4–7 August. Retrieved from http://www.uwex.edu/disted/conference/Resource_library/proceedings/09_20002.pdf

Raynes-Goldie, K. (2012). *Privacy in the age of Facebook? Discourse, architecture, consequences.* (Doctoral dissertation, Curtin University, Perth, Australia). Retrieved from http://www.k4t3.org/2012/09/13/privacy-in-the-age-of-facebook-discourse-architecture-consequences/

Raynes-Goldie, K., & Lloyd, C. (2014). Unfriending Facebook? Challenges from an educators' perspective. In M. Kent & T. Leaver (Eds.), *An education in Facebook: Higher education and the world's largest social network* (pp. 153–161). New York, NY: Routledge.

Roberts, J.B., Crittenden, L.A., & Crittenden, J.C. (2011). Students with disabilities and online learning: A cross-institutional study of perceived satisfaction with accessibility compliance and services. *Internet and Higher Education, 14,* 242–250.

Sachs, D., & Schreuer, N. (2011). Inclusion of students with disabilities in higher education: Performance and participation in student experiences. *Disability Studies Quarterly, 31*(2).

Schroeder, J., & Greenbowe, T.J. (2009). The chemistry of Facebook: Using social networking to create an online community for the organic chemistry. *Innovate: Journal of Online Education, 5*(4), 1–7. Retrieved from http://www.innovateonline.info/pdf/vol5_issue4/The_Chemistry_of_Facebook-_Using_Social_Networking_to_Create_an_Online_Community_for_the_Organic_Chemistry_Laborat ory.pdf

Sparks, R.L., & Lovett, B.J. (2013). Learning disability documentation in higher education: What are students submitting? *Learning Disability Quarterly, 37*(1), 54–62. Retrieved from http://dx.doi/10.1177/0731948713486888

Sugar, W., Martindale, T., & Crawley, F.E. (2007). One professor's face-to-face teaching strategies while becoming an online instructor. *Quarterly Review of Distance Education, 8*(4), 365–385.

Tade, S.J., & Ondrey, J.A. (2015). YouTube your course. *Paper Presented at the Minnesota eLearning Summit,* July 30. Twin Cities, MN: University of Minnesota.

Tay, E., & Allen, M. (2011). Designing social media into university learning: Technology of collaboration or collaboration for technology? *Education Media International, 48*(3), 151–163.

Teclehaimanot, B., & Hickman, T. (2011). Student–teacher interaction on Facebook: What students find appropriate. *TechTrends, 55*(3), 19–30. Retrieved from http://dx.doi/0.1007/s11528-011-0494-8

Van de Bunt-Kokhuis, S., & Bolger, M. (2009). Talent competences in the new eLearning generation. *eLearning Papers No 15*, June. Retrieved from http://www.elearningeuropa.info/files/media/media19740.pdf

Waits, T., & Lewis, L. (2003). *Distance education at degree granting post secondary institutions: 2000–2001*. Washington, DC: US Department of Education, National Center for Educational Statistics, NCES 20003–017.

Wentz, B., Jaeger, P.T., & Lazar, J. (2011). Retrofitting accessibility: The legal inequality of after-the-fact online access for persons with disabilities in the United States. *First Monday, 16*(11). Retrieved from http://www.firstmonday.org/htbin/cgiwrap/bin/ojs/index.php/fm/article/view/3666/

Williams, J. (2006). The Lectopia service and students with disabilities. *Paper Presented at the Proceedings of the 23rd Australasians Society for Computers and Learning in Tertiary Education Conference: Who's Learning Whose Technology?* Sydney.

15 A phenomenology of media making experience

Disability studies and wearable cameras

D. Andy Rice

This chapter reflects on the place of social media and miniature wearable cameras in teaching documentary production within disability studies (DS). I consider two related processes through my case study. First, I describe how a new course in DS and urban planning at the University of California, Los Angeles (UCLA) called *Documentary production for social change: Mobility in Los Angeles* enfolded social media platforms into collaborative video making and outreach assignments. Second, I discuss how one group of six students came to repurpose the wearable GoPro camera from the company's branded social media aesthetic style to represent the commute of a classmate who walked with a crutch. I argue that my students' video, *Access game* (2014), came to meld critical DS theories of representation with the politics of an emergent film movement about which they knew little, dubbed 'slow cinema'. I then reflect on the future possibilities of this conjuncture.

Technologies made available as social media since the late 1990s have opened new low-cost pathways for producing and distributing non-fiction videos, making it possible to teach critical media literacy to university students through production practice. Whereas a late 1990s production process entailed the use of handheld, tape-based camcorders, non-linear editing on a very expensive desktop computer, and DVD/VHS one-at-a-time distribution, video production circa 2015 allows for tapeless recording on smartphones that most students already own, cloud storage, simultaneous editing at multiple consumer laptops, and instantaneous, global sharing through websites including YouTube, Vimeo, Tumblr, and Facebook. Compared to analogue production processes encumbered by heavy, expensive equipment, I view digital video making that makes use of social media tools as significantly more accessible for persons with physical disabilities. However, social media videos that aim for impact and high view counts, as I suggest later in this chapter, often celebrate ablism and speed in their aesthetics, a dilemma for DS approaches to representation. This chapter focuses on the ways that university students in a new DS course negotiated social media conventions as they learned a video production process and created a non-fiction work about the commutes of students with disabilities.

My class, *Documentary production for social change: Mobility in Los Angeles*, cross-listed in DS and urban planning at UCLA, built on successes using a hybrid educational model that combined 'face-to-face meetings with interactive social media between meetings' (Yaros, 2012, p. 58). We used the Google Drive platform to mediate student collaborations on video projects, and Facebook, Twitter, and campus message boards to get the word out about our end of quarter screening. Student assignments blended traditional documentary production techniques with experiments wearing GoPro camcorders to record movement in novel ways.

GoPro, a company founded by visual artist and tech entrepreneur Nick Woodman in 2002, is best known for producing a rugged miniature HD camera that can be mounted to an arm, chest, head, surfboard, bike, or moving vehicle. The company has also established itself as an extreme sports branded content creator under the tagline *GoPro: Be a hero,* and it happened to come of age with the rise of YouTube as a platform for commercial video distribution and marketing.

Judging from videos on the GoPro YouTube Channel, however, the company seems unaware of – or actively hostile to – the political possibilities of using its technology to represent the everyday lives of persons with disabilities. Rather, the company brand provides an uber-ablist imagery around which other individual producers and fan groups can orient their own YouTube presence.[1] Videos blend the personal orientation dominant in the YouTube media ecology with the romantic tropes of adventure tourism. A 2014 upload titled *The adventure of life in 4K,* for instance, included shots taken from the chest of an ice climber, the DJ of a rock concert, a cowboy upon a galloping horse, a driver racing a Lamborghini at night in Japan, a scientist descending into a volcano, and a marine rescue-worker saving an orca from a tangled fishing line, all quickly-cut and set to a score of heart-thumping drums and high-pitched, staccato violin (GoPro, 2014). This video emphasises spectacular movement in wearable camera footage taken by individuals as the centre of collective identity associated with the brand. Notably, I could not find a single representation of an individual with a disability in this or dozens of other GoPro branded videos.[2] Company messaging is not disability inclusive,[3] a bias through which we may interpret the single line anonymously voiced at the beginning of the *Adventure of life in 4K* upload. 'Life is either an incredible adventure or it's nothing at all', states an unironic male with a vaguely Australian accent. Life with disabilities, of course, can be an incredible adventure – and likely constitutes a regular, unrepresented part of the lives of camera-wearing skydivers, BMX racers, skateboarders, etc. who routinely teeter on the edge of bone-crunching accidents – but by not including subjects with disabilities, the company's videos position disability and an event-worth-wearing-a-camera-to-record as mutually exclusive categories.

Rather, as I suggest in my case study, I see wearable camera media makers with physical disabilities potentially leading the way in crafting new, thought-provoking aesthetic styles attentive to time in everyday life. My teaching emphasised observational and participatory traditions of practice, critical theories gleaned from DS, and the subversive qualities of the long take in digital culture, to prime students to imagine alternative uses for wearable cameras. We used social media tools primarily to aid in a collaborative production process rather than accelerate the proliferation of student work or model their aesthetic choices. The group I focus upon here included 'Tomas', a student who walked with a crutch and wore a camera on a chest mount to record portions of his commute. The recordings that the group included in their final video resembled, in pace and politics, the aesthetic strategies at the centre of the emergent slow cinema movement, which, as I argue later, dovetails in suggestive ways with writing on representing everyday life in what Snyder and Mitchell termed 'the new disability documentary cinema' as well as Vivian Sobchack's disability-inclusive media phenomenology (Sobchack, 1992, 2004; Snyder & Mitchell, 2006). Hearkening back to the film theories of Andre Bazin, Gilles Deleuze, and Paul Shrader about the viewer's experience of radically unmoored subjectivity in the real-time of the long take, slow cinema has re-emerged in concert with slow food, slow medicine, slow cities, etc., as an emblem of resistance against the imperative of speed in twenty-first-century global capitalism and its dominant social media forms.[4]

Sometimes referred to as 'contemplative cinema', slow cinema tends to emphasise cyclical time over linear action, mood or affective texture over character development, observed sensory experience over interviews, existential doubt over narrative resolution, and mundane everyday activity over depictions of violence (Koehler, 2009; Romney, 2010; Jaffe, 2014; Lim, 2014). The languorousness beckons a manner of attention unfamiliar to viewers accustomed to the quick-cutting norms of commercially oriented videos, making space for thought in the midst of viewing. Crucially from a DS perspective, the pace of living emerges as the empathic centre of slow cinema works rather than a particular character's motives, desires, or abilities. This is a conjuncture not yet commented upon in either film studies, where most of the major slow cinema works centre on pastoral life, spiritual matters, or manual labour (MacDougall, 2006; Grimshaw & Ravetz, 2009; Romney, 2010; Jaffe 2014; Lim, 2014), or DS, in which questions of representation of disability in media predominate over experiments in film/video-making practice (Longmore, 2001; Sobchack, 2004; Snyder & Mitchell, 2006; Mogk, 2013).

By repurposing wearable recording systems marketed to extreme sports enthusiasts, my case study suggests that persons with physical disabilities can shoot footage of their everyday lives that compels viewers to imaginatively embody an approximation of their phenomenological experience. Representing duration in living with a disability, in the context of a social media economy that valorises speed, can be both a politics of resistance and a means for creating new forms of cinematic empathy. Given that my course led students of diverse majors and abilities to collaborate on videos through a social media platform, Tomas's footage, as I show later in the chapter, became an invaluable resource for our collective learning and teaching, both about living with disability and media aesthetics. In the later sections, I describe the course, the use of social media, and the process through which students decided to represent part of Tomas's everyday experience using a long take with a wearable camera. I conclude with reflections on the potentials and pitfalls for teaching with social media and wearable cameras in DS classrooms.

ASPIRE Lab is an initiative at UCLA to teach socially engaged media production as a form of project-based, service learning in interdisciplinary capstone classes. ASPIRE (The Academy for Social Purpose in Responsible Entertainment), headed by film producer and social entrepreneur Peter Samuelson, is a non-profit organisation that partners with universities to develop media-focused coursework for students who generally want to pursue careers outside of the film and television industry. Sensing a gap between student engagement with digital media in everyday life and media production course offerings outside of the film school, the Division of Undergraduate Education (DUE) at UCLA entered into an agreement with ASPIRE to develop several pilot seminars for liberal arts majors. I designed and taught the first, *Documentary production for social change: Mobility in Los Angeles,* a seminar that led 24 students from 17 different majors to work together on a series of videos about the commuting issues of UCLA affiliates. Across the 10-week course, each student completed a one-to-two minute portrait of a space, pairs of students made four-to-five minute portraits of a UCLA commuter, and groups of four to six integrated several of the short portraits into an issue-focused documentary project. Final works included an interactive map combining 13 video portraits of UCLA commuters with highlighted routes, and shorts on the perceptions of diverse bus commuters, infrastructure for bicycle commuters in LA, and Access Services for students with disabilities, *Access game,*[5] my focus here.

I decided to harness 'easy-to-use' social web platforms to facilitate the praxis ends of the class. DS scholars have noted ways that social media platforms have opened new avenues for employment, friendship and learning for some persons with disabilities (Ellis & Goggin, 2014), and education scholars have reported success in using social media to facilitate student engagement and class solidarity in university lecture classes (Elavsky, 2012; Yaros, 2012). However, uncritically using the tools offered by for-profit social media companies in a DS course may fail to acknowledge – or even amplify – inequities suffered by labourers making digital devices for subsistence wages, users forced to sign away control of their personal data for access to software, and persons with disabilities such as dyslexia or blindness, for whom the shift to a communication culture dominated by text messages and visual imagery is not liberating at all (Lanier, 2013; Ellis & Goggin, 2014; Sandoval, 2014; McRae, Chapter 16 this volume). Teaching with and through social media-enabled communications embeds 'contradictory dynamics', in digital culture theorist Felix Stalder's terms, between the free flow of information characteristic of voluntary communities and the opacity of proprietary, for-profit providers of social media infrastructure (Stalder, 2012, p. 248). The social web remains 'decentralized, ad hoc, cheap, easy to use, community oriented, and transparent' for many purposes (Stalder, 2012, p. 248), but as of 2010, 12 of the 13 most visited social media sites, including YouTube, were for-profit companies – even 'contemporary slaveholders and slave masters', in Christian Fuch's characterisation – that extract data from social media exchanges carried out on their platform as a commodity to be sold to advertisers (Fuchs, 2012, p. 212; Fuchs, 2014, p. 60).

The commercialisation of the web has further implications in considering a platform like YouTube, where video is the medium around which communities cohere. DS and film studies critiques of commercial cinema tropes – including identification with action-oriented, white, male protagonists; passive female char-acters; fast-paced editing, etc. – may be applied as well to much social media video, like the GoPro channel described earlier (Longmore, 2001; Sobchack 2004; Cartwright, 2008). Yet given that social media technologies 'crucially intersect conceptions of contemporary life and agency' for most students (Elavsky, 2012, p. 76), and can still arguably function as common carrier 'advertising platforms without determining their [communities'] communicative content' (Feenberg, 2014, p. 116), I see a role for educators to model commons-based uses of social media and value the inclusive possibilities in networked technologies. As Andrew Feenberg (2014) points out, the only tools available for the construction of alterna-tive visions of our social world are those already embedded in our everyday lives. Especially valuable for small groups of differently abled, busy students, social media tools centralise the asynchronous, geographically disparate communications of group members, and allow student collaborators a way to imagine identifying and extending their core ideas to networks outside of the classroom.

I incorporated work with social media platforms into assignments in two ways. First, like 'social impact' documentary filmmakers who post in-progress updates on Facebook, Twitter, and Tumblr to build audiences, students in the course worked together to develop a digital flyer, press release, and outreach campaign for their final screening as they fine-tuned their documentaries. Social media outreach led students to consider how their work might contribute to public dialogue outside the university about sustainability and issues faced by commuters with disabilities. In part due to these activities, we drew a crowd of around 60 for the final screening, with stakeholders in DS, campus transportation planning, sustainability initiatives, and active transit activism in attendance. Their presence enriched discussion at the conclusion of student films, and students routinely identified this event as a highlight of the course in evaluations.

Second, my class shared video files using Google Drive as a closed, social media platform. They could access one another's planning documents and watch cuts of videos uploaded by their classmates to the site, but these activities were restricted to members of the class. Some documentary subjects only allowed their stories to be filmed for the purposes of classroom assignments, and all of the groups needed time to craft the representations of subjects in an ethical manner. Using Google Drive gave us the flexibility to screen uploaded videos together in class, as well as in small group settings outside of class time on any device with an internet con-nection, a significant advantage over having to play from tapes or DVDs. YouTube served as a convenient platform for sharing completed videos with allied groups and individuals. And the group that produced the interactive map hyperlinked clickable icons to the YouTube videos, creating a representation that included work done by every student in the class.[6]

While these were exciting ways for DS students to learn both critical media literacy and social engagement, I was wary of validating social media aesthetic norms now dominant on sites like YouTube. Miniature digital cameras afford inti-mate, serialised, personal video styles drawn from everyday life that, in combina-tion with a site like YouTube, seem to beckon a particular kind of performance.

YouTube advises individual producers to create 2–10 minute videos regularly on a theme, and to work consistently over years to accumulate loyal subscribers to their channels (YouTube, 2014b). These structuring norms are powerful, and they have long-range ideological implications as a network expands. Whenever a YouTube producer uploads a new video, an email automatically goes out to all of their subscribers, who function as a commodity for sale to advertisers. On monetised channels, YouTube and the individual YouTube producer share the advertising revenues generated when a user clicks play on sponsored content (YouTube, 2014a). The site does not differentiate between a lone viewer clicking a YouTube video and a screening of the same video for an audience of many people. In this way, the architecture of the site encourages producing for-profit videos for individual consumption. And it is striking that in spite of the myriad possibilities a tiny camera opens to experimenting with aesthetics as the grounds for new communities, the dominant style on YouTube (typified by popular channels like Jenna Marbles and Ray William Johnson), is a domestic version of the direct address entertainer of late night talk shows. Many students in my class regularly watched such YouTube channels in their free time. In direct address videos, the individual speaks to the camera (and to imagined viewers by extension) in a high energy, hyper-expressive, quick-talking style about dilemmas with personal grooming, popular culture, or topics suggested by fans, for instance, in ways that echo culturally recognisable types (snarky critic, video gamer, d.i.y. fashionista, etc.). These videos tend to use jump cuts to move from one shot to the next, suggesting an improvisational style before the camera in the production phase that is then condensed in the editing. When many viewers watch such channels, the audiovisual aesthetics they employ *come to function as proprietary social media technologies*. Individuals-as-direct address performers and the audiences they cultivate now constitute an array of YouTube products for sale to advertisers. Few YouTube personas drift into the realms of political activism or formal experimentation. And in the classroom, it takes a good deal of teaching work to establish that such aesthetic styles are the product of particular social and historical contexts and not reflections of the world or just the choices of individual video makers. I ask students to craft their own aesthetics to be in tune with a more inclusive, accessible, and/or politically activated social context than such models tend to offer.

It is worth noting that makers with physical disabilities, like YouTuber comedian and travel show host Zach Anner, have created commercially successful, disability-inclusive personas using the direct address style. Anner has cerebral palsy – 'which I think is the sexiest of the palsies', he cracks – and appears in all of his videos addressing the camera from his wheelchair.[7] In keeping with DS scholars whom have identified the benefits of social media for persons with disabilities, Anner extols the tools that allow him to create his YouTube show. 'I'm a creative person, and it's only because we're in this age where the technology is so good that I'm actually able to say what I want to say and do what I want to do', he says before knowingly digressing into a comment on 'the implications for porn' (Dobi, 2012). Anner offers himself up as an adventuresome, affable, smart, white, male companion who understands the facts of his life as assets for joking within his show – a product in keeping with the dominant, direct address aesthetic style on YouTube. Still, he manages to use humour to critique the rhetoric of pity/ inspiration often attached to the disabled body 'doing'.

While Anner's work merits further consideration, the direct address style that emphasises verbal commentary is at odds with the slow cinema, wearable camera aesthetics I am theorising here. As viewers, we understand Anner's everyday life primarily through the witty things he says to the camera – excursions provide Anner new environments in which to perform his show persona. We never sense how he perceives or the time in which he experiences the world. Wearable camera videos, on the other hand, rarely feature the faces or voices of the makers because the cameras face outward as the subject moves through space. The camera orientation eschews the kind of verbal commentary and facial performance that is central to videos about the self in front of the camera. The result, to use a pithy phrase from Nick Paumgarten's (2014) *New Yorker* article about wearable camera adventure videos, 'is not as much a selfie as a worldie' (p. 46). I contend that this difference between selfie and worldie opens possibilities for a turn toward a slow cinema, audiovisual phenomenology led by persons with disabilities, a potential intimated in my class by Tomas's participation in the video about his commute.

Tomas could not afford to rent an apartment in West LA near campus, so he commuted from his family's home in the San Fernando Valley 14 miles north of UCLA. The Valley is a 30-minute drive from UCLA in light traffic, but the commute can take up to 90 minutes during rush hour. As a sophomore, Tomas drove to school. However, the cost of gas and parking compelled him as an upperclassman to use Access Services, a program run by LA County in coordination with taxis and specially designed vans to provide rides for persons with disabilities. His daily commute with Access was around two hours each way given that they frequently had to pick up other riders en route. The interconnections across Tomas's commute, use of disability services, family economics, and housing constraints touched on key questions in the class, so I encouraged him to document his experiences moving through space by wearing a camera on a chest mount. In screening these shots in class as raw footage, we collectively experienced the striking sensation of moving at Tomas's everyday pace.

I want to note here that the strategy Tomas employed may be applicable more broadly for other persons with dexterity or motility impairments. Miniature cameras may also be mounted to wrists, ankles, arms, or crutches, or worn on the forehead like a miner's light. Unlike my previous critique of the ableist GoPro social media campaign, seeing in these novel, fragmented ways within a disability-rights context is neither spectacular nor ableist. Rather, the new angles of view place the spectator in close proximity to previously inaccessible everyday experiences, eliciting unfamiliar sensations of empathy for and/or identification with subjects creating the images on screen. Given the history of stereotypically negative representations of disability in popular media (Longmore, 2001; Snyder & Mitchell, 2006; Mogk, 2013), disability rights activists may consider the possibilities for reappropriating wearable and other miniaturised cameras embedded in smartphones and the like to take ownership over social media representations of stories about living with disability.

Prior to the widespread availability of wearable cameras, moreover, Snyder and Mitchell (2006) fleshed out a theoretical framework for a 'new disability documentary cinema' in keeping with the politics of slow cinema and the use of wearable cameras I am describing here. Snyder and Mitchell argued that showing the 'routine activities' of persons with disabilities in their own time – a pace unrepresented in profit-driven Hollywood productions and social media videos alike – constituted 'the essence of the argument' of a cinema committed to making 'an ordinary life with disability imaginable and even palatable to a society that holds a bankrupt tradition of disability imagery' (pp. 173–174). At least in my class, Tomas's footage became central to class discussions about disability and access *because* wearing the camera and sharing the footage he recorded allowed other 'temporarily able-bodied' (TAB) students an affecting, unsentimental way to empathise with his everyday experiences.

It was actually Tomas's collaborators who first brought his wearable camera footage to my attention, a fact that speaks to the intersubjective nature of collaborative documentary work. Tomas had not shown much of the footage he shot in class, nor used the editing software on his own to put together his video assignments. Dexterity impairments, unfamiliarity with the software platform and the distance Tomas lived from campus perhaps added to the formidable challenge all students face in learning how to see and think as filmmakers. Tomas sat for an interview with his collaborators for the project, provided insider information about Access Services, recorded his commute, identified two additional subjects for the film and interviewed the director of the Office for Students with Disabilities (OSD) at UCLA, who provided context about the number and range of students they served. Other members of the group edited the video, a task that may have been more accessible had the class used a bug-free, cloud-based video editing application. Social media editing platforms may address some of these barriers to accessibility and collaboration, if costs remain low, but we were not able to use one when I taught this course.

Screening the wearable camera footage in class with some shots extending for several minutes at a time opened a dialogue about how to include such material in a final, tightly edited film. While some students stated that several seconds of a few shots would do, others countered that Tomas's footage needed to play out in real-time, at least for a while. They and Tomas were moved by the way that the long duration of the shots seemed to compel them – sometimes with discomfort and anxiety – to imaginatively embody the pace and manner of Tomas's walk. The group settled on a strategy after our discussion. The video would employ conventional shot pacing with an interview for the first part of Tomas's commute, then transition to a wearable camera scene that played at length with no interview, music, or commentary. Other group members recorded Tomas as he began the journey to UCLA, transferred to an OSD campus shuttle once at UCLA and arrived at the building where he was having class – footage ultimately condensed into roughly the first two and a half minutes of *Access game* (see Figure 15.1). Then came the minute-long, wearable camera shot – the longest in the film.

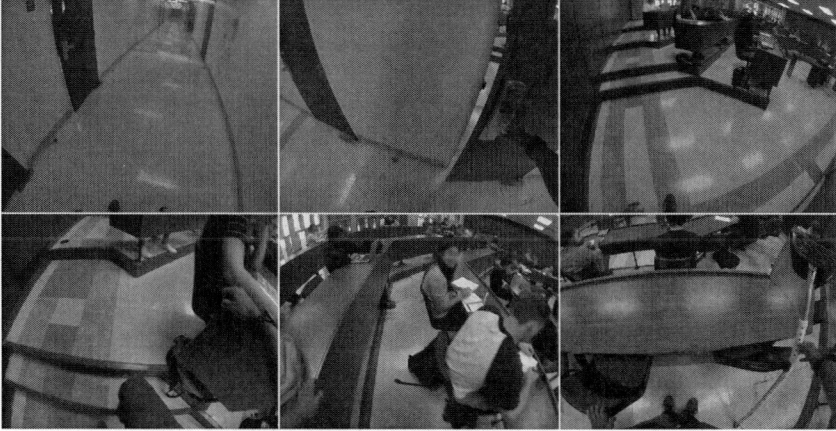

Figure 15.1 Series of video stills from *Access game* (2014)

Tomas opens the classroom door and walks to a seat in the centre of the room, about 40 feet away and elevated two stairs above the ground level. Unlike the social media videos that employ wearable cameras to represent many ways of hurtling through space, we are here beckoned to attend to the small details of the classroom through the perspective of *this* student who walks with a crutch. He is a few minutes late. We hear the muffled voice of the professor off-screen and clicks as the camera jostles back and forth with Tomas's gait. His hand reaches in the frame, grabs a desk corner and shakes under strain as he steps up the first and then second stair. More time passes. Students in the class keep their eyes on the lecturer as Tomas moves by, except for one young woman, who turns her head toward him and smiles. The slow and poignant unfolding of these details invites us to empathise with Tomas though we do not see his face, nor really even what he sees. The camera is not, after all, aligned with his eyes, but with his chest. What we see is a specific embodiment of time, accumulated moments that suggest a lifeworld.

In discussion at the end-of-quarter public screening, TAB audience members spoke most often and most passionately about the effect of this shot, as though they were still working out their unmoored, somewhat contradictory feelings of empathy and shame. One veteran filmmaker stated that he had never before seen a shot from such a point of view, and felt that he had seen the world momentarily as though he were Tomas. A senior administrator took the shot as evidence that such classrooms – and by extension many other parts of campus – were 'not that accessible'. When TAB viewers saw *as* and *through* Tomas's subjective expression of movement, the barriers to accessibility in the classroom revealed themselves without comment. In a paper turned in at the end of the quarter, Tomas reflected that he 'hadn't slightest clue' about video making before the class, but could now say that he was 'in a rather well-made documentary' that he was proud to share. Tomas was able to express, to adapt Snyder and Mitchell's (2006) description of phenomenology in DS, 'the meaningful influence of disability upon [his] subjectivity and upon cinematic technique itself' (p. 170).

As in other slow cinema works, the shot I have described aimed to catalyse critical and ethical thinking by reorienting the viewer's manner of attention in the real-time of the screening. But Tomas's wearable camera scene attempted to approximate *his* experience of space rather than a disembodied experience of the world. Wearable cameras offer a means for employing long takes in accordance with theories gleaned from DS like Snyder and Mitchell's work described earlier, as well as media phenomenology about representing the lived body, sans exotic adventure destination, romance, or pity. A 'thick and *radical description* of experience is a turn toward articulating not only another kind of bodily being', argued Sobchack (1992) about the variability of subjective viewing experience, 'but also a healthy and adult polymorphousness, a freedom of becoming' (p. xv). Wearable cameras offer the long take aesthetic a different way of expressing the phenomenological world, more closely tied to the body *wearing* the camera so as to represent its manner of motility in space in the midst of activities. Tomas's long take beckoned viewers to search the frame for points of interest while slowly realising a pace of movement not as symbol, but as index, as 'the disturbing presence of lives [*behind* the camera] halted at a set moment in their duration, freed from their destiny' to tweak Bazin's characterisation of cinematic ontology for a social media age (Bazin, 1967, p. 14).

Conclusion

While *Access game* has not 'gone viral' or garnered conversation in the comments section of its YouTube page, I consider the video to represent a successful use of social media in a DS class. Students effectively used the Google Drive social media platform to share schedules, ideas, and rough cuts of projects so as to include those who lived far from campus, like Tomas. The class employed social media to share news of screening events and then finished works with a broader public, enhancing students' overall sense of solidarity and civic engagement. *Access game* screened in several venues after the quarter, including a community arts group in Downtown LA, an Orange County school district considering how to develop access services for their students with disabilities, and the UCLA library during Undergraduate Research Week. One senior who enrolled in the course because of her interest in film studies actually took a job in Access Services in her hometown as a direct result of seeing and discussing *Access game* over the quarter (she worked on a video about bicycle commuters). Two of the other students who worked on *Access game* have subsequently pursued DS-focused video projects as independent studies with me. Such outcomes do not make for sexy social media impact statistics, but I think they are suggestive of the kinds of affections, cares, and relationships that can develop in a DS course that uses social media and critically experiments with video aesthetics and collaborative documentary practice to catalyse public-oriented, intersubjective thinking. In this way, even though Tomas was not the most vocal or directive member of the class, the footage he contributed constituted an important kind of leadership, a direction for new thinking about representing and living in our collective social world.

I have also argued that in a DS class focused on digital media making, aesthetics *are* social media technologies. Aesthetics beckon a particular community and manner of attention, working in concert with or, in this case, somewhat at-a-slant to the norms of easy-to-use network platforms like YouTube. From this vantage, measuring success in terms of metrics can be dangerous. Counting YouTube views per week or noting numbers of petitions signed depends, in effect, on valuing first and foremost what one's media work is *able* to do, and how fast it is able to do it. Social impact media, like advertising, can make haste to harness audience attention through recourse to quickly identifiable, verbally driven, mythic tropes (the evil corporation, the victim turned activist as an up-by-the-bootstraps narrative, the disabled body doing as inspiration, etc.) that have been historically quite detrimental to persons with disabilities. As an alternative strategy, DS production curricula on 'slow cinema for social media' could make use of the possibilities for collaboration offered by lightweight, easy-to-use, wearable, networked digital tools, while opening up an inclusive, non-didactic space for developing a 2.0 version of Snyder and Mitchell's phenomenology-based, 'new disability documentary cinema'.

Notes

1 By affiliating with the branded content of the company channel, these producers take up niche markets within the broader GoPro social media ecology. Their monetised channels suggest that they seek to profit by this affiliation – or at least to make enough money to support a stint of watersports, snowboarding, or cliff diving – and so tend to mimic the fast-cutting, montage style associated with the company. See, for instance, *RealLifeHD* (https://www.youtube.com/channel/UC1H70dZhqBBL_hywR66v4sg), *MicBergsma* (https://www.youtube.com/user/micbergsma), 'CB Filmz' (https://www.youtube.com/user/cbomb19), *Be the adventure,* (https://www.youtube.com/channel/UCtEXh6yxM12HXzvNLquGYCw), and *skatepunk2425* (https://www.youtube.com/user/skatepunk2425), all of which emphasize montages with pop music featuring young, white men recording themselves, friends, and 'babes' as they travel and/or participate in extreme sports (Accessed 1 September 2015).
2 The company listed 185 videos as of 1 September 2015 on its YouTube Channel, none of which explicitly represent individuals with disabilities: https://www.youtube.com/playlist?list=PLSSPBo7OVSZvJtRrcF5CVSjRkmH9eNWA3
3 One exception to this general sentiment would be the case of Aaron 'Wheelz' Fotheringham, a self-titled 'extreme sitter' who occasionally wears a camera as he flips his way around skateboarding parks on his wheelchair (Fotheringham, 2013).
4 Scholars continue to debate whether to think of slow cinema as a genre, movement, or set of aesthetic characteristics. I am using the term to refer to an aesthetic movement. Oft-mentioned fiction directors include Apichatpong Weerasethakul, Tsai Ming-liang, Abbas Kiarostami, Chantal Ackerman, Béla Tarr, and Gus van Sant, with references back to Italian neo-realism and the films of Yasujiro Ozu, Robert Bresson, and Carl Theodor Dreyer. I would also consider films by Rea Tajiri, Julie Dash, Charles Burnett, and Zeinabu Davis within this rubric, and sensory ethnographic works such as Lucien Castaing-Taylor and Ilisa Barbash's *Sweetgrass* (2009), Castaing-Taylor and Verena Paravel's *Leviathan* (2012), Sharon Lockhart's *Lunch break* (2008) and *Four exercises in Eshkol-Wachman movement notation* (2011), Stephanie Spray and Pacho Velez's *Manakamana* (2013), and David MacDougall's *Doon school chronicles* (2000–2004).

214   *D. Andy Rice*

5 A final cut of the student film *Access game* (2014) is accessible at this web address: http://www.uei.ucla.edu/aspirestudentwork.htm
6 The interactive commute map is viewable here: http://aspirelab.squarespace.com/final-videos/
7 Since 2010, Anner has collaborated with two friends on producing regular videos for a variety of YouTube shows, including a travel series called *Riding shotgun* and a Soul-Pancake-sponsored show on religious institutions called *Have a little faith.* As of June 2015, Anner's channel had over 165,000 subscribers, and he had moved to Los Angeles to pursue widened commercial opportunities. Anner is featured in an epilogue of Dan Dobi's documentary *Please subscribe: A documentary about YouTubers* (2012).

References

Bazin, A. (1967). *What is cinema?* Translated by H. Grey. Berkeley: University of California Press.

Cartwright, L. (2008). *Moral spectatorship: Technologies of voice and affect in postwar representations of the child.* Durham: Duke University Press.

Dobi, D. (Director). (2012). *Please subscribe: A documentary about YouTubers.* Dobi Media.

Elavsky, C. M. (2012). You can't go back now: Incorporating "disruptive" technologies in the large lecture hall. In H. S. Noor Al-Deen, & J. A. Hendricks (Eds.), *Social media: Usage and impact* (p. 75). Lanham, MD: Lexington Books.

Ellis, K., & Goggin, G. (2014). Disability and social media. In J. Hunsinger, & T. M. Senft (Eds.), *The social media handbook* (p. 126). New York: Routledge.

Feenberg, A. (2014). Great refusal or long march: How to think about the internet. In C. Fuchs, & M. Sandoval (Eds.), *Critique, social media and the information society* (p. 109). New York, NY [u.a.]: Routledge.

Fotheringham, A. (2013, September 15). *Aaron Wheelz Fotheringham – WCMX – Airborne.* YouTube: http://www.youtube.com/watch?v=YEXsDdhgX-s

Fuchs, C. (2012). The contemporary world wide web: Social medium or new space of accumulation. In D. Winseck, & D. Yong Jin (Eds.), *The political economies of media: The transformation of the global media industries* (p. 201). London: Bloomsbury Academic.

Fuchs, C. (2014). Critique of the political economy of informational capitalism and social media. In C. Fuchs, & M. Sandoval (Eds.), *Critique, social media and the information society* (p. 51). New York, NY [u.a.]: Routledge.

GoPro. (2014, September 29). *GoPro HERO4:The Adventure of Life in 4K.* YouTube: http://www.youtube.com/watch?v=wTcNtgA6gHs

Grimshaw, A., & Ravetz, A. (2009). *Observational cinema: Anthropology, film, and the exploration of social life.* Bloomington: Indiana University Press.

Jaffe, I. (2014). *Slow movies: Countering the cinema of action.* New York; London: Wallflower Press.

Koehler, R. (2009). *Sweetgrass* and the Future of Nonfiction Cinema. *POV on PBS.* Retrieved September 1, 2015 from http://www.pbs.org/pov/sweetgrass/future_of_nonfiction_films_koehler.php.

Lanier, J. (2013). *Who owns the future?* New York: Simon and Schuster.

Lim, S. H. (2014). *Tsai ming-liang and a cinema of slowness.* Honolulu, HI: University of Hawai'i Press.

Longmore, P. (Ed.). (2001). *Screening stereotypes: Images of disabled people.* Lanham, MD: University Press of America.

MacDougall, D. (2006). *The corporeal image: Film, ethnography, and the senses.* Princeton, NJ: Princeton University Press.

Mogk, M. (2013). *Different bodies: Essays on disability in film and television.* Jefferson, NC: McFarland and Company.

Paumgarten, N. (2014, September 22). We are a camera: Experience and memory in the age of GoPro. *The New Yorker,* 44–52.

Romney, J. (2010). In search of lost time. *Sight and Sound,* 43–44.

Sandoval, M. (2014). Social media? The unsocial character of capitalist media. In C. Fuchs, & M. Sandoval (Eds.), *Critique, social media and the information society* (p. 144). New York, NY [u.a.]: Routledge.

Snyder, S. L., & Mitchell, D. T. (2006). *Cultural locations of disability.* Chicago; London: University of Chicago Press.

Sobchack, V. (1992). *The address of the eye: A phenomenology of film experience.* Princeton, NJ: Princeton University Press.

Sobchack, V. C. (2004). *Carnal thoughts embodiment and moving image culture.* Berkeley: University of California Press.

Stalder, F. (2012). The social media reader. In M. Mandiberg (Ed.), *The social media reader* (p. 340). New York; Chesham: New York University Press.

Yaros, R. A. (2012). Social media in education: Effects of personalization and interactivity on engagement and collaboration. In H. S. Noor Al-Deen, & J. A. Hendricks (Eds.), *Social media: Usage and impact* (p. 57). Lanham, MD: Lexington Books.

YouTube. (2014a). *Earn money with YouTube.* Retrieved November 10, 2014, from https://www.youtube.com/yt/creators/earn-money.html

YouTube. (2014b). *Grow Your Audience.* Retrieved November 10, 2014, from https://www.youtube.com/yt/creators/grow-audience-bootcamp.html

16 Blackboard as in/accessible social media

Updating education, teaching and learning

Leanne McRae

Introduction

When Tim Berners-Lee formulated his ideas for the world wide web, he held a 'grand vision' for this application as an environment of and for flexibility. He confirmed these ideals in 2010 by writing, 'The Web should be useable by people with disabilities. It must work with any form of information . . . and it should be accessible from any kind of hardware that can connect to the Internet' (Berners-Lee, 2010, p. 82). Via this vision, a popular imagining of the web as free and democratic has become potent. However, as the web has evolved, it has become increasingly difficult to hold onto Berners-Lee's vision as it becomes clearer that many people remain disabled by some forms of digitisation and unable to access the web effectively. Disabled people using assistive technologies often bear the brunt of built-in accessibility problems.

In education, these conditions become acute as web-based learning management systems (LMSs) such as Blackboard are increasingly the dominant manner by which course material is delivered, assignments are marked and grades are accessed. Yet despite the tremendous attraction in thinking about education in online environments as productive and progressive, the digital is not the answer to all educational investments. In particular there remain significant problems in the delivery of equitable and accessible content to diverse users of the online environment. For disabled students, the digital is both enabling and disabling. It can generate empowerment within the learning environment, but can also block effective and timely engagement with content. Disabled students must retrofit their education by adapting and modifying their technological interactions with course content, situating a radical re-inscription of how learning is deployed and thinking is mobilised.

Space for understanding these complex experiences with LMSs is frequently squeezed out by the chorus of congratulations from the champions of e-learning. Instead of celebrating the hyperbole of online learning spaces as transformative, this chapter is careful to consider the thoughtful and rigorous ways in which digitisation can assist and resist educational outcomes. Without due consideration of how this access is managed and how web literacies are activated on and through digital and assistive devices, teaching and learning will become impoverished.

Just as universities must ensure their physical spaces are accessible to disabled students, so too must the digital environment (Ellis & Kent, 2014). Via this investigation into online education and the tropes of accessibility for disabled students, a more energetic engagement with digital learning platforms can merge with understandings of universal design to mobilise an effective and transformative curriculum for all students.

With LMSs taking on an increasingly central role in university education, it is vital that disabled students have equal access to these platforms. In the context of this book, this chapter will explore the role of the LMS as a specialised form of social media in its own right, with a focus on the difficulties faced by students with vision impairments accessing Blackboard in particular. It questions the codification of digitisation as inherently enabling by rethinking the languages that define social media and LMSs as intuitive and effective learning spaces.

In addition, the chapter considers the terminology surrounding online educational forums in relation to disabled students. Significantly, it continues to amend the narratives that shape and define disabled people by using the phrase 'disabled people/students' rather than 'people/students with disabilities' in consistency with the reasoning mapped out in Jane K. Searle's (2014) book *E-Learning and disability in higher education: Accessibility research and practice:*

> Referring to 'disabled students' [is] preferable to 'students with disabilities' because the term 'people with disabilities implies that the person's impairment or condition causes them to be 'disabled' (and consequently that it is their responsibility to overcome it), whereas 'disabled person' implies that the person is disabled not necessarily by their condition or impairment, but by society and its inability or reluctance to cater effectively for that person (and consequently that society must effect change to remove that disability).
>
> (p. 5)

This is not just a linguistic distinction; it is a key feature of the social model of disability, where 'disability is not random or natural, but a social accomplishment . . . created by a disablist society, through the perpetuation of barriers to the participation of persons with impairments' (Swartz & Watermeyer, 2006, p. 3), and a determinate of how institutions, programmers and developers, teachers and other students understand, speak about, and deploy disability inside and outside the classroom. The argument in this chapter is therefore aimed at reinterpreting the rhetoric of digitised learning spaces to situate the social model of disability centrally within understandings of disability, digitisation, and education.

A turning point in my teaching career

In 2013 I was teaching the second year university unit *Virtual communities and online social networks*. The unit was conducted fully online and, unbeknownst to me, a student with vision impairment was struggling to access the various digital platforms we used to facilitate student engagement in course content – his screen reader could not keep up with the quick exchanges. After the student reached out to me via email, I sought assistance from the University's Disability Office to see what advice they might have for us – both teacher and student. I was advised only to refer the student to them, and I felt powerless. I wanted to intervene. I wanted to find a way to make the process and the participation accessible to him and any future students with disabilities I might have. Unfortunately, this did not eventuate and the student withdrew from the unit.

The disenfranchisement of this student remains a troubling axis point around which I ponder my role as a teacher and instructor to this day. It has also inspired this chapter – to investigate the ways I might have been able to assist this student and to explore how learning technologies and LMSs, such as social media, interface with people with disability. The objective of this investigation is to consider the ways LMSs in online education can both help and hinder disabled people in a digitised environment. While LMSs are widely integrated into educational frameworks and are a core method for accessing course content, there is little in the way of training for staff in the principles of universal design for effective mobilisation of content. Rather, it is assumed that the digitised environment will provide flexibility for disabled students to modify and manage their own learning – and that it is the responsibility of the designers of the LMS to provide an accessible template for use.

University-based access

As a result of popularised web rhetoric, disabled people are often singled out as exemplars of Berners-Lee's vision of web democracy and archetypal of the potentials for the digital environment to enhance and transform lives. Stories like those of Kathy Bell (2015) in *The Guardian* who wrote about how a tablet has enabled her son to communicate are uplifting (see also Alper & Haller, Chapter 10 this volume). Disabled people using a platform, tablet, or app that allows them unprecedented communication makes for good headlines and is socially and personally cathartic (see Hynan et al., Chapter 21 this volume). However, these popular stories play into prevailing ideologies of technology, disability, and access where digitisation results in social and individual transformation. The potentials of the web to both hinder and help disabled people is embodied in the World Wide Web Consortium (W3C), directed by Tim Berners-Lee, which has developed and implemented Web Accessibility Initiative (WAI) guidelines designed to address the issues of web accessibility by acknowledging that website design may block access for some users. These guidelines offer a way to begin breaking down the distinctly ableist trajectory of web rhetoric, design, and development (see Hollier, Chapter 2 this volume).

A core design principle is 'web for all' which advocates making 'human communication, commerce and opportunities to share knowledge . . . available to all people, whatever their hardware, software, network infrastructure, native language, culture, geographical location or physical and mental ability' (W3C, n.d.). The W3C also developed Web Content Accessibility Guidelines, the most recent version – WCAG 2.0 – state that websites should comply with the four principles of being perceivable, operable, understandable, and robust. These guidelines embed protocols to facilitate universal design. Importantly, they create conditions where access for disabled people is not an aside to be managed exclusively by third-party technologies like screen readers or other assistive tools retroactively deployed in the programming to make a platform or site compatible, but are centrally situated as part of product development. Access is inbuilt and all users benefit from universal design that is reflexive and careful across platforms and content. E-learning tools and applications should make accessing, processing, and deploying information easier not harder.

However, in 2010, Muwanguzi and Lin reported a 2000 study in the United States by Schmetzke which 'found that 23 out of 24 university websites audited in the United States did not comply with Web Accessibility Initiative [W3C] (WAI, 1999) guidelines' (p. 45). By 2014 Michalska, You, Nicolini, Ippolito, and Fink reported that '41% of university websites do not meet the Web Accessibility in Mind standards' (p. 995). Most significantly, Muwanguzi and Lin (2010) affirm that among colleges and universities in the United States, 'the needs of students with disabilities did not appear to be considered in the interface design of web pages or the organization of web content' (p. 45). Michalska et al. (2014) confirm that 'common violations of section 508, ADA and WCAG include no alternate text on images, inaccuracies with screen readers, meaningless alternative texts, and illogical header organization' (p. 995), demonstrating the continued marginalisation of the needs of disabled students within the delivery of online information at universities.

What does this mean for students with vision impairments?

This data is particularly significant when connected to the experiences of students with vision impairments. In a general context, WHO (World Health Organization) statistics report, for example, that 'about 314 million people worldwide are visually impaired' (Buzzi et al., 2010, p. 327) – this does not account for the myriad of disabilities that impact the diverse populations of the globe, which can include a whole range of physical and mental impairments and illnesses (see Kent, Chapter 14 this volume). Within educational frameworks, the inadequacies gain further focus when considered amongst the data for disabled students. Getzel and Thomas reported in 2008 that 'approximately 25% of youth with disabilities participate in postsecondary education after exiting high school' (p. 77), indicating significant levels of drop-out and an impoverishment of opportunity and future outcomes. In 2009, Shebilske, Alakke, and Narakesari reported that 'of Americans with low vision or blindness who are 25 years old or over, 4.5 million have less than a high school diploma, 6.0 million have a high school diploma or a GED, 5.4 million have some college education, and 3.6 million have a bachelor's degree or higher' (p. 989). In Australia, the number of students with disabilities participating in higher education have increased, but, in 2008, were still only identified as 4.1% of all students (Goggin, 2010, p. 471).

Many of these students require assistive technologies to access online materials, but there remain significant problems with the integration of these platforms and formats with the university delivery systems. 'In one study, 60 percent of students with visual impairments were found to be not benefitting from assistive technology' (Wong & Cohen, 2011, p. 132) – assistive technology like screen readers that translate online text into a 'readable' format for blind users. This was mainly due to a lack of education on behalf of both users and teachers about the capabilities of these devices when interfacing with the internet. However, this also means that many students are blocked from effective and efficient learning experiences due to a culture of inaccessibility built into ways of thinking about the online environment and the education of disabled students.

The disabling nature of these interactions is located in the way in which assistive technologies that students might use to access the web and LMSs are retrofitted into the development and design of platforms – here they unevenly sit within the suite of tools available to ease student access. Assistive technologies can range from low-tech to high-tech tools, from magnifying devices through to text-to-speech software and screen readers. Increasingly, for those with hearing impairment, the smartphone has become an assistive tool, with many users reporting 'the only thing I don't use my phone for is making calls – everything else about it gives me incredible access to the world around me' (Mager, 2015, para. 2). This demonstrates the ways in which disabled people innovate and deploy techniques and technologies in ways that are unpredictable and transformative. This is an invention motivated by necessity as a result of popular platforms not addressing the needs of the disabled, and solutions being found to disabling environments.

However, while disabled people continue to rewrite and recode the social to make it less disabling, developers have continued to ignore their needs, despite innovations like speech synthesis, for example, being around since the 1930s (Ghaoui, Mann & Ng, 2001, p. 139). These continuing attitudes prevail due to a lack of transparency around how disabling digital environments can be and the innovations disabled people deploy to manage and mediate these blockages.

Blackboard as LMS as social media

Blackboard is now one of the most commonly deployed LMSs in universities and higher education institutions 'with more than 20 million users across 20,000 organisations' (Empson, 2014, para. 1). It boasts a suite of tools to add value to students' online learning experiences and particularly claims that it offers 'learners accessibility through mobile devices, assignments at their fingertips through easy navigation, [to] keep them informed of dates and events through multi-modal notifications, and connected to the academic community through collaborative spaces' (Blackboard, n.d.b).

Blackboard invokes the rhetoric of social media in its claims to provide energetic and effective learning spaces along with streamlined management of student records, assignments, grades, and even plagiarism detection. In this context, Blackboard itself, like many LMSs, can be seen as a form of specialised social media. It allows a shared place online for both formal and social interaction, it allows for content to be posted, linked to, and commented upon. While a counter-argument can be made about the lack of open access to the system and the established hierarchy between users (in this case teachers and students), many disabled people would argue that for them this is always a feature of social networking. This discourse is most often situated in the understanding of the inherent flexibility and personalisation of online environments where the mobilities of text, links, images, and interfaces offers the potential for tailor-made interactions with unit material, online discussions, and learning outcomes. Within this rationalising, students are able to construct just-in-time delivery of their education by mobilising text, hyper-linking their literacies, and posting their preferences.

Blackboard – accessibility

Blackboard makes serious claims about its level of accessibility for disabled students. It offers evidence of their compliance to the Web Content Accessibility Guidelines (WCAG) as of December 2012 and confirms that they have gold level certification for non-visual access issued by the National Federation of the Blind (NFB) (Blackboard, n.d.a). This was an important step for the company – in 2010 studies reported that Blackboard failed to meet a number of accessibility standards, particularly for blind students. However, as Kent (2015) wryly notes, 'Thirteen years is a long time to wait for an accessible version of the software' (para. 1), demonstrating how disabled students continue to be an afterthought in the design and delivery of Blackboard tools. This lack of consideration places responsibility for access squarely with the student in the management of their embodiment rather than with the institution or the developers altering the environment to facilitate multiple styles of educational interfacing.

In 2010 Conway reported a number of failures in Blackboard navigation for sight impaired users including 'the login page failed the checklist in three out of four criteria. Main features missing are the lack of a "Contact us" link, and accessibility features placed in very small print at the bottom of the page' (p. 18). Conway (2010) also affirmed that websites should feature resizing and accessibility options prominently (p. 18) and noted that Blackboard did not appear to conform to these guidelines. Conway (2010) further identified that 'the tab key moves through the page [but] it is difficult and sometimes impossible to know where you are because there is no set sequencing to the tab movements' (p. 19). This is particularly disabling for people using screen readers which read web pages sequentially, and it barely addresses the WCAG Guidelines that confirm pages should be navigable without a mouse. Lambert (2013), also assessing the site for visually impaired users, found that

> Blackboard Learn is moderately well executed. However, until things like the captcha, inaccessible email bodies, and confusing links are rectified, Blackboard Learn will not be a complete solution for independent learning for those who are users of screen access technology.
>
> (p. 32)

In his study, Lambert (2013) discovered varying results using Blackboard depending on the assistive technology used, be it VoiceOver (for Macintosh users), JAWS for Windows, and Windows-Eyes. Nevertheless, each demonstrated significant lacks in particular areas, namely account creation, email composition, and confusing links. Lambert (2013) was particularly articulate in affirming that 'creating e-learning that is accessible has to do with making the whole environment accessible and not just the tools themselves' (p. 3). By rethinking the ways in which access is understood, universal design can become normalised.

Blackboard – teaching, design and disability

However, this rethinking cannot only involve IT support and platform developers. It must include university hierarchies, and it must include teachers and curriculum designers. This latter group will need skills in not only managing the Blackboard environment so that the materials they upload do not further disable students using assistive technologies, but so that they can also design reflexive syllabi that facilitate flexibilities in knowledge, assessment, time management, and learning outcomes. Without such training, Blackboard will continue to alienate, block, and disengage disabled students.

Instead of replicating mainstream ideologies about digitisation, disability, and education, teachers and university hierarchies need to acknowledge the ways in which digital environments are not equitable for all users. Teachers need reflexive, engaged, and situated training in Blackboard management for disabled students. These skills must be privileged along with managing Grade Center and Turnitin workshops that often fill up university training programmes and professional development. Muwanguzi and Lin (2010) affirm that 'online instructors have little knowledge about the special needs that students with disabilities have in working with web-based educational media' (p. 45). Disabled students' learning experiences are compromised in part because most educators lack 'the design skills or technical expertise to do more than implement the most rudimentary modification strategies' (Simoncelli & Hinson, 2008, p. 51). Teachers need to be instructed on strategies that can assist in situating universal design within their curriculum and building it into the materials they draw upon. But this can only be effective if a commitment to universal design is embraced by university hierarchies. Importantly, Conway (2010) identified that 'while there are a number of features that are static on Blackboard, due to its use of a content management system, there are ways that staff may ensure that accessibility is maximised for students' (p. 22). These strategies include a series of interventions that staff can deploy as a way to ease the accessibility issues of disabled students:

> Some methods that may be used include: ensuring that there are a variety of access methods used for lecture materials including audio recordings of lectures accompanied by a transcript would enable individuals with both hearing and visual impairments to maximise their learning potential. . . . Items such as PDF files are notoriously inaccessible to screen-reading software; therefore an

HTML version should also be included. Descriptive content for any graphics should also be included in ALT-text format so that screen-reading software may describe the item to the user.

(Conway, 2010, p. 22)

Teachers are able to increase the accessibility of the blackboard platform through simple choices related to font. Michalska et al. (2014) advise using 'standard san serif fonts such as Arial and Helvetica' (p. 996) and a font size between 9 and 12 (p. 996). They also advise a black and white colour contrast (p. 997). These are all things that teachers can do within Blackboard to make navigation and read-ing easier for disabled students, particularly those with sight impairment. While these may appear to be cosmetic interventions, the building of consciousness into curriculum design and Blackboard layout can serve to reshape how education is delivered and managed. In reflexive negotiation of 'the command-and-control imposition Blackboard represents' (Goggin, 2012, p. 14), teachers and curriculum designers can reframe the structures and strategies of education.

Awareness of the need – for example, 'to ensure clear and consistent navigation, rows or all navigational links . . . always . . . placed in the same location on all web pages and in the same sequence, which will help to avoid user disorientation' (Michalska et al., 2014, p. 996) – will make educators conscious of the specific experiences involved in using assistive technologies. While teachers will have little control over the situation of navigational tools in Blackboard, such knowl-edge does provide insight into the difficulties disabled students face and can allow teachers to mitigate them with understanding and allowances. For blind students, for example, 'although typical tasks in education do not seem time sensitive or complex, visual impairments make them so' (Shebilske, Alakke & Narakesari, 2009, p. 988). Buzzi et al. (2010) found that 'visually impaired users searching the Web for a specific piece of information took an average 2.5 times longer than sighted users' (p. 329), indicating the basic barriers screen-reading technology can create when having to read dynamic or poorly designed websites. Teachers becoming aware of these difficulties can create an assistive framework for learn-ing within the unit content and its outcomes, while university hierarchies can press for universal design from Blackboard as well as the way in which digital interfaces are activated on home sites and localised technologies. Through these means, third-party technologies can function to access Blackboard content, while better design and a conscious curriculum can create conditions for more effective useability within Blackboard.

Universal universities

All of these existing and potential problems with Blackboard and e-learning more generally exist in the ambivalence taken towards education and universal design by LMS development and university hierarchies. The tensions between the opportunities that digital formats provide for flexible and dynamic learning management and the potential for crippling inaccessibility dance together to create an environment where dialogue about disabled students is allocated to disability specialists and not widely populated and percolated through the academic sphere. This will always mean that accessibility for disabled students remains an after-thought instead of embedded in the core design principles that are supposed to be activated and embodied in the W3C guidelines governing online sites. Disabled people 'have been pioneers in the use of the Internet' (Goggin, 2015, p. 327) but their needs remain retrospectively engaged rather than on the cutting edge of tech-nology design and application. Kent (2015) affirms that 'disability access needs to be built into the design process at the beginning, not retrofitted' (para. 16).

This built-in approach is at the core of effective accessibility for disabled stu-dents. If universal design is effectively deployed, these issues are significantly mitigated. However, universal design is neglected in digital environments where mobility and perceived flexibility of text, platform, audio-visual media, and hyper-links translates into a custom-made viewing or browsing experience. These atti-tudes ignore the ways in which assistive technologies must actually make the virtual environment less dynamic for the disabled person to read the web. Screen-reading software, for example, 'can only navigate virtual environments that can be re-configured to be accessed in sequential and linear rather than parallel formats' (Muwanguzi & Lin, 2010, p. 44). Web 2.0 is notoriously problematic for sight impaired users and sits in counterpoint to a universally accessible and therefore useable web environment.

Ellcessor (2014) argues that 'the technological imagination of web accessibility is located between ideologies of ability, web technology, and assistive technol-ogy; it defines what is desirable and practical' (pp. 451–452). It is in this space that a rethink of accessibility in online learning needs to take place. This involves reframing the relationship between digitisation, mobility, comprehension, and cur-riculum. It means creating a universally designed learning environment where 'assistive technology will no longer be required to make up for inadequacies in curriculum' (Simoncelli & Hinson, 2008, p. 54). It will mean that 'adaptability is subtle and integrated into the design' (Simoncelli & Hinson, 2008, p. 50) so that assistive technology is not retrofitted into interfaces but is mobilised as part of the way learning is visualised and achieved. Ultimately, it means that knowledge of accessibility, useability, universal design, and assistive technologies need to be more thoroughly integrated into the knowledge base of teachers and curriculum designers. It cannot be the exclusive responsibility of IT experts and Blackboard developers. Instead, teachers, administrators, and university hierarchies need to think about how they may begin to intervene in the delivery and design of their curriculum to make disability, access, and useability a visible and coherent part of learning design.

Conclusion

In chapter 14 of this volume, Mike Kent explores the interactions between disabled people and traditional social media in a higher education environment. However, with the increasingly central role played by more formal LMSs such as Blackboard in both blended and fully online learning and teaching, it is important to consider the role that these systems play as social media in their own right and the implications of this understanding for ensuring access to all students, regardless of disability.

Myths about the liberation of information and the flexible accessibility of the internet and web for disabled people need to be counteracted. The digital interfaces utilised by universities to deliver course content need to reflexively deploy the principles of universal design rather than relying on reverse-engineered technologies to add value to the browsing experience of disabled students. Core recognition of the function and framework of an equitable education must be redefined so that disabled students are not left to manage, fund, and intervene in their own education with devices that may or may not be leveraged by software engineers. Instead, their devices should open opportunities rather than shut them down. Yet current design and development of LMSs and educational interventions in curriculum are lacking. Rather than leaving disabled students to manage on their own, rather than shielding teachers from considering their virtual experiences, universal design needs to be more visible. Only then can the consideration of curriculum design and how it might codify accessibility begin to ease the burden on disabled students – leaving them to focus on learning rather than managing technology, third-party tools, and navigational interventions.

References

Bell, K. (2015, July 18). An iPad gave my son with disabilities a voice – and changed his life. *The Guardian*. Retrieved from http://www.theguardian.com/commentisfree/2015/jul/17/ipad-disability-voice-app-quality-of-life

Berners-Lee, T. (2010). Long live the web. *Scientific American*. Retrieved from http://www.cs.virginia.edu/~robins/Long_Live_the_Web.pdf

Blackboard. (n.d.a). Accessibility at Blackboard. Retrieved from http://www.blackboard.com/accessibility.aspx

Blackboard. (n.d.b). Blackboard learn, benefits. Retrieved from http://anz.blackboard.com/sites/international/globalmaster/Platforms/Blackboard-Learn.html

Buzzi, M. C., Buzzi, M., Leporini, B., & Akhter, F. (2010). Is Facebook really 'open' to all? *In IEEE International Symposium on Technology and Society (ISTAS)*, 7–9 June, NSW (pp. 327–36). DOI: 10.1109/ISTAS.2010.5514621

Conway, V. (2010). Web accessibility issues with Blackboard at Edith Cowan University. *eCulture, 3*. Retrieved from http://ro.ecu.edu.au/cgi/viewcontent.cgi?article=1099&context=eculture

Ellcessor, E. (2014). <ALT='Textbooks'>: Web accessibility myths as negotiated industrial lore. *Critical Studies in Media Communication, 3*(15), 448–463.

Ellis. K., & Kent, M. (2014). Facebook, disability and higher education: Accessing the digital campus. In M. Kent and T. Leaver (Eds.), *An education in Facebook: Higher education and the world's largest social network* (pp. 196–204). New York, NY: Routledge.

Empson, R. (2014). Education giant Blackboard buys MyEdu to help refresh its brand and reanimate its user experience. *TechCrunch*, posted January 16. Retrieved from http://techcrunch.com/2014/01/16/education-giant-blackboard-buys-myedu-to-help-refresh-its-brand-and-reanimate-its-user-experience/

Getzel, E. E., & Thomas, C. A. (2008). Experiences of college students with disabilities and the importance of self-determination in higher education settings. *Career Development for Exceptional Individuals, 31*(2), 77–84. DOI: 10.1177/0885728808317658

Ghaoui, C., Mann, M., & Ng, E. G. (2001). Designing a humane multimedia interface for the visually impaired. *European Journal of Engineering Education, 26*(2), 139–149. DOI: 10.1080/03043790110034401

Goggin, G. (2010). 'Laughing with/at the disabled': The cultural politics of disability in Australian universities. *Discourse: Studies in the Cultural Politics of Education, 31*(4), 469–481. DOI: 10.1080/01596306.2010.504363

Goggin, G. (2012). Borderlands or enclosures?: Technology, the university, and cultural studies. *The Review of Education, Pedagogy, and Cultural Studies, 34*(8), 8–22. DOI: 10.1080/10714413.2011.643727

Goggin, G. (2015). Communication rights and disability online: Policy and technology after the World Summit on the Information Society. *Information, Communication and Society, 18*(1), 327–341. DOI: 10.1080/1369118X.2014.989879

Kent, K. (2015). Disability and eLearning: Opportunities and barriers. *Disability Studies Quarterly*, 35(1). Retrieved from http://dsq-sds.org/article/view/3815/3830

Lambert, R. (2013). A tale of two PCs: An evaluation of access platforms for the bling utilizing the "Blackboard learn" learning management system. UNLV Theses/Dissertations/Professional Papers/Capstones. Retrieved from http://digitalscholarship.unlv.edu/cgi/viewcontent.cgi?article=3004&context=thesesdissertations

Mager, W. (2015, January 27). Smartphones make deaf life easier but at the expense of what? [Web log post]. Ouch Blog. *BBC News*. Retrieved from http://www.bbc.com/news/blogs-ouch-31004325

Michalska, A. M., You, C. X., Nicolini, A. M., Ippolito, V. J., & Fink, W. (2014). Accessible webpage design for the visually impaired: A case study. *International Journal of Human-Computer Interaction, 30*(12), 995–1002. DOI: 10.1080/10447318.2014.925771

Muwanguzi, S., & Lin, L. (2010). Wrestling with online technologies: Blind students' struggle to achieve academic success. *International Journal of Distance Education Technologies, 8*(2), 43–57.

Searle, J. (2014). *E-Learning and disability in higher education: Accessibility research and practice.* London: Routledge.

Shebilske, W., Alakke, G., & Narakesari, S. (2009). University students using a screen reader for education tasks. *Proceedings of the Human Factors and Ergonomics Society 53rd Annual Meeting* (pp. 985–9). San Antonio, ASA, October 19–23. DOI: 10.1177/154193120905301510

Simoncelli, A., & Hinson, J. M. (2008). College students' with learning disabilities personal reactions to online learning. *Journal of College Reading and Learning, 38*(2), 49–62. DOI: 10.1080/10790195.2008.10850308

Swartz, L., & Watermeyer, B. (2006). Introduction and overview. In B. Watermeyer, L. Swartz, T. Lorenzo, M. Schnieder & M. Priestley (Eds.), *Disability and social change: A South African agenda* (pp. 1–7). Cape Town: HSRC Press.

W3C. (n.d.). W3C mission. Retrieved from http://www.w3.org/Consortium/mission

Wong, M. E., & Cohen, L. (2011). School family and other influences on assistive technology use: Access and challenges for students with visual impairments in Singapore. *British Journal of Visual Impairment, 29*(2), 130–144. DOI: 10.1177/0264619611402759

17 Dyslexics 'knowing how' to challenge 'lexism'

Craig Collinson and Owen Barden

Introduction

Lexism (Collinson, 2012, 2014) is an alternative conceptualisation of what defines dyslexics. Much as ableism and racism entail prejudice against specific culturally constructed groups, lexism is the Othering of, and discrimination against, dyslexics. Lexism is the result of normative attitudes and beliefs of literacy – that literacy should only be 'done' a certain way. We use the new concept of lexism to reassess some assumptions around literacy and dyslexia, and then to examine the way social media can act as enabling technologies which unsettle these normative assumptions. Drawing on a study of the digitally mediated social network Facebook, we argue that, under the right conditions, social media can provide spaces for dyslexics[1] to contest dominant literacy ideology, whilst engaged in active, critical learning about and through multiple literacies. Craig (Collinson, 2012) has argued that it is normative practices and assumptions associated with literacy (lexism) that define dyslexics, rather than a psychomedical impairment (dyslexia). This new way of conceptualising how dyslexics are defined creates new means of questioning existing discourses. Owen (Barden, 2012, 2014a) has argued that dyslexics can access and evidence knowledge in multimodal forms, via social media, which challenge traditional, restricted models of literacy. Our question is the extent to which Facebook provides opportunities for dyslexics to challenge lexism or bypass its normative assumptions. We recognise that social media can be disabling as well as enabling (Ellis & Kent, 2011; Hollier, 2012). Lewthwaite (2011) highlights attitudinal barriers – including scrutiny from others and the consequent perceived need to present and maintain a normative identity – which Merchant (2012) agrees may entrench rather than rebalance social inequalities and divisions in educational settings. But we give one example of a classroom-based project which precipitated authentic learning about and through literacy and which we believe could be replicated by other teachers or researchers in contexts similar to the one we describe.

The chapter begins by noting key features of our approach to 'dyslexia'. We then introduce the concept of lexism to illustrate the ways in which our text-rich society has constructed and maintained dyslexia as a disability. We go on to argue that a social model of literacy, together with the emergence of new literacy practices which are frequently socio-technologically mediated, prompt reconsideration of the relationship between dyslexia, literacy and learning. To do so, we draw on the philosopher Gilbert Ryle's classic (1949) work *The concept of mind* and his observations on the distinction between propositional knowledge (which includes literacy) and other ways we might define intelligence, and the importance of not confusing or conflating the two. Ryle calls this distinction 'Knowing how and knowing that'. We show how this work both enables us to unpick dominant conceptualisations of literacy (and hence what underpins lexist attitudes), and helps illustrate the shifting emphasis on procedural over declarative knowledge which some attribute to the expansion of Web 2.0 technologies (Dede, 2008; Kress, 2010; Lankshear & Knobel, 2003). We contend that deficit models of dyslexia and literacy can be explained through conceptual confusion between the 'knowing how' and 'knowing that' of literacy, meaning that too often educators focus on the technicalities of literacy and correcting perceived skill deficits, forgetting that literacy is a social act whose primary function is to allow us to communicate and develop knowledge of other things. We then present evidence from an empirical classroom study of five dyslexic students' educational Facebook use which suggests that rather than being defined and constrained by perceived literacy deficits related to 'knowing that', the dyslexic students can be seen to be highly motivated and adept in learning the 'knowing how' necessary for developing critical digital literacies. In the actions of the five dyslexic students in this study, we find support for Meyer and Rose's (2005, p. 1) claim that:

> students 'on the margins,' for whom current curricula are patently ineffective, can actually lead the way to true reform because they help us understand weaknesses in our educational system and curricula that impede teaching and learning for all. The needs of diverse learners who have until now been disenfranchised in a print-centric world can drive us to discover, develop, and apply the astonishing power of new media to expand educational opportunities.

Dyslexia

Dyslexia is usually defined as a specific learning difficulty (SpLD) which principally affects an individual's acquisition of literacy skills. The cause of the difficulty is usually said to be located within the individual's neurology – their brain structure and function. Biological variations in such things as volume of grey and white brain matter, hemisphere symmetry and the localisation of speech and language operations are held to produce cognitive variations in functions such as phonological awareness, speed of information processing and working memory capacity (Frith, 2002, 1999). These variations are usually described as deficits or weaknesses. The cognitive deficits are used in turn to explain observable behavioural differences, such as impaired ability to read, spell and write. Most discourse around dyslexia thus reflects and reinforces a psychomedical paradigm which blames certain individuals' failure to conform to conventional ways of learning on their 'faulty' brains.

In this chapter we take a different view. Adopting a social model of disability (Oliver, 1990), we contend first that human beings are diverse creations, and second that societies create and sustain the concept of disability through structures of thought and environment. Natural human variation implies that we should anticipate a wide range of aptitudes in literacy ability and in cognitive faculties, yet our sociocultural environment discriminates against those who, through no fault of their own, find it difficult to meet societal and curricular literacy demands, that is, our normative practices and assumptions of literacy. Reid Lyon (2001) and Stanovich (1994) remind us that reading is not a natural process and should not be thought in such terms. Assuming that it is, and that there should therefore be a literate norm, leads to the reification of dyslexia – the idea that we will be able to 'find' dyslexia in dyslexic people's brains if only we look hard enough. However, in over a century of research, with hundreds of books and thousands of scholarly articles published, we still do not have a satisfactory neurobiological or psychological explanation of dyslexia. Some recent neuroimaging evidence even suggests that looking for neuro-anatomical determinants of dyslexia might be mistaking causes for effects, because of the influence of the environment and experience on neuroanatomical and hence cognitive development (Kraftnick, Flowers, Luetje, Napoliello, & Eden, 2014).

In other words, literacy is not an evolutionary given. It is only when literacy becomes a cultural artefact and expectation that we can talk of dyslexics or others with literacy difficulties. Thus, it has been argued that normative practices and assumptions of literacy are what *ipso facto* define some as dyslexic, and as these are culturally constructed so too must be 'dyslexia' (Collinson, 2012). Dyslexia can only exist in cultures which privilege literacy, like ours. Dyslexia is not simply *influenced* by the environment, as Frith's (1999, 2002) causal modelling framework indicates – the sociocultural environment *co-constructs* dyslexia through dependence on the written word. As Kress notes (2003, p. 1, original italics) '*The world told* is different to *the world shown*' and it is not difficult to imagine cultures where the dominant mode of communication for education is (or was) song or images, as in prehistoric times. An Ancient Egyptian who could not decode hieroglyphs, for example, might have been labelled as 'dyspictoric'. Such a label does not exist in our culture because alphabetic literacy is prized in education to a far greater extent than a facility for images. Our alphabet is less than 2,000 years old and universal schooling is less than 200 years old. A social model perspective on dyslexia and literacy thus accounts for the fact that reading and writing are (in evolutionary terms) recently invented, unnatural processes which are difficult to learn for a large minority of the population. Extrinsic cultural forces have interacted with the neurologies of individuals in the minority to co-construct the difficulty (McDermott & Varenne, 1995). This minority is labelled 'dyslexic', but the label is a product of the cultural privileging of reading and writing over a very short time span (Ehardt, 2008; Kress, 2000). The collective noun we use here to encapsulate the normative practices and assumptions of literacy which 'Others' dyslexics is lexism. What we mean by lexism is set out in the following section, in relation to the more familiar concept of ableism. What is of particular interest to us is the way social media – where compositions frequently combine abbreviated or unorthodox spellings and grammar forms with other modes of representation such as icons, emoji, graphics, animation, sound and video – unsettle some of the assumptions underpinning lexism.

Lexism and ableism

'Ableism' is a term for the prejudicial belief that non-disabled people are superior to disabled people. Ableist tendencies are not restricted to deeply ingrained prejudices against disabled people themselves, they extend to prejudices about certain ways of being and doing. Thomas Hehir puts it this way (2002, p. 3):

> the devaluation of disability results in societal attitudes that uncritically assert that it is better for a child to walk than roll, speak than sign, read print than read Braille, spell independently than use a spell-check, and hang out with non-disabled kids as opposed to other disabled kids, etc. In short, in the eyes of many educators and society, it is preferable for disabled students to do things in the same manner as non-disabled kids.

The dominant dyslexia discourse, rooted in the psychomedical paradigm, can be seen to be underpinned by ableist assumptions about literacy and learning. The educational and social environment is hostile towards dyslexics – those whose mental and cognitive abilities, in the domain of literacy and memory, fall out of the scope of what is considered normal and acceptable. These students may have strengths in other domains, such as practical problem solving, working in three dimensions, or creative non-linear thought, but these are frequently sidelined in the interests of developing traditional literacy skills so that dyslexics can be seen to – paraphrasing Hehir – at least be trying to 'do things in the same manner as non-dyslexic kids'.

In this way, ableist assumptions and disabling attitudes contribute to a self-fulfilling prophecy based on low expectations. 'Dyslexia' can therefore be understood simply as failure to meet social expectations in literacy. The cultural and educational privileging of a particular set of literacy skills, and thus their high social value, together with a school system which assumes that all students can and should learn those literacy skills at the same time and in the same ways as their peers, casts as deviant and defective the dyslexic students who do not satisfy these normative expectations. It is these prejudicial normative attitudes, expectations and practices that Collinson (2012) terms lexism, and which we can think of as a specific, pervasive form of ableism. Having outlined what we mean by lexism, we now go on to detail an instance of students challenging lexism through their use of Facebook.

'Knowing how' and 'knowing that'

In this section we draw on the work of philosopher Gilbert Ryle (1949), who stressed the long-standing tendency in Western thought to confuse the capacity for propositional knowledge ('knowing that') with original thought ('knowing how').

Something of interest to us is the way changing notions of 'what counts' as literacy, combined with evolving, technologically mediated social literacy practices, suggest that the deficit discourse of dyslexia may indeed be 'barking up the wrong tree' (Moores, 2004, p. 1).

There are many definitions of 'digital literacies' (Merchant, 2007) but they have in common an emphasis on 'knowing how' (Ryle, 1949) to evaluate, manage, use and share electronic texts, rather than on the 'knowing that' of traditional, formal schooled literacy. Tasks more reliant on memory and rote learning can be thought of as 'knowing that'. These tasks are a normative practice within formal compulsory education, and dyslexics so often struggle with them. Social normative assumptions of literacy thus lead to a perception of some strange discrepancy between dyslexics' 'intelligence' and their ability to engage with rote learning aspects of literacy. However, this is a conceptual confusion, failing to distinguish 'knowing how' from 'knowing that'. Original thought can be considered 'knowing how', and social media literacies require this capacity more than 'knowing that' (Dede, 2008; Kress, 2010). In a benchmark text, Lankshear and Knobel (2003, p. 173), declared that 'practices of knowing that reflect a range of strategies for assembling, editing, processing, receiving, sending and working on information and data to transform resources of "digitalia" into "things that work"' are now coming to the fore. In other words, digital literacies, including those needed for social media, emphasise 'knowing how' to construct, interpret rework and circulate multimodal texts, and this shift in emphasis may favour dyslexics who struggle with the more traditional 'knowing that' dimensions of literacy.

Ryle's argument that we so often confuse – knowing how with knowing that (what he terms the 'intellectualist doctrine') – can be synthesised with Street's (1984) arguments about literacy ideology. Ryle's conception of an intellectualist doctrine emphasising 'knowing that' chimes with Street's critique of societal literacy norms reflecting the ideologies and standards of dominant social groups, including teachers and academics. We would add that these hegemonic forces create lexism, and that lexism then defines 'Others' and discriminates against dyslexics. Social media, however, provide opportunities for dyslexics to develop agency by exploiting new forms of literacy, beyond the control of policy makers and the arbiters of 'school' literacy. In tune with Lankshear and Knobel's observation, these new forms rely to a far greater extent than school literacies on 'knowing how' to use texts rather than 'knowing that' (for example) a particular spelling or grammar rule ought to be applied in a particular place.

Challenging lexism

Remedial literacy programmes prescribed for dyslexic students epitomise curricula embedded in and constitutive of normative literacy practices. Lexist attitudes and assumptions try to force dyslexic students to conform to dominant, traditionalist literacy norms through highly structured interventions, often based on intensive, repetitive skill-and-drill pedagogies usually based on synthetic phonics. Such programmes aim to get students to 'know that' each letter or combination of letters corresponds to a spoken sound or sounds. There is no doubt that these programmes can be effective for some learners, but their effectiveness is not universal and even where they are effective they are often not well loved. Craig, who is dyslexic himself, has direct experience of these programmes and he often found provision paternalistic, oppressive, patronising and superficial. Craig can remember one specialised teacher outside the school sector with fondness, gratitude and respect. However, this teacher was notable precisely because she rejected the condescending attitudes Craig had experienced from other teachers, and encouraged understanding of written language (knowing how) over and above rote learning (knowing that).

Owen's experience of teaching dyslexics and of training specialist dyslexia teachers on an MA programme professionally accredited by the British Dyslexia Association suggests that there is usually little time given over to reading for reading's sake. Some teachers on the MA programme might, for example, report permitting their students a few minutes reading a book of their own choice during a lesson if the student had performed well on the other tasks. Despite evidence indicating that high interest in reading is actually a common feature of 'successful dyslexics' (Fink, 1995), what might motivate students to read more – and so learn more – was often either ignored or subservient to the normative interests of the intervention.

Owen was dissatisfied and uneasy with this approach to both developing literacy and, especially, attempts to use it with the 16–17-year-old students at the Sixth Form College[2] where he worked as a specialist tutor. Owen therefore instigated a project which would see a group of five dyslexic students learning about and through literacies, with this learning mediated by the social networking site, Facebook. The students' regular 'study support' classroom was reconfigured as 'an inquiry-oriented learning environment that positioned students as active collaborators investigating their learning, personal responsibility, and construction of identities as self-sufficient learners' (Greenleaf & Hinchman, 2009, p. 11). Over the five weeks of the project lifespan, the students researched online the topic of dyslexia, and co-constructed a group Facebook page by posting links, documents, videos and so on they had both found and made. The space was dissociated from the institutionalised norms associated with 'doing' literacy in school contexts, with 'no requirements concerning "correctness," style or format' (West, 2008, p. 588). Describing the sequence of events in the classroom during one of the project sessions will demonstrate how adept the students were at the 'knowing how' of literacies, despite each having undergone standardised assessments of literacy which indicated impaired abilities (when measured against culture-specific statistical norms) for the 'knowing that' aspects of literacy. Freed from the expectations of school literacy, the students engaged enthusiastically in reading, writing, sharing and commenting on a large variety of multimodal texts, for example by scaffolding reading of a difficult text by watching an associated video first. They often used a somewhat knowing humour as well as unorthodox literacy practices, such as abbreviating 'cool' to 'kwl' when typing. Their prolific engagement with texts belies the stereotype that dyslexics are not motivated to read and write. Counter to lexist notions of literacy as an individual skill, it also highlights the social nature of literacy, of reading and writing as profoundly collective endeavours (Barden, 2012).

Classroom snapshot – 10 December 2010, 12:24–12:46

The following vignette is constructed from multiple data sources used over five 95-minute sessions – participant-observation, video recording, semi-structured interviews, dynamic screen capture and think-aloud protocols. Together these yielded over 70,000 words of transcript and eight hours of video. As such the snapshot is a credible summary of part of a fairly typical 'lesson' in the classroom used for the empirical study. Extensive accounts of the methodology and methods are given in Barden (2013) and Barden (2014b) respectively.

The five students are sat in a row, each working individually on a PC. One of the students, Chloe, is researching visual stress. This is a term for the perceptual distortions, such as the words appearing to move or blur on the page, that many dyslexics experience when trying to read. She watches a video by an eminent academic expert in the field, reads the user comments posted below the video and then triangulates this data by looking at some reputable sites including the Dyslexia Research Trust. Chloe 'knows how' to use the video to scaffold her subsequent reading of written text. Satisfied that this information is both trustworthy and of interest to her peers, she posts a link to the Dyslexia Research Trust site on the group Facebook page. Chloe has processed and evaluated the text before sharing it via social media. Having read the linked article and looked at another related video on the Facebook page, another student, Josh, decides to make a Powerpoint presentation illustrating the visual stress he experiences when reading. A third student, Charlotte, observes Josh and, intrigued, starts making her own Powerpoint movie, similar to Josh's. Having received the texts shared by their peers, Josh and Charlotte work on that information, transforming it and sharing the new projects via their screens. In her post-project interview, Charlotte revealed that she had never made a Powerpoint movie before. Following Josh's inadvertent prompt, Charlotte began to teach herself how to make a Powerpoint movie to communicate the visual distortions of text she experiences as part of her dyslexia:

> I thought I could do a little PowerPoint on the dyslexic . . . but then I needed to figure out how to do it . . . and then I put into PowerPoint like 'This is what it looks like when I'm reading a book' and then I put it into a little thing because what happens is the middle of the page disappears . . . and then I had to make the middle of the writing white and then I think I made it grey afterwards because it didn't work properly because I wanted it to like flash up and like on and off.

Freed from the constraints of normative literacy demands and lexist assumptions, these students are engaged in critical, authentic learning by and through multiple literacies. Wheeler (2012a, 2012b), citing Illich's (1970) assertion that 'Most

learning is not the result of instruction. It is rather the result of unhampered participation in a meaningful setting', argues that authentic learning involves complex,
sustained, collaborative tasks with multiple possible outcomes, products which are
useful in their own right, and real-world relevance. Co-constructing the group's
Facebook page over five weeks, reading, making, discussing and sharing a wide
variety of texts (including *inter alia* Powerpoint movies and dyslexia research
websites) related to a self-determined topic and aims, fulfils these criteria. Contrary to lexist representations of dyslexics as literacy 'strugglers' or even 'failures', through co-construction of their group Facebook page, we see the students
assembling, editing, processing, receiving, sending and working on a range of
multimodal texts transforming these resources into 'things that work' to educate
themselves and others about dyslexia (Lankshear & Knobel, 2003). The students
were able to concentrate on using and extending their knowledge of 'knowing
how' (to make a Powerpoint movie, for instance) to construct a text in order to
communicate their understanding and experiences of dyslexia, rather than on the
superficial, rote, 'knowing that' which governs so much dyslexia tuition. This strategic use of critical digital literacies further strengthens the challenge to lexism – in
Chloe's research and Josh and Charlotte's creative, constructive response to it, for
example, we see the trio exploiting their 'capacity to find out truths for themselves
and their ability to organise and exploit them, when discovered' (Ryle, 1949, p. 27)
via a combination of traditional and new literacies. Of course, the students needed
adequate 'knowing that', declarative literacy knowledge in order to engage with
these texts. The significance for us is that the authentic learning experience motivated the students to engage in, and even enjoy, substantial amounts of reading and
writing, the very things dyslexics are supposed to struggle with, dislike and avoid.

Our contention is that rather than authentic, motivating literacy experiences
being a reward or by-product of normative intervention – as is all too often the
case – such experiences should in fact be the foundation of literacy and learning. Social media provide a wealth of potential authentic literacy and learning
experiences. Moreover, technological innovations such as 3D printing, haptics,
holograms, virtual and augmented reality suggest an imminent and growing challenge to the dominance of the written word as the privileged mode for learning
in formal education (Kress, 2003). Such innovations may help 'level the playing
field' (Barden, 2014a) for dyslexic students, who have hitherto often found themselves on the margins (Meyer & Rose, 2005).

Conclusion

In this chapter we have sought firstly to highlight hegemonic lexist assumptions
embedded and enacted in both the dyslexia discourse and the practices of formal
education. We have argued that these assumptions rest on lexism, which arises from
an historic conceptual confusion, a failure to adequately distinguish 'knowing how'
from 'knowing that'. We suggest that this fundamental confusion has led to the prevalence of a variety of lexist, normalising and discriminatory practices. We question
how inclusive purportedly inclusive practices can really be if their overriding purpose

is to make dyslexics honouree non-dyslexics, rather than embracing diversity and recognising that there is nothing necessarily inherently superior in text-based epistemologies compared with other modes of thinking, learning and communicating.

This has led us to two conclusions. First, that if we adopt a social model of literacy, focusing on shared literacy events and practices rather than individual technical skill, we can see that the students in this study were, contrary to lexist expectations and stereotypes, highly motivated to learn about and through literacies, using social media. Second, that continued technological innovation, continually evolving ideas about 'what counts' as literacy, and epistemological shifts afforded by the richly multimodal semiotic domain of social media suggest the *potential* for greater inclusion and agency for dyslexic students.

Although we cannot generalise from this single case, our conclusions suggest to us some pedagogical factors others may wish to consider in relation to social media in educational contexts. Firstly, the students' use of Facebook and related digital media prompts reconsideration of the roles of teachers and learners. Teachers and learners are likely to bring different, but potentially complementary, technology skill-sets into the classroom. These factors suggest a possible return to the literal Roman meaning of 'pedagogue', as someone who 'walks with' or leads the students towards intended learning. It also prompts consideration of heutagogy – self-directed learning (Wheeler, 2011) – and if, when and how this should be incorporated into the classroom setting. Following from this, teachers may wish to reflect on their views on 'what counts' as literacy and how their students learn best in a social media age, as there are opportunities to use new literacies both in their own right and to foster traditional literacy skills (Leander, 2009; Veater, Plester, & Wood, 2011; Waller, 2013). The primary role of the teacher in such settings may not necessarily be as subject-expert, but rather as facilitator and mediator (Somekh, 2007), providing a direction, an appropriate degree of challenge, and equality of access to the relevant technology (Davies, 2009). Third, the group Facebook page can be conceived of as a kind of collaborative blog. It has been argued that blogging involves learning in an important and distinctive way, namely the 'read-write-think-and-link' (Richardson, 2006 cited in Davies & Merchant, 2009, p. 88). Blogging and, by extension, Facebook, can be used in the classroom to co-construct knowledge and develop critical literacy (Davies & Merchant, 2009). Opportunities for developing critical digital literacy through social media involve encouraging students building on existing practices and knowledge, whether obtained through formal or informal education, and identifying 'barriers and enablers' to participation in new literacies (Willett, 2009, p. 21; also Davies, 2009). Facer (2011, p. 69) suggests that the critical digital literacy all students will need in the near future for social and academic success has three elements – discernment (ability to judge the quality and relevance of information), multiliteracy (appreciation of the affordances and limitations of different technologies, materials and modes), and responsibility (awareness of the consequences of the ways in which they manage, circulate and control information). The empirical study we drew on for evidence in this chapter could be replicated, or at least approximated, in order to promote critical digital literacy and challenge lexism.

Notes

1 We recognise that some are uncomfortable with the label 'dyslexic'. There is no nomen-
clature which pleases all parties. One of the authors, Craig, is dyslexic himself and
refuses to be labelled 'a person with dyslexia'. Our position is that we accept the existence of 'dyslexics' – those people Othered by lexism – but question 'dyslexia' as an
explanation of perceived literacy difficulties.
2 Sixth form colleges are an intermediate stage between compulsory schooling and higher
education in England and Wales. They predominantly teach 16–19-year-olds academi-
cally demanding A-level programmes which are generally a prerequisite for university
entry.

References

Barden, O. (2014a). Facebook levels the playing field: Dyslexic students learning through
digital literacies. *Research in Learning Technology, 22*, 18535. [online]. Retrieved from
http://dx.doi.org/10.3402/rlt.v22.18535
Barden, O. (2014b). Winking at Facebook: Capturing digitally-mediated classroom learning. *E-Learning and Digital Media, 11*(6). Retrieved from http://www.wwwords.co.uk/
elea/content/pdfs/11/issue11_6.asp
Barden, O. (2013). New approaches for new media: Moving towards a connected methodology. *Qualitative Research Journal, 13*(1), 6–24. DOI: 10.1108/14439881311314496
Barden, O. (2012). '. . . If we were cavemen we'd be fine': Facebook as a catalyst for critical literacy learning by dyslexic sixth-form students. *Literacy, 46*(3), 123–132. Retrieved
from http://doi.wiley.com/10.1111/j.1741–4369.2012.00662.x
Collinson, C. (2014). 'Lexism' and the temporal problem of defining 'dyslexia'. In D. Bolt
(Ed.), *Changing social attitudes toward disability: Perspectives from historical, cultural,
and educational studies* (pp. 153–161). Abingdon, Oxon: Routledge.
Collinson, C. (2012). Dyslexics in time machines and alternate realities: Thought experi-
ments on the existence of dyslexics, 'dyslexia' and 'Lexism'. *British Journal of Special
Education, 39*(2), 63–70.
Davies, J. (2009). A space for play: Crossing boundaries and learning online. In V. Car-
rington & M. Robinson (Eds.), *Digital literacies: Social learning and classroom prac-
tices* (pp. 27–42). London: SAGE/UKLA.
Davies, J., & Merchant, G. (2009). Negotiating the blogosphere: Educational possibilities.
In V. Carrington & M. Robinson (Eds.), *Digital literacies: Social learning and classroom
practices* (pp. 81–94). London: SAGE/UKLA.
Dede, C. (2008). A seismic shift in epistemology. *EDUCAUSE Review, 43*(3), 80–81.
Retrieved from http://www.educause.edu/EDUCAUSE+Review/EDUCAUSEReview
MagazineVolume43/ASeismicShiftinEpistemology/162892 [Accessed August 5, 2011]
Ehardt, K. (2008). Dyslexia not disorder. *Dyslexia, 15*(4), 363–366.
Ellis, K., & Kent, M. (2011). *Disability and new media*. New York & Abingdon, Oxon:
Routledge.
Facer, K. (2011). *Learning futures: Education, technology and social change*. Abingdon,
Oxon: Routledge.
Fink, R. P. (1995). Successful dyslexics: A constructivist study of passionate reading. *Jour-
nal of Adolescent and Adult Literacy, 39*(4), 268–280.
Frith, U. (2002). Resolving the paradoxes of dyslexia. In G. Reid & J. Wearmouth (Eds.),
Dyslexia and literacy (pp. 45–68). Chichester: Wiley.
Frith, U. (1999). Paradoxes in the definition of dyslexia. *Dyslexia, 5*(4), 192–214.

Greenleaf, C., & Hinchman, K. (2009). Reimagining our inexperienced adolescent readers: From struggling, striving, marginalized, and reluctant to thriving. *Adolescent & Adult Literacy*, *53*(1), 4–13. Retrieved from http://onlinelibrary.wiley.com/doi/10.1598/JAAL.53.1.1 [Accessed September 13, 2012].

Hehir, T. (2002). Eliminating ableism in education. *Harvard Educational Review*, *72*(1), 1–33.

Hollier, S. (2012). Sociability: Social media for people with a disability. *Media access Australia*. [online]. Retrieved 12 June 2014 from http://www.mediaaccess.org.au/sites/default/files/files/MAA2657-%20Report-OnlineVersion.pdf

Kraftnick, A.J., Flowers, D.L., Luetje, M.M., Napoliello, E.M., & Eden, G.F. (2014). An investigation into the origin of anatomical differences in dyslexia. *The Journal of Neuroscience*, *34*(3), 901–908. DOI: 10.1523/JNEUROSCI.2092–13.2013

Kress, G. (2010). *Multimodality: A social semiotic approach to contemporary communication*. Abingdon, Oxon: Routledge.

Kress, G. (2003). *Literacy in the new media age*. London & New York: Routledge.

Kress, G. (2000). Multimodality. In B. Cope & M. Kalantzis (Eds.), *Multiliteracies: Literacy learning and the design of social futures* (pp. 153–161). London & New York: Routledge.

Lankshear, C., & Knobel, M. (2003). *New literacies: Changing knowledge and classroom learning*. Buckingham & Philadelphia: Open University Press.

Leander, K. (2009). Composing with old and new media: Toward a parallel pedagogy. In V. Carrington & M. Robinson (Eds.), *Digital literacies: Social learning and classroom practices* (pp. 147–164). London: SAGE/UKLA.

Lewthwaite, S. (2011). *Disability 2.0: Student dis/connections: A study of student experiences of disability and social networks on campus in higher education*. Unpublished thesis submitted to the University of Nottingham. Retrieved from http://etheses.nottingham.ac.uk/2406/1/Final_Thesis_Accessible.pdf

Lyon, G.R. (2001). Why reading is not a natural process. *Orton Insight*, Autumn, 1–5.

McDermott, R., & Varenne, H. (1995). Culture 'as' disability. *Anthropology & Education Quarterly*, *26*(3), 324–348.

Merchant, G. (2012). Unravelling the social network: Theory and research. *Learning, Media and Technology*, *37*(1), 4–19. DOI: 10.1080/17439884.2011.567992

Merchant, G. (2007). Writing the future in the digital age. *Literacy*, *41*(3), 118–128. DOI: 10.1111/j.1467–9345.2007.00469.x

Meyer, A., & Rose, D.H. (2005). The future is in the margins: The role of technology and disability in educational reform. In D.H. Rose, A. Meyer & C. Hitchcock (Eds.), *The universally designed classroom: Accessible curriculum and digital technologies* (pp. 13–35). Cambridge, MA: Harvard Education Press.

Moores, E. (2004). Deficits in dyslexia: Barking up the wrong tree? *Dyslexia, 10*(4), 289–98. DOI: 10.1002/dys.277

Oliver, M. (1990). *The politics of disablement*. London: Palgrave Macmillan.

Ryle, G. (1949). *The concept of mind*. London: Penguin.

Somekh, B. (2007). *Pedagogy and learning with ICT: Researching the art of innovation*. London & New York: Routledge.

Stanovich, K.E. (1994). Annotation; does dyslexia exist? *Journal of Child Psychology and Psychiatry*, *35*(4), 579–595.

Street, B. (1984). *Literacy in theory and practice*. Cambridge: Cambridge University Press.

Veater, H., Plester, B., & Wood, C. (2011). Use of text message abbreviations and literacy skills in children with dyslexia. *Dyslexia, 17*(1), 65–71.

Waller, M. (2013). More than Tweets: Developing the 'new' and 'old' through online social networking. In G. Merchant, J. Gillen, J. Marsh & J. Davies (Eds.), *Virtual literacies: Interactive spaces for children and young people* (pp. 126–141). New York & London: Routledge.

West, K. C. (2008). Weblogs and literary response: Socially situated identities and hybrid social languages in English class blogs. *Journal of Adolescent & Adult Literacy, 51*(7), 588–598. DOI: 10.1598/JAAL.51.7.6

Wheeler, S. (2012a). *Authentic learning*. [blog post]. *Learning with e's*. 28th November. Retrieved 13 June 2014 from http://steve-wheeler.blogspot.co.uk/2012/11/authentic-learning.html

Wheeler, S. (2012b). *10 characteristics of authentic learning*. [blog post]. *Learning with e's*. 29th November. Retrieved 13 June 2014 from http://steve-wheeler.blogspot. co.uk/2012/11/authentic-learning.html

Wheeler, S. (2011). Digital age learning. [online]. Retrieved 15 August 2011 from http:// steve-wheeler.blogspot.com/2011/07/digital-age-learning.html

Willett, R. (2009). Young people's video production as new sites of learning. In V. Carrington & M. Robinson (Eds.), *Digital literacies: Social learning and classroom practices* (pp. 13–26). London: SAGE/UKLA.

Part V

Community

18 'Talking my language'

The AthletesFirst project and the use of blogging in virtual disability sport communities

Andrea Bundon

> I would love to see more athletes discussing issues within the Paralympic Games! Not just the Games but the movement or the community so to speak. That's what I would love to see, discussions around that.
>
> (Mary, Paralympian and project participant)

Introduction

The AthletesFirst project was how my teammate Courtney and I responded to what we perceived to be a critical need in the disability sport community. Observing the rapidly rising popularity of blogging with amateur athletes – in 2010 it was de rigeur for athletes trying out for the Canadian Olympic and Paralympic teams to have blogs – we decided to create a blog of our own that would provide athletes with disabilities with an *online* space for the types of discussions that we felt were currently missing in *offline* sport networks. We recruited four athletes who would join us in the venture by contributing weekly posts and serving as a pseudo-editorial board and, together, we launched www.AthletesFirst.ca.

The focus of this chapter is on athletes with disabilities and the formation of virtual communities through the use of blogging and other digital platforms. Drawing on the online conversations from the AthletesFirst blog as well as interviews with blog writers and readers, I explore the following questions: Why do athletes with disabilities go online and participate in virtual communities? What do these online interactions offer that offline ones do not? And, most importantly, what can virtual communities offer, not only to athletes, but more specifically to athletes *with disabilities*? In addressing these questions, I illustrate how AthletesFirst provided a space that was disability-centred and where athletes with disabilities could find others who were 'talking their language'. Finally, I argue for a definition of community that is not tied to physical space but that also encompasses online networks of individuals linked by reciprocal and supportive relationships.

Background

The AthletesFirst project was conceptualised using a participatory action research (PAR) framework. PAR research is not defined by a particular set of methods but rather is characterised by adherence to core principles or values that guide the research process (Greenwood, Foot Whyte, & Harkavy, 1993). PAR research: (1) acknowledges the capacity of research participants to identify issues/research topics that are meaningful to them and their communities; (2) exposes how power operates in research projects and adopts practices that seek to redistribute power more equitably; (3) endeavours to build capacity and support growth in communities involved as well as amongst research participants and researchers; and (4) aims to translate knowledge into action that facilitates positive change in the community involved (Cargo & Mercer, 2008; Evans et al., 2009; Ponic, Reid, & Frisby, 2010; Reid & Brief, 2009; Stoudt, Fox, & Fine, 2012).

PAR research projects disavow the notion that distance leads to objectivity and hence to legitimacy in research practices and offer instead a 'scientific counter-story; a radical imagination of public science, conducted by and for the people most intimately affected by inequity' (Stoudt et al., 2012, p. 181). Within the field of disability studies, interest in PAR stems from an acknowledgement that people with disabilities have historically been denied meaningful roles in academia and other research undertakings (Goodley & Moore, 2000; Kitchin, 2000). In this sense, PAR is a response to the call by disability activist Mike Oliver for more emancipatory disability research, which he argued would facilitate 'the empowerment of disabled people through the transformation of the material and social relations of research production' (cited in Barnes, 2003, p. 6).

PAR-based projects generally evolve out of long-term engagement with communities and ongoing conversations between community members. In this instance, the catalyst for the AthletesFirst project was a discussion that I had with Courtney while driving home from a para-nordic skiing training camp. Courtney, an athlete with a visual impairment, was pursuing a spot on the Canadian Paralympic Team for the 2010 Vancouver Paralympic Games. I had recently joined her in this endeavour as her 'sighted race guide' and the training camp had been our first together. A long-time competitive athlete myself, I was confident in my skiing and racing ability, but I had just spent the entire week feeling like a total novice as I tried to negotiate the policies, practices, and politics of a disability sport program. On the ski trails, I was her guide, but on the ride home, it was Courtney who took the lead as she explained to me the nuances of disability sport.

A four-time Paralympian (soon to be five), Courtney's understanding of the complex ways in which disability is conceptualised within a largely able-bodied sport system was incredibly sophisticated and deeply personal. She was, for example, painfully aware of what Purdue and Howe (2012) have termed the 'Paralympic paradox', the pressure on para-athletes to downplay impairments and showcase abilities in order to impress non-disabled audiences and earn the respect of non-disabled athletes and coaches while simultaneously maintaining their disabled identities and demonstrating their solidarity for others with disabilities. Other issues we discussed were the classification system,[1] the funding of sighted race guides and other sport assistants, and the elimination of certain events from the Paralympic Games. These were not merely policies to Courtney, they were policies that had direct implications on her sport participation, her ability and her eligibility to compete, and even influenced how she identified as a person with a disability. Furthermore, as our conversations continued, it became clear to both of us that despite the fundamental role these issues had in shaping how people with disabilities participate in sport and their experiences whilst in the sport system, they were topics that were very rarely discussed by athletes with disabilities during the course of their daily training and competitions.

Though Courtney and I would have struggled at the time to identify the reasons that these types of conversations were so rare amongst our teammates, we suspected it had something to do with the 'mainstreaming' of disability sport. In the mid-1990s, Sport Canada started a process for integrating disability sport into the mainstream (a.k.a. able-bodied or non-disabled) sport system (Howe, 2007; Legg, 2003). This transition, which included transferring funding earmarked for disability sport from the Canadian affiliates of the International Organizations of Sport for the Disabled (i.e. the Canadian Amputee Sports Association, the Canadian Blind Sport Association and the Canadian Cerebral Palsy Sports Association) to national sport organisations (i.e. Athletics Canada and Swim Canada) occurred gradually over a period of approximately ten years. This move was harmonious with the Canadian policy environment of that era that advocated for the integration rather than segregation of people with disabilities within mainstream social programs[2] and it was also aligned with initiatives simultaneously taking place in other nations with established Paralympic programs including Great Britain and Australia. Furthermore, it was consistent with the International Paralympic Committee's (IPC) strategy to pursue closer ties with the International Olympic Association (IOC).[3]

Though this move towards inclusion and mainstreaming was largely framed as a positive step for disability sport (inclusion always is) and as an opportunity to move disability sport towards a more elite, performance-based model, it had other implications as well. For example, whereas previously an athlete with a disability's first affiliation was to a disability-centred sport organisation (for example, the Canadian Wheelchair Sport Association) now, his or her primary affiliation was to a sport-specific organisation (for example, Swim Canada). Or, to phrase it differently, athletes with disabilities went from being majority stakeholders in organisations that had a very good understanding of disability issues and disability politics to being minority stakeholders in sport organisations that had historically very little association with disability communities. Furthermore, the change dismantled existing networks of athletes with disabilities as, for example, athletes went from belonging to one organisation where they were in regular communication with others who shared their same impairment to being spread across a number of organisations based on the sport in which they competed. Courtney and I hypothesised that the new configuration of the sport system, with athletes with disabilities merging into pre-existing able-bodied sport organisations, was one of the reasons that few athletes were discussing disability-related issues. Courtney's personal experience was that, within this context, athletes with disabilities were reluctant to raise issues that might mark them as different from their able-bodied counterparts or that might lead coaches to label them as 'difficult' (for a good discussion see Bundon & Hurd Clarke, 2015). This concern, in addition to the relatively low numbers of athletes with disabilities compared to non-disabled actors in the associations meant that there was very little opportunity or incentive for athletes with disabilities to engage in debates about the 'politics' of disability sport. The AthletesFirst project was our attempt to try to address that gap and provide athletes with disabilities with online opportunities to connect with others and explore topics unique to their sport experiences. It was also an opportunity to explore if and how online platforms could support the (re)formation of the disability sport networks that had been lost to athletes in the process of mainstreaming.

Methods

The AthletesFirst project started with two contributors, grew to include a six-person blog team, and eventually engaged a global audience. The findings presented here are derived from 25 semi-structured interviews conducted with blog team members, others who read, wrote for, liked, shared, or commented on the AthletesFirst blog. The interviews were supplemented by fieldnotes, 34 posts, and 339 comments made on the blog itself, and by conversations about the blog on Twitter and Facebook. The sample consisted of athletes, coaches, volunteers, sport assistants, administrators, and spectators: 12 were female and 13 were male, 17 participants had a disability and eight did not, and 14 were competitive para-athletes and six were Paralympians. The group included individuals with amputations and other limb injuries, cerebral palsy, epilepsy, multiple sclerosis/neural diseases, spinal cord injuries, and visual and hearing impairments: 22 participants had Facebook accounts, 17 had Twitter accounts, and 13 were bloggers. Though given the choice to use a pseudonym, all participants choose to be identified by their real names.

The AthletesFirst blog

The first post went up on the AthletesFirst blog on 28 November 2011. Entitled *Language and sport* it was a point/counterpoint written by Courtney and Josh, both Canadian Paralympians. Courtney argued for the use of the term 'adaptive' to describe sports done by people with disabilities stating that it was the sport that needed to be modified and not the athlete. Josh made his case for the prefix 'para' explaining that 'para' was a brand that could unify disability sport from the grassroots level to the Paralympic Games. That post attracted only three comments including one by me, the blog's administrator. It was, however, widely read and distributed via social media networks to athletes, coaches, volunteers, and sport administrators. Over the next 14 months, the blog team would continue to write such posts with the aim of engaging an audience in critical discussions regarding the policies and practices of disability sport. During that time, our blog would be visited 9,500+ times by 6,500 readers from 97 countries and the comments filled 200 printed pages.

Though some question whether blogs should strictly be considered 'social media' on the basis that blogging predates Web 2.0 technologies and also because

blogs do not intrinsically require users to form social networks of friends and followers in the way that Facebook or Twitter do, I draw on Baumer, Sueyoshi, and
Tomlinson's (2011) and Keller's (2012) work to argue that blogs are co-created
social and discursive spaces formed through exchanges between authors and audiences. This was certainly the case for AthletesFirst where there was considerable
interaction and collaboration between the blog team and others who visited, read,
and commented on the site. These interactions occurred not only on the blog itself
but also sharing, liking, and messaging on Facebook and Twitter.

Findings

Creating online spaces for conversations that do not happen offline

When the first post went up on AthletesFirst, the blog team distributed the link
using our personal social media accounts. Given our mode of advertising, it was
not surprising that most of our early readers were people we also knew offline
and were our teammates, family members, and friends. Though it is common to
romanticise the potential of the internet to connect individuals who would not
otherwise meet in the 'real world', empirical evidence indicates that online social
networks most commonly overlap with offline social networks (Subrahmanyam,
Reich, Waechter, & Espinoza, 2008). This was certainly our experience and
two of the first people to read the blog and join the online conversations were
known to Courtney and me. Mary began competing in para-nordic skiing after
sustaining an acute brain injury and her partner, Kathy, was a coach with our
local ski club's para-nordic program. When Mary and Kathy read that first post
in which Courtney and Josh debated the use of the terms 'adaptive' and 'para',
they were intrigued by the views presented by the writers. Here is how Kathy
described her reaction:

> I got excited about it and I thought 'Wow, that's interesting' and you know, I
> kept reading [AthletesFirst]. I've really enjoyed the different perspectives. It's
> given me food for thought. It's even challenged my thinking in some areas.
> Cause you don't realize! You're going along 'tickity boo' and you think you
> have an idea of how people are feeling and you think it's a certain way, but then
> you see these kinds of posts and it's like 'Oh! I never thought of it that way.'

Mary elaborated that the attraction for her was seeing the divergent opinions
expressed by two authors that she would have previously assumed to have fairly
heterogeneous views: 'I find it really interesting that within the same community
you can have such vast ideas as to what a word means or what a label means!'
Reading the post prompted Mary and Kathy to reflect upon the assumptions they
themselves were making, specifically about the language they were using in their
sports clubs.

As previously stated, Mary and Kathy were known to Courtney and me and
their engagement with the AthletesFirst blog does not prove that blogging

can lead to the formulation of new communities of athletes with disabilities that would not exist were it not for social media technologies. However, their responses do illustrate how rare it was within their (our) offline network to engage in reflexive and challenging conversations. Courtney had very strong opinions about the 'right terminology' for talking about disability sport, but she had never discussed it with Kathy or Mary and, quite frankly, her daily interactions with them on the ski trails did not lend themselves to these kinds of discussion. Instead, each went along 'tickity boo' confident that the team as a whole had a common vision for the program, shared similar values and beliefs, and was speaking the same language.

For sociologists of sport, this finding is not surprising. It has long been observed that athletes are not encouraged to be critical thinkers and are commonly excluded, directly and indirectly, from discussions about the policies and practices that directly affect them (Kihl, Kikulis, & Thibault, 2007). Throughout our project, blog team members and participants supported this observation and described the barriers they had personally encountered when attempting to have these kinds of conversations within their sports organisation. For example, it was Courtney's experience that athletes were rewarded for focusing their attention solely on their sport performance. As she described it:

> So many athletes just want to focus on competing. When issues come up – like when fighting for equal access and stuff like that – so many [athletes] go 'I can't fight the fight *and* train *and* balance my life.' . . . I don't think that athletes that are competing are thinking like that. And I don't blame them because they're thinking of a whole lot of other things that in their immediate environment are a lot more important. . . . The political and intellectual part of it gets pushed aside because it doesn't impact on making your performance better. If anything, it can detract from it because if you are perceived to be causing problems, it's going to be harder on you. It's not encouraged.

Josh was even more explicit in his condemnation of not so subtle ways that athletes are discouraged from critically engaging with these of topics. He explained that he became involved in AthletesFirst because he wanted to see if online platforms, like blogs, might provide new and 'safer' avenues for athletes to express their opinions. He said:

> In the athlete community there is this sense [that] almost every athlete has ideas [about] how you can make the system better. But they always have some kind of a stick held above them – speak out and you won't make the team, make suggestions and you will be benched, and so on. So I thought [blogging] was a good way to have some meaningful debates and dodge some of the political consequences.

Though the earlier statements describe how and why athletes' voices often go unheard in the sport system, they do not address the implications this might have specifically for athletes with disabilities. This next section explores how the integration of para-sport into mainstream sport systems under the logic of inclusion has isolated and silenced athletes with disabilities and, second, how blogs like AthletesFirst can address this isolation by providing an alternative space for formulating shared identities and for connecting individuals with others who 'speak their language'.

'Talking my language': Finding others online who understand

A thread that wove through many of the online conversations on AthletesFirst was that athletes with disabilities felt isolated. The relatively low number of athletes with disabilities within sport organisations meant that they frequently spent a lot of time training alone and, in many instances, they were working with clubs or coaches who had limited experience with athletes with disabilities. For example, Rachael competed in wheelchair racing and had raced at the 2012 Paralympic Games. At the time she was interviewed she was living in a small town and was the only wheelchair athlete in the area. She described the crucial role of online social networks in helping her to establish and maintain relationships with others who could provide emotional support and motivation when she was struggling in training.

> Where I live there is no para-athletics. I am forced to train by myself. . . . . .
> There is nothing. I'm either in a roller in my basement or on the road because
> there is no track that I can use. . . . It's hard to stay motivated when you are
> training that way. . . . I started the blog and I don't post on it every day but
> every once in a while, you know, if I have a thought or I need to vent, I'll
> write a post. And it comes in handy. . . . There is some frustration because I'm
> the only para-athlete in athletics in [my city]. . . . Having social networking
> is a huge thing. . . . To just [be able to] say, 'Listen, this is what is going on.
> I'm frustrated.'

Rachael described an extensive and integrated use of social media that included a personal Facebook page, a professional 'athlete' Facebook page, a Twitter profile and a blog. Though she viewed each of these platforms as having a different purpose (for example, she used her blog to update fans on her competition results while her personal Facebook was for sharing messages with friends), there was considerable overlap in these networks and collectively they provided her with emotional support and a channel for extending support to others.

Arguably Rachael, as a member of the Canadian Paralympic Team, was already part of a community of para-athletes. For her, social media and online communication was a means of maintaining and supplementing these relationships when physical co-presence was not possible. However, for others with disabilities, newly come to sport, reading AthletesFirst and other online forums was part of finding an 'affirmative solidarity' (Meekosha, 2002, p. 80). For example, Shelley Ann, a woman with a visual impairment who had just started competing in para-triathlon, was reading AthletesFirst and had this reaction to the blog:

I thought 'Whoa! These are people who are talking my language. . . . I don't remember whose blog post it was but someone wrote [in the comments] 'Right on sistah' and I thought 'Yeah!' There are different times I have said to myself 'You're talking my language.' It's a gathering where everyone is signing from the same hymnbook.' . . . It give us [athletes with disabilities] a forum where we can discuss issues that are particular to us.

'*You feel like you already know them*': Online and offline communities

Shelley Ann described feeling validated because others were 'talking her language' and she came to value the AthletesFirst blog as a forum for discussing issues particular to athletes with disabilities. But just because people share an interest in a particular subject, it does not necessarily follow that they feel connected to or kinship with the people with whom they are conversing. The difference between using online networks to gather information about a certain subject matter versus being part of a community that interacts through online communication and social media platforms is demonstrated by Rachel's story. Rachel was a woman living in the United States whose vision had deteriorated over time and who turned to Facebook to find information about running with a guide:

> When I first started I was just trying to find guide running [on Facebook] . . . I was [asking] 'where are the visually impaired runners?' 'Oh, we have a whole group' {laughs}. . . . And that's really where I started meeting people – *C Different* and the *Challenged Athletes Foundation* was on there. It was just this huge network.

Rachel went on to explain that after meeting other athletes with disabilities via Facebook groups, she continued conversing with them using group posts, instant messaging and email. Communicating purely online, they answered her questions, connected her with guides in her area, and coached her through her first race. Soon they were making arrangements to meet in person at a race. Rachel described the experience:

> This past weekend I went to Washington DC and there were at least eight of them that I met on Facebook and then met in person. . . . We put a name and face together and had an amazing weekend . . .. You feel like you already know them. When we were introduced to each other, we immediately hugged each other like we were best friends.

Rachel's online community was not confined to one website or one form of social media but was integrated across a number of platforms with the same individuals posting in multiple Facebook groups, following each other on Twitter, cross-posting to each other's blogs, and communicating one-to-one using email and private messaging. Her description was consistent with my own observations of the online behaviours of the AthletesFirst readers. Though blogs do not have the same 'friend' or 'follower' model used by Facebook and Twitter, there were frequent indications that readers had ties with each other that extended well beyond the blog itself. For example, in their comments on the blog, readers would reference something they had read on another's Facebook page or Twitter account. Furthermore, during interviews, participants discussed their relations with other readers and described connections that extended across multiple social media networks and that also bridged the online/offline divide. In some instances, these relationships started with an offline encounter and online communication was subsequently used to continue the relationship. One example of this was provided by Leona, a competitive goalball player who stated that she stayed in contact with a large number of goalball athletes via Facebook and Twitter in a way that enriched their offline relationships:

> I have connected with people [offline] who have become friends over the Internet . . .. Like the people that I have competed with in goalball that played for other provinces that you sort of see just twice a year and just kind of have a brief conversation with. But then the whole next year you are talking with them through texts or Facebook or by email and then you see them again next year and you have a whole big conversation. It's like being reunited with a friend because you've been able to establish a stronger relationship and you're able to be in each other's daily lives even though you might be provinces or countries away.

Other participants described online encounters that led to offline meetings. For example, Darren and Rachel both described seeking out other para-athletes at races because they had been following them on Twitter and knew they would be in attendance. Like Leona, they rejected a hierarchy that ranks face-to-face contact as more authentic or valuable than online communication and instead spoke about how *all* forms of communication were essential to maintaining their connections with and their sense of belonging to a disability sport community. This finding is consistent with the existent literature that reports that connectivity (Baym, 2010; Rheingold, 2014), an important element of virtual communities, is strongest when group members supplement group communication with private, one-to-one dialogues. While these dyadic exchanges are not visible to the other members of the group, they 'provide a social mesh that underlies and helps to connect the broader Web of interconnection within the group more closely' (Baym, 2010, p. 90).

'I type and I erase': High standards and thoughtful replies

The final finding addresses what happens when people felt connected to the people with whom they were interacting with online. It was a feeling of commitment that drove many of the conversations on the AthletesFirst blog and that also shaped the overall tone of the blog. While much has been made of the *potential* for sophisticated, democratic discussion in online forums, the empirical evidence more commonly points to online conversations that are shallow, cruel, or even hateful (Suler,

2004). One only has to read the comment section of an online newspaper and it very quickly becomes obvious that the individuals writing there do not feel part of any online community and are more interested in attacking one another than in having conversations. However, though much of the communication that occurs online is aggressive and derogatory, there are exceptions and, as noted by Rachael, AthletesFirst was one of those:

> Sometimes you'll see comments on newspapers or those types of things where there is no filter. Someone is just pissed off and they are writing. Whereas blogs like AthletesFirst or even my personal Facebook page, people think before they speak.

Lelainia agreed with this position and stated that she felt people took care with what they posted on AthletesFirst and this compelled her to reply in kind:

> I type and then I erase. I write some more and then I think about it. I mean I think it's because of the bar being set so high there. . . . They [other respondents] are really trying to offer something meaningful when they write their response. . . . And you know, maybe they agree with it and maybe they don't but it doesn't really matter. It's the fact that the conversation is happening which is the point I think.

Overwhelmingly when asked about the 'tone' of the AthletesFirst blog, participants used the following terms: respectful, responsible, and thoughtful. Meyrick described reading the blog and composing his responses as a 'valuable part of my week' and others said they stayed up late at night composing their replies or reading others' posts. While considerable attention has been paid to research into the 'online disinhibition effect' (Suler, 2004), the phenomenon whereby individuals act out in online forums because they feel they are anonymous and distanced from the others involved in the conversation, what I observed was quite the opposite. Participants felt a responsibility to give fair consideration to opinions that differed from their own and to really engage with the topic. As Lelainia pointed out, and as the early comments by Mary and Kathy also indicate, blog participants did not believe that reaching a consensus or winning an argument was the goal, instead they placed a very high value on listening to others and having the opportunity to share their own stories and opinions. The result was conversations that were both thoughtful and thought-provoking.

Conclusion

The interviews, the discussions on AthletesFirst, and my own observations from five years of guiding athletes with visual impairments at the Paralympic Games and other international events do seem to confirm that the move to an integrated system of sport delivery did, as intended, result in a more performance-focused and professionalised disability sport system. However, what also became apparent while working on this project, and consistent with the existing literature (see Howe, 2007), was that though national sporting bodies had adapted to include disability sport in their organisations, the extent to which athletes with disabilities were truly *integrated* is debatable. In most instances, athletes with disabilities were expected to adjust to the norms of their new governing bodies while very few changes were made to the structure or culture of the organisations they joined. Another consequence of the move was that athletes with disabilities went from being the primary stakeholders of disability-centred sport organisations to being minority stakeholders in sport-centred organisations where they had to compete against able-bodied athletes for attention and resources. As Courtney had identi-fied early in the project, and as others later confirmed during interviews and blog posts, this left many athletes with disabilities in a difficult position of constantly having to advocate on their own behalf from within a sport system that has little understanding of disability-related issues or politics (an issued explored in more depth in Bundon & Hurd Clarke, 2015). Furthermore, as described by Rachael and Rachel, they felt alone.

It was the opportunity to make connections online that were not locally available to them that made the AthletesFirst blog and other online networks particularly valuable to athletes with disabilities. As described by the participants in this proj-ect, athletes with a disability went online to find the support that was absent in their immediate, offline networks. Using online communication, they interacted one-to-one and one-to-many and through the repetitions of these interactions, they formed networks that took on more enduring qualities. These networks became sources of support for the athletes and provided them with channels to extend support to others. Furthermore, because these interactions occurred in cyberspace and were largely on public or semi-public platforms (blogs, Facebook, and Twitter), they were visible to individuals who were just starting to get involved with disability sport. Thus these online conversations provided a way for outsiders to become insiders by joining the online conversations.

The literature on online social networks is replete with debates about the defi-nition of community. Scholars have argued both for and against the use of the word 'community' to describe online forums, newsgroups, networks of video gamers, Second Life gatherings etc. One side contends that 'online formations cannot be considered communities when participants can simply log out or turn off when they choose' (Hine, 2000, p. 19), while the opposing side points to the strength and solidarity that individuals get from their online networks (Chayko, 2007; Hine, 2000; Rheingold, 2014). Although these debates about the definition of community might be interesting theoretically, in many ways they miss the mark. The point is not to assess whether online relationships are superior to offline ones (or vice versa) or even to determine whether time spent online is time stolen from 'real world' interactions. The real task is to uncover if and how digital technologies enable the formation of communities that were previously impossible.

Though historically most communities have been geographically bound, communities are increasingly being understood as networks of individuals who share identities, interests and practices and who have reciprocal relationships (Baym, 2010; Rheingold, 2014). It is notable that none of these criteria *require* the physical co-presence of community members. In fact, I would contend that the participants in the AthletesFirst project fulfilled all the criteria for 'a community' in their online activities – they affirmed a shared identity as athletes with disabilities, they explored topics of common interest, and they discussed their shared sport practice. Furthermore, they demonstrated reciprocal relations in the form of offering and accepting emotional support (as described by Rachael) and sharing knowledge and material resources (as exemplified by the assistance Rachel received when she first looked for guide runners and started travelling to races). Finally, they described feeling connected and committed to others in the online networks as was seen in Lelainia's comment detailing how she felt obliged to spend time on posts and make a thoughtful reply because others had taken time with contributions. Most importantly, *none of this would have been possible in an offline-only context*. As was previously discussed, the participants were not only geographical dispersed, but even when they were part of the same local networks (as was the case with Mary, Kathy, Courtney, and me), the opportunities and incentives to engage in community-forming activities were absent. As Courtney and Josh indicated, in offline environments, the athletes were either preoccupied with the practicalities of training and competing or were concerned about the repercussions of engaging in potentially controversial conversations.

My conclusion is not that AthletesFirst was in and of itself a community but rather that it was a tool that contributed to the connectivity essential to communities. It provided a space where athletes with disabilities (and their supporters and allies) could congregate to have discussions about sport and about their involvement in it. These conversations, along a multitude of other online and offline encounters, were one way in which athletes with disabilities found others who were 'talking their language' and came to understand themselves as part of a larger disability sport community.

Notes

1 The International Paralympic Committee's Layman's Guide to Classification states that classification is a system 'to minimise the impact of impairments on sport performance and to ensure that the success of an athlete is determined by skill, fitness, power, endurance, tactical ability and mental focus' (IPC, 2012, p. 2). To provide an example, Courtney is classified as a B3 athlete in the sport of para-nordic. This means she has been assessed as having sight loss that meets the minimum 'cut-off' but has more usuable visual acuity than athletes in the B1 and B2 classes. Thus when Courtney races with against athletes classified as B1 or B2, they are either given a head start or their finish times are adjusted at the end of the race.
2 In the 2004 document *Sport for persons with a disability* produced by Sport Canada, it was reported that there were at that time 159 distinct programs being delivered by government departments and agencies that had the express goal of promotion the 'inclusion' of people with disabilities in Canadian society.

3 A strategy that culminated with the signing of the 'One Bid, One City' agreement by the IPC and IOC in 2001. This agreement requires that Olympic host cities also agree to stage the Paralympic Games and is seen by many as ensuring the ongoing viability of the Paralympic Games.

References

Barnes, C. (2003). What a difference a decade makes: Reflections on doing 'emancipatory' disability research. *Disability & Society, 18*(1), 3–7.

Baumer, E. P. S., Sueyoshi, M., & Tomlinson, B. (2011). Bloggers and readers blogging together: Collaborative co-creation of political blogs. *Computer Supported Cooperative Work, 20*(1), 1–36.

Baym, N. (2010). *Personal connections in the digital age.* Cambridge, UK: Polity Press.

Bundon, A., & Hurd Clarke, L. (2015). Honey or vinegar? Athletes with disabilities discuss strategies for advocacy within the Paralympic Movement. *Journal of Sport and Social Issues, 39*(5), 351–370.

Cargo, M., & Mercer, S. L. (2008). The value and challenges of participatory research: Strengthening its practice. *Annual Review of Public Health, 29*, 325–350.

Chayko, M. (2007). The portable community: Envisioning and examining mobile social connectedness. *International Journal of Web Based Communities, 3*(4), 373–385.

Evans, M., Hole, R., Berg, L. D., Hutchinson, P., & Sookraj, D. (2009). Common insights, differing methodologies: Toward a fusion of indigenous methodologies, participatory action research, and white studies in an urban aboriginal research agenda. *Qualitative Inquiry, 15*(5), 893–910.

Greenwood, D. J., Foot Whyte, W., & Harkavy, I. (1993). Participatory action research as a process and as a goal. *Human Relations, 46*(2), 175–192.

Goodley, D., & Moore, M. (2000). Doing disability research: Activist lives and the academy. *Disability & Society, 15*(6), 861–882.

Hine, C. (2000). *Virtual ethnography.* Thousand Oaks, CA: Sage.

Howe, P. D. (2007). Integration of Paralympic athletes into Athletics Canada. *International Journal of Canadian Studies, 35*, 133–150.

IPC (2012). *Layman's Guide to Classification in Paralympic Winter Sports.* November 15, Bonn, Germany: International Paralympic Committee

Keller, J. M. (2012). Virtual feminisms: Girl's blogging communities, feminist activism, and participatory politics. *Information, Communication & Society, 15*(3), 429–447.

Kihl, L. A., Kikulis, L. M., & Thibault, L. (2007). A deliberative democratic approach to athlete-centred sport: The dynamics of administrative and communicative power. *European Sport Management Quarterly, 7*(1), 1–30.

Kitchin, R. (2000). The researched opinions on research: Disabled people and disability research. *Disability & Society, 15*(1), 25–47.

Legg, D. (2003). The impact of disability sport and recreation organization in Canadian adapted physical activity. In R. Steadward & G. Wheeler (Eds.), *Adapted physical activity in Canada* (pp. 115–139). Edmonton, AB: University of Alberta.

Meekosha, H. (2002). Virtual activists? Women and the making of identities of disability. *Hypathia, 17*(3), 67–88.

Ponic, P., Reid, C., & Frisby, W. (2010). Cultivating the power of partnerships in feminist participatory action research in women's health. *Nursing Inquiry, 17*(4), 324–335.

Purdue, D. E. J., & Howe, P. D. (2012). See the sport, not the disability: Exploring the Paralympic paradox. *Qualitative Research in Sport, Exercise and Health, 4*(2), 189–205.

Reid, C., & Brief, E. (2009). Confronting condescending ethics: How community-based research challenges traditional approaches to consent, confidentiality, and capacity. *Journal of Academic Ethics, 7*(1), 75–85.

Rheingold, H. (2014). *Net smart: How to thrive online.* Cambridge, MA: The MIT Press.

Stoudt, B. G., Fox, M., & Fine, M. (2012). Contesting privilege with critical participatory action research. *Journal of Social Issues, 68*(1), 178–193.

Subrahmanyam, K., Reich, S. M., Waechter, N., & Espinoza, G. (2008). Online and offline social networks: Use of social networking sites by emerging adults. *Journal of Applied Developmental Psychology, 29*(6), 420–433.

Suler, J. (2004). The online disinhibition effect. *Cyberpsychology & Behaviour, 7*(3), 321–326.

19 Posting autism

Online self-representation
strategies in Tistje, a Flemish blog
on *Living on the spectrum from
the front row*

*Anneleen Masschelein
and Leni Van Goidsenhoven*

Introduction

Online communities and blogs are increasingly popular among autistic[1] people and have even become the touchstones of 'autism culture' and 'autism- and
neurodiversity-advocacy'. In this chapter, we will indicate how autobiographical
narratives and self-representations have influenced the conceptualisation of autism
in the second half of the twentieth century. The advent of the internet continues this
tradition, but lowers the threshold, making the forum broadly available for a wide
range of subjects on the spectrum. The internet greatly facilitates social interaction,
community and advocacy, but our focus is more on the specific advantages and
limitations of individual internet use for people living on the spectrum. Moreover,
we will also examine some of the implications of computer and internet metaphors
to describe an autistic mind. In a close reading of the popular Flemish blog or 'sailing diary' of Tistje – a young man on the spectrum who plays an important role in
the Belgian autism self-advocacy movement – supplemented with data from participatory observation and online interviewing (Brownlow & O'Dell, 2002), we
explore how autism can be read, reproduced and reconsidered in this digital field.[2]
We examine what blogging means for Tistje, how it affects his sense of social connection and his sense of self and whether there is any overlap between online and
offline worlds. In so doing, we not only focus on the specific content of this online
autie-biography,[3] but we also pay attention to the creative and material (or formal)
aspects of the blog. This will bring us, ultimately, to the question of whether the blog
can be read as a kind of 'prosthesis' in the cultural sense of the term (Coffey, 2004)
of an autistic mind.

The emergence of identity on the autism spectrum

Autism, a neurological development spectrum disorder, is deeply embedded in
medical, social and cultural contexts. The term was first used in 1911 by Paul
Eugen Bleuer to indicate specific behavior with schizophrenic patients, then

coined as a distinctive classification and disorder in 1943 by Leo Kanner and Hans Asperger. Subsequently, it has been examined by different medical and psychiatric traditions. Over the years autism became an exemplary psychiatric niche spectrum disorder of the late twentieth and early twenty-first century and a flexible signifier, simultaneously a medical diagnosis and a sociocultural construction (Nadesan, 2005; Hacking, 2010). For a long time, autistic people were the object of psychiatric and medical inquiry but had no voice at all in academic or public contexts. This changed in the late 1980s and early 1990s with the appearance of (auto)biographies by people living on the autism spectrum like Temple Grandin and David Eastham. These texts led to a significant shift in the discursive context surrounding the diagnostic category and received a lot of public attention. The life stories of people on the spectrum gave voice to 'new' and 'different' perspectives that contradicted the idea that people with autism have diminished subjectivity and raised interest in the way in which 'the autistic mind' functions (see Sacks, 1996; Smith, 1996; Lombardo & Baron-Cohen, 2011). In this way, self-representations are at the basis of an emerging 'autism culture' or 'autism (self-)advocacy'.

This entailed an important shift from autism as an abstract category to a focus on people living on the spectrum as an amorphous, inclusive and heterogeneous identity group that shape not only themselves but also the signifier 'autism' in culture (Straus, 2013; Waltz, 2013). The perspective thus shifts from what a person might do or be despite his or her autism, to what someone can be or do starting from or thanks to autism. This helped create a flourishing community in which autism is interpreted as a variety of the human brain – a neurodiversity – rather than an impairment. As a result, the question of self-definition, self-representation and self-expression of people with autism became all the more urgent, leading to an explosion of autobiographies, self-help books, artworks, music, blogs and websites.

'Autistic utopia'

All these forms of self-expression and self-definition do more than just allow subjects to communicate about their selves and autism. They show how autistic people 'inhabit the identities that have been ascribed to them and how they appropriate and/or resist autistic ascriptions in their efforts to promote their sense of personal well-being' (Nadesan, 2005, p. 179). In this way, the self-expressions and representations feed into the current conceptualisation of autism and lead to activism. As forms of socio-political action, the self-expressions and self-definitions of autistic subjects have fundamentally altered the autism discourse on four main levels. First, the self-narratives have revisited medical and therapeutic ideas, for instance about autism and hyper-sensory sensitivity (Osteen, 2008). They also play a role in countering some medical research programs (mainly in the US) that present autism as 'a terrifying epidemic that threatens children and families, which can only be addressed through finding a cure' (Waltz, 2012, p. 143). Second, widespread stereotypes such as 'flapping hands', 'bouncing heads' and 'little savant professors' in popular culture are demythologised and reversed (e.g. Higashida's [2013] *The reason I jump*). On a third level, the self-narratives influence the academic or scientific discourse on autism, which has shifted from speaking about autism in terms of 'shortcomings', 'disorders' and 'insufficiencies' towards terms such as 'condition', 'neuro-divergent' and 'difference'. Fourth, the most performative aspect of these forms of self-expression and self-identification is the construction of agency and socio-political validation. By engaging in debates about policy and research about autism, the autism community itself can make a non-medicalised autistic identity culturally available and debatable. The formation of this community manifests itself in the use of words as 'we' versus 'them', 'auties', 'aspies', 'our world', 'our autism blogs' etc. and in intertextual references to a body of work on autism and to other self-narratives.

The emergence of an autism community and self-advocacy movement shares a number of similarities with other disability movements (see Davis, 2002; Shakespeare, 2006). In his famous text, *On our own terms: Emerging autistic culture* (1999), the Dutch self-advocate Martijn Dekker suggests that the autism self-advocacy movement can learn from achievements of previous disability advocates.[4] He draws parallels between autism culture and the deaf or blind community on the one hand and psychiatric survivors' movements on the other hand. However, as Davidson and Orsini (2013) rightly point out, although autistic self-advocates are influenced by and can fall back on previous and ancestral disability movements, 'the nature of autism means that for some autistic people, unlike members of other disability communities, social interaction of any kind can be challenging' (p. 10). This points to an intriguing paradox at the heart of the concept of an 'autism community' – although autistic people often express anxieties and difficulties with functioning in any group and behaving like a neuro-typical social person, there is nonetheless an extreme desire for contact with other people and for countering the myth of loneliness (see also Biklen, 2005). The need for an autism community is also of great importance to react against one-sided statements about autism. Diversity is a cornerstone for autistic people, who stress that 'no one – neither autistic nor non-autistic people – speaks for everyone on the autism community [and spectrum]. Therefore, it is essential to attend to a range of voices, not just the loudest ones' (Osteen, 2008, p. 298). Reflecting on this paradox, Dekker proposes an 'autistic utopia' in which society would be 'organised around [the] individual' (n.p.).

Internet and autism communities

Thus far, a lot of critical attention has been devoted to written and published autobiographies by people with autism, or autie-biographies as they are sometimes called (see Smith, 1996; Capps & Ochs, 2002; Murray, 2008; Osteen, 2008, 2013; Savarese & Savarese, 2010). In many countries, publishers like Jessica Kingsley Publishers specialise in books about autism, among which a substantial part are 'self-narratives' and 'handbooks for peers'. This entails institutional and commercial aspects that raise many questions – who is published, what are the criteria for selection, to what extent do publishers interfere with their manuscripts, what are the genres in which texts are presented? Apart from narrative or poetical demands related to the (often implicit) genre conventions of life writing, autobiography or illness narratives, there are also marketing or commercial strategies involved. Compared to this, the internet is a much more accessible medium for self-expression and distribution of narratives.

Blogging and its advantages for people on the autism spectrum

Self-expression and personal narratives are omnipresent in what is called 'the blog'. In general, a blog or Weblog can be described as an online journal or diary, i.e. a user-authored site that takes the form of regularly updated web pages, listed in reverse chronological order that can be commented upon by readers. Blogs are not the earliest form of social media; their roots as a sub-set of social media can probably be traced back to the late 1990s, when Bruce and Susan Abelson worked on a project to bring diary writers together, which ultimately lead to *Open diary*, a social networking site that united the writers into an online community (Kaplan & Haenlein, 2010, p. 60). Similarly, the term 'blog' only came into existence in the late 1990s. Blogs, as social networking tools, may vary widely in nature, content and form, but most frequently they provide a combination of online diaries (i.e. confessional stories) and descriptive commentaries or information on a particular subject. Social processes (i.e. self-representation, self-disclosure) are at the heart of this online networking tool – blogging is an experimental form of social communication in which the blogger and the readers/followers are closely related through the act of online writing and reading. Moreover, a blog creates readers/followers, just as much as readers/followers create the blog.[5] A blog is thus a sort of social networking tool, but nevertheless varies from contemporary social media as for instance Facebook, Twitter and Pinterest. Both blogs and Facebook, Twitter and Pinterest could be interpreted as social media – online places where people can interact with each other. Nevertheless, the way one uses a blog or the more 'protocol-oriented sites', like Facebook, Twitter and Pinterest, is quite different. Current popular social media, such as Facebook, is strongly structured, allows one to develop an extremely large (but not that strong) community, is most of the time personality-centred and contains mediated compilations (i.e. the 'timeline' keeps updating). Whereas, blogs or user-authored sites are less structured and algorithm-driven than 'protocol-oriented sites', like Facebook etc. Furthermore, a blog allows one to develop a rather strong and cohesive community, is more topic-centred, allows longer posts and permits the blogger to stay in control of the discussions on his or her blog. According to Smith and Watson (2014), '*user-authored sites* observe some protocols, they are looser and may be minimal' (p. 89). As Henry Jenkins (2006) and other scholars have noted, Internet 2.0 and social media (and especially blogs) enable the formation of communities and activism. Especially for people with disabilities, 'dependence of technology' can lead to 'independence to become an active citizen' (Gray, cited in Reeve, 2012, p. 98). Likewise, digital social networking tools like a blog offer a number of important advantages for people on the autism spectrum: (1) the accessibility or lower threshold for telling (self-)narratives, (2) enabling interaction or the importance of community formation and (3) the comfortable mediation of the interface, which we will briefly outline.

The accessibility or lower threshold for telling (self-)narratives

One of the obvious advantages of a blog or online journal is that it can give visibility to authors who would never foster the idea of publishing their work or muster the courage to approach a publisher. For this reason, the internet clearly provides opportunities for minority groups. According to autobiography specialist Philippe Lejeune (2000):

> the *struggle for life* is much softer there [on the Internet] than in the world of books. From the very beginning, one can be 'visible' and stay that way without ever being 'seen'. Lack of success does not lead to elimination. The Internet proposes a kind of genetic stratigraphy of selection, as opposed to the world of publishing that only knows winners.
>
> (p. 395 – our translation)

Stories on blogs can question and play with traditional notions of authorship. Most bloggers use nicknames or avatars and experiment with the tension between anonymity, privacy and public space. Moreover, online blog stories are not tampered with (by editors) and usually have a different structure than classical, print autobiographies. Often they are more figurative, expressive or associative than narrative. They can be changed, adapted or deleted at any moment. As a result, computer and internet writing can be regarded as more flexible and ludic and 'it can be related to a new way of communicating' (Lejeune, 2000, p. 16 – our translation).

Enabling interaction or the importance of community formation

Secondly, the internet is 'essential in the facilitation of communication of adults on the autism spectrum' (Dekker, 1999, n.p.). Dekker traces the history of autistic involvement with the internet back to 1991, when a first 'mailing list' (the oldest form of group communication on the internet) *SJU autism and developmental disabilities list* (AUTISM List) was founded by Ray Kopp and Dr. Zenhausern. As a reaction against this medical (and cure-focused) list, Autism Network International (ANI), the first self-advocacy organisation, was founded by Jim Sinclair and Donna Williams. In the following decades, various new forms of communities emerged, such as virtual meeting rooms like chatrooms, blogs, online bulletin boards etc. that in turn transformed into creative neuro-shared spaces. Other 'autistic spaces' that developed are Independent Living on the Autism Spectrum (InLv founded by Dekker in 1996) and Autism Self-Advocacy Network (founded by Ari Ne'eman and Scott Robertson in 2006). On YouTube and *Second Life* as well, autism groups are present, e.g. Amanda Baggs and Brigadoon: the Autistic Island. Brigadoon, founded by John Lester, is a place within *Second Life* where one can be and make virtual contact with others. It is a commercial system for which one pays monthly. On both these platforms, communication is broader than mere language.

Since autistic subjects repeatedly express a preference for the written word over face-to-face conversations, these online platforms facilitate contact between people with autism from all over the world, provided of course that they are able to communicate, preferably in English (Singer, 1999; Broekhuis, 2010; Tistje, personal communication, 20 October 2014; van Gelder, 2014). However, there are also difficulties for people with developmental disorders and learning disabilities. To begin with, not everyone is able to understand or study English and thus to co-operate in the large self-advocacy movements (most of which are situated in the US and the UK). In other words, the global village of the world wide web is by no means without borders, linguistic and/or geographical. As a result, different language areas started to create their own – much smaller – autism communities, for instance the VVA [Flemish Autism Organisation] in Belgium.[6] More fundamentally, however, for many subjects living on the autism spectrum any form of communication can be extremely difficult. A delicate issue in this respect is the criticism on these self-advocacy voices from parents with autistic children who are (and will) not able to communicate or write at all. They feel that the autism community and self-advocates are not representative for their children and sometimes go as far as to doubt whether the self-advocates are in fact autistic at all. The English-speaking self-advocate Ari Ne'eman countered this critique:

> What concerns me is that sometimes that perspective is utilized not to make an argument that there should be broader representation or to do more to reach individuals with more severe degrees of impairment in one area of life or another, it's a way of attacking the idea of self-advocacy altogether or, even worse, the whole area of rights and dignity for people with low levels of ability.
>
> (Ne'eman in Waltz, 2013, p. 143)

The comfortable mediation of the interface

Finally, in his text on autism self-advocacy, Dekker (1999) raises an issue that brings us to a third advantage for people on the autism spectrum, namely that '[t]he Internet is for many high functioning autistics what sign language is for the deaf' (n.p.). In this statement, we encounter the role of the medium or the interface itself. Several aspects of the internet may be especially attractive for people with autism as the longstanding association of the functioning of the 'autistic mind' with the way computers work in a sense suggests.

Computer and internet metaphors

The autism–computer analogy goes back quite far. From the very beginning, machine metaphors (among others, see Waltz, 2003) have been used – mostly in a negative and de-humanising sense – as in Bettelheim's famous case study *Joey: A mechanical boy* (1959). Moreover, the American Psychiatric Association's *Diagnostic and statistical manual of mental disorders* (5th ed.) mentions 'stereotyped or repetitive motor movements' (American Psychiatric Association,

2013, 299.00 [F84.00]) in its diagnostic criteria for autism spectrum disorder. On blogs written by parents of autistic children, phrases like 'he will literally talk like a videogame' (Sandradodd, n.d., n.p.) or 'his brain is like a computer that never shuts off' (Fitzgerald, 2014, n.p.) also abound. As computer culture progressed, however, the negative connotations have begun to make way for more positive ones. Autistic people are often thought to thrive in professional computer environments.[7] Moreover, Temple Grandin re-appropriates the computer metaphor. In her second autie-biography (1996), she already points out that she is thinking in pictures instead of in language and compares her mind with a 'library of video memories' (p. 6). In a following text, *My mind is a web browser: How people with autism think* (2000), she extends this explanation by comparing her mind with the world wide web: 'A web browser finds specific words; by analogy, my mind looks for picture memories that are associated with a word. It can also go off on a tangent in the same way as a Web browser, because visual thinking is non-linear, associative thinking' (p. 14). Furthermore, many autistic people indicate that 'the computer and communication via the computer occurs in an "auti-way"' (AutSider, 2003, n.p.). The preference for computer narratives and conversations on digital social media tools can thus be related to aspects of the interface. The computer minimises the external stimuli and paraverbal signals like intonation, tone, body language, light, smell, noise, etc. that must be processed simultaneously with the verbal information. Moreover, as Lejeune (2000) points out: 'The computer is credited with a kind of therapeutic ear that purifies what one has to say, thanks to the neutrality of the typography, that allows one to objectify oneself, to escape from oneself, to put a distance' (p. 28 – our translation). Online narratives are often fragmentary rather than linear and hyperlinks create associations with other texts, ideas, images or movies. The dynamism and multimodality of online writing allow for a different, arguably more intuitive, way of writing and representing. All these elements can have a positive effect on identity (re)construction and representation. It is not a surprise, then, that Dekker (1999) links his utopian ideal of society for autistic people, based on respect, individuality and non-hierarchical organisation to the internet:

> The most successful and famous instance of a non-hierarchical today is the Internet (indeed a 'society' in which many autistic people thrive). The Internet is effective and unlimited in its growth precisely because of the lack of hierarchy: it is a distributed, redundant network. Even though the Internet is an organisation of computers, not of humans, this could well serve as a model to organise a new kind of human society compatible with the autistic way of being.
>
> (n.p.)

Other more traditional metaphors for autism, like the fortress metaphor, animal, military and puzzle metaphors (see Waltz, 2003) suggest in some way the existence of a 'true' or 'real' person 'behind' the 'autism facade'. This entails a negative view on autism as a disease from which a person should be freed or relieved. By contrast, the idea of a 'normal' or 'non-autistic' personality hidden behind a facade (or a ghost in the machine) is entirely absent in the postmodern machine-, computer- or internet-tropes used to describe autistic people and their ways of thinking. These metaphors fit within the ideology that governs more brain-centred autism research (EEG, CAT, MRi scans that promise to lay bare and map autistic brains or 'autism genotypes') and also entails possibly dangerous connotations. Conceiving of a person primarily as a series of algorithms can reinforce the idea of the reduced humanity of the autistic person. The enormous effect of the machine/internet metaphor has led to the temptation to objectify autistic subjects and to stereotypical representations of them in terms of mathematical brains, computer nerds and emotion-less robots (see Osteen, 2008).

In addition to reservations about technologically loaded metaphors, some disability studies scholars (who are mainly focusing on physical impairments and disability, thorough enquiry on technology, mental illnesses and disabilities and who have yet not received a lot of scholarly attention) also deconstruct the idea of the internet as a place of freedom that offers unlimited space to anarchic, countercultural and communal logics as a romantic myth. They point especially to the fact that 'the history of disability technology [is] one of normalisation, cure and rehabilitation' (Goodley, 2011, p. 167) which implies a predominantly medical model. The idea of using computer technology to 'fix' the subject is also found in computer therapies and apps that aim to normalise people with severe autism, for instance by teaching them to communicate verbally. Finally, an important nuance is that the 'promised inclusion' of the internet and other technologies is only apparent, because 'disability is both highly visible and curiously invisible in its digital landscapes' (Goggin & Newell, 2003, p. 110). There is no real or substantial confrontation between a disabled and non-disabled person because you meet the avatar or online identity – nobody is really and directly confronted with otherness, and the bodily, psychological and social aspects of disability are again ignored (see Goodley, 2011; Reeve, 2012). The internet creates rather a 'utopian thinking emphasising the *overcoming* of bodily limitations' (Goggin & Newell, 2003, p. 111 – our emphasis). Goggin and Newell, therefore, speak of the myth of the promised digital inclusion: 'While the internet has brought changes to the lives of many people with disabilities, they have also been firmly kept in the margins online or just left offline. More subtly too, the internet has also ushered in new dimensions of control' (p. 210).

In spite of their strong reservations, however, Gerard Goggin and Christopher Newell (2003) and Donna Reeve (2012) argue that digital culture certainly could also be a promising domain to gain insight in the implications of disability on subjecthood. To make this more concrete, we will now turn to an actual blog by a Flemish blogger on the autism spectrum in order to acquire more insight in how the blog influences both the individual and social aspects of the blogger. Our reading of the blog will take, as a starting point, the proposals made by Smith and Watson (2014) for reading blogs and will be supplemented by personal information from the blogger.

Blogging as autie-biographical act: The case of Tistje:
Living on the spectrum from the front row

As a case study, we will examine a blog by 'Tistje', a Flemish autism advocate, who is present on various online platforms and within the Flemish autism community, or the VVA. The blog, called *Living on the spectrum from the front row,* has been online since 7 February 2009 and is regularly updated.[8] Tistje is a pseudonym that is polysemous – an abbreviation of '(au)tist' as well as a reference to 'tist', a dialect word that means 'weirdo'; the diminutive form '-je' is a term of endearment, that connotes a loving or mild attitude.[9] The blog occupies a prominent position within the Flemish autism community, as can be gathered from the number of visitors (more than 470,000 at the time of writing) and by references to it by the autism community (i.e. VVA) as well as autism experts (i.e. Peter Vermeulen). Moreover, the blog has led to requests for paid articles. The blog posts can be tagged by keywords and may include hyperlinks to other websites or blogs, different typographic elements and images, either still or moving. Tistje's blog, made on wordpress, follows the same pattern. The posts vary in length, sometimes the texts are long and have been published on other fora, such as the VVA, sometimes they are shorter, containing more personal reflections or reminiscences. Often they contain book reviews or mindmaps visualising how a problem can be dealt with. The posts are, because of the interface, well structured – every post has a date, title, keywords and possibilities to respond.

The blog contains many paratexts that seem mostly chosen or created by the author himself (Smith & Watson, 2014, p. 85). The homepage opens with a grid of nine possible ways of entry: 'quotes by author' contains an alphabetic list of quotes related to autism or mental disability from a wide range books about autism, literary works and interviews with important cultural icons. 'Own work – thematic articles' contains a list of 18 themes related to living with autism, that in turn offers hyperlinks to blog posts related to the theme. 'Conferences' offers summaries of public lectures. The entry 'Alphabet' opens up shorter reflections on various keywords (e.g. 'being alone', 'being glad', 'Fingerspitzengefühl' or 'hope', which occurs twice) or phrases (e.g. 'Happiness, as in the vicinity of "happiness"'). The entry 'Most read articles' refers to a grid entitled 'Shop Window' that does not entirely overlap with the 'most read' list in the sidebar on the right. 'Published articles' contains longer articles published elsewhere that also feature in the entry 'Own work'. 'Five questions to. . .' collects interviews with various experts in autism. 'My bookshelf' refers to book reports of 25 recent publications and 'Just missed/archive' summarises blog posts from the preceding months. In the sidebar on the right, a standard feature of blogs, there is succinct information about the author, who describes himself as an 'experienced worker and writer', a calendar, a summary of recent and most read posts, a grid of keywords and links to responses. It also provides a lot of hyperlinks to other websites and blogs, ordered thematically, as well as to other online platforms on which the author is active. The sidebar ends with archives and a visitor count. On the top side of the blog some of the categories on the main pages are repeated: 'Just missed', 'Shop window' and 'My bookshelf'. 'Everything in a row' provides a grid to the entries present in the opening grid and 'Thumbs up' gives some praise for the blog.

Tisjte's blog as a moving target

On his blog Tistje talks about his life on the spectrum, outings, experiences with medication, therapy and labels but also his attachment to language, social relations etc. He also regularly discusses 'autie-blogs', social media and the tension between public and private. Moreover, he frequently posts extensive reports of conferences, books and articles on autism. Thus, on the one hand, anecdotal and autobiographical, the blog is 'an experience blog written by an ordinary guy from the dinner table with a view on the choices' (Tistje.com, 2012, January 28). On the other hand, it is a thematic, informative site with numerous longer critical, reflective pieces and even internally contradictory pieces on autism. This is related to an explicit ethical and activist stance – rather than bringing a 'triumph story', the goal of the blog is to gather as much information as possible, to share experiences and to give insight in an ongoing quest for being himself (Tistje.com, 2012, October 21). This is also expressed in the use of dynamic metaphors: the blog is called a 'sailing diary' and in one of his more autobiographical posts, Tistje talks about the importance of walking:

> On my way to the sea, on a walk, my thinking not really comes to rest but it comes to a different rhythm. Lines are being drawn. One way or the other knots that must be cut are disentangling. Or solutions emerge.
>
> (Tistje.com, 2012, November 6)

As a result, the blog is more than just self-expression; Tistje is a 'moving target' (Smith & Watson, 2014, p. 71) who speaks of a responsibility towards oneself, blogging, and autism as disability and identity. Through blogging Tistje discovers that his identity is fluid:

> for besides autism I also have a physical disability, I'm a person with a character, temper, personality, education, influence of society etc.
>
> (Tistje.com, 2013, August 7)

> Blogging has made me more aware of being more than someone with autism or someone with a disability, but that I have a huge amount of different dimensions. That I'm a son, brother, partner, man etc. That I'm educated, experience worker, someone with hobbies. When I write a text I not only do so as a person with autism but as a multicolored, pluriform whole, all of which is part of the 'I'.
>
> (Tistje, personal communication, 20 October 2014)

This can be related to Haraway's idea of cyborg politics as a political act that is a struggle against perfect communication and language. She says that:

> [c]yborg writing must not be about the fall, the imagination of a once-upon-a-time wholeness before writing, before Man. Cyborg writing is about the power to survive, not on the basis of original innocence, but on the basis of seizing the tools to mark the world that marked them as other. The tools are often stories, retold stories, versions that reverse and displace the hierarchical dualisms of naturalized identities.
>
> (Haraway, 2000, p. 311)

Different ideas coincide with different writing styles – lyrical and prosaic, scientific and precise ways of writing can occur even within one post. The coexistence of styles can be linked to the use of pseudonyms or avatars. First and foremost, they create a distance that alleviates tensions in his private life when some relatives felt that his writing was too personal (Tistje, personal communication, 20 October 2014). Second, they allow him to try out different identities, to rewrite them and confront them, to allow the contradictions to co-exist (Turkle, 1995, p. 186–189; Haraway, 2000, p. 310–316). All the posts are carefully edited; however, it is quite striking that the author uses a lot of neologisms like 'screendriver', 'sailing diary', 'brainpickers' and 'othersmaking'. Moreover, the more autobiographical texts are often associative. The titles are sometimes wryly funny, for instance 'Why "You don't seem to be autistic" is not really a compliment', 'Cat vomit, once my favourite dish', 'On a safari through autism-land' or 'Who reads this, gets autism'. More recently, Tistje also includes mindmaps to explain himself (Tistje.com, 2014 October 7) or to order quotes from others in a visual pattern, e.g. 'If you want to unload yourself, what do you do' (Tistje.com, 2014, November 30). Tistje also borrows words from others to voice ideas about autism or outside positions, both autism specialists like Donna Williams, Temple Grandin, Peter Vermeulen and literary authors like Arnon Grunberg, David Foster Wallace, Salman Rushdie, Fernando Pessoa and Marcel Proust. Tistje's blog as a whole can be regarded as a dynamic mindmap in which various aspects of himself and his influences are 'voiced'.

Cyborg identity and different forms of interaction

A crucial difference between blogs and written diary writing is the focus on interaction. The aim of online writing is not only 'inwards' but also 'outwards' (Lejeune, 2000, p. 28). As Smith and Watson put it:

> Studying the presentation of online lives makes clear that both the self and its presentation are only apparently autonomous, as many life narrative theorists, as well as media theorists, argue. In fact, online lives are fundamentally relational or refracted through engagement with the lives of their significant

others: the lives presented are often interactive; they are co-constructed; they are linked to others.

(Smith & Watson, 2014, p. 70–71)

As pointed out earlier, computer-mediated interactivity is a significant theme in digital media and can also stimulate utopian ideas. In autism studies (Davidson, 2008) as well, the interaction possibilities in a networked environment are usually embraced, however, digital interaction is rarely defined or critically examined. In the wake of Sally J. McMillan (2002), it is interesting to define it as a 'multifaceted concept that resides in the users, the documents and the systems that facilitate interactive communication' (p. 175). McMillan makes a useful distinction between 'user-to-user interaction', 'user-to-document interaction' and 'user-to-system interaction'.

User-to-user interaction occurs when Tistje addresses his readers with phrases like 'attentive readers will have noticed' or when he writes a blog post answering questions that he received via email. Moreover, in the responses Tistje – often using the name Sam – also interacts with others:

> One of the biggest misunderstandings is [. . .] that autism would be a synonym of not being social. Although autistic social being differs quite a lot from ordinary interaction. Autistic social being is more often geared towards the exchange of knowledge rather than sharing feelings or expanding stories, and also more often occurs via a material interface. Like written or virtual. People with autism are therefore social, but in a different way.
>
> (Tistje.com, 2013, June 18)

In one of his posts, Tistje describes loneliness as an important consequence of his autism (Tistje.com, 2013, July 1). The blog has alleviated this by allowing him to communicate:

> The reactions of visitors and readers on my blog are in my opinion important for identity formation. With some readers, there has been a long mail conversation, that in some case has led to a 'live' meeting. Sometimes, I say, because I'm not a big fan of 'offline'-conversations.
>
> (Tistje, personal communication, 20 October 2014)

However, the tension between the individual and the community aspect of the blog remains palpable on the blog. One way to resolve this is the function of the blog as a way of communicating information, which can work in two ways. As Tistje wrote: 'As opposed to others I have no interest at all in how other people are doing. Not even you, dear reader. I do like to hear whether I can learn something from you or others' (Tistje.com, 2011, June 15).

According to Tistje, autistic communication is more geared towards the exchange of knowledge: 'It more often starts from a shared interest (or shared interests) than with people without autism, that tend to start more from a shared relation in their social network or from a relational activity' (Tistje, personal communication, 21 January 2015). He experiences profound pleasure in gathering information about autism and structuring it: turning it into mindmaps, translating it and commenting on texts. This can be related to 'user-to-document' interaction, a remarkable feature of the blog. As pointed out earlier, 'the stability [and structure] of the written word [and the interface] can be a form of survival for those on the AS' (Henderson et al., 2014, p. 507). More than just a form of survival, moreover, the blog enables the writer to play with lettertypes, hyperlinks and visual material.

This can be regarded as another way of expressing the fragmentary and associative cyborg identity (Haraway, 2000). Due to the strict format of the blog, however, fragmented self-representation also coincides with a high degree of structure and linking. For Tistje, the material form of the blog itself is highly stimulating:

> The blog has changed my view of myself. [. . .] because I like collecting texts, getting an overview and I love layout and typography. I used to make thematic books and clip books, but those are too static. Once they're finished, I can't use them anymore. [. . .] With a blog I can keep experimenting. [. . .] this gives me space to learn. [. . .] It stimulates my creativity.
> (Tistje, personal communication, 20 October 2014)

The third aspect, the 'user-to-system' interaction can be seen in the particular relation of Tistje to the blog form, that allows for creativity and dynamism. At the same time, the constrained format may offer a form of relief because it limits options and avoids chaos. Moreover, blogging requires that the author masters certain technical aspects like hosting, cms systems and java. In this way, Tistje, who is unfit for work, acquired not only self-esteem but also an offline, socio-economic identity:

> Once the blog was there, I was a blogger. I regained energy to broaden my world. For example going to an exhibition or film or event. Whereas I would not go otherwise, I now went there 'to write a review as a blogger.' This stimulated my sense of initiative and social skills. I regarded it as a kind of work. In a later stage a number of blogs were published and I made money with them.
> (Tistje, personal communication, 20 October 2014)

Thus, while the blog identity is fragmentary and dynamic, and social interaction is preferably limited to online communication and via avatars, blogging has also offered Tistje a positive identity of 'the blogger' that has offline consequences in that it has led to (a certain amount of) social and economic integration. In this case, therefore, the critical remarks of disability scholars regarding the actual integration of disabled people through online identities and communities, must be qualified.

More than screendrivers

Both the quantitative success of the blog and Tistje's responses to our questions indicate that there is a degree of overlap between online and offline world, but on the whole it is the separation between the two that facilitates his interaction with both worlds. However, in spite of the positive effects of blogging, Tistje is aware of some of the negative consequences of blogging and the internet. In a post entitled 'More than screendrivers' he says, 'we are something more than computer users'. He also criticises the representation of people with autism as 'gamers' or 'softwaretesters' (see the employment project of 'Passwerk') (Tistje.com, 2012, October 6). In other posts he reflects on questions of privacy – e.g. in 'What it's like to make love to an autist' (Tistje.com, 2013, September 1) or 'About people who are quick to take offence' (Tistje.com, 2014b, June 18). In the online interview, moreover, Tistje demonstrates his awareness of the social aspects of blogging: the fact that online communication demands, 'a lot of insight in the context and the subtle social-emotional meaning of words for others', that it remains visible for a long time and that it can have a profound impact on use of time and relations. However, he concludes that his main pleasure lies in blogging as an activity itself, 'Just like my partner/wife likes knitting a sweater or quietly reading a book, I knit a text or am puzzling with the layout of my blog' (Tistje, personal communication, 20 October 2014).

Conclusion

For many reasons, blogging has become an important tool for self-representation, community and advocacy that seems particularly well suited for quite a number of people living on the autism spectrum. Although this aspect of online life writing and autie-biography has not yet been examined in depth, bloggers and advocates like Tistje and Dekker have reflected on the use of the internet. In general, two aspects of autie-blogging in particular seem beneficiary. First of all, the threshold to tell one's story and to reach out to an audience seems to be much lower compared to the institutional barriers of the publishing press. Moreover, despite and also thanks to the constraints of the format, blogging allows for creativity and associativity in the different posts. Second, the distance created by the computer interface and by the use of an avatar or pseudonym, makes it easier for people with autism to interact and communicate. Online, written contact eliminates some of the additional stimuli that can make real life interaction difficult for people with autism.

These two aspects are also found in the literature on disability and social media and do not seem to be exclusive or specific for subjects with autism. In our close reading of Tistje, a popular Flemish blog, we have tried to focus on a number of aspects that struck us in reading the blog and that in our view have not yet received attention in the literature. First, the multimodality – the rich mix of styles and types of information present in the blog – facilitates a type of communication that focuses mainly on the collection and sharing of divergent types of information. According to Tistje, this is an important feature of autistic communication. The different styles also give rise to humour and wordplay and to more personal reminiscences that do not fall under the category of the exchange of information and that open up the uniqueness of the blogger's identity and voice. Second, the openness and fragmentation of the presentation of information can be related to the fragmented identity construction that is typical for blog writing in general, but it also reveals a particularly creative and associative mind. As Tistje himself indicates, the blog stimulates his creativity and opens his world, leading him to discover new things. Moreover, he experiences a lot of pleasure in the materiality of his blog – working on the information, playing with the layout, typography, design and the careful way in which the material is connected.[10]

The blog as a whole – the wide range of the information and quotes, the careful execution and ordering of texts, the humour and the inventiveness of the language – does not present a unified theory of living with autism. It reflects the working of a mind and a pattern of thinking, not in a static or linear manner, but in a dynamic way. Because the blog, as a kind of creative cocoon, enables him to make contact and even to acquire a professional identity, we may wonder whether it does not have a prosthetic function for Tistje, like a pair of glasses. If we adopt McLuhan's optimistic and ambivalent approach to prosthesis, we could state that a prosthesis as an artificial mediator can be understood as a double movement of simultaneously extending and amputating – see: (McLuhan, 1994 [1964]; Coffey, 2004). Obviously, this prosthetic function of the blog is not limited to people with autism, nor are all blogs necessarily prostheses. We consider a blog 'prosthetic' when the author's online life appears equally, if not more, intense than his offline life and his online personality seems clearly different from his real life personality: when, moreover, the formal aspects are used in such a way that they personalise the impersonal, when the standardised blog format and this activity entails a certain sensual experience or pleasure (i.e. pleasure of materiality) in itself. In Tistje's case, the blog remedies some of the difficulties related to his autism but at the same time also marks it as an 'amputation' or 'default of origin' (Coffey, 2004), i.e. as a genetic condition of otherness. However, in as far as it has become a part of himself, not in an organic way, but in a conscious way, the blog also functions as an extension that marks his identity and opens up an ethics and activism that nonetheless remains profoundly individual.

Notes

1 The term 'autistic' (and later on also the term 'autism') is used here to reflect the preference of the author Tistje (cf. case study) and covers the full diversity of the spectrum. For discussions about self-definitions of autism, see Osteen (2008) and Waltz (2013).
2 We have followed Tistje from July 2014 until March 2015. The blogger was aware of our online research and has read and commented on the article several times.
3 'Autie-biography' is a portmanteau word of 'autism' and 'autobiography'. Importantly, the term has been coined by the autism community itself (cf. Couser, 2009, p. 5; Couser, 2012, p. 152). Analogous with this genre indication, we will use the term 'autie-blog'.
4 Martijn Dekker is the first Dutch-speaking autism self-advocate who interacts with the more well-known English-speaking autism self-advocates (for instance Jim Sinclair, Donna Williams, Ari Ne'eman). His text *On our own terms: Emerging autistic culture* was written for the first international autism conference in 1999 (*Autism '99*).
5 For more exhaustive studies on blogging, see Carolyn Miller and Dawn Shepherd (2004), who identified blogging as a distinctive genre that provides social action. In their view, the blog is a new rhetorical opportunity. Susan C. Herring et al. (2004) also

investigated blogs as a distinctive genre with close attention to the social aspects of the medium. She focused more specifically on the characteristics of blog authors, their reasons for blogging, the frequency of posts and the usage of blog features.

6 Obviously, this has implications on the fragmentation of autism culture and community: 'Diversity is a good thing, but there are not yet many attempts to avoid duplicate efforts and collaborate in furthering common goals among the various organisations' (Dekker, 1999, n.p.). Although it is not the aim of this chapter, it could be interesting to compare the different contexts, impacts, aims and functions of the many online autism communities out of different language areas and countries.

7 This characteristic is strategically highlighted in the Flemish employment project 'Passwerk' that, according to its website, 'uses the qualities of people with an autism spectrum disorder with a normal intellectual capacity for testing software.' http://www. passwerk.be/ (Schoitsch, 2010).

8 All translations from the blog will be our own and are as accurate and literal as possible.

9 Tistje sometimes uses another pseudonym, Sam Peters; his real name is not known.

10 We prefer the word 'materiality' over 'formal aspects' to emphasise a pleasurable, almost sensual experience of colour, form and the ability to play with various (standardised) aspects of the format. This could be linked to high sensitivity as a feature of autism.

References

American Psychiatric Association. (2013). *Diagnostic and statistical manual of mental disorders* (5th ed.). Washington, DC: American Psychiatric Publishing.

AutSider. (2003, May 3). Is het Internet een informatiebron voor mensen met autisme? [Web log post]. Retrieved November 5, 2014 from http://www.autsider.net/documentatie/artikelen/internet%20en%20Autisme.htm

Bettelheim, B. (1959). Joey: A 'Mechanical Boy'. *Scientific America, 200*(3), 116–120.

Biklen, D. (2005). *Autism and the myth of the person alone.* New York: New York University Press.

Broekhuis, W. (2010). *Alleen met mijn wereld. Hoe ik leerde leven met autisme.* Amsterdam: Uitgeverij Nieuwezijds.

Brownlow, C., & O'Dell, L. (2010). Ethical issues for qualitative research in on-line communities [Electronic version]. *Disability & Society, 17*(6), 685–694.

Capps, L., & Ochs, E. (2002). *Living narrative: Creating lives in everyday storytelling.* Harvard: Harvard University Press.

Coffey, S. (2004). Prosthesis in *The University of Chicago: Theories of Media: Keywords Glossary*. Retrieved April 2, 2015 from http://csmt.uchicago.edu/glossary2004/prosthesis.htm

Couser, G. T. (2009). *Signifying bodies: Disability in contemporary life writing.* Ann Arbor: The University of Michigan Press.

Couser, G. T. (2012). *Memoir: An introduction.* Oxford /New York: Oxford University Press.

Davidson, J. (2008). Autistic culture online: Virtual communication and cultural expression on the spectrum. *Social and Cultural Geography, 9*(7), 791–806.

Davidson, J., & Orsini, M. (2013). Critical autism studies: Notes on an emerging field. In J. Davidson & M. Orsini (Eds.), *Worlds of autism: Across the spectrum of neurological difference* (p. 1–28). Minnesota: University of Minnesota Press.

Davis, L. J. (2002). *Bending over backwards: Disability, dismodernism, and other difficult positions.* New York: New York University Press.

Dekker, M. (1999). *On our own terms: Emerging autistic culture*. Retrieved October 15, 2014 from http://web.archive.org/web/20050617075621/http://www.aspiesforfreedom.com/wiki/index.php/Emerging_autistic_culture

Fitzgerald, C. (2014, August 8). Autism in our family [Web log post]. Retrieved October 13, 2014 from http://www.huffingtonpost.com/courtney-fitzgerald/autism-in-our-family_b_5626993.html

Goggin, G., & Newell, C. (2003). *Digital disability: The social constructing of disability in new media*. Oxford: Lanham Rowman & Littlefield.

Goodley, D. (2011). *Disability studies: An interdisciplinary approach*. London: Sage.

Grandin, T. (1996). *Thinking in pictures and other reports from my life with autism*. New York: Vintage Books.

Grandin, T. (2000). My mind is a web browser: How people with autism think. *Cerebrum, 2*(1), 14–22. Retrieved October 13, 2014 from http://www.grandin.com/inc/mind.web.browser.html

Hacking, I. (2010). Autism fiction: A mirror of an internet decade? [Electronic version]. *University of Toronto Quarterly, 79*(2), 632–655.

Haraway, D. (2000). A cyborg manifesto: Science, technology and socialist-feminism in the late twentieth century. In D. Bell & B. M. Kennedy (Eds.), *The cybercultures reader* (p. 291–324). London/New York: Routledge.

Henderson, V., Davidson, J., Hemsworth, K., & Edwards, S. (2014). Hacking the master code: Cyborg stories and the boundaries of autism [Electronic version]. *Social and Cultural Geography, 15*(5), 504–524.

Herring, S. C., Scheidt, L., Bonus, S., & Wright, E. (2004). Bridging the gap: A genre analysis of weblogs [Electronic Version]. *Proceedings 37th Annual HICSS Conference*. Big Island, Hawaii, p. 1–11.

Higashida, N. (2013). *The reason I jump*. Translated by K. Yoshida & D. Mitchell. London: Hodder & Stoughton.

Jenkins, H. (2006). *Convergence culture: Where old and new media collide*. New York: University New York.

Kaplan, A. M., & Haenlein, M. (2010). Users of the world, unite! The challenges and opportunities of social media. *Business Horizons, 53*(1), 59–68.

Lejeune, P. (2000). *Cher écran . . . Journal personnel, ordinateur, Internet*. Paris: Seuil.

Lombardo, M. V., & Baron-Cohen, S. (2011). The role of the self in mindblindness in autism. *Consciousness and Cognition, 20*(1), 130–140.

McLuhan, M. (1994 [1964]). *Understanding media: The extensions of man*. Cambridge: The MIT Press.

McMillan, S. J. (2002). Exploring models of interactivity from multiple research traditions: Users, documents, and systems. In L. Lievrouw & S. Livingstone (Eds.), *The Handbook of new media* (p. 163–182). London: Sage.

Miller, C., & Shepherd, D. (2004). Blogging as social action: A genre analysis of the weblog. In L. K. Gurak, S. Antonijevic, L. Johnson, C. Ratliff, & J. Reyman (Eds.), *Into the blogosphere: Rhetoric, community, and culture of weblogs*. Retrieved October 13, 2014 from http://blog.lib.umn.edu/blogosphere/blogging_as_social_action_a_genre_analysis_of_the_weblog.html

Murray, S. (2008). *Representing autism: Culture, narrative, fascination*. Liverpool: Liverpool University Press.

Nadesan, M. H. (2005). *Constructing autism: Unravelling the 'truth' and understanding the social*. New York: Routledge.

Osteen, M. (Ed.). (2008). *Autism and representation*. New York: Routledge.

Osteen, M. (2013). Narrating autism. In J. Davidson & M. Orsini (Eds.), *Worlds of autism: Across the spectrum of neurological difference* (p. 261–284). Minnesota: University of Minnesota Press.

Reeve, D. (2012). Cyborgs, cripples and iCrip: Reflections on the contribution of Haraway to disability studies. In D. Goodley, B. Hughes, & L. J. Davis (Eds.), *Disability and social theory: New developments and directions* (p. 91–111). Hampshire: Palgrave Macmillan.

Sacks, O. (1996). Foreword. In T. Grandin (Ed.), *Thinking in pictures and other reports from my life with autism* (p. xiii–xviii). New York: Vintage Books.

Sandradodd. (n.d.). Video games and autism [Web log post]. Retrieved October 13, 2014 from http://sandradodd.com/special/videogames.html

Savarese, R. J., & Savarese, E. T. (Eds.). (2010). Autism and the concept of neurodiversity. *Disability Studies Quarterly, 30*(1).

Schoitsch, E. (Ed.). (2010). Computer safety, reliability, and security. *29th International Conference, SAFECOMP 2010*. Vienna, Austria, September *2010 Proceedings*. Vienna: Springer.

Shakespeare, T. (2006). *Disability rights and wrongs*. New York: Routledge.

Singer, J. (1999). Why can't you be normal for one in your life? From a problem with no name to the emergence of a new category of difference. In M. Corker, & S. French (Eds.), *Disability discourse* (p. 59–67). Buckingham: Open University Press.

Smith, S. (1996). Taking it to a limit one more time: Autobiography and autism. In S. Smith, & J. Watson (Eds.), *Getting a life: Everyday use of autobiography* (p. 226–246). Minnesota: University of Minnesota.

Smith, S., & Watson, J. (2014). Virtually me: A toolbox about online self-representation. In A. Poletto, & J. Rak (Eds.), *Identity technologies: Constructing the self online* (p. 70–96). Madison Wisconsin: University of Wisconsin Press.

Straus, J. N. (2013). Autism as culture. In L. J. Davis (Ed.), *The disability studies reader* (4th ed., p. 460–484). New York: Routledge.

Tistje. (2011, June 15). Wat gaat er beter? [Web log post]. Retrieved December 1, 2014 from http://tistje.com/2011/06/15/wat-gaat-er-beter/

Tistje. (2011, November 6). De wandeling [Web log post]. Retrieved December 1, 2014 from http://tistje.com/2012/11/06/de-wandeling

Tistje. (2012, January 28). Hoe Tistje.com er kwam [Web log post]. Retrieved December 1, 2014 from http://tistje.com/2012/01/28/hoe-tistje-com-er-kwam/

Tistje. (2012, October 21). Ieder zijn tempo [Web log post]. Retrieved December 1, 2014 from http://tistje.com/2012/10/21/ieder-zijn-tempo/

Tistje. (2013, August 7). Hoe is het om te vrijen met een autist(e)? [Web log post]. Retrieved December 1, 2014 from http://tistje.com/2013/08/07/hoe-is-het-om-te-vrijen-met-een-autiste/

Tistje. (2014a, June 18). Op Safari door autismeland [Web log post]. Retrieved December 1, 2014 from http://tistje.com/2013/06/18/op-safari-door-autismeland/Tistje.com/2013/07/01

Tistje. (2014b, June 18). Is het leven eerlijk? [Web log post]. Retrieved December 1, 2014 from http://tistje.com/2014/06/18/is-het-leven-eerlijk/

Tistje. (2014c, October 7). Tistje in een mindmap [Web log post]. Retrieved December 1, 2014 from http://tistje.com/2014/10/07/tistje-in-een-mindmap/Tistje.com/2014/11/30

Tistje. (2014d, October 20). Personal communication.

Tistje. (2015, January 21). Personal communication.

Turkle, S. (1995). *Life on the screen: Identity in the age of the internet*. New York: Simon & Schuster.

Van Gelder, E. (2014). *Ik ben niet vreemd, ik heb autisme. Leven met een autismespectrum- stoornis*. Leersum: Uitgeverij Village.

Waltz, M. (2003). *Metaphors of autism, and autism as metaphor: An exploration of repre- sentation*. Retrieved October 15, 2014 from http://www.inter-disciplinary.net/ptb/mso/ hid/hid2/waltz%20paper.pdf

Waltz, M. (2013). *Autism: A social and medical history*. London: Palgrave Macmillan.

20 From awareness to inclusion

Creating bridges with the disability community through social media and civil society in Japan

Muneo Kaigo

From awareness to inclusion: An introduction

A number of Japanese municipalities have begun communicating with their constituents via Facebook. Using Facebook has some obvious benefits for local governments – it provides quicker service for citizens, greater accountability, and offers lower costs for information technology and server maintenance. Facebook also offers greater opportunities for interactivity among citizens, civil society, and the government. However, adopting Facebook also has some potential problems – requesting citizens to adopt Facebook for communication may intimidate or prohibit citizens with low levels of digital literacy from accessing information, communication might be lost if Facebook services fail, postings might be 'trolled' (harassed) by other Facebook users, and there are concerns about personal (or private) information being shared with Facebook. For people with disabilities, insufficient funds to afford a computer or internet connection along with inaccessible platforms has seen unnecessary exclusion (see also Shava, Chapter 13 this volume). In considering the merits and risks of implementing Facebook services, many Japanese municipalities have decided that there are more benefits than risks. These local governments are planning or starting Facebook pages to provide a forum for citizens and government so that they can exchange ideas (MIC, 2013). This chapter focuses on one of these cases in Tsukuba city in the Ibaraki prefecture, Japan, specifically on the Facebook page of the *Tsukuba civic activities cyber-square* experiment.

The aim of this chapter is to provide an overview of the state of social networking sites (SNS) usage in Japan and the regulatory and social context for the disability community in Japan. Given disability benefits and issues related to inclusion are handled at the local government level in Japan (Stevens, 2013), the advantages of the *Tsukuba civic activities cyber-square* experiment to people with disabilities are particularly significant. This chapter also provides a future outlook on the possibilities of social media usage in Japan for people with disabilities through participation of civil society organisations.

Social Networking Sites (SNS) in Japan:
From mixi to Facebook

The use and history of SNS have been well defined and documented in many nations, and platforms have been compared in different contexts (Boyd & Ellison, 2007; Raacke & Bonds-Raacke, 2008). While sites such as Facebook and MySpace dominated early in a Western context, in Japan users favoured the local SNS *mixi*. *mixi* is a Japanese SNS that was founded in 2004 and was the dominant platform in Japan until 2011, before gradually giving way to global platforms such as Twitter and Facebook. Takahashi (2010) documented Japanese audience engagement with SNS in the social context to consider 'geographical and cultural variations' (p. 17). She conducted an ethnographic study of users of the Japanese SNS *mixi* and MySpace. Takahashi observed that Japanese *mixi* users had more of a collective dynamic in comparison to MySpace users who were more focused on the individual.

We live in a networked society characterised by daily online communication and interconnectedness (Wellman & Haythornthwaite, 2002). Social media as virtual communities (Baym, 2010; Wellman et al., 2003) have the traits of shared space, practice, resources and support, and identities and interpersonal relationships. Previous research has explored how online social networks and virtual communities might provide improvements in civil society (Jennings & Zeitner, 2003; Livingstone & Markham, 2008; McAtee & Wolak, 2011; Shah, Cho, Eveland, & Kwak, 2005; Shah, McLeod, & Yoon, 2001).

Neilsen Netview Japan (2013) reported in March 2013 that among the various SNS in Japan, Facebook had become the leading platform and had the most unique visitors, totalling 17,515,000. In contrast, *mixi*, had 4,468,000 visitors in the same month. As a result of this increase in Facebook users, organisations and municipalities in Japan have initiated projects to implement Facebook usage. The SNS with the largest and growing user base can provide the most effective platform for communication. Facebook can also be useful for the disability community by providing a new channel of communication for accessing and disseminating information. Online activity by people with disabilities through SNS such as Facebook can potentially lead to more civic engagement among the disability community and facilitate better understanding of the community by those that are non-disabled.

Awareness of the disability community and
social media in Japan

Vera Mackie (2002) argues that in Japan 'active citizenship is intimately tied to access to public space' and along with 'obstacles to their usage of public space' (p. 210) people with disabilities are excluded from notions of Japanese citizenship. While people with disabilities have experienced exclusion and lack of access, a number of recent incentives have sought greater civic inclusion for this group (Mackie, 2002). Mackie argues that celebrities with disabilities and the media have been vital in raising the public profile of people with disabilities and the importance of access to public space. As other chapters in this volume argue (see Parent & Veilleux, Chapter 7; Bennett et al., Chapter 9; Ellis, Chapter 11 this volume), online and social media is increasingly becoming an important site of public accommodation and access.

Changing social attitudes towards disability

Gottlieb (2001) argues the rapid uptake of the internet in Japan since the 1990s 'facilitated the increasing politicisation of the disability rights movement' (p. 992). Before social media, various online communities in Japan provided opportunities for people with disabilities to communicate, to create personal bridges, and to have strong personal bonds online (see Gottlieb, 2001). A popular early example of a disability-focused online community is the website SenSui which was established in 1995 and gave information related to navigating around Japan with a disability and on the existence of associations for people with disability in Japan (see Kobayashi, 2007). Although the disability community was often neglected in some online situations, other online environments have allowed people with disabilities in Japan to freely communicate and have social exchange with people who have no disabilities due to the anonymity that accompanied these environments.

Alongside this anonymity, some Twitter accounts among individuals with disabilities in Japan have gained prominence in cyberspace. One example in Japan is the famous writer Hirotada Ototake (@h_ototake) who has over 660,000 Twitter followers. The journalist and former teacher was born without arms and legs due to tetra-amelia syndrome. He also wrote a memoir *No One's Perfect* in 1988. This was turned into a feature film in 2013. However, most Japanese with disabilities and their families, may not want to be identified as having disabilities. In Japan, any information related to this is handled with both caution and sensitivity by local authorities or schools and other organisations. Disability groups using internet communications platforms for disability social justice have been able to leverage this cultural ethos to agitate for change, particularly regarding the language the mainstream media use to report disability issues (Gottlieb, 2001).

Haller's (2010) observations about the ways mainstream media misrepresentation of people with disabilities can lead to misconceptions of the community as a whole applies to the Japanese media. For example, the Japanese traditional media have misrepresented people with disabilities – they have often been illustrated as being comparatively inferior to non-disabled people or lacking in value and vulnerable, much like the way the disability community has been misrepresented in the traditional media in other nations. Traditional media often reduce and stigmatise people with disabilities into the following perspectives: medical, heroic or the 'supercrip', charity, and disability rights (Haller, 2010). Where interpersonal interactions between non-disabled people and the disability community are not adequate enough to eradicate media stereotypes, the advent of social media has allowed the disability community to relay accurate information regarding important issues or events. As Haller (2010) notes, these services can be utilised for free speech, sharing, and online organising. In addition, SNS liberate the flow of information related to the disability community (Haller, 2010).

It has also been argued that people with disabilities have not received proper attention throughout the digital revolution, and diffusion of Web 2.0 in particular, when considering accessibility and usability (Ellis & Kent, 2011). The ableism that is pervasive in our sociocultural environments required petitions for change in the absences of accessibility in these new communication platforms (Ellis & Kent, 2011). However, to date, legislation has not been able to overcome the inaccessibility of social media for a disabled audience. In spite of these issues, social media such as Facebook are a recognised tool for people with disabilities to keep up to date with issues and initiate civic engagement (see Zdrodowska, Chapter 2; Parent & Veilleux, Chapter 7; Bieling et al., Chapter 8; and Masschelein & Van Goidsenhoven, Chapter 19; this volume). Japanese local governments have started several initiatives for such activities by using Facebook and hope that these tools will provide a new communication platform for the disability community.

Regulations related to the disability community in Japan

In post–World War II Japan, laws and regulations were passed to support people with disabilities. On 21 May 1970, the *Basic Act for Persons with Disabilities* (Shōgaisha Kihonhō, No. 84) was established, consisting of four chapters that cover general provisions, basic measures to support independence and social participation of the disability community, prevention of injuries and diseases causing disability, and the establishment of a commission on policy for persons with disabilities. In 2004, support for developmental disabilities was re-recognised and the Act was amended to emphasise the protection of rights and hence revise the law to protect people with disabilities against discrimination. The previous laws relating to disability in Japan, the *Act on Welfare of Physically Disabled Persons* (Shintai Shōgaisha Fukushihō, No. 283, February 26, 1949) and the *Act on Mental Health and Welfare for Persons with Developmental and Physical Disabilities* and *Act on Welfare for Persons with Intellectual Disabilities* (Seishin Hoken oyobi Seishin Shōgaisha Fukushi ni Kansuru Hōritsu, No. 23 established on May 1, 1950; Chiteki Shōgaisha Fukushi Hō, No. 37, March 31, 1960) now complement the *Basic Act for Persons with Disabilities* to provide services and support every day and social life for those with disabilities in Japan.

Local legislation also supplements the support of the disability community in Japan. For instance, Ibaraki prefecture passed the *Ordinance for Building a Happy Life Together Among People with Disabilities* and *no Disabilities in Ibaraki Prefecture* (Shōgai no Aruhito Naihito mo Tomoni Ayumi Shiawase ni Kurasutameno Ibarakiken Zukuri Jōrei) on March 2014. This was enforced on 1 April 2014 to support inclusive education in schools and provide employment opportunities for people with disabilities in Ibaraki.

In contrast to the advances in legislation through the development and implementation of these laws, Japanese society has been lagging behind in actual inclusion. For instance, the diffusion of barrier-free architecture is still in the process of further development, even in urban areas, and more progress is needed in the more rural areas of Japan. Although one cannot frequently observe open discrimination towards the disability community in Japan today, the general reservation and avoidance of people with disabilities in society and everyday situations is a stigma that remains. Further inclusion is an agenda that needs to be addressed in Japan.

SNS for municipalities in Japan

The architecture of SNS such as Facebook provides a convenient platform for promoting municipalities – Japanese municipalities have been relatively proactive with adopting these new ICTs. The case of Takeo city in Saga prefecture in southern Japan is a noteworthy example – the city had been using their Facebook page as their main internet presence from 2011 until this year (2015) (Nagasawa, 2011; Nishinippon Shimbun, 2015).

Takeo city had been very progressive in using social media such as Twitter in the past. During the flooding in the Takeo area on 12 June 2011, the mayor and other workers sent out disaster information about road blocks and flooding, and subsequently were able to raise over one million yen in donations in part thanks to their Twitter usage (Takeo City, 2011). Although successful with social media usage, due to the change in government from 2015, Takeo city now provides information mainly through their website. Nevertheless, many Japanese local governments evaluated the Takeo case very positively. The Takeo case encouraged the development of the *Tsukuba civic activities cyber-square* experiment in Tsukuba city.

Tsukuba civic activities cyber-square experiment

Tsukuba city is located in the Ibaraki prefecture approximately 30 miles north of Tokyo. The municipal government of Tsukuba has been working with the University of Tsukuba and Intel Corporation to create the Facebook site *Tsukuba civic activities cyber-square*. Its aim is two-fold – to help nurture future human resources and cultivate entrepreneurship and to activate communities and create a healthy civic life. Within this context, the Tsukuba municipal government began an experiment in 2012 promoting cooperation among citizens through Facebook. It created a 'cyber-square' to promote online and offline networking among civic activities and civic-oriented groups and to help visualise the various civic activities that endeavour to create a better civil society (Kaigo & Tkach-Kawasaki, 2012). As consultant and chair of this project at the University of Tsukuba, I have worked side by side with the municipal government of Tsukuba to help realise their vision.

Tsukuba city had the highest number of Facebook users in Ibaraki, with approximately 10,860 users in October 2011. The Tsukuba experiment was initiated in January 2012 and completed its initial experimental phase in June 2012. The *Tsukuba civic activities cyber-square* has now been integrated into the daily operations of the government of Tsukuba.

A previous study (Kaigo & Tkach-Kawasaki, 2012) focusing on the possibilities and problems of complementary communication channels demonstrated how usage of the *Tsukuba civic activities cyber-square* enhanced civil society and how SNS can provide information and connect citizens. The main obstacle to initiating usage of SNS by the Tsukuba municipal government stemmed from fears of offending others, or making a mistake in posting, and/or having posts of inappropriate information through social media. For example in 2011, a Japanese hotel restaurant worker was posting private information of television celebrities onto Twitter and this was reported in the mainstream media (*Yumeijin ga raiten Twitter ni toukoushitara*, 2011), gossip tabloids, and tabloid television. Such information essentially lured 'trolls' to harass the account holder and the online exchange was highlighted as a spectacular, negative example of social media and the internet in general by the Japanese mass media.

These negative examples in Japan resulted in delaying or prohibiting the adoption of social media in many organisations. They also created a general fear of using social media among those with low digital skills or information technology literacy. To overcome these concerns *Tsukuba civic activities cyber-square* at the Tsukuba municipality created guidelines for the appropriate use of SNS. Their guidelines stipulated the need to use a SNS that insists users have user accounts with their actual names, control or prohibit posts of slanderous information, avoid leaks of secret, private information or post opinions that can be misinterpreted, and avoid posts about uncertain facts and therefore avoid mistakes.

The *Tsukuba civic activities cyber-square* built a solid following of people who are interested in civic activities and can be mobilised in disseminating information about volunteering in the case of a disaster (Kaigo & Tkach-Kawasaki, 2012). SNS in Japan can play an important role in filling in the gap between the ordinary citizen and government, allowing for more transparency and creating a community of people that have common interests. People within a similar environment, with similar characteristics, and similar experiences, tend to form communities together. Facebook users with similar orientations or interests are more likely to become friends online.

The possibilities of using SNS for government and civic activities is an attractive option, and the *Tsukuba civic activities cyber-square* experiment is an example of how municipalities are endeavouring to initiate usage of SNS platforms such as Facebook to better communicate and to create cyber communities within Japan (Kaigo & Tkach-Kawasaki, 2012).

Facebook and inclusion of people with disabilities in Japan

Despite all the elements that society creates to impede inclusion, SNS such as Facebook are perceived to provide the most convenient platforms for civil society organisations to operate networks in relation to the disability community in Japan today, *Tsukuba civic activities cyber-square* is such an example. However, there are other administrative issues that such websites and their hosts face. The Division for Civic Activities that operates the *Tsukuba civic activities cyber-square* is a separate section of the municipal government from the one that deals with issues concerning people with disabilities and organisations which are handled by the Welfare Division for Persons with Disabilities in the Tsukuba municipal hall. This separation of these divisions is similar in most Japanese municipalities (Kaigo, 2014).

The Welfare Division for Persons with Disabilities of the Tsukuba municipal government has not yet been able to independently initiate integrating any social media or Facebook usage into their operations, so the *Tsukuba civic activities cyber-square* is the main point of contact for online networking in the Tsukuba area for individuals and organisations involved with people with disabilities. For example, the Sakura Centre for Persons with Disabilities (Shōgaisha Sentā Sakura) located in Tsukuba independently operates a Facebook page that introduces many of their activities, and is connected with the *Tsukuba civic activities cyber-square,* aiming to expand their connections with other civil society organisations involved with people with disabilities.

From November 2014, the *Tsukuba civic activities cyber-square* began pro-active communications with these organisations that handle matters relating to people with disabilities to complement other social media portals for activities concerning people with disabilities in Tsukuba and Ibaraki. The main obstacles prior to these communications were the barriers of jurisdiction within the munici-pality and the general concerns of communication about people with disabilities due to social stigma in Japan and societal concerns about being unintentionally identified through social media usage. These obstacles have hindered extensive communications with organisations that support persons with disabilities (Kaigo, 2014). However, it appears the *Tsukuba civic activities cyber-square* has overcome these obstacles, and since November 2014 commenced postings in relation to these organisations by the active online community managers of the Division for Civic Activities.

Table 20.1 indicates the three-month list of civic-activities-related-posts by the Division for Civic Activities onto the status of the *Tsukuba civic activities cyber-square* website from 10 September 2014 through to 10 December 2014, indicating the engagement metrics provided by the Facebook Insight interface available for community managers. The metrics of reach (the number of people who have seen any content associated with the page), likes (the number of people who have clicked 'like' in relation to the page), comments (the number of people who have com-mented on the page), and shares (the number of people who have shared the page), as well as an indication of whether or not the topic was in relation to the disability community is provided.

Upon comparing the means of the reach, likes, comments, and shares of the postings, the results display no statistical difference between topics of the disabil-ity community and other topics. In other words, the reach and online engagement in the status of the *Tsukuba civic activities cyber-square* between topics were equally engaged online (Table 20.2). Although this is an isolated case with lim-ited data, results indicate that social media has successfully bridged the activities related to people with disabilities into an online community that has interest in

Table 20.1 Reach and online engagement of the *Tsukuba civic activities cyber-square* (10 September 2014–10 December 2014)

Date of posting	Topic of posting on status	Reach	Likes	Comments	Shares	Topic on disability
18-Sep-14	Child support club	560	29	0	0	N
22-Sep-14	Citizen volunteer system	818	46	3	0	N
24-Sep-14	Lantern festival	791	50	0	0	N
26-Sep-14	U. Tsukuba symposium	693	21	4	3	N
3-Oct-14	Funding campaign	602	37	2	0	N
8-Oct-14	Protect environment	402	21	0	0	N
16-Oct-14	Enjoy autumn	830	48	0	0	N
21-Oct-14	Mothers' support	556	22	0	0	N
22-Oct-14	Activity Festival on November 1	1190	53	0	2	N
28-Oct-14	Flower planting	618	36	0	0	N
28-Oct-14	Shrine flower planting	724	46	0	1	N
31-Oct-14	Sports day report	785	55	2	0	N
6-Nov-14	Cooking class for kids	637	49	0	0	N
14-Nov-14	Wheelchair dancing	578	53	0	1	Y
19-Nov-14	Sign language seminar	734	40	0	1	Y
20-Nov-14	Tenji (Japanese Braille) seminar	513	28	0	1	Y
21-Nov-14	Tenji interview	520	41	0	0	Y
25-Nov-14	NPO funding contest	705	27	0	0	N
26-Nov-14	Teaching words to kids	574	36	0	1	N
27-Nov-14	Kimono class for kids	478	29	0	0	N
28-Nov-14	NPO Gathering in February	316	8	0	0	N
28-Nov-14	NPO gathering (2)	434	26	0	0	N
1-Dec-14	Kimono class (2)	603	43	0	0	N
2-Dec-14	NPO gathering (3)	531	30	0	0	N
3-Dec-14	Computers for the Hearing Loss	980	59	1	2	Y
4-Dec-14	Computers for the Hearing Loss (2)	458	20	0	0	Y
5-Dec-14	Cooking konyaku (potato jelly)	777	39	0	0	N
6-Dec-14	Children in Palestine	464	35	0	0	N
9-Dec-14	NPO gathering (4)	494	28	0	0	N

Table 20.2 Means and standard deviations of reach and online engagement of the *Tsukuba civic activities cyber-square* (10 September 2014–10 December 2014)

Posting	Reach		Likes		Comments		Shares	
	M	SD	M	SD	M	SD	M	SD
Other topics	704.08	388.59	35.5	11.84	0.46	1.1	0.5	1.22
On disability	630.5	195.65	40.17	14.67	0.17	0.4	0.83	0.753

civic activities. One can observe that the reach and comments of topics on disability were somewhat lower than other topics, yet one can also find that there were more likes and shares of posts related to the disability community. Although more data collection is necessary to make any conclusions, this indicates that although Facebook users of this community may be hesitant to make any comments on the posts, they are less reluctant to show that they like the post and share the post with their friends.

Conclusion

This chapter started with a brief overview of the current state of SNS usage in Japan in relation to civil society, it then examined the history of disability rights legislation in Japan, and briefly explained the social context. It was illustrated how, in certain cases, social media usage in Japan can provide potential bridges between the disability community and civil society organisations. Given the importance of access to public space to notions of citizenship in Japan, and the increasing use of Facebook by local governments, the visibility of and engagement with disability-related posts on the *Tsukuba civic activities cyber-square* is significant.

The evidence procured through the Facebook Insight interface of the case study indicates how posts related to disabilities and civil society on the *Tsukuba civic activities cyber-square* gained equal amounts of online engagement when compared to the other posts in the same period. Posts related to the disability community had more likes and were more likely to be shared when compared to the other posts in the same period.

For a significant period now, Japanese people have been aware of the need to improve social inclusion for people with disabilities. Public announcements, various commercials by different entities, along with changes in formal education and internet activism (see Gottlieb, 2001), have all endeavoured to create a society with awareness of this necessity of inclusion. Currently, SNS such as Facebook demonstrate an ability to create the necessary human connections or bridges among a large variety of civic activities oriented individuals and organisations. The findings in this study can help better realise inclusion of the disability community into Japanese society.

Posting information about activities designed to support people with disabilities can be engaged online by users with high civic activity orientation, and such engagement can potentially proliferate much more widely online, if given enough time and effort. Research questions coming out of this chapter can be phrased as follows:

• Can social media be employed as a bridge to facilitate connection and inclusion for the disability community in Japan?
• Can social media usage lead to stronger personal bonding among those with disabilities in the future?

This experiment on government and civil society SNS usage in Japan is an ongoing project and more progress needs to be made and observed to make more inference into the future. Further evidence and data from other case studies are necessary to examine the research questions. However, the new research questions are important and perhaps will determine how social media can navigate the future direction for the social inclusion of the disability community in Japan.

Acknowledgements

I would like to thank Mike Kent, Katie Ellis, and the anonymous reviewers of this chapter for their constructive comments, and the municipal government of Tsukuba for generously providing the data used in this study. Parts of this study are based on a conference paper at CeDEM Asia 2012. The author would also like to acknowledge that this study was supported by JSPS KAKENHI, grant number 25330394.

References

Baym, N. K. (2010). *Personal connections in the digital age*. Cambridge, UK: Polity.

Boyd, D., & Ellison, N. B. (2007). Social network sites: Definition, history, and scholarship. *Journal of Computer-Mediated Communication, 13*(1), 210–230. doi: 10.1111/j.1083–6101.2007.00393.x

Ellis, K., & Kent, M. (2011). *Disability and the new media*. New York and London: Routledge.

Gottlieb, N. (2001). Language and disability in Japan. *Disability & Society, 16*(7), 981–995.

Haller, B. (2010). *Representing disability in an ableist world: Essays on mass media*. Louisville, KY: The Advocado Press.

Jennings, M. K., & Zeitner, V. (2003). Internet use and civic engagement: A longitudinal analysis. *Public Opinion Quarterly, 67*(3), 311–334.

Kaigo, M. (2014). Social media and red tape. In P. Parycek, M. Sachs & M. Skoric (Eds.), *CeDEM Asia 2014: Proceedings of the international conference for e-democracy and open government – Asia 2014*. Krems: Edition Donau-Universitat Krems, 217–223.

Kaigo, M., & Tkach-Kawasaki, L. (2012). Social media usage for civil society in Japanese municipalities. In P. Parycek, M. Sachs & M. Skoric (Eds.), *CeDEM Asia 2012: Proceedings of the international conference for e-democracy and open government – Asia-2012*. Krems: Edition Donau-Universitat Krems, 59–70.

Kobayashi, I. (2007). Web-based disability information resource in Japan. *Journal of Technology in Human Services, 25*(1–2), 199–200.

Livingstone, S., & Markham, T. (2008). The contribution of media consumption to civic participation. *British Journal of Sociology, 59*(2), 351–371. doi: 10.1111/j.1468–4446.2008.00197.x

Mackie, V. (2002). Embodiment, citizenship and social policy in contemporary Japan. In R. Goodman (Ed.), *Family and social policy in Japan*. Cambridge: Cambridge University Press, 200–229.

McAtee, A., & Wolak, J. (2011). Why people decide to participate in state politics. *Political Research Quarterly, 64*(1), 45–58. doi: 10.1177/1065912909343581

Ministry of Internal Affairs and Communications, Japan (MIC) (2013). *Heisei nijugonendo jōhō tsushin hakusho* [Information and communications white paper 2013]. Tokyo: Ministry of Internal Affairs and Communications, Retrieved from http://www.soumu.go.jp/johotsusintokei/whitepaper/h25.html

Nagasawa, S. (2011, July 29). Sagaken Takeoshi, shiyakushono koushiki saitowo Facebook page ni iko [Takeo, Saga municipal hall page transferred to Facebook]. *Internet Watch*. Retrieved from http://internet.watch.impress.co.jp/docs/news/20110729_463979.html

Nielsen Netview (2013). *Sumatofon wo shoyu shiteiru 10 dai danjo, 20 dai joseino 6 wari ijouga omoni sumatofon de SNS wo riyou* [Male and female teens, over 60 percent of females in their 20s use smartphones for SNS]. Retrieved from http://www.netratings.co.jp/news_release/2012/03/10206-sns.html

Raacke, J., & Bonds-Raacke, J. (2008). MySpace and Facebook: Applying the uses and gratifications theory to exploring friend-networking sites. *Cyberpsychology & Behavior, 1*(2), 169–174. doi: 10.1089/cpb.2007.0056

Shah, D., Cho, J., Eveland, W., & Kwak, N. (2005). Information and expression in a digital age: Modeling internet effects on civic participation. *Communication Research, 32*(5), 531–565. doi: 10.1177/0093650205279209

Shah, D. V., McLeod, J. M., & Yoon, S. H. (2001). Communication, context, and community: An exploration of print, broadcast, and internet influences. *Communication Research, 28*(4), 464–506. doi: 10.1177/009365001028004005

Stevens, C. (2013). *Disability in Japan*. London: Routledge.

Takahashi, T. (2010). MySpace or Mixi? Japanese engagement with SNS (Social Networking Sites) in the global age. *New Media and Society, 12*(3), 453–475. doi: 10.1177/1461444809343462

Takeo City. (2011). *Heisei 23 Nen Koushin Jokyou* [Updates of 2011]. Retrieved from http://www.city.takeo.lg.jp/updateinfo_h23.html

Takeoshi ga Facebook ka haishi "Kodomokyoikubu" shinsetsu [Takeo's children education department replaces Facebook department]. (2015, May 26). *Nishinippon Shimbun Morning Edition*. Retrieved from http://www.47news.jp/smp/localnews/saga/2015/05/post_20150526021858.html

Wellman, B., & Haythornthwaite, C. A. (Eds.). (2002). *The internet in everyday life*. Malden, MA: Blackwell Publishing.

Wellman, B., Quan-Haase, A., Boase, J., Chen, W., Hampton, K., Isla de Diaz, I., & Miyata, K. (2003). The social affordances of the internet for networked individualism. *Journal of Computer-Mediated Communication, 8*(3). doi: 10.1111/j.1083–6101.2003.tb00216.x

Yumeijin ga raiten Twitter ni toukoushitara [Tweeted about a celebrity visit to our restaurant]. (2011, January 19). *Asahi Shimbun Evening Edition*, 6.

Part VI
New directions

21 Self-representation considerations for people who use Augmentative and Alternative Communication (AAC) and social media

Amanda Hynan, Janice Murray and Juliet Goldbart

> My laptop is completely lifeless, flatlined, I feel sick. . . . All I'll have to commu-
> nicate with now is a battered old alphabet board that won't reach around the globe
> the way I need it to.
>
> (Martin Pistorius, 2011)

Introduction

As Martin Pistorius reflected, people with disabilities increasingly rely on ICT for communication. In this chapter we will initially outline the ramifications for self-representation within the highly specialised field of augmentative and alternative communication (AAC) before moving on to consider existing psychological and sociological theories underpinning identity formation. The focus will be on the development of identity during adolescence and young adulthood and the impact of online opportunities, especially for young people with disabilities.

This chapter is informed by a UK-based qualitative research project that developed a grounded theory of internet and social media use by people who use AAC (Hynan, 2013; Hynan, Murray, & Goldbart, 2014; Hynan, Goldbart, & Murray, 2015). Twenty-five young people (aged 14–24) who use AAC took part in face-to-face interviews in order to address an identified gap in the UK literature regarding the self-reported experiences of engagement within online digital environments. This chapter uses selected data from that research project to discuss online self-representation considerations within this niche population.

Defining AAC

AAC is an interdisciplinary clinical and research field that supports individuals who find it difficult to use natural speech (due to a range of acquired or developmental conditions) to use multi-modal communication strategies that focus on maximising and developing an individual's ability to integrate residual speech skills with forms of AAC (Marshall & Goldbart, 2008; Clarke, Newton, Petrides, Griffiths, Lysley, & Price, 2012). Whilst AAC-mediated conversation is slower than typical, it offers many ways to support successful communication and interaction (Smith & Murray, 2011).

AAC can augment or act as an alternative to natural speech and writing. AAC modes are differentiated between 'unaided' or 'aided' communication depending on whether a person uses additional equipment. 'Unaided' forms refer to gesture or sign language whilst 'aided' forms fall into two broad categories – low-tech (not requiring an additional power source, e.g. a communication book) or high-tech (requiring a battery or power source). High-tech forms range from simple, single message devices to complex, flexible computer-based devices that usually have a form of voice output which is either digitised (recorded speech) or synthesised (produced by text-to-speech software). In the UK these are often referred to as voice output communication aids (VOCAs), in the USA they are referred to as speech-generating devices (SGDs). Since the 1980s, AAC technology has developed dramatically, moving from large, heavy, dedicated devices with robotic voices (developed to withstand sustained use) through many subsequent design iterations. A two-tier market has developed within the last few years – on one side dedicated devices have incorporated mainstream technology design, and, on the other, mainstream mobile devices have incorporated specialised speech output software. This has resulted in broader consumer choice, wider accessibility solutions and lowered costs. However, mainstream devices do not always have the same level of robustness or accessibility, and voice output App designers may not fully understand the orthographic literacy and language domain difficulties of some people who use AAC (Smith, 1992; Browning, 2002; Sturm & Clendon, 2004).

Face-to-face conversations and AAC

Various factors can impact on AAC-mediated face-to-face conversations and naturally speaking partners often need to adopt supportive strategies in areas such as repairing misunderstandings, changing topic, starting conversations and turn-taking (Clarke & Wilkinson, 2007, 2008; Clarke, Bloch, & Wilkinson, 2013). Disruption within the social organisation and ratification of turn-taking (Goffman, 1964), which is typically characterised by no overlaps and minimal gaps (Sacks, Schegloff, & Jefferson, 1974), can lead to the naturally speaking partners underestimating the ability of the person using AAC. Well-intentioned compensatory behaviours may be adopted, leading to domination of the conversation by the speaking partner, and the person using AAC thereby taking a more passive role (Clarke & Wilkinson, 2008). Todman, Alm, Higginbotham, and File (2008) say perceptions of people who use AAC often focus negatively on their slow rates of communication, and opportunities to contribute are often denied within fast-moving interactions. People who use AAC have also expressed great frustration with the effect of the slowed rate of communication (Judge & Townend, 2013) and maintaining attention during conversations can also be problematic for both parties (Thistle & Wilkinson, 2012).

A final consideration here is the disruption placed on narrative and humour generation for individuals who use AAC. The issues already outlined can lead to discourse within face-to-face conversations becoming skewed towards transactional (discussing concrete needs) rather than interactional (sharing experiences) communication (Waller, 2006). Narratives and storytelling support friendships and expressions of social identity, as well as making sense of experiences (Grove & Tucker, 2003). Narratives support friendships by acting as a bridge by which experiences can be shared – Balandin, Berg, and Waller (2006) and Ballin and Balandin (2007) explored the topics of social closeness, connectedness and loneliness in those with a communication disability and found having established bonds with people across a range of contexts is more important than the size of the network of friends and associates. However, narratives on VOCAs tend to be stored as monologues or chunked sequences (Reddington & Coles-Kemp, 2011) that are time consuming to prepare and need to be constantly altered to mark the progress of time. As a result, many people who use AAC rely on close communication partners to tell stories on their behalf once they have indicated a topic area (Waller, 1992). These issues illuminate the importance of exploring how people who use AAC may be able to take advantage of digital communication to augment their social relationships through increased self-representation opportunities.

Technological advances within the field of AAC and online opportunities

VOCAs started to develop within the dedicated AAC industry in earnest during the 1980s/90s with the advent of more readily available computer technologies, speech synthesis programmes and alternative access methods. By 2007, totally integrated communication aids were available from many manufacturers, meaning single machines could operate as a combined communication aid and personal computer or act as an interface with an external computer (Chapple, 2011). Within the last few years, voice output Apps on mainstream mobile devices have been developed (Higginbotham & Jacobs, 2011) which has increased opportunities for people who need AAC-based software to engage with mainstream social media.

Social media use by people who use AAC

The increased opportunities available for using online communication has triggered AAC-focused social media research, although to date it has been limited to specific countries and contexts and may be reported incidentally within the context of more broadly focused topic areas (Atanasoff, McNaughton, Wolf, & Light,

1998; Cohen & Light, 2000; Rackensperger, Krezman, McNaughton, Williams, & D'Silva, 2005; Dattilo, Estrella, Estrella, Light, McNaughton, & Seabury, 2008; Sundqvist & Ronnberg, 2010; Garcia, Loureiro, Gonzalez, Riveiro, & Sierra, 2011).

To summarise some of the available findings, it would appear that being online may have significant benefits for people who use AAC. Within an online study to explore perceptions of leisure for people who use AAC, one participant reported:

> having access to the Internet has opened up my world.
>
> (Dattilo et al., 2008, p. 25)

Further, survey information looking at communication opportunities in college from seven students who used AAC, reported using email was:

> the most effective way of being understood by others.
>
> (Atanasoff et al., 1998, abstract)

Gandell and Sutton (1998) compared the communication interactions between a person who used AAC and a typically speaking communication partner using a specialised form of email. They found that email facilitated greater interaction within the communication exchange for the person who used AAC than was seen within the monitored face-to-face conversations. In another study, Sundqvist and Ronnberg (2010) found that a software programme that supported symbol-based email exchanges enhanced social contact for children, aged 6–13 years, who use AAC. In Australia, Raghavendra, Wood, Newman, and Lawry (2012) conducted qualitative interviews with a cohort of 15 children (mean age 14.6 years) with physical disabilities (five with communication difficulties, one of whom used AAC). They found that they were using the internet for a variety of purposes but the extent and frequency of use was lower than similarly aged children in the general population. Friends were the main people contacted online and the digital skills of parents, siblings and friends influenced levels of use. In another study, a tailored one-to-one intervention programme to facilitate social participation for 18 young people with disabilities through use of the internet and social networking (Raghavendra, Newman, Grace, & Woods, 2013) contained five participants with complex communication needs who used AAC. By comparing pre-post design quantitative data collected within this sub-group it was shown that the intervention had successfully supported the use of email, Skype and online safety awareness as well as increasing the number of online communication partners among lifelong companions and paid staff (Grace, Raghavendra, & Newman, 2014).

Hyatt (2011), an experienced user of AAC, says her iPad has changed her social opportunities and allowed her to share a depth of communication about areas of her life which would not have been possible on her single-function VOCA. Larned (2012), another person who uses AAC, suggests being able to use written communication can expand social interactions. Stevens (2011), who also uses AAC, writes about his experiences of using mobile phone technology through his hybrid VOCA and also talks about his iPad, describing them as fundamental tools for his sense of dignity and self-worth.

The aims of the research project reported within this chapter were to understand and contextualise perceptions of access and use of the internet and social media and to explore the implications for self-representation and social participation by people who use AAC (Hynan, 2013; Hynan et al., 2014; Hynan et al., 2015).

Identity formation and self-representation

Psychological and sociological identity theories during adolescence and young adulthood

Adolescence and young adulthood are regarded as key stages for identity exploration as bonds to parents weaken and peer relationships become more significant (Smith, 2005; Mesch & Talmud, 2010), with the time between 18–25 years of age being very significant (Arnett, 2004). Erikson's (1963, 1968) theory of psychosocial development suggests the exploration of *ego identity* happens in developmental stages across the lifespan and involves the competent resolution of various conflicts. He suggests that during adolescence (12–18 years) the experience of identity versus role confusion is a key factor characterised by an exploration of a sense of self. Young adulthood (19–40 years) is characterised by intimacy versus isolation where the development of close relationships with others is deemed important to counteract isolation and loneliness.

Marcia (1980) suggests adolescent identity should be seen as a self-created internal concept formed when an individual can physically, cognitively and socially begin to examine childhood constructs and create their own passageway to adulthood. If well-developed, the individual has a sense of stability and internal validation, but if under-developed, may need to externally validate a sense of self. It is pertinent to consider the role that social media may play in terms of identity development as it is known to be popular within the adolescent and young adult age demographic (Ofcom Consumer Experience Report, 2012).

Identity formation and self-representation within the context of social media

The growing popularity and integration into young people's lives of social media is opening up new dynamics. Livingstone (2008) discusses how adolescents are not necessarily using social media to displace face-to-face communication but find it adds an additional dimension to existing local ties. The development of the internet has provided a theoretical space within which researchers can consider and debate online identity theory. Livingstone (2008) points out that one facet of the role of social media in the lives of typically developing adolescents is to offer an:

> exciting yet relatively safe opportunity . . . to construct, experiment with and present a reflexive project of the self in a social context.
>
> (p. 396)

Goffman (1959) discussed the presentation of self in everyday life as individual performances that can be broadened and manipulated to affect audience reaction.

Central to Goffman's discussion is the idea that an individual plays a part and creates a performance which s/he hopes observers will take seriously. Livingstone (2008) suggests young people pay great attention to the presentation of self within social media sites due to the convergence of multimedia that are offering young people opportunities to construct their presentation of self in ways not seen before.

Zhao, Grasmuck, and Martin (2008) investigated identity construction on Facebook and cite the work of Stone (1981) who, in similarity with the ideas of Goffman (1959), suggests individuals make 'announcements' which are then 'placed' by others and identity is established when the two coincide. Zhao and colleagues carried out content analysis on the Facebook profile data of 63 university students and concluded that a Facebook identity is formed around a continuum. It ranges from the implicit visual end where the self is portrayed as a social actor predominantly through photographs (the 'watch me' self that shows without telling) to the explicit narrative 'first person self' where descriptions are used to illuminate information. The mid-point is the enumerative (or 'self as consumer'), the space on Facebook where an individual lists what they like in terms of cultural material (music, books, films, etc.). Users can control their audiences through filters, but Zhao et al. suggest most people tend to present a 'hoped for' self, a socially constructed identity the individual believes s/he can establish within the given context. One of their conclusions is that:

> the Internet provides new resources and opportunities for identity production that can be used to overcome some limitations inherent in face-to-face situations.
>
> (p. 1831)

They suggest that these 'digital selves' are real in many ways to Facebook users and can enhance a person's self-image and increase chances to make connections in the offline world that have concrete consequences. They also suggest being able to perform acts of resistance through a Facebook profile and use the 'hoped for' self to influence and convince others of what to think about the individual. Livingstone (2008) suggests (in line with Mead's (1934) distinction between 'I' and 'me') that social media is definitely about 'me' as it reveals the self as it is entrenched within a social peer group, and Ellis (2010) suggests that the self as a product of communication and social interaction has a contemporary currency within the context of Facebook.

Online identity and physical disability

Self-concept is a-multi-dimensional psychological construct built on what people think of themselves, covering issues such as physical appearance, social acceptance and other areas. Oyserman, Elmore, and Smith (2012) suggest individuals align their perceptions of themselves within social contexts to establish self-concepts and rely on memories of the past, perceptions of the present and future, and on information from the senses about what they sound like, look like and how they physically interact with their environment. Much of the work being carried out looking at issues of online identity and physical disability has debated whether being online can be a 'levelling ground' offering people with physical disabilities the opportunity to show their abilities without being defined by their bodily appearance (e.g. Bowker & Tuffin, 2002, 2007). Seymour and Lupton (2004) carried out interviews with people with physical disabilities about online communication. One of the aspects they explored was the potential for online communication to remove the focus on physical appearance and potentially discriminatory attitudes. Their interview-based research found the participants were not interested in removing references to physical disabilities but instead sought to reinstate their physical identity within their interpersonal online discussions.

In citing this research, it is important to understand that any suggestions made about the 'body-less' potential of online communication is related to ideas of challenging societal discrimination and must not be confused with ideas of lowered self-concept. Shields, Murdoch, Loy, Dodd, and Taylor (2006) carried out a systematic review to examine the literature base for evidence of lowered self-concept perceptions of young people who have cerebral palsy. They found there was insufficient evidence to conclude young people with cerebral palsy have lower global self-concept than peers without disability across most domains, although young girls with cerebral palsy may have lowered self-concept in the domains of physical appearance, social acceptance and athletic and scholastic competence.

In summary, adolescent/young adult identity development is perceived to be characterised by seeking to establish a self-identity through role exploration and presentation of the self beyond childhood constructs, with a goal to build intimate and close relationships. The world of online communication has opened up novel opportunities to enrich this exploration through multimodal channels and new ways for controlling the presentation of self, leading to the construction of 'digital selves' that may have concrete consequences in an offline world. An investigation of self-representation and online identity within the context of people with physical disabilities and complex communication needs must acknowledge the impact of the 'body' within digital self-presentation opportunities, whilst being mindful not to suggest this is connected with lowered self-esteem.

Morris (2003), Rabiee, Sloper, and Beresford (2005) and Wickenden (2009) all comment on the lack of self-report research with disabled young people with complex communication needs and state that much of the research carried out within this niche population has relied on data from family or caregivers. Therefore very little research exploring the potential implications of online identity and physical disability has included people with additional, complex communication needs. In light of these considerations for the current state of knowledge, we move on to present selected data from the UK-based project exploring the use of the internet and social media with 25 young people (aged 14–24) who use AAC (Hynan, 2013; Hynan et al., 2014; Hynan et al., 2015). One of the aims was to explore concepts of self-representation.

The use of online social media by young people who use AAC: A specific study

The qualitative research study followed the constructivist grounded theory approach outlined by Charmaz (2006), and led to the generation of a grounded theory of internet and online social media use by young people who use AAC (Hynan et al., 2015). Over a period of 18 months, 25 young people aged between 14 and 24 years were identified who wanted to contribute to the research (12 females; mean age 20.04 years). There were variations within the participants' profiles in terms of physical access methods, cognitive and orthographic literacy abilities and the types of AAC methods they used. Fifteen of the participants were supported by a communication partner, e.g. a parent or a speech and language therapist (SLT), during their interviews and all have been given pseudonyms to protect their privacy. Concurrent data collection and analysis followed the coding steps suggested by Charmaz (2006) and utilised memo writing and theoretical sampling. Data were collected through semi-structured interviews (duration 30–120 minutes) guided by topic themes identified through the literature review and a pilot study with a user of AAC. One participant contributed data via an online blog and another requested the questions in advance of their interview in order to pre-prepare responses. Data have been transcribed as follows – non-verbal communication is marked with single speech marks with a written description of how this was non-verbally communicated in brackets, e.g. 'yes' (nods head), VOCA-generated communication is indicated by speech parenthesis, e.g. "Yes", and naturally spoken speech is not marked in any way. One participant used an alphabet board to finger spell her answers and this data has been transcribed using the protocol outlined by von Tetzchner and Basil (2011), e.g. *s-p-e-l-l-e-d w-o-r-d-s*.

Findings

Self-representation

During the interviews, participants described being able to use online social media to tell people things about themselves and to exercise choice over what they shared with people.

Carol was supported during her interview by her SLT.

SLT:	What is good about Facebook?
Carol:	(points to self)
SLT:	about you
Researcher:	oh because you can give news about you to your friends
Carol:	'yes' (nods head)
Email question:	Tell me about your profile on Facebook?
Peter:	"I have a photo of me at Chelsea which my sister took. I include things I like, where I live, places I have been"

Email question: Have you added any description about yourself onto your profile?

Peter: "Yes I have included things I like such as cricket, Chelsea, theatre, family information, where I have been"

Caroline contributed to the research through a blog site and this data is italicised.

I like choosing different photos for my Facebook profile. I used to have photos of my Ginger cat, now I have Doctor Who characters.

Carol sometimes preferred to use Makaton signs (http://www.makaton.org/) during her interview rather than her VOCA. She was supported by her SLT.

Researcher: On your Facebook profile have you got your own picture?
SLT: (using Makaton signs to support speech) your own photo
Carol: FRIEND (Makaton sign)
SLT: friend, a photo of you and a friend
Carol: 'yes' (nods head)
[not consecutive]
Researcher: do you put photographs on Facebook
Carol: 'yes' (nods head)
Researcher: of things that you have been doing
Carol: "prom 2011"
Researcher: what have you got as your profile picture?
Keith: "I got a picture of Pikachu"
[not consecutive]
Keith: "I like Facebook because I like seeing me holding Pikachu"
[not consecutive]
Researcher: what information do you tell people about yourself, how much do you tell people?
Keith: "a lot"
Ben was supported during his interview by his teaching assistant in mainstream secondary school.
Researcher: do you have a photo of yourself as your profile photograph on Facebook?
Ben: "one I was on holiday"
Researcher: have you got profile information
Ben: 'yes' (nods head)
Teaching assistant: what have you got on it sweetheart?
Ben: "Like I know French, English, Portuguese"
Researcher: what kind of things do you put on [Facebook]?
Moira: "anything, well I am mixed person"
Researcher: Do you use as part of your business [referring to Facebook]. Do you have any customers from your websites on there?

Harriet:	'yes' (nods head) *I h-a-v-e o-n-l-y j-u-s-t s-t-a-r-t-e-d m-y b-u-s-i-n-e-s-s*
Researcher:	Right, so it's quite a new area. So you wouldn't necessarily use Facebook as part of your business. Is Facebook more personal?
Harriet:	*I d-o a-d-v-e-r-t-i-s-i-n-g . . . I h-a-v-e a-l-l t-h-e j-o-b-s I h-a-v-e d-o-n-e*
Researcher:	Okay and with your status, what kind of things do you tell people about?
Will:	"What I think"
Nancy:	"it good show pictures"
	[referring to Facebook]

Decreased misunderstanding and perceived equality

Participants also gave descriptions of how being online improved the ability to be understood by others and helped support perceptions of equality.

Email question:	What advice would you give to someone who uses AAC about using the internet and Facebook?
Peter:	"It's a really good way for people to get to know you better and understand you"
Nancy:	"people understand me better in writing"
Researcher:	okay, so can I just check that I've understood that, so you're saying when you can write things down you can give people more information and they can understand you better
Nancy:	yeah

Caroline's blog

I read what everyone is up to, I like or write comments, and look at photos. I like that because I communicate equally with everyone.

Researcher:	when you say it helps you to talk to people, you can say more
Moira:	"It shows people that how they have to wait to hear what I say"

Expressing humour and creating narratives

Participants described how online social media was helpful for expressing humour and offering alternative ways of creating self-narrative.

Harriet:	*I a-l-s-o p-u-t s-i-l-l-y s-t-u-f-f o-n m-y F-a-c-e-b-o-o-k*
Researcher:	. . . you've got a picture of yourself
Harriet:	*I-t-'s m-e l-e-a-n-i-n-g o-n s-h-o-p-p-i-n-g t-r-o-l-l-e-y*
	(Harriet usually uses a wheelchair but has created an image of herself using a trolley)

Harriet mentioned the timeline feature of Facebook as useful for keeping a record of old activities.

Researcher: You love it . . . I must get into Timeline then

Harriet: Y-o-u c-a-n l-o-o-k r-e-a-l-l-y o-l-d

Discussion

The opinions expressed by the participants would suggest that the technological advances that have facilitated the use of the internet and social media have added an additional dimension to the self-representation opportunities of people who use AAC. The reported perception of being understood more clearly suggests that it is an important additional support for face-to-face communication and facilitates alternative ways of expressing self-identity.

Keith is literate and uses an AAC device to turn text to speech but the device-generated speech has limited levels of intonation. In face-to-face conversation, Keith uses a highly intonational form of verbal communication, in addition to his AAC device, allowing certain emotions and phrases to be understood by people who know him very well and Ben moved to England as a small child from another European country.

All the participants discuss their profiles in some way but for this discussion the data from Keith, Ben and Peter will be explored in more depth. All of these participants have deemed it important to express something specific within their Facebook profiles. Keith likes seeing himself holding Pikachu, Ben wants people to appreciate he knows other languages and Peter wants to include things he likes such as the Chelsea football club. Both Ben and Peter want to show people places they have visited.

Erikson (1963, 1968) suggested an important part of adolescence is the development of a sense of self through role exploration and adolescents often align themselves with particular cultural signifiers as part of this process (fashion, music, subcultural groups etc.). Keith may be highlighting a self-perceived characteristic to others by using an internationally recognised icon within his profile picture and Ben is keen to signal his culturally diverse background. This presentation of the 'digital self' may be supporting their ability to self-create internal concepts (Marcia, 1980) and performing a role, as Livingstone (2008) suggests, of offering adolescents a relatively safe, but still exciting space, within which to project an image of the self within a social context.

As discussed earlier, Goffman (1959) and Stone (1981, cited by Zhao et al., 2008), both suggested individual performances are used to influence the perceptions of others. Zhao et al.'s (2008) analysis of how university students manage the continuum of a Facebook identity, from an implicit visual portrayal through photographs to a more explicit narrative where descriptions illuminate information, holds true with the participants in this research. Zhao et al. also suggested the use of Facebook can have concrete consequences within the offline world, which is supported by the data from Moira, Nancy and Caroline. All three have suggested that they can use social media to change others' perceptions – Moira suggests it shows people that they have to wait to hear what she has to say and it allows her to show different facets of her 'mixed' personality, Nancy feels it changes people's ability to understand her and Caroline reports that she likes communicating equally with everyone. Harriet's use of Facebook is particularly interesting in terms of Zhao et al.'s (2008) suggestion that a Facebook identity can be used to perform acts of resistance. By creating an ironic image of herself pushing a shopping trolley she is creating a joke with those who know her well as a wheelchair user. However, she may also be using the image to make a political statement about supermarket trolley design. She also uses her Facebook status to present herself as a business woman who creates and designs websites.

Establishing intimate relationships to counteract feelings of isolation is also identified by Erikson (1963, 1968) as a key stage of identity development in young adulthood. The perceptions expressed by Will, Peter and Carol illustrate how Facebook may be a useful tool for allowing them to interact more intimately with others. Will suggests that he is able to use Facebook to show people what he thinks and Carol points to herself when asked how she feels about Facebook. Peter suggests it is a good way for people to 'get to know you better and understand you'. This may illustrate how social media could be an important element in alleviating the propensity of AAC-mediated conversations to favour transactional rather than interactional communication (Grove & Tucker, 2003; Waller, 1992, 2006). Using social media to support self-representation resonates with the research presented earlier in the chapter from three people who use AAC – Hyatt (2011) said that it increased the depth of communication, Stevens (2011) said that it enhanced his sense of dignity and self-worth and Larned (2012) felt that it expanded social interaction to communication. Larned also felt that the written word:

> has a power all of its own to change hearts and win friends.
>
> (newsletter)

In line with Mead's (1934, cited by Livingstone, 2008) distinction of 'me' and 'I', the currency of social media, especially Facebook, offers opportunities to explore the more public concept of 'me' within a social context (Ellis, 2010). This phenomenon is shown within this research to have perceived benefits in terms of exploring self-representation for people with profound physical disabilities and complex communication needs. This must be recognised and prioritised within intervention; however, the broader findings from this study showed that there are considerable challenges across many areas for people who use AAC to achieve digital inclusion (Hynan et al., 2015). Evidence for enhanced self-representation via social media cannot be ignored, as self-report and sharing personal experiences are important aspects of developing a social identity (Grove & Tucker, 2003). The use of social media by people who use AAC must not be seen as the 'icing on the cake', but rather as a fundamental cultural right within our contemporary digital society.

References

Arnett, J. J. (2004). *Emerging adulthood: The winding road from the late teens through the twenties*. New York, NY: Oxford University Press.

Atanasoff, L. M., McNaughton, D., Wolf, P. S., & Light, J. (1998). Communication demands of university settings for students who use augmentative and alternative communication (AAC). *Journal on Postsecondary Education and Disability, 13*(3), 32–47. Retrieved from: http://scholar.google.co.uk/scholar?q=atanasoff+1998&btnG=&hl=en&as_sdt=0%2C5

Balandin, S., Berg, N., & Waller, A. (2006). Assessing the loneliness of older people with cerebral palsy. *Disability and Rehabilitation, 28*, 469–479.

Ballin, L., & Balandin, S. (2007). An exploration of loneliness: Communication and the social networks of older people with cerebral palsy. *Journal of Intellectual and Developmental Disabilities, 32*, 315–326.

Bowker, N., & Tuffin, K. (2002). Disability discourses and online identities. *Disability and Society, 17*(3), 327–344.

Bowker, N., & Tuffin, K. (2007). Understanding positive subjectivities made possible online for disabled people. *New Zealand Journal of Psychology, 36*(2), 63–71.

Browning, N. (2002). Literacy of children with physical disabilities: A literature review. *Canadian Journal of Occupational Therapy, 69*(3), 176–182.

Chapple, D. (2011). The evolution of augmentative communication and the importance of alternate access. *Perspectives on Augmentative and Alternative Communication, 20*(1), 34–37.

Charmaz, K. (2006). *Constructing grounded theory: A practical guide through qualitative research*. London, Thousand Oaks and New Delhi: Sage Publications.

Clarke, M. T., Bloch, S., & Wilkinson, R. (2013). Speaker transfer in children's peer conversation: Completing communication-aid-mediated contributions. *Augmentative and Alternative Communication, 29*(1), 37–53.

Clarke, M. T., Newton, C., Petrides, K., Griffiths, T., Lysley, A., & Price, K. (2012). An examination of relations between participation, communication and age in children with complex communication needs. *Augmentative and Alternative Communication, 28*(1), 44–51.

Clarke, M. T., & Wilkinson, R. (2007). Interaction between children with cerebral palsy and their peers 1: Organizing and understanding VOCA use. *Augmentative and Alternative Communication, 23*, 336–348.

Clarke, M. T., & Wilkinson, R. (2008). Interaction between children with cerebral palsy and their peers 2: Understanding initiated VOCA-mediated turns. *Augmentative and Alternative Communication, 24*, 3–15.

Cohen, K., & Light, J. (2000). Use of electronic communication to develop mentor-protégé relationships between adolescent and adult AAC users: Pilot study. *Augmentative and Alternative Communication, 16*, 227–238.

Dattilo, J., Estrella, G., Estrella, L. J., Light, J., McNaughton, D., & Seabury, M. (2008). 'I have chosen to live life abundantly': Perceptions of leisure by adults who use augmentative and alternative communication. *Augmentative and Alternative Communication, 24*(1), 16–28.

Ellis, K. (2010). Be who you want to be: The philosophy of Facebook and the construction of identity. *Screen Education, 58*, 36–41. Retrieved from: http://search.informit.com.au/documentSummary;dn=209659174211287;res=IELHSS.

Erikson, E. H. (1963). *Childhood and society* (2nd ed). New York, NY: Norton.

Erikson, E. H. (1968). *Identity: Youth and crises*. New York, NY: Norton.

Gandell, T., & Sutton, A. (1998). Comparison of AAC interaction patterns in face-to-face and telecommunications conversations. *Augmentative and Alternative Communication, 14*, 4–10.

Garcia, T. P., Loureiro, J. P., Gonzalez, B. G., Riveiro, L. N., & Sierra, A. P. (2011). The use of computers and augmentative and alternative communication devices by children and young with cerebral palsy. *Assistive Technology: The Official Journal of RESNA, 23*(3), 135–149.

Goffman, E. (1959). *The presentation of self in everyday life*. New York, NY: Penguin.

Goffman, E. (1964). The neglected situation. *American Anthropologist, 66*(6, part 2), 133–136.

Grace, E., Raghavendra, P., & Newman, L. (2014). Learning to use the internet and online social media: What is the effectiveness of home-based intervention for youth with complex communication needs? *Child Language Teaching and Therapy, 30*(2), 141–157.

Grove, N., & Tucker, S. (2003). Narratives in manual sign by children with intellectual impairments. In S. von Tetzchner & N. Grove (Eds.), *Augmentative and alternative communication: Developmental issues* (pp. 229–255). London and Philadelphia: Whurr Publishers.

Higginbotham, J., & Jacobs, S. (2011). The future of the Android operating system for augmentative and alternative communication. *Perspectives on Augmentative and Alternative Communication, 20*(2), 52–56.

Hyatt, G. W. (2011). The iPad: A cool communicator on the go. *Perspectives on Augmentative and Alternative Communication, 20*(1), 24–27.

Hynan, A. (2013). *How I use the Internet and online social media: Experiences of young people who use augmentative and alternative communication (AAC)* (Ph.D. thesis). Manchester Metropolitan University.

Hynan, A., Goldbart, J., & Murray, J. (2015). A grounded theory of internet and online social media use by young people who use augmentative and alternative communication. *Disability and Rehabilitation, 37*(17), 1559–1575.

Hynan, A., Murray, J., & Goldbart, J. (2014). 'Happy and excited': Perceptions of using digital technology and social media by young people who use augmentative and alternative communication. *Child Language Teaching and Therapy, 30*, 175–186.

Judge, S., & Townend, G. (2013). Perceptions of the design of voice output communication aids. *International Journal of Language and Communication Disorders, 48*(4), 366–381.

Larned, D. (2012). Discovering empowerment through writing. ConnSense bulletin. Retrieved from: http://aac-rerc.psu.edu/index.php/publications/list/page/4

Livingstone, S. (2008). Taking risky opportunities in youthful content creation: teenager's use of social networking sites for intimacy, privacy and self-expression. *New Media Society, 10*, 393–411.

Marcia, J. (1980). Identity in adolescence. In J. Adelson (Ed.), *Handbook of adolescent psychology* (pp. 159–187). New York, NY: Wiley and Sons.

Marshall, J., & Goldbart, J. (2008). 'Communication is everything I think.' Parenting a child who needs augmentative and alternative communication (AAC). *International Journal of Language and Communication Disorders, 43*(1), 77–98.

Mead, G. H. (1934). *Mind, self and society*. Chicago, IL: University of Chicago Press.

Mesch, G., & Talmud, I. (2010). *Wired youth: The social world of adolescence in the information age*. London, UK: Routledge.

Morris, J. (2003). Including all children: Finding out about the experiences of children with communication and/or cognitive impairments. *Children and Society, 17*(5), 337–348.

Ofcom. (2012). The consumer experience report. Ofcom. Retrieved from: http://stakeholders.ofcom.org.uk/binaries/research/consumer-experience/tce-12/Consumer_Experience_Researc1.pdf

Oyserman, D., Elmore, K., & Smith, G. (2012). Self, self-concept and identity. In M. Leary & J. P. Tangney (Eds.), *Handbook of self and identity* (2nd ed) (pp. 69–104). New York, NY: The Guilford Press.

Pistorius, M. (2011). *Ghost boy*. London: Simon and Schuster.

Rabiee, P., Sloper, P., & Beresford, B. (2005). Doing research with children and young people who do not use speech for communication. *Children and Society, 19*(5), 385–396.

Rackensperger, T., Krezman, C., McNaughton, D., Williams, M. B., & D'Silva, K. (2005). 'When I first got it, I wanted to throw it off of a cliff': The challenges and benefits of learning AAC technologies described by adults who use AAC. *Augmentative and Alternative Communication, 21*(3), 165–186.

Raghavendra, P., Newman, L., Grace, E., & Woods, D. (2013). 'I could never do that before': Effectiveness of a tailored internet support intervention to increase the social participation of youth with disabilities. *Child: Care, Health and Development, 39*(4), 552–561.

Raghavendra, P., Wood, D., Newman, L., & Lawry, J. (2012). Why aren't you on Facebook? Patterns and experiences of using the internet among young people with physical disabilities. *Technology and Disability, 24*, 149–162.

Reddington, J., & Coles-Kemp, L. (2011). Automatically generating stories from sensor data. *Proceedings of the 2011 International Conference on Intelligent User Interfaces (IUI2011)* (pp. 407–410). Retrieved from: http://www.cs.rhul.ac.uk/home/joseph/papers/IUI2011.pdf

Sacks, H., Schegloff, E., & Jefferson, G. (1974). A simplest systematics for the organization of turn-taking for conversation. *Language, 50*(4, part 1), 696–735.

Seymour, W., & Lupton, D. (2004). Holding the line online: Exploring wired relationships for people with disabilities. *Disability and Society, 19*(4), 291–305.

Shields, N., Murdoch, A., Loy, Y., Dodd, K.J., & Taylor, N. (2006). A systematic review of the self-concept of children with cerebral palsy compared with children without disability. *Developmental Medicine and Child Neurology, 48*(2), 151–157. Retrieved from: http://onlinelibrary.wiley.com/doi/10.1017/S0012162206000326/pdf

Smith, M. M. (1992). Reading abilities of nonspeaking students: Two case studies. *Augmentative and Alternative Communication, 8*, 57–66.

Smith, M. M. (2005). The dual challenges of aided communication and adolescence. *Augmentative and Alternative Communication, 21*(1), 67–79.

Smith, M. M., & Murray, J. (2011). Parachute without a ripcord: The skydive of communication interaction. *Augmentative and Alternative Communication, 27*(4), 292–303.

Stevens, S. (2011). Have you seen my new mobile phone? Merging AAC with mobile telephony. *Communication Matters, 25*(3), 5–7.

Sturm, J., & Clendon, S. (2004). Augmentative and alternative communication, language and literacy: Fostering the relationship. *Topics in Language Disorders, 24*(1), 76–91.

Sundqvist, A., & Ronnberg, J. (2010). A qualitative analysis of email interactions of children who use augmentative and alternative communication. *Augmentative and Alternative Communication, 26*(4), 255–266.

Thistle, J. J., & Wilkinson, K. M. (2012). What are the attention demands of aided AAC? *Perspectives on Augmentative and Alternative Communication, 21*(1), 17–22.

Todman, J., Alm, N., Higginbotham, J., & File, P. (2008). Whole utterance approaches in AAC. *Augmentative and Alternative Communication, 24*(3), 235–254.

von Tetzchner, S., & Basil, C. (2011). Terminology and notation in written representations of conversations with augmentative and alternative communication. *Augmentative and Alternative Communication, 27*(3), 141–149.

Waller, A. (1992). *Providing narratives in an augmentative communication system* (Ph.D. thesis). University of Dundee, Scotland.

Waller, A. (2006). Communication access to conversational narrative. *Topics in Language Disorders, 26*(3), 221–239.

Wickenden, M. (2009). 'Talking to teenagers: using anthropological methods to explore identity and lifeworlds of young people who use AAC'. *Communication Disorders Quarterly, 32*(3), 151–163.

Zhao, S., Grasmuck, S., & Martin, J. (2008). Identity construction on Facebook: Digital empowerment in anchored relationships. *Computers in Human Behavior, 24*, 1816–1836.

22 Disability, social media and religious discourse

An Arabian example

Najma Al Zidjaly

Cultural contextualisation

Social media have been credited with playing a major role in creating religious and political change in the Middle East (e.g. Eickelman & Anderson, 2003; Howard et al., 2011; Stepanova & Eurasia, 2011, Gerbaudo, 2012). The role that Arab people with disabilities might have played, or continue to play, in such historic, changing times merits examination. This is all the more disconcerting as research overwhelmingly looks favourably upon the role that social media (and technology in general) have played in the formation of the new identity of Arabs. Researchers studying the impact of technology on disability, however, are divided on how they conceptualise the benefits of technology. Mainly they either foreground what technology can do for people with disabilities (i.e. highlighting the cultural tool), thereby backgrounding the agency of the users, or they generalise the claims with no substantiation or documentation of actual usage. Research about social media (or technology in general) and Arabs with disability is almost non-existent, save my decade-long ethnographic examination of how a now 47-year-old man with quadriplegia from Oman named Yahya, the focus of this chapter, has managed to create personal and social inclusion through Yahoo chatrooms and through Microsoft PowerPoint (Al Zidjaly, 2007, 2009, 2010, 2011a, 2011b, 2015).

In Oman, an Islamic social monarchy located in the Arabian Gulf, the situation of the roughly estimated 60,000 people with disabilities is inconclusive. Despite government efforts to implement the social model of disability, both the medical model and what I loosely term the 'test from God' model of disability (which derives from the holy book of Islam) and their accompanying stigma have long prevailed, as in many other cultures of the Arab world (see Al Zidjaly, 2015). People with (physical) disabilities have always been excluded to an extent from the larger society due to Oman's mountainous typography; the sequestration, however, intensified with the onset of modernisation in Oman in 1970. Omanis have struggled to see how disability could fit in with modern Oman (this comment on disability and modernisation has also been noted about the West (e.g. Barnes, 1990, 2012; Oliver, 1990; Borsay, 2005). This scuffle materialised much to the dismay of the Omani government, which in 2008 ratified the United Nation's Convention on the Rights of People with Disabilities and fashioned its own Disability and Rehabilitation Law. Accordingly, Omani legislation proclaims that disability is a social problem not just a medical predicament. They, however, have yet to implement this belief in reality, and, as a consequence, people with disabilities in Oman – especially those with physical disability – continue to be stigmatised, marginalised and concealed, much more than in the past, given the outdated societal and religious misconceptions of disability, which equate disability with dependency, futility and pitifulness. This has resulted in a double bind with two contradictory discourses – on the one hand, the Omani government informs Omanis with disabilities that they are a crucial component of the Omani society. On the other hand, psychological and cultural barriers continue to thrive, resulting in haphazard disability policies and in the continuation of a society where disability causes are relegated as family, not government, concerns.

Against this disabling backdrop, Yahya turned to technology as a means of agency. Yahya was 19 years old when he had a car accident that rendered him a quadriplegic for life. He is, however, able to press on computer keyboards or iPads with the knuckle of his right index finger. In Al Zidjaly (2015), I document Yahya's journey with technology which started in 2000. At first, Yahya used technology as a tool to make sense of his disability through creating music videos (via Microsoft PowerPoint) that delve into societal taboo discourses that touch upon his disability and the effect it had had on his masculinity in particular. Next, Yahya used technology to create inclusion within family circles. Later, through contributing to Yahoo political and religious chatrooms online, he created inclusion with the international community with the aim, as he proclaimed in playback sessions (Tannen, 2005), 'to showcase that there is more to him than his physical disability.' When Yahoo chatrooms ceased to exist and WhatsApp launched in 2012, Yahya found himself compelled to take note of other fellow Omanis whom he has long shunned, as they could never comprehend his disability. As WhatsApp is a free smartphone messenger app, it was immediately adopted by Omanis to create private communities to discuss social and political concerns (unlike Yahoo online chatrooms, WhatsApp chat groups are by invitation only). This provided Yahya an opportunity to continue his spiritual teachings which he had started online, but this time with Omanis, by drawing upon the cultural practice of daily creating and sharing multimodal texts that get to be distributed nationally. Rather than engaging in typical religious or political discourse, however, Yahya's artistic creations are spiritual in nature. In addition, his creations do not disclose his identity as a man with quadriplegia; they do, however, indirectly engage in disability discourse. This was motivated by two concerns – Yahya is aware of the societal, demeaning discourses concerning him as a man with a physical disability, and he believes that to change how disability is viewed in his disabling, albeit unintentionally, society, Omanis' higher consciousness must be shifted first. Yahya's decision not to disclose his disability with Omanis he engages with on social media is further discussed in the next section.

Theoretical contextualisation

Disability has not fared well in traditional religious discourse across cultures (Anderson, 2006). Spiritual discourse (especially from the Buddhism perspective), on the other hand, has managed to reconcile disability with religion (Bejoian, 2006). Therefore, Yahya concluded that a prerequisite to changing disability discourse in Oman (and Arabia at large) is to first highlight the spiritual side of Islam. This was all the more crucial given that traditional Islamic misrepresentations of disability are accentuated by far more condescending cultural misunderstandings. Both discourses have failed to disrupt the antiquated model of disability which, according to Lewis (2000), equates disability with uselessness and, as in the Arabian context, pitifulness. Yahya's awareness of his body with quadriplegia as a 'performing agent' (Sandahl & Auslander, 2005) was an additional factor to undisclose his identity as a man with a disability on social media. The distressed body that Yahya is cognisant of has been the subject of numerous sociological accounts of living with physical disability. Murphy (1990), for instance, in his lived experience with paralysis, demonstrates the contradictory effect that his paralysed body has had on his identity. While his body had lost the ability for non-verbal communication, the bodily and emotional distress communicated loud and clear. A body with paralysis, Becker (1995) argues, cannot help but reflect physical and emotional anguish. Even when not seen, the word 'disability' conjures 'commotion' not just in public, as argued by Sandahl and Auslander (2005), but also on social media, as I found the case to be in Arabia. In Oman, for example, the typical response when referencing a person with a disability is 'poor them'. This connotation is not only demeaning, but, as Yahya explained in playback sessions, it also renders it nearly impossible for people with disabilities to manage the discrepancy between their real selves and virtual selves, a major predicament with living with disability according to sociologist Goffman (1963). In Yahya's words, 'it makes it hard to transcend disability and showcase ability.'

Social media (e.g. WhatsApp) has provided Yahya an opportunity to focus on his actions (creating multimodal texts that are shared nationally) instead of his disability. In doing so, it has assisted, instead of hindered, Yahya's ultimate goal, i.e. to change the discourse on disability in the Middle East by first shifting higher consciousness. As the 'ideology of the physical' that 'constructs an imagined bridge between bodily difference and individual abilities' (Mitchell & Snyder, 1997, p. 13) is but a lived reality in Oman, Yahya creates works of art that indirectly, not directly, engage with disability, until his mark is made. Only then, he declares, he will disclose his identity and demonstrate to his society that has long treated him as inconsequential that disability is indeed a social, not a medical or physical, concern.

To understand the exact role Yahya plays in attempting to bring about religious and, in due course, (disability) change, I introduce to critical disability studies the theory of mediated discourse analysis (Scollon, 2001), which foregrounds agency by highlighting actions instead of tools. I thus theorise all multimodal texts (on and off social media) as mediated actions that are social and historical. They are to be conceived not as mere vehicles of expression or as tools of representation, as they have been constructed in traditional research, but instead as social actions taken by social actors to strategically generate identities and outcomes, including inciting change (see Al Zidjaly, 2011c). Actions are always mediated through language or technology (e.g. WhatsApp). This theorisation is crucial in introducing an element of action to the discourse on technology (or art) and disability, as the shift in conceptualising works of art (created by technology and shared on social media) as by-products to conceptualising them as actions highlights the power of art (and social media) in igniting change; it further centralises the agentivity of the creator of the works of art (and the users of technology) in the process of propelling transformation (i.e. it demonstrates how social media can be used to create transformation in the lives of its users). I moreover suggest contextualising multimodal texts physically, socially and culturally (Scollon & Scollon, 2003; Al Zidjaly, 2014); contextualising the data (i.e. viewing multimodal [textual and visual] texts on WhatsApp as mediated actions that advance a new way of conceiving Islam – and by extension disability) surpasses analysing what visual texts mean to investigating how they are used to affect various kinds of identities – Blommaert (2005) makes a similar argument regarding verbal texts. Doing so enables capturing not just how social media is used by a person with a disability in the Middle East to create change, but also how technological tools can be used to alleviate disability by masking, temporarily, the physical body . . . until Yahya decides to disclose it himself.

Agency through WhatsApp

In the spirit of participatory research, in this section, as per Yahya's request, I provide four examples that Yahya himself has selected that, according to him, 'demonstrate his creativity, showcase his capabilities, and illuminate his transformative ideas, instead of centralizing his physical disability.' These four examples are representative of the kind of multimodal mediated actions Yahya creates via Textgram and shares on WhatsApp groups he participates in nationally. One of these WhatsApp chat groups is an assembly named the Omani Creative which houses some of the most established Omani leaders and intellectuals – I also am part of the group; it was me who invited Yahya to join the group in 2014. The particular set was selected for two reasons. First, it represents the four major elements of spiritual discourse which can collectively reconcile disability with religion – divine love, oneness, justice and kindness. Second, these four texts are Yahya's most circulated across Oman from 2014–2015 when the data for this chapter were collected. The four mediated actions are aimed at centralising the forlorn, spiritual side of Islam which Muslims have assigned to Sufism, often treated as a distinct sect that many 'true' Muslims, especially in the Arabian Gulf, do not concede. Yahya's highest concern is to summon up the spirituality of Islam – to enable Muslim Arabs to first learn the true essence of their religion instead of making mere movements through religious motions (e.g. rather than highlighting the act of prayer, Yahya aims to teach how best to pray); and second, most illuminatingly, to introduce a new discourse of disability in Arabia, a discourse that highlights the social aspect of disability instead of the physical. These actions are thus intended to, directly, create the ultimate shift in consciousness aimed at altering how Omanis engage with and practise Islam and, indirectly, highlight the cause of disability in a creative manner through social media.

To ignite the desired shift, Yahya intertextually references (and meta-comments on) prior religious texts and actions, established cultural practices and events. In so doing, Yahya – someone with a disability who has long believed to be agentless by his society's standards – is able to recontextualise what Bakhtin (1981) terms 'authoritative discourses' (i.e. discourses un-open for discussion) to 'internally persuasive discourses' (i.e. discourses open for discussion). Thus far, none of the members of the Omani Creative group (save myself) are aware of Yahya's disability; some though are aware of his online teachings from the days of the Yahoo chatrooms. For the time being, and for the reasons conferred in the previous sections, Yahya prefers to centralise his creative actions and ideas rather than his disability which, according to him, Omanis cannot see past. Once he establishes himself as a contending intellectual authority, as he had managed to achieve online in Yahoo chatrooms, he will disclose his disability. In so doing, he intends to demonstrate that not only is there more to him than his disability (which was afforded to him by his creative use of technology) but that disability is indeed a social construction, contrary to mainstream beliefs in Oman. Yahya trusts that only when the higher consciousness of Arabs is raised, the old narrative of disability that is widely practised in Arabia shall transform.

Note that the provided interpretations of the four examples in this section are based on Yahya's own explanations in playback sessions and in recorded chat discussions on WhatsApp of his artistic works aimed to reconciling religion with disability, albeit covertly. The focus in the following mediated actions, therefore, is not so much on Yahya's identity as a man with a disability from the Middle East but, rather, on his transformative ideas, as per Yahya's own request.

The four mediated actions

Mediated action 1: Divine love

The most important relationship one can have is with God, or, in traditional spiritual discourse, the universe. Moreover, the quality of one's experience in life is in direct proportion to the quality of one's relationship with the creator of the universe. This is a chief teaching of spiritual traditions, including Islam. The nature of this connection, however, eludes the majority of traditional Muslims, especially in the Arabian Gulf, as Muslim Arabs are theoretically masters of the act of worship; yet, practically, they find the quality of the act of worship a mystifying concept. These assertions, which might at first seem threatening, are based on a decade-long ethnographic examination of Islamic behaviour and teachings I have conducted as an Arab cultural anthropologist; the assertions, as aforementioned, have also been discussed with Yahya. Hence, Yahya during the first week of joining WhatsApp, created a mediated action that addresses the nature of the connection with God and, indirectly, his disability.

Mediated action 1 (see Figure 22.1) was originally crafted to share with family and friends through WhatsApp showing Yahya's conceptualisation of the nature of humans' connection with God. When it catapulted nationally into popularity, for months Yahya chose the text as his WhatsApp profile to symbolise the strength of his character and his main philosophy of life. The mediated action is created through linguistically referencing an iconic line of classical Arabic poetry: 'Whose essence is filled with God is seldom weighed by burdens.' Thus, it serves one well to be mindful of God. The blue sky acts not just as the background, but also visually invokes the creator of the universe. The blue sky additionally symbolises Yahya's quest for physical freedom. Indirectly and visually, Yahya's disability is further alluded to by his choice of an image of a burdened soul: the image both represents life challenges and his disability, which he indeed conceives of as a load he is able to transcend through his filled-with-God heart. The romantic red heart references the nature of the connection between God and people: that one should fall in love with God (as Sufism preaches), rather than merely worship God out of habit (as traditionally practised in Arabia). This falling in love concept, symbolised by an image of a red heart, was a new discourse that took a great many WhatsApp users by surprise, rendering the action worthy of national distribution. As a result, a number of discussions were initiated on WhatsApp that intertextually referenced the traditional Islamic concept of worship and invoke new means of not just talking about God but also of conceiving God – Yahya was able to reintroduce a close God that one can fall in love with. Only through falling in love can one triumph over any challenge, including disability – this is the main message.

This early multimodal action of Yahya, which still at times serves as his profile image for the app, is an attempt to encourage others to revisit their relationships with God, and ultimately, revisit their relationships with others in need to overcome adversity. Due to its iconic status, Yahya signs off the image in yellow with his first and last name.

Mediated action 2: Oneness

In addition to engaging with issues of relating with God, Yahya addresses the concept of oneness. Traditional religious discourse, especially in the Islamic culture, and particularly during the current unrest in the Middle East, thrives on sectarianism. Spiritual discourse, on the other hand, transcends dissimilarities – it advocates oneness. Non-sectarianism and tolerance have also been main tenants of Omani nationalism. The Omani government, since the Omani renaissance in 1970 under the leadership of Sultan Qaboos bin Said, has been adamant about peace and lenience, the two pillars of a modern, stable society. This has been all the more crucial given the cultural background of Oman as an Arabian empire that governed colonies in Africa and Asia in the past, resulting in Omani nationals who belong not only to various religious sects but also to different ethnic backgrounds (and various types of abilities). Thus, Omanis have grown accustomed to not heeding

Figure 22.1 Mediated action 1: Divine love

ethnic, religious and other types of sectarianism. This national discourse, however, found itself under attack in 2015, a natural outcome of the unrest across Arabia. When it appeared as though Omanis were succumbing to outside pressures that highlight differences and, accordingly, were beginning to turn to divisiveness after 45 years of unity and oneness – a serious national shift with dangerous consequences – Yahya was moved to act. He created an action intended to engage in the Omani national and spiritual discourse of unity – oneness.

In mediated action 2 (see Figure 22.2), Yahya attempts to unite Omanis, and bring to halt once and for all divisive discourses that have spread across WhatsApp, through a reminder of Omani national discourse – loyalty, tolerance and religious unity. The mediated action thus intertextually references the Omani government discourse while simultaneously engaging with the then destabilising political discourses from the outside. It also indirectly reminds Omanis of the need to treat all Omanis (including those with disabilities) as one. This action is addressed both to other Omanis, warning them of the dangers of falling prey to sectarian attempts, and also to outsiders, reassuring them of the failure of their actions. To arrive at the intended outcomes, Yahya creates an action made up of two images – a map of Oman and an official portrait of the Sultan of Oman, thereby harkening back the identity of Oman as the land of peace and tolerance (and inclusion of all), and the instructions of the leader of Oman to whom Yahya, as a spokesperson of Omanis, pledges loyalty. Linguistically, Yahya sums up the identity of Omanis as an Islamic nation with various sects, including Sunna, Shia and Ibadhi, the most prominent sects in Oman, and as a nation who loves its leader and Oman – an undivided nation who believes that 'together we stand, divided we fall'. Although this famous phrase – taken from the lyrics of the British alternative band Pink Floyd – does not appear in mediated action 2, it was the motivating factor behind making this action, as Yahya professed in playback sessions. The verbal and visual elements of the action combined together appear to have worked, affecting public discourse the way Yahya intended – sectarian and ethnic discussions on WhatsApp around the time this action was created and shared have quieted down, rendering it successful in reminding Omanis of taking pride, as they have always done, in being diverse and accepting of all.

Mediated action 3: Justice for all

An additional pillar of spirituality that is addressed by Yahya's mediated WhatsApp actions, which indirectly alludes to disability rights, is justice. Without justice, Yahya declares, peace cannot exist. In truth, one of the chief teachings he advocates is that Islam, unlike what many Muslims and Westerners might think, is a religion of justice first and peace second, as peace can only be a by-product of justice and not vice versa. This new way of defining Islam has caught the attention of a great many Muslim Arabs who have grown up believing it is the other way around. As a result, Yahya not only supports just causes, he actively promotes them, as demonstrated by mediated action 3 (see Figure 22.3), which he shared on WhatsApp in 2014.

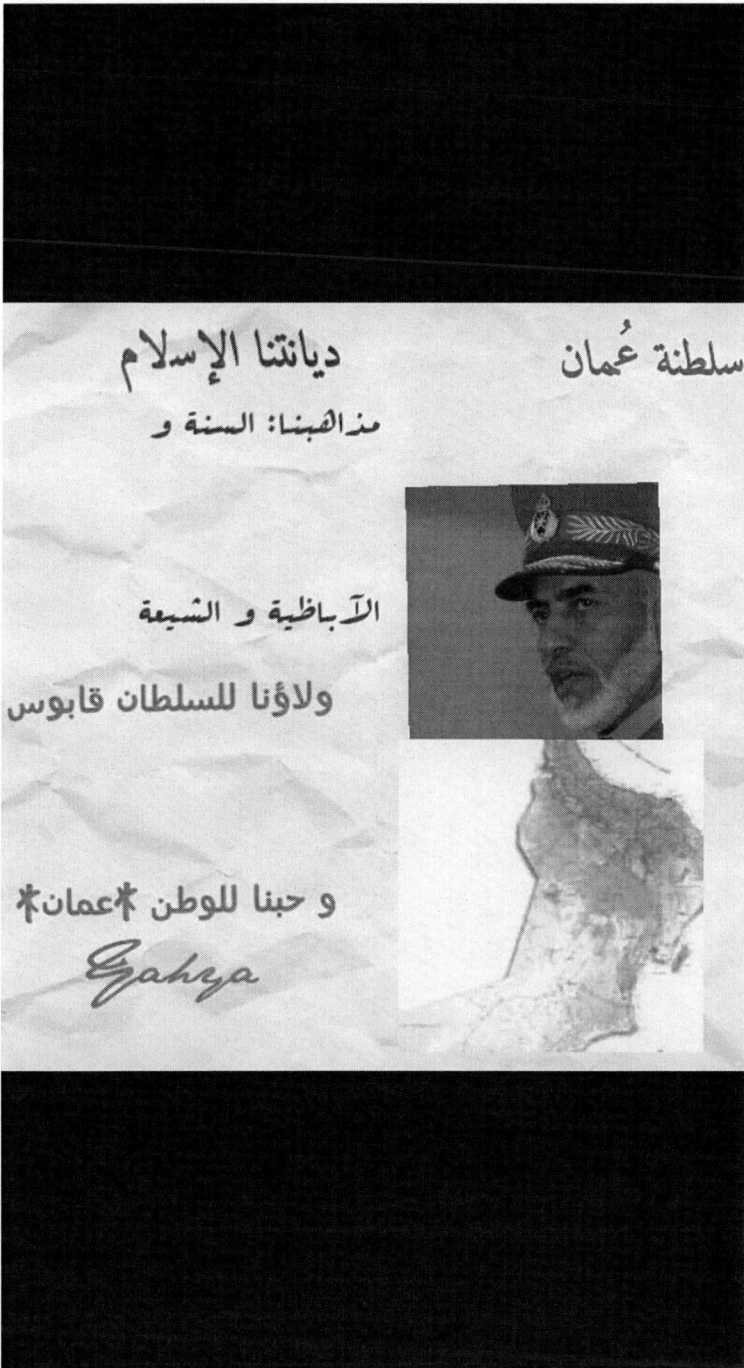

Figure 22.2 Mediated action 2: Oneness

Figure 22.3 Mediated action 3: Justice for all

This mediated action symbolises a call for action in the face of political corruption, which has been a serious concern in Oman since the Arab Spring in 2011, and which has now become all the more mobilised. Therefore, Yahya's mediated action still makes the rounds on WhatsApp every few weeks whenever more reports about the corruption of certain Omani government officials surface. It should be noted that Omanis distinguish between the leader of Oman – whom Omanis adulate – and officials in the Omani government who might/do not carry out the instructions of the leader of Oman to the letter. The created mediated action 3 is simplified into three images – the top and bottom images are of the leader of Oman (the symbol of justice, acceptance and spirituality) whom Yahya pledges allegiance to, and the middle image is of an audience. In the top image, the leader of Oman is greeting both Omanis and appointed government officials. The centre image symbolises the audience related to the leader's instructions of serving Omani people, not their own personal interests. In the bottom image, the Sultan of Oman is captured in mid speech. What he is depicted as saying is represented by a quote Yahya coins in both English and Arabic that sums up all the instructions of the leader of Oman, and which most government officials have denied – justice for all. That is, not just for the rich and the elite but for all Omanis, including those with disabilities. In fact, this particular mediated action did lead to long discussions of disability rights in Oman. It is further a reminder (and a warning) to government officials to abide by the laws of the government of Oman as per the instructions of the leader of Oman, including putting into effect the laws of disability inclusion that the Omani government introduced in 2008. Representing it both in Arabic and English signals the universality of the call.

Mediated action 4: Kindness

Teaching the importance of kindness is an additional method by which Yahya aims to make Islamic religion a daily practice of love and compassion, not of habit. This particular message was one that Yahya came upon online and decided to share with his WhatsApp groups, especially since it is a famous quote by American satirical author Mark Twain, written, according to Yahya, in a 'patronising' language that Omanis can relate to.

While the message (see Figure 22.4) is problematic within disability studies, as it conjures up antiquated, demeaning constructions of people with disabilities, Yahya insisted on its inclusion in this chapter as it directly alludes to disability; it is also one of his creations that has led to a plethora of debates on the unacceptable reality of disability in Oman. With its inclusion Yahya further aims to highlight the discrepancy between disability discourse in the Western culture and the Middle East with its disabling linguistic constructions to date (i.e. people in Oman still use terms such as crippled, deaf and blind instead of people with physical, hearing or visual disability). Furthermore, in the Middle East, people still point out physical attributes in relation to 'the mainstream' abled bodies, much like old cultural discourses pointed out by Mitchell and Snyder (1997). Thus, although Yahya does not prefer centralising his disability, it is a part and parcel (but not the entirety)

Figure 22.4 Mediated action 4: Kindness

of his identity. In the discussion that ensued following the sharing of this action, Yahya explained that the reference to 'deaf' and 'blind' is metaphoric, not literal, indicating the universality of kindness and its power to get through all even those with blinders and those with closed minds. Yahya's love for the English language was a second motivator to share this widely circulated action on Omani What-sApp. Yahya chose this particular message to indicate his mastery of the English language, leading him to be appointed as the unofficial English instructor of the Creative Group. This was, and still is, as it keeps being recycled across WhatsApp, a call for Muslim Arabs to practise compassion not metaphorically, but literally. The action is also an indirect reminder of the cause of disability and the necessity to support Omanis with disability in gaining rights – that it is the kind thing to do. In Yahya's own words, 'doing the kind thing is doing the right thing, which Omanis and the Arab world in general are lagging behind, especially when the rights of people with disabilities are concerned.' The kind or the right thing to do in the Middle East is to move disability rights from theory (i.e. policies at the government level) to reality (i.e. to put them into daily practice).

Concluding remarks

In Al Zidjaly (2015, p. 195), I state:

> The consensus among disability researchers is that disability studies is at a crossroads. The path ultimately taken will shape its future in two ways: It

can secure its survival by redefining and extending its historical role in alleviating disability, or, if boundaries are not pushed and human agency is not foregrounded, we can ensure the field's demise.

In this chapter, I provided an example that demonstrates how boundaries can be pushed and agency can be foregrounded; in turn, I answered a number of calls put forth in critical disability studies. I have further presented a rare case study from the Middle Eastern context where disability rights largely remain an untranslatable, theoretical discourse. I approached the study from the perspective that human agency has been conspicuously absent from the discourse on social media and disability. In providing an analysis of how one man with quadriplegia attempts to ignite change through social media, I advocate a refocus of the analytical lens – we need to foreground the agency of people with disabilities by examining the discourse and actions they take in real life. I further advocate conducting longitudinal, multimodal and ethnographic research, of which I have provided an example here.

The findings of this chapter cannot be generalised to cover all people with disabilities and more research is needed in the Middle East. The chapter, however, contributes to documenting an historic time in the world and the role that one person with a disability, likely one among many around the world, is trying to play to ignite religious and, in due course, disability change. Although I have formerly documented how Yahya has established himself as a religious authority among online friends through his Yahoo chatrooms contributions (see Al Zidjaly, 2015), the larger effects of his WhatsApp actions are yet to be measured. Yahya, however, is steadily gaining the trust and admiration of his WhatsApp peers and is inciting debates, indicating that his intended path to move disability policies in Oman from theory to practice (and to demonstrate that disability is indeed a social concern) might be underway already. This is owing to Yahya's mediated actions that create inclusion in an excluding society in a creative manner afforded to him by social media's ability not to disclose his physical attributes. Until further notice.

Acknowledgements

Research for this chapter was made possible by strategic grants at Sultan Qaboos University, Oman. The funded project (SR/ART/ENGL/15/01) is titled, *The impact of social media on Omani youth: A multimodal project.*

Many heartfelt thanks to Cynthia Gordon, Katie Ellis, Mike Kent and two anonymous reviewers for their valuable comments on an earlier draft of the paper. Many profound thanks also to Yahya Belushi for sharing his wisdom with the world.

References

Al Zidjaly, N. (2007). Alleviating disability through Microsoft PowerPoint: The story of one quadriplegic man in Oman. *Visual Communication, 6*(1), 73–98. doi:10.1177/1470357207071466

Al Zidjaly, N. (2009). Agency as an interactive achievement. *Language in Society, 38,* 177–200.

Al Zidjaly, N. (2010). Intertextuality and Islamic identities online. In R. Taiwo (Ed.), *Handbook of research on discourse behavior and digital communication: Language structures and social interaction* (pp. 191–204). Hershey, PA: IGI Global.

Al Zidjaly, N. (2011a). Managing social exclusion through technology: An example of art as mediated action. *Disability Studies Quarterly, 31*(4). Retrieved from http://dsq- sds.org/article/view/1716

Al Zidjaly, N. (2011b). Can art lead to social change? A mediated multimodal inquiry. *Multimodal Communication, 1*(1), 65–81.

Al Zidjaly, N. (2011c). Multimodal texts as mediated actions: Voice, synchronization and layered simultaneity in images of disability. In S. Norris (Ed.), *Multimodality in practice: Investigating theory-in-practice-through-methodology* (pp. 190–205). London, UK: Routledge.

Al Zidjaly, N. (2014). Geosemiotics: Discourses in place. In S. Norris & C. D. Maier (Eds.), *The reader in multimodality* (pp. 63–76). Berlin, Germany: De Gruyter.

Al Zidjaly, N. (2015). *Disability, discourse and technology: Agency and inclusion in (Inter) action.* London, UK: Palgrave Macmillan.

Anderson, R. (2006). Faith in access: Bridging conversations between religion and disability. *Disability Studies Quarterly, 26*(3). Retrieved from http://dsq-sds.org/article/view/719/896

Bakhtin, M. M. (1981). *The dialogic imagination: Four essays*. Edited and translated by C. Emerson, & M. Holquist, Austin, TX: The University of Texas Press.

Barnes, C. (1990). *Cabbage syndrome: The social construction of dependence.* Bristol, UK: Falmer.

Barnes, C. (2012). *The social model of disability: Valuable or irrelevant?* In N. Watson, A. Roulstone, & C. Thomas (Eds.), *The Routledge handbook of disability studies* (pp. 12–29). London, UK: Routledge.

Becker, A. L. (1995). *Beyond translation: Essays toward a modern philology*. Ann Arbor, MI: University of Michigan Press.

Bejoian, L. (2006). Non-dualistic paradigms in disability studies and Buddhism: Creating bridges for theoretical practice. *Disability Studies Quarterly, 26*(3). Retrieved from http://dsq-sds.org/article/view/723/900

Blommaert, J. (2005). *Discourse: A critical introduction.* Cambridge, UK: Cambridge University Press.

Borsay, A. (2005). *Disability and social policy in Britain since 1750.* Basingstoke, UK: Palgrave Macmillan.

Eickelman, D. F., & Anderson, J. W. (Eds.). (2003). *New media in the Muslim world: The emerging public sphere.* Bloomington, IN: Indiana University Press.

Gerbaudo, P. (2012). *Tweets and the streets: Social media and contemporary activism.* New York, NY: Pluto Press.

Goffman, E. (1963). *Stigma: Notes on the management of a spoiled identity.* Englewood Cliffs, NJ: Prentice-Hall.

Howard, P. N., Duffy, A., Freelon, D., Hussain, M. M., Mari, W., & Maziad, M. (2011). *Opening closed regimes: What was the role of social media during the Arab Spring?* Seattle: PIPTI. Retrieved January 1, 2014 from http://pitpi.org/index.php/2011/09/11/opening-closed-regimes-what-was-the-role-of-social-media-during-the-arab-spring/

Lewis, V. A. (2000). The dramaturgy of disability. In S. Crutchfield & M. Epstein (Eds.), *Points of contact: Disability, art, and culture* (pp. 93–108). Ann Arbor, MI: University of Michigan Press.

Mitchell, D., & Snyder, S. (1997). *The body and physical difference: Discourses of disability (The body, in theory: Histories of cultural materialism)*. Ann Arbour, MI: University of Michigan Press.

Murphy, R. F. (1990). *The body silent*. New York: Henry Holt.

Oliver, M. (1990). *The politics of disablement*. Basingstoke, UK: Macmillan.

Sandahl, C., & Auslander, P. (2005). *Bodies in commotion: Disability and performance (Corporealities: Discourses of disability)*. Ann Arbour, MI: University of Michigan Press.

Scollon, R. (2001). *Mediated discourse: The nexus of practice*. London, UK: Routledge.

Scollon, R., & Scollon, S. (2003). *Geosemiotics: Discourses in place*. London, UK: Routledge.

Stepanova, E., & Eurasia, P. (2011). The role of information communication technologies in the 'Arab Spring': Implications beyond the region. *PONARS Eurasia Policy Memo* No. 159.

Tannen, D. (2005). *Conversational style: Analyzing talk among friends*. Norwood, NJ: Ablex.

23 Using social media to advance the social rights of people with disability in China

The Beijing One Plus One
Disabled Persons' Cultural
Development Centre

*Jian Xu, Mike Kent, Katie Ellis
and He Zhang*

Introduction

With the increasing take up of digital technology in China, various social groups are presented with new opportunities to seek equality and participation. With digital devices such as computers and smartphones, and digital literacy as simple as reading and writing online texts, particularly in conjunction with social media, Chinese non-professional citizens can self-represent and speak to the public directly using personal and experiential knowledge. Voluntary online self-representations of diverse forms are able to portray a range of social concerns as well as demonstrate activist and advocacy potentials. A prominent example of this, particularly as it relates to people with disabilities, can be seen in the activities of the Beijing One Plus One Disabled Persons' Cultural Development Centre (OPO) over the last ten years. The OPO is an NGO and a non-official disabled persons organisation (DPO) run by and for people with disabilities.

   This chapter looks at social media in China through the online activities of the OPO to explore issues of disability and Chinese language social media. This topic is often overlooked in the current disability studies and social media literature, particularly in an English language context. As such, this chapter aims to outline the research available and identify what is distinctive about disability and social media in China. While the chapter broadly focuses on the social position of people with disabilities in China, the discussion highlights the specific position of people with vision impairments and blindness.

Disability in China

Although a significant portion of the world's disabled population live in China, the country has only ever undertaken two national disability surveys, one in 1987 and one 19 years later in 2006. Data from these two representative surveys show that the number of people with disabilities rose from 52.7 million in 1987 to 84.6 million in 2006 (Zheng et al., 2011). While these surveys reflect an increasing incidence of disability, the definition of disability used to collect the data is limited and the actual amount of people with disabilities is likely to be much higher (Sagli et al., 2013), particularly because autism and multiple disabilities were excluded (see Aubié, 2014).

Blindness and vision impairment in China

Recent figures suggest China has 17 million people with a vision impairment, 5 million of whom are totally blind (The Economist, 2013). While this figure constitutes 18 per cent of the world's total population of blind people, it represents a mere 0.4 per cent of the Chinese population (World Health Organisation, 2015).

People in China with vision impairments usually use one of four types of screen readers which support Chinese in order to access online- and computer-based information. Non-visual desktop access (NVDA) is an open source screen reader that supports both Braille display output and languages other than English. While NVDA originated in the United States, the other three readers are Chinese designs. The Sunshine Screen Reader was developed by the government-affiliated China Braille Press while the Yongde Screen Reader and Zhengdu Screen Reader were both developed by non-official programmers.

Yeh, Tsay, & Liang (2008) have been critical of the inadequacies of most commercially available screen readers such as JAWS when it comes to supporting Chinese characters. They argue that despite being available to many people with vision impairment internationally, refreshable Braille displays do not support Chinese characters (Yeh, Tsay, & Liang, 2008). Wang et al. (2010) note that the Braille or screen reader inputs that do exist, such as the Sunshine Screen Reader, still rely on the user understanding pinyin – a linguistic system for representing standard Mandarin in the Roman alphabet developed during the 1950s.

Social disablement

Although China's Disabled Person's Act states 'all aspects of social life should be open to persons with disabilities' there is no mechanism for the enforcement of this law and people with disabilities in China continue to experience significant social disadvantage (Braddock & Parish, 2001, p. 16). People with vision impairments and blindness experience restrictions of activity surrounding access to education, employment and public space in China. These restrictions are often due to a lack of accessible communication practices, an inaccessible built environment and discriminatory attitudes.

During the 1960s and 1970s a number of initiatives to improve the social position of people with vision impairment were implemented in China. Several cities including Shanghai, Beijing and Guangzhou installed raised concrete bumps along the footpath to assist pedestrians with vision impairments to 'navigate the city unassisted' (Crouch, 2015). However, the 'mang dao' (blind paths) footpath system was not maintained and present day hurdles such as bikes and scooters being left on the footpath represent a significant danger to vision impaired people attempting to navigate the city.

Similarly, linguists developed a new two-cell Braille system to translate Chinese into Braille. The system adopted a similar approach to pinyin and represented both phonetics and tones. However, as Crouch observes, 'for many, the system never lived up to its potential – some vital school texts have never been translated into Braille, and the Ministry of Education did not begin offering a Braille/electronically-assisted Gaokao college entrance exam until [2014]' (Crouch, 2015).

Access to higher education is particularly difficult for people with vision impairment, with only three of China's 2000 universities allowing admission to people with significant vision impairment. Between 2002 and 2013 a mere 60 students who are blind attended university in China (The Economist, 2013). Discriminatory attitudes play a key role in whether a person who is blind has access to education. For example, the Shandong provincial education bureau denied a student's request for the provision of the Gaokao exam in an accessible format because:

> Even if [the student] takes the exams, she would be unable to participate in class like normal students and since ordinary universities cannot provide Braille textbooks, she cannot receive a normal education in ordinary schools.
>
> (Shandong Province Bureau of Education
> cited in Human Rights Watch, 2013)

Despite people with disabilities gaining the right to attend mainstream schools in China in 2008, vocational opportunities for people with vision impairment are limited and unofficial policy encourages people to become masseuses or musicians (Crouch, 2015; The Economist, 2013; Human Rights Watch, 2013; Tatlow, 2013). In 2012, 17,000 people with vision impairments trained to become massagers (The Economist, 2013). Fu Gaoshan established the OPO because he wanted to avoid this vocation:

> the initial idea of establishing a DPO is very simple, because I don't want to be a massager. I would like to try a different occupation, do something innovative and make disabled people more respected in society.
>
> (Paper.oeeee.com, 2013)

A social approach to disability

Although a changing attitude toward people with disabilities has been identified by various theorists (see Fjeld & Sagli, 2011; Kohrman, 2005) and a China Disabled Persons' Federation (2008) report following the 2006 national survey noted 'attention should be given to functional barriers and social adaptability' (cited in

Fjeld & Sagli, 2011, p. 34), there is little evidence of a government-sanctioned social approach to disability. Fisher, Li, & Fan (2012) note that social inclusion initiatives often fall to NGOs rather than to the Chinese government.

In two articles published in 2005, researchers including Huang and Guo (2005) proposed and developed a social perspective towards disability in China to counter the dominant medical approach (see Oliver, 1996). They pointed out that the medical perspective places hopes solely on professionals such as doctors and educators in order to find 'a technological "fix" for all impairments' (Guo, Bricout, & Huang, 2005 p. 52), neglecting that the group actually 'values integrity, wholeness and choice over a relentless drive towards reconstruction' (Guo, Bricout, & Huang, 2005 p. 52). Aubié (2014) characterises the Chinese Government's approach to disability policy as 'patchy' and suggests Civil Society Organisations run by disabled people such as the OPO have the potential to be 'dramatically more effective' (p. 1) in changing the social position of people with disabilities in China.

A number of disability inclusion social incentives have been initiated in China including the prioritisation of information technology access for students with disabilities (Zhao, 2011). However a joint World Health Organisation and World Bank report observed that access to assistive technology is a particularly significant unmet need (World Health Organisation & World Bank, 2011). Since 2004, the Ministry of Industry and Information Technology has been co-hosting the annual China Information Accessibility Forum with the China Disabled Persons' Federation, the Internet Society of China and the China Foundation for Disabled Persons. The forum aims to provide a platform for different societal actors, including the government, research institutions, NGOs and IT companies, to collaborate with each other to promote the development of China's barrier-free information technologies and their applications (UNESCO, 2012). In the development programmes of the 11th Five-Year Plan (2006–2010) and the 12th Five-Year Plan (2011–2015) formulated by the China Disabled Persons' Federation, information accessibility, education, employability and the rights of people with disability are priority national planning tasks.

Theorising Chinese blogsphere to social media

A number of researchers see blogging as a transformative force to cause social, cultural and political changes in China. Zhang and Clarke (2008) argue that blog-enabled connections allow ordinary people to access alternative information and exchange ideas on sensitive matters in China's heavily controlled media environment. Esarey and Xiao (2008) take the popularisation of blogging in China as 'a major breakthrough toward the formation of a Chinese public sphere, albeit a virtual one' (p. 755). They argue blogging allows people to speak truth not only to peer bloggers and the public, but also to those in power. Xiang Zhou's content analysis of blogs, addressing the controversial dismissal of the Shanghai Party leader Chen Liangyu, concludes that bloggers' responses to the politically sensitive event 'paint a relatively promising picture of the blogosphere as a platform for personal expression in political discussion and online civic messages from diverse perspectives, relatively independent of official media' (Zhou, 2009, p. 1016).

Haiqing Yu (2007) argues that bloggers are 'not merely spectators or consumer', but have become 'active participants in the production of symbolic values by being part of a culture of circulation' (p. 428). She believes that bloggers' seeming apolitical cultural practices also have political implications in the long-term as they could influence the way people think about politics, culture and society in China. As other chapters in this collection show, blogging should be seen as a legitimate form of social media in its own right (see Ellis, Chapter 11; Bundon, Chapter 18; and Goldfarb & Armenta, Chapter 12 this volume). In the context of the OPO, blogging remains a very active area of online interaction, and across the NGO sector they still make up one of the 'big four' of online spaces for interaction behind QQ, Weibo and the NGO's own websites (Wang, 2015). However, since 2009, an additional new wave of Chinese language social media became available, and been embraced by the broader NGO sector, and the OPO (Wang, 2015).

Chinese social media

China has seen a social media boom during recent years. According to official statistics on social media as of June 2014, social networking sites (such as Qzone and Renren), microblogs (such as Sina Weibo and Tencent Weibo) and instant messaging service (such as Wechat and QQ) made up the most popular types of social media platforms in China. Up to 33.7 per cent of internet users use all the three types of platforms at the same time (CNNIC, 2014). These platforms are made additionally potent through the rapid rise in the availability of smartphone capable of accessing them (Crouch, 2015).

This rapid growth can be attributed to a convergence of both technological progress and economic transformation in China. On one hand, the Chinese government has stepped up the information network infrastructure building in a bid to support the IT industry since 1995 (Yu, Asur, & Huberman, 2011). China's number of internet users has increased to 668 million with an internet penetration rate of 48.8 per cent (CNNIC, 2015), and has led the developing countries in the world (International Telecommunication Union, 2013). On the other hand, Fuchs (2015) points out that China's six most accessed internet platforms, namely Baidu, QQ, Taobao, Sina, Hao123 and Weibo, all rise as private businesses under the context of a vigorous private sector economy (Fuchs, 2015). However, despite the massive user scale and multiplying variety, Chinese social media platforms and uses remain scarcely researched compared to their American counterparts (Chu & Choi, 2010). Most studies are concentrated on QQ, Renren, Sina Weibo, and WeChat.

QQ

QQ is an instant messaging service popular in China. It was introduced by parent company Tencent in 1999 and has over 800 million active accounts (Skuse, 2014). In 2004 QQ was ranked as 'having the greatest social impact' by Chinese internet companies (see Koch et al., 2010). Koch et al. (2010) argue that part of the success of QQ can be attributed to its 'Chineseness' and the promotion of its use 'as central to Chinese youth and modern Chinese culture' (p. 267). QQ has expanded beyond an instant messaging service to include online games, music, shopping, microblogging, movies and voice chat.

In 2009 Tencent launched barrier-free designs for its products including the QQ.com portal, Qzone, QQmail and the QQ instant messaging software. In its barrier-free statements for QQ.com and Qzone, it provides hotkey instructions, the screen readers it supports (NVDA, Zhengdu Screen Reader and the Yongde Screen Reader), and channels for feedback (email address and a feedback webpage). In October 2015 Tencent donated this Information Barrier-free Standards for Mobile Terminals to the China Information Barrier-free Product Alliance.

Renren

Renren was founded in 2005, and was originally called Xiaonei or 'inside the school' in English. In 2009 it rebranded itself as Renren or 'everybody'. It is often referred to as the Chinese Facebook (Bai, Yao & Dou, 2015; Yu & Xie, 2012), and mirrors some of its US-based counterparts' functionality and developmental history. However, as both Li (2011) and Chu and Choi (2010) observed, the network differs from Facebook in how it is used by its members. It has been labelled the first and most influential social network in China (Bai, Yao, & Dou, 2015), although it is now no longer the most popular network being used in the country (Chu & Choi, 2010). However, a search of both the Renren website and also the Chinese language Baidu search engine finds no accessibility policies for people with disabilities or even discussions around this topic.

Sina Weibo

Weibo, the domestic microblogging service, is one of the most widely used social media sites in China. Sina.com launched the first Weibo in 2009, followed by Tencent, Netease and Sohu in 2010. Sina Weibo shares a range of interface and functional characteristics with the US-based Twitter. Sina Weibo users can post and repost messages of up to 140 characters, give comments, use hashtags to start or join in topic discussions, etc. However, researchers comparing the two sites have discovered some distinct aspects of Sina Weibo. Due to the signification of the Chinese language, 140 Chinese characters can convey a great deal of information and nuances beyond the English equivalent (Rauchfleisch & Schäfer, 2015; Sullivan, 2012; Wang, 2015).

Researchers recognise Weibo's provision of an open space for public dialogues as well as opportunities to participate in public affairs. The Chinese public on Weibo can deviate from the official and hegemonic discourses around socio-political issues of common concern and contest mainstream representations of them. Weibo users make alternative narratives, which valorise personal feelings, experiences and memories in expressing values and ideologies (Wang, 2013) and building the national image (Du, 2014), history (Zhao & Liu, 2015) and geo-identity

(Wang, 2015). Sina Weibo users are found to be strategic and creative in responding to and navigating through censorship restrictions. They switch between multiple public spheres to sustain dialogues on sensitive issues (Rauchfleisch & Schäfer, 2015), and use personal micro-narratives instead of straightforward rebuttals to rearticulate insights and depoliticise tasks to achieve activist goals (Gleiss, 2015). Although a search of 'people with disabilities' on Sina Weibo reveals thousands of individual and organisational accounts, there is no accessibility policy for visually impaired users launched on the website.

WeChat

WeChat, also known as 'Weixin', literally translates as 'micro-message' in English. It is a popular mobile messaging app (similar to WhatsApp or LINE) and is becoming the most popular social media platform in China (Roberg, 2014). Released by Tencent in January 2011, WeChat provides hold-to-talk voice messaging, text messaging, broadcast (one-to-many) messaging and sharing photos and videos. In the second quarter of 2015, WeChat had 600 million monthly active users (Millward, 2015), and its overseas users had surpassed 100 million (Hong, 2015). Its popularity is partly due to Tencent's many users of its other services, such as QQ. Just as Yu (2007) and Du (2014) highlight the unique national features of the blogosphere and Sina Weibo respectively, Kuo (2014) situates WeChat as a uniquely Chinese form of social media. WeChat allows users to send voice messages of up to one minute in length. The audio service does not require the user to use either their hands or eyes to type and read textual messages, which is convenient for people with vision impairment to send and receive messages.

OPO protest blogging and social media

The OPO embraces the 'tactical form of resistance' identified by Yu where Chinese bloggers adopt a playful tone to deconstruct the mainstream culture (Yu, 2007, p. 429). For Yu, the Chinese blogosphere is characterised by spoof, parody and popular resistance. The OPO has launched a number of performance-based protests against large companies who discriminate against people with disability. These protests embody the 'playful spirit' identified by Yu: a spirit which communicates 'confidence in their role as media consumers-cum-producers' (p. 431) with a high level of technical and cultural expertise. This technical and cultural expertise is important, as we discuss later, in the OPO's goal to empower people with disabilities to express independent voices and establish networks, to improve their employment skills and entrepreneurial abilities and to promote the advocacy of social and legal issues regarding disability in China.

Parkson and blogging

After two women were denied entry to a large Parkson department store in Nanchang, the capital city of Jiangxi province in China, because one used a wheelchair, the OPO, together with another DPO – China-Dolls Care and Support Association (CDCSA) – organised a small-scale protest against Parkson's unfair treatment of people with disabilities. On 20 October 2009 volunteers put four cut-outs of human figures, two in wheelchairs and two holding walking sticks (see Figure 23.1), at the entrance of Parkson's Fuxingmen store in Beijing. The figures carried a Chinese message translated as 'You pretend I don't exist' (Xinhuanet.com, 2009). The protest put pressure on Parkson to openly apologise for its discrimination towards people with disability.

While the protest was reported by the mainstream media the following day, the real intensity occurred on social media where the story was shared amongst networks of people with disabilities indignant at Parkon's discrimination against people with disabilities.

On 21 October, OPO posted two news items on its official website. One titled 'Volunteers protest against Parkson's discrimination on the disabled – you pretend I don't exist', reporting details of the protest (Yijiayi.org, 2009a). They also published a joint open letter to Parkson with CDCSA, demanding Parkson openly acknowledge its discrimination and make an apology (Yijiayi.org, 2009b). The two news items were reposted on the official blog of OPO's China Disability Observatory (CDO; 2009a, 2009b) programme. Members of each blog community widely

Figure 23.1 Four cardboard cut-outs of human figures, two in wheelchairs and two holding walking sticks at the entrance to the Parkson's Fuxingmen store in Beijing

reposted the two news items as well as the reporting of other media outlets on the protest on personal blogs and Bulletin Board Systems (BBS), such as the Tianya Forum, China's most popular BBS with more than 100 million registers. Public sentiment against Parkson's unfair treatment of the disabled galvanised online, adding group pressure on Parkson to make an apology. On 22 October 2009, only two days after the protest, Parkson released a letter of apology on its official website, openly apologising to people with disabilities and pledging a commitment to improving service in the future (Yijiayi.org, 2009c).

Pizza Hut and social media

The OPO organised another successful protest in 2013 when Pizza Hut released an online advertisement featuring a 'confused' shrimp ball wearing sunglasses and holding a cane. The ad was intended to be a play on words because 'shrimp' and 'blind' have the same pronunciation in Putonghua. However, images of people with vision impairments wearing t-shirts with the words 'I'm not a blind ball' protesting at Pizza Huts in Beijing, Guangzhou, Shijiazhuang, Qingdao and Zhengzhou spread online, with the Weibo thread #PizzaHutsShrimpBallAdvertisement housing the distribution of the images and discussion on the topic. OPO posted the images and commentary from its own Weibo account. Pizza Hut subsequently withdrew the offensive ad and apologised on Weibo. Ironically, this social media apology was in an image format inaccessible to users who rely on screen readers to access the internet. Following the incident and problematic apology, the OPO drafted guidelines for the ethical representation of disability and encouraged the media to challenge public prejudice (Aubié, 2014; personal communication).

The OPO, UN and voice donors on social media

In 2008 China ratified the United Nations Convention on the Rights of Persons with Disabilities (UNCRPD). This convention sets out a series of human rights for people with disabilities and strategies for implementing these rights (see Shava, Chapter 13 this collection). Where government policy has been accused of contravening this convention (see Aubié, 2014), the OPO has been proactive in monitoring the implementation of the UNCRPD in China, even submitting a shadow report to monitor the Chinese government's implementation of the UNCRPD (Hallett, 2015).

In 2014 the OPO partnered with the United Nations and the social media site WeChat to produce audio books of the UNCRPD and Invisible Rights, a joint OPO and Harvard Law School publication explaining the social rights of people with vision impairments in China under the UNCRPD. The document was written by people with vision impairment and the audio book created through a crowd-sourced voice donor programme where fluent Chinese speakers read aloud sections of the relevant documents in the public 'voice donor' account on WeChat. The compiled recordings were distributed to DPOs and schools for people with vision impairment. According to the United Nations (2015), this crowd-sourced voice donor programme produced in excess of 100 audio books, which were used by over three million people. Significantly, three million people contributed one-minute audio clips to the initiative.

Skills employment and social media

Following the previous success of its website- and blog-based protests, OPO embraced the most popular social media platforms, Weibo and WeChat, to enhance its profile in the media, promote interaction with the public and attract volunteers and other resources. OPO uses social media to send out content to the mobile devices of their subscribers on a daily basis, receive subscribers' feedback and reply to the subscribers.

In China, grassroots NGOs such as OPO have struggled to compete with government-affiliated NGOs for media coverage due to a lack of funding and the government's control. As Jing Wang (2015) observes:

> they cannot compete with government-affiliated NGOs for media coverage. The lack of media coverage makes NGOs invisible to each other and to the general public. We do not get to hear their stories, learn about the causes they are promoting, and respond to their needs. Many NGOs toiled quietly until their thin workforce burned out. Social media arrived in China around 2009, providing NGOs an alternative means of communication to break this vicious cycle.
>
> (p. 18)

The OPO uses social media to bring together a community of people with disabilities and through that community add volume to their concerns. In addition to advocacy work and community building, the OPO also focuses on the promotion of people with disabilities' skills and employability. OPO offers radio production, photography and stenographer training for people with both vision and physical impairments. These skill-training programmes aim to foster people with disabilities' sense of personal initiative, develop their occupational skills, build up their networks with society and increase their competence and competitiveness in future education and employment.

Voice of the Blind (VOB) is an OPO-affiliated online community radio network that provides a digital audio broadcasting platform for people with vision impairment. Its predecessor was the 1+1 Sound Studio established in 2006. 1+1 Sound Studio was the first registered media run by people with disabilities at the 2008 Beijing Paralympics. Two of the studio team members became the first Chinese journalists with disabilities to gain press accreditation as Paralympics reporters, eventually leading to their paid employment. In addition to extending the broadcasting channel of the radio programmes produced by 1+1 Sound Studio, OPO established an online platform for visually impaired people to broadcast and share personal productions in order to create a digital radio network that enables self-representation, audience participation and social networking. The online nature of the platform allows it to reach beyond China to other Chinese language communities. People can upload user-generated audio productions to any relevant section of the VOB website, comment on these programmes and share them on China's social media platforms. Again, significantly, this use of social media allows the site content to be easily and effectively shared and reposted.

Conclusion

Over ten years, OPO has developed from a radio production centre (the 1+1 Sound Studio, for people with disabilities) into one of China's leading DPOs. The success of OPO is primarily due to its proactive policy advocacy through a series of change-making actions discussed in this chapter. The past decade of the organisations' activities also parallel first the use of blogs in China and then more recently the growth of other more widely distributed social media. This can be seen in the organisations' evolving online activities, from the blog- and website-based protest against Parkson in 2009, and the company's response posted on its own website, to the social media-based protest against Pizza Hut in 2013, and that company's fumbled Weibo-based response, to the more recent move from direct activism to advocacy in partnering with WeChat and the crowd-sourced voice donor project.

People with disabilities still face severe disadvantage in Chinese society. However, the advent of social media and its ability to enable non-government NGOs to, in the words of Jing Wang (2015), 'break out of their communications bottleneck' (p. 1) gives the country a greater opportunity for the social and economic positioning of people with disability to better reflect on the rhetoric of the country's ambitions as set out in China's Disabled Person's Act for all aspects of life to be open to people with disabilities.

References

Aubié, H. (2014). The rise of disability rights advocacy in China: Now is the time for more international support. Retrieved 20 October 2015, from https://www.academia.edu/8764274/ The_Rise_of_Disability_Rights_Advocacy_in_China_Now_is_the_Time_for_More_ International_Support

Bai, Y., Yao, Z., & Dou, Y. (2015). Effect of social commerce factors on user purchase behaviour: An empirical investigation from Renren.com. *International Journal of Information Management, 35*, 538–550.

Braddock, D. L., & Parish, S. L. (2001). Introduction: The formation of disability studies. In G. L. Albrecht, K. D. Seelman & M. Bury (Eds.), *Handbook of Disability Studies* (pp. 1–68). Thousand Oaks, CA: Sage.

China Disability Observatory. (2009a). 致百盛集团的公开信 (Joint open letter to Parson). Retrieved from http://oporadio.blog.sohu.com/134547385.html

China Disability Observatory. (2009b). 志愿者在百盛门前抗议残障歧视—百盛，你说你的眼里没有我 (Volunteers protest against Parkson's discrimination on the disabled – you pretend I don't exist). Retrieved from http://oporadio.blog.sohu.com/134547385. html

China Disabled Person's Federation. (2008). CDPF: About us. Retrieved from http://www. cdpf.org.cn/english/about1us/200804/t20080409_267487.html

Chu, S., & Choi, S. (2010). Social capital and self-presentation on social networking sites: A competitive study of Chinese and American youth generation. *Chinese Journal of Communication, 3*(4), 402–420.

CNNIC. (2014). 2014年中国社交类应用用户行为研究报告 (2014 Research Report on Social Media User Behaviour in China). Retrieved from http://www.cnnic.net.cn/hlwfzyj/ hlwxzbg/sqbg/201408/P020150401351309648557.pdf on 19 October, 2015.

CNNIC. (2015). 第36次中国互联网络发展状况统计报告(36th Statistical Report on the State of the Chinese Internet's Development). Retrieved from http://www.cnnic.net.cn/ hlwfzyj/hlwxzbg/hlwtjbg/201507/P020150723549500667087.pdf on 19 October, 2015.

Crouch, E. (2015, 16 July). Sightless in Shanghai – Being blind in a 21st century Chinese megacity. Retrieved from http://www.thatsmags.com/china/post/10638/sightless- in-shanghai-being-blind-in-a-21st-century-chinese-megacity-1

Du, S. (2014). Social media and the transformation of 'Chinese nationalism': 'Igniting positive energy' in China since the 2012 London Olympics (Respond to this article at http://www.therai.org.uk/at/debate). *Anthropology Today, 30*(1), 5–8.

The Economist. (2013). Feeling their way Chinese Braille. *The Economist, 408*, 40.

Esarey, A., & Xiao, Q. (2008). Political expression in the Chinese blogophere: Below the radar. *Asian Survey, 48*(5), 752–772.

Fisher, K. R., Li, J., & Fan, L. (2012). Barriers to the supply of non-government disability services in China. *Journal of Social Policy, 41*(1), 161–182.

Fjeld, H., & Sagli, G. (2011). Disability, poverty and healthcare: Changes in the canji ('dis-ability') policies in the history of the People's Republic of China. In A. H. Eide & B. Ingstad (Eds.), *Disability and poverty: A global challenge* (pp. 31–54). Bristol, UK: Polity Press.

Fuchs, C. (2015). Baidu, Weibo and Renren: The global political economy of social media in China. *Asian Journal of Communication,* 1–28. doi:10.1080/01292986.2015.1041537

Gleiss, M. S. (2015). Speaking up for the suffering (br) other: Weibo activism, discursive struggles, and minimal politics in China. *Media, Culture & Society, 37*(4), 513–529.

Guo, B., Bricout, J. C., & Huang, J. (2005). A common open space or a digital divide? A social model perspective on the online disability community in China. *Disability & Society, 20*(1), 49–66. doi:10.1080/0968759042000283638

Hallett, S. (2015). 'Enabling the disabled': The growing role of civil society in disability rights advocacy. In A. Fulda (Ed.), *Civil society contributions to policy innovation in the PR China: Environment, social development and international cooperation* (pp. 173–195). Houndmills, UK: Palgrave Macmillan.

Hong, K. (2015). WhatsApp rival WeChat surpasses 100 million user accounts outside China. *The next web.* Retrieved from http://thenextweb.com/asia/2013/08/15/ whatsapp-rival-wechat-surpasses-100-million-user-accounts-outside-china/

Huang, J., & Guo, B. (2005). Building social capital: A study of the online disability community. *Disability Studies Quarterly, 25*(2). Retrieved from http://dsq-sds.org/article/view/554/731

Human Rights Watch. (2013, July 2013). "As long as they let us stay in class": Barriers to education for persons with disabilities in China. Retrieved from https://www.hrw.org/ sites/default/files/reports/china0713_ForUpload.pdf

International Telecommunication Union. (2013). Measuring the information society 2013. Retrieved from http://www.itu.int/en/ITU-D/Statistics/Documents/publications/ mis2013/MIS2013_without_Annex_4.pdf

Koch, P., Koch, B. J., Huang, K., & Chen, W. (2010). Beauty is in the eye of the QQ user: Instant messaging in China. In G. Goggin & M. McLelland (Eds.), *Internationalizing internet studies: Beyond Anglophone paradigms* (pp. 265–284). London, New York: Routledge.

Kohrman, M. (2005). *Bodies of difference: Experiences of disability and institutional advocacy in the making of modern China.* Berkeley, CA: University of California Press.

Kuo, L. (2014). WeChat is nothing like WhatsApp – and that makes it even more valuable. Retrieved from http://qz.com/179007/wechat-is-nothing-like-whatsapp-and-that-makes-it-even-more-valuable/

Li, L. (2011). Social network sites comparison between the United States and China: Case study of Facebook and Renren Network. Paper presented at the Business Management and Electronic Information (BMEI) Conference, Guangzhou, 13–5 May. Volume 1, 825–827.

Millward, S. (2015). WeChat rockets to 600M monthly users. *Tech in Asia.* Retrieved from https://www.techinasia.com/wechat-monthly-active-users-q2–2015/

Oliver, M. (1996). *Understanding disability: From theory to practice.* Houndsmill, Basingstoke, UK: Macmillan.

Paper.oeeee.com. (2013). "一加一": 残障人也是公民 (One Plus One: People with disability are also citizens). Retrieved from http://paper.oeeee.com/nis/201312/23/157136.html

Rauchfleisch, A., & Schäfer, M. S. (2015). Multiple public spheres of Weibo: A typology of forms and potentials of online public spheres in China. *Information, Communication & Society, 18*(2), 139–155.

Roberg, M. (2014). The top 5 social media networks in China. Retrieved from http://maximize socialbusiness.com/5-top-social-media-networks-china-12918/

Sagli, G., Zhang, J., Ingstad, B., & Fjeld, H. E. (2013). Poverty and disabled households in the People's Republic of China: Experiences with a new rural health insurance scheme. *Disability & Society, 28*(2), 218–231. doi:10.1080/09687599.2012.699281

Skuse, A. (2014). WeChat: The Chinese chat app stealing Weibo's thunder. Retrieved from http://edition.cnn.com/2014/02/27/business/tencent-wechat-unseats-sina-weibo/index.html

Sullivan, J. (2012). A tale of two microblogs in China. *Media, Culture & Society, 34*(6), 773–783.

Tatlow, D. K. (2013, 4 November). Disabled Chinese struggle for a good education, and acceptance. *The New York Times.* Retrieved from http://sinosphere.blogs.nytimes.com/2013/11/04/disabled-chinese-struggle-for-a-good-education-and-acceptance/

UNESCO. (2012). Access to scientific information and access for persons with disabilities discussed in China. Retrieved from http://www.unesco.org/new/en/communication-and-information/resources/news-and-in-focus-articles/all-news/news/access_to_scientific_information_and_access_for_persons_with_disabilities_discussed_in_china/#.VjaurPsmym6

United Nations Development Program. (2015). UNDP and WeChat promote the rights of people with disabilities. 17 May. Retrieved from http://www.cn.undp.org/content/china/en/home/presscenter/articles/2015/05/undp-uses-social-media-to-promote-the-rights-of-people-with-disa.html

Wang, C., Wang, X., Qian, Y., & Lin, S. (2010). Accurate Braille-Chinese translation towards efficient Chinese input method for blind people. 5th International Conference on Pervasive Computing and Applications, Birmingham City University.

Wang, J. (2015). NGO2.0 and social media praxis: activist as researcher. *Chinese Journal of Communication, 8*(1), 18–41.

Wang, W. Y. (2013). Weibo, framing, and media practices in China. *Journal of Chinese Political Science, 18*(4), 375–388.

Wang, W. Y. (2015). Remaking Guangzhou: Geo-identity and place-making on Sina Weibo. *Media International Australia Incorporating Culture and Policy, 156*(Aug), 29–38.

World Health Organisation. (2015). Blindness as a public health problem in China. Retrieved from http://www.who.int/mediacentre/factsheets/fs230/en/

World Health Organisation, & World Bank. (2011). World report on disability. Retrieved from http://www.unicef.org/protection/World_report_on_disability_eng.pdf

Xinhuanet.com. (2009). Retailing giant Parkson apologizes over disabled controversy in China. Retrieved from http://news.xinhuanet.com/english/2009–10/22/content_12301389.htm

Yijiayi.org. (2009a). 志愿者在百盛门前抗议残障歧视——百盛，你说你的眼里没有我！(Volunteers protest against Parkson's discrimination on the disabled – you pretend I don't exist). Retrieved from http://www.yijiayi.org/list.php?gmod=ds&mid=1&lid=49&nid=40

Yijiayi.org. (2009b). 致百盛集团的公开信 (Open letter to Parkson). Retrieved from http://www.yijiayi.org/list.php?gmod=ds&mid=1&lid=49&nid=41

Yijiayi.org. (2009c). 中国百盛集团致：广大消费者 (Open letter to customers from Parkson China). Retrieved from http://www.yijiayi.org/list.php?gmod=ds&mid=1&lid=49&nid=43

Yeh, F., Tsay, H., & Liang, S. (2008). Human computer interface and optimized electromechanical design for Chinese Braille display. *Mechanism and Machine Theory, 43*(12), 1495–1518. doi:10.1016/j.mechmachtheory.2008.01.006

Yu, H. (2007). Blogging everyday life in Chinese internet culture. *Asian Studies Review, 31*(4), 423–433. doi:10.1080/10357820701710724

Yu, L., Asur, S., & Huberman, B. A. (2011). What trends in Chinese social media. arXiv preprint arXiv:1107.3522.

Yu, S., & Xie, Y. (2012). Preference effects on friendship choice: Evidence from an online field experiment. *Population Studies Centre Research Report 12–780*. Ann Arbor, MI: University of Michigan.

Zhang, J. G., & Clarke, J. (2008). Blogging in China: A force for social change. *Australian Journalism Review, 30*(1), 3–11.

Zhao, H., & Liu, J. (2015). Social media and collective remembrance: The debate over China's great famine on Weibo. *China Perspectives, 2015*(1), 41–48.

Zhao, J. (2011). China special education: The perspective of information technologies. In P. Ordóñez de Pablos, J. Zhao & R. Tennyson (Eds.), *Technology enhanced learning for people with disabilities: Approaches and applications* (pp. 34–43). Hershey, PA: Information Science Reference.

Zheng, X., Chen, G., Song, X., Liu, J., Yan, L., Du, W., Pang, L., Zhang, L., Wu, J., Zhang, B., & Zhang, J. (2011). Twenty-year trends in the prevalence of disability in China. *Bulletin of the World Health Organization*. Retrieved from http://www.who.int/bulletin/volumes/89/11/11–089730/en/

Zhou, X. (2009). The political blogosphere in China: A content analysis of the blogs regarding the dismissal of Shanghai leader Chen Liangyu. *New Media and Society, 11*(6), 1003–1022.

Index

Ryan, Sara 25–38
Ryle, Gilbert 228, 230–1

Samuelson, Peter 206
Screen Australia study 150
Searle, Jane K. 217
self-directed learning 235
self-representation: identity formation
    and 291–3; users of augmentative and
    alternative communication (AAC)
    294–6, 297
sender-receiver model of communication 141
Shava, Kudzai 176–86
Shifman, Limor 43
Shrader, Paul 205
Sina Weibo: in China 323–4
Sinclair, Jim 259, 269*n*4
Singer, Peter 60
slacktivism 37
slow cinema 203, 205, 209–10, 212–13,
    213*n*4
Smith, Iain Duncan 57, 71*n*2
Snyder Center for Aphasia Life
    Enhancement (SCALE) 138–9
Sobchack, Vivian 205, 212
*Sociability: Social media for people with a
    disability* (Hollier) 79, 81, 86
social activism: designing accessibility
    113–14; Twitter and 59–63
social inclusion: disabled persons in Japan
    279–82
social justice 115–16*n*4
social media: accessibility barriers
    of 81–3; assistive technology (AT)
    evolution 77–8; background 1–3;
    Blackboard learning management
    system 220–1; in China 322–4; cloud
    integration of 83–6; collaborative
    147–8; core values 2–3; digital
    accessibility 4–6; disability activism
    and 90–1; disability advocacy 146–7,
    156–7; disability stories 3; emergency
    management agencies 122–3, 126;
    evolution of 77; Facebook and
    online learning 193–5; George Takei
    incident 50–2; identity formation and
    self-presentation within 291–3; Japan
    275–8; Lorm devices for accessibility
    114–15; mainstreaming the deaf cause
    21–3; mobile technologies and 95–6;
    personal engagement with 79–81;
    potential for online education 193–5,
    198–9; purposes of users 80; tools 81–2;

usage for learning disability 26–8;
    use with augmentative and alternative
    communication (AAC) 294–8; word
    cloud of disability and 6; *see also
    Daredevil* (television show)
Social Media Emergency Response Bill
    (HR4263) 121, 126
social media in Zimbabwe: accessibility
    184–5; affordability 185; availability
    184; challenges for future 185–6
Social Movement of the Deaf and their
    Friends 18–21
social networking sites (SNSs): in China
    322–4; from *mixi* to Facebook 275;
    municipalities in Japan 278; usage in
    Japan 274
Sparrowhawk, Connor 25; *see also*
    #107days campaign
speech-generating devices (SGDs) 133,
    134, 136, 142, 288
Stalder, Felix 206
Stephens, Christina 165–9, 173–4
STM (*Société de Transport de Montréal*):
    customer service 97–8; Facebook group
    89; Facebook page 99*n*1; paratransit
    users 94–5; social media use 99*n*2
Sufism 306, 308
suicide: veterans 161, 169–71, 173, 174
supercrip: pity narratives 43
supercrip frame 42

Takei, George 50–2
television: accessing and accessible 150;
    disability advocacy 146–7; transmedia
    environment 148; *see also Daredevil*
    (television show)
Tistje 255, 268–9; blog as moving target
    264–5; *Living on the spectrum from the
    front row* 263–8; *see also* autism
transmedia storytelling 147–8
transmission model: communication 141
Transport mésadapté: activism 95–6,
    98; collaboration with Québec Human
    Rights Commission 98; creation of 91;
    growth of 97, 99; membership growth
    98–9; Montréal's public transit 89, 90,
    91; participants of 93–5; stories shared
    on 97–8
traumatic brain injury 138, 169
Tsukuba civic activities cyber-square
    experiment: Facebook 274, 278,
    279–82; Japan 278–9; reach and online
    engagement of 281